Family Therapy:
An Overview
Second Edition

Family Therapy:
An Overview
Second Edition

IRENE GOLDENBERG
U.C.L.A. Neuropsychiatric Institute

HERBERT GOLDENBERG
California State University, Los Angeles

BROOKS/COLE PUBLISHING COMPANY
Pacific Grove, California

Printed in the United States of America

10 9 8 7

Library of Congress Cataloging in Publication Data
Goldenberg, Irene

Family therapy.

Bibliography: p.
Includes index.
1. Family psychotherapy. I. Goldenberg, Herbert.
II. Title.

RC488.5.G64 1985   616.89′156   84-21387

Sponsoring Editor: *Claire Verduin*
Editorial Assistant: *Pat Carnahan*
Production Editor: *Ellen Brownstein*
Manuscript Editor: *Katherine McAvity*
Permissions Editor: *Carline Haga*
Interior and Cover Design: *Vernon T. Boes*
Art Coordinator: *Michèle Judge/Rebecca Ann Tait*
Interior Illustration: *Publisher's Art Service*
Photo Editor: *Judy Blamer*
Typesetting: *Allservice Phototypesetting Co. of Arizona*
Printing and Binding: *The Maple-Vail Book Manufacturing Group*

For our families of origin
. . . who stimulated our drive and
sensitivity,

And for the family we created
. . . who enriched our understanding
and, above all, taught us
humility,

And for our children's families
. . . whose contributions we look
forward to discovering.

PREFACE

Family therapy is a growing, exciting field, complete with competing theories, innovative and sometimes controversial techniques, and a host of competent and charismatic clinicians. We are delighted to be a part of what is going on, especially if we can help organize the considerable family-therapy literature so that the reader is simultaneously informed and stimulated.

In our first edition, we set ourselves the task of providing a broad introduction to the field, offering what we believed to be a balanced presentation of the major theoretical underpinnings and clinical practices that were then current. Rather than simply detailing a how-to-do-it set of technical procedures, we attempted to provide an overview of the evolving viewpoints, perspectives, values, intervention techniques, and goals of family therapy. Students, fellow professors, and clinical colleagues responded favorably to our efforts, supporting our view that such a book was needed to help systematize a growing field.

This second edition attempts to retain what others have suggested were the main strengths of the first edition—its concise, readable quality and its unbiased presentation. Beyond that, we believe this present effort offers a broader and deeper perspective. More specifically, this edition is much enlarged (from a previous 9 chapters to the current 13 chapters) with more detailed examinations of current theories and practices. The four theoretical models offered in the first edition have now been expanded to six models, to more accurately reflect current thinking in the field. While all four models were described briefly in one chapter previously, we have amplified our presentation here into six separate chapters, and augmented the much expanded theoretical foundation with numerous clinical examples, brief case studies, and vignettes of actual family therapy sessions.

To be effective in helping couples and entire families to change, we continue to believe that therapists must first have some grounding in the general principles of family living. They need to be familiar with how families operate as a social system, how they develop "rules" for living together, and how they deal with the ever-changing tasks that must be met by a family going through its life cycle. Therapists need some basic theoretical understanding of what causes dysfunction within families and of how to distinguish those families who are undergoing a time-limited crisis from which they will reorganize and recover independently from those families who are severely dysfunctional and who will not recover without therapeutic intervention. Learning about these fundamental theoretical issues should precede the learning of specific family-therapy theories and techniques, and we have organized Part One (The Structure and Process of Family Systems) around such issues.

Part Two (Historical and Theoretical Foundations) and Part Three (The Practice of Family Therapy) are intended to lead the reader from family theory to practice in what we consider a logical sequence. Part Four (Training and Evaluation) is devoted to nuts and bolts issues—where and how to get training in family therapy and how practice in marital and family therapy is regulated in the United States. The text concludes with an issue of concern to theoreticians, researchers, and practitioners alike—the effectiveness of family therapy. A detailed glossary of terms is included at the end of the book to facilitate the reading and minimize interruptions.

We have written this book as a survey of the field of family therapy, covering its historical roots as well as its current major theories and techniques. The book is directed toward readers in the fields of psychology, education, counseling, social work, psychiatry, nursing, and theology. We recognize that, in each of these groups, learning to become a practitioner comes at different points in the educational training. Therefore, this book can serve as a base of information in an introductory or advanced undergraduate course, but it will also be helpful in a graduate course and for the practicing professional.

A number of colleagues in various related fields who have an interest in teaching family therapy have been most generous in reviewing earlier drafts of this text in an effort to improve the final product. We wish particularly to thank Eric Bermann, University of Michigan at Ann Arbor; David Capuzzi, Portland State University, Portland, Oregon; Nancy Elman, University of Pittsburgh, Pittsburgh, Pennsylvania; and Barbara Wickell, University of Illinois at Chicago Circle.

Rosa M. Silva deserves special recognition for swiftly and expertly translating a handwritten manuscript into its final typed form. Kathleen Austin earns our thanks for her help with the genogram in Chapter 11 of this book. Thanks too to Serena Stier, who first whetted our appetite for the therapeutic possibilities of family intervention. Our friends at Brooks/Cole have been an ever-available source of guidance and support, and we would like them to know how much we appreciate their efforts.

What we both learned about working together, while writing the first edition, continued to apply to this current undertaking. Our different experiences, viewpoints, and styles notwithstanding, this book brought with it the challenge of producing a fulfilling joint effort. What more appropriate task for a couple of family therapists!

Irene Goldenberg
Herbert Goldenberg

CONTENTS

Contents

Contents

Family Therapy:
An Overview
Second Edition

PART ONE

The Structure and Process of Family Systems

CHAPTER ONE

Patterns of
Family Interaction

A family is far more than a collection of individuals occupying a specific physical and psychological space together. A family is a natural social **system,**[1] with properties all its own, one that has evolved a set of rules, **roles,** a power structure, forms of communication, and ways of negotiation and problem solving that allow various tasks to be performed effectively. Within such a system, individuals are tied to one another by powerful, durable, reciprocal emotional attachments and loyalties that may fluctuate in intensity over time but nevertheless persist over the lifetime of the family. Entrance into such an organized system occurs only through birth, adoption, or marriage, and, despite a possible temporary or even permanent sense of alienation from one's family, one can never truly leave except by death.

Whether traditional or innovative, adaptive or maladaptive, efficient or chaotically organized, a family inevitably attempts to arrange itself into a functioning group. Initially all members share a common household and strive to engage in cooperative behavior in order to meet survival and developmental needs. Later, as children grow up and separate from their family of origin, households may multiply, but family ties continue to exert influence on the behavior of family members over several generations. Affection, loyalty, and durability of membership are what characterize all families and distinguish them from all other social systems (Terkelsen, 1980). Whatever the composition or structure of the family—**nuclear family, blended family** (stepfamily), **single-parent family,** childless couple, **common-law family, extended family,** three-generation units living under one roof or apart—no one form may be designated as either more or less "family" than the other. Regardless of format—or of ultimate success—all families must work at promoting positive relationships

[1]Terms printed in **boldface** are defined in the Glossary at the back of the book.

among members, attend to the personal needs of all constituents, develop strategies for dealing with external stress, cope with maturational changes (for example, children growing up and leaving home; death) as well as unexpected crises (for example, divorce, acute illness, accidents), and in general organize themselves in order to get on with the day-to-day problems of living.

It should be clear from the above that family systems may be studied from three perspectives—structurally, functionally, and developmentally (Freeman, 1981). Structurally we might look at the **dyadic** nature of the husband–wife, the sibling–sibling, and the parent–child subsystems, as well as the **triadic** mother–grandmother–daughter or father–son–daughter subsystems. (Each of these subarrangements has its own **boundaries,** needs and expectations, which will be discussed in detail in Chapter 2.) Since everyone in a family operates within a role network, we might look too at how roles are assigned—whether they are assigned primarily by age and sex or acquired by family status or personal characteristics (for example, the role of family leader or family **scapegoat**). Also, how does the family develop norms for its own behavior and for the acceptable behavior of its individual members? How does the family cope with norm violation by a member? Functionally, we are interested in how a family organizes to protect, care for, and educate children; how it creates a physical, social, and economic setting that promotes individual development; how affectionate bonds within the family are nourished and strengthened; how modeling by parents prepares children to relate successfully to the outside world. Developmentally, as we shall see later in this chapter, we are concerned with the family's developmental stages (for example, the newly married couple, the family with adolescents, the family in later life). Families, like individuals, go through a life cycle during which different **developmental tasks** must be mastered and new adaptational strategies applied. Family transaction patterns form the matrix within which the psychological growth of individual family members takes place.

ADOPTING A FAMILY PERSPECTIVE

Personality theorists, academicians interested in the development of psychopathology, and psychotherapists have all been interested in and aware of the consequences of early family relationships on adult behavior. Ever since Freud's early theoretical psychoanalytic formulations, attention has been drawn to family conflicts and alliances (the **Oedipus complex** in boys is one example) as contributing factors in an individual's personal growth as well as in any possible manifestation of later **neurotic** symptoms. However, Freud did not utilize his awareness of the interactional nature of behavior in his psychoanalytic treatment. That is, he acknowledged the influence (and sometimes the powerful impact) of family dynamics, but he chose to help individuals resolve their personal, **intrapsychic** conflicts; he did not deal directly with changing the properties of the family system. By producing changes in the person's psychic organization, Freud hoped to evoke behavioral changes, including

4

changes in response to others, that would ultimately lead others to change their response patterns to the patient. Thus, most psychotherapists, following the lead of Freud and others, would treat a distressed individual but refuse to see that person's spouse, believing that as the patient's behavior changed, a corresponding change would occur in the spouse and ultimately in the couple's relationship. Unfortunately, this was frequently not the case.

Over the last 30 years, an alternative view of human problems and their alleviation has slowly emerged—namely, that an individual who exhibits **dysfunctional** behavior (for example, behavior associated with excessive anxieties, depression, alcoholism, sexual disturbances, **schizophrenia**) may simply be a representative of a system that is faulty. Moreover, the causes and nature of an individual's problem may not be clear from a study of that person alone but can often be better understood when viewed in the context of a family social system that is in disequilibrium.

Our understanding of what a person does, what his or her motives are for doing it, and how that behavior can be changed therapeutically takes new forms as we shift from the individual to the broader context in which that person functions. From this new vantage point, psychopathology or dysfunctional behavior is more the product of a struggle between persons than the result of opposing forces within a single individual (Haley, 1963). When the locus of pathology is defined as internal, the therapist is likely to focus on the individual. On the other hand, if the dysfunctional behavior is seen as the product of a faulty dyadic or triadic relationship, then it is the relationship that becomes the focus of the therapist's attention and intervention strategies. Helping couples or entire families alter their transactional pattern replaces seeking ways to uncover and decipher what goes on within "the mysterious black box"— the mind of the single individual. Family therapy, directed at changing the system—the family members' characteristic pattern of interacting with one another, their style and manner of communication, and the structure of their relationship—allows individual family members to experience a new family environment and a new social context and to begin to change their behavior in response to such new experiences.

More than simply a new treatment method, family therapy represents a "whole new way of conceptualizing human problems, of understanding behavior, the development of symptoms, and their resolution" (Sluzki, 1978, p. 366). Haley (1971b) argues that the perspective of family therapy demonstrates a **paradigm** shift, a discontinuous break with past ideas, calling for a new set of premises and new methods for collecting and understanding forthcoming data.

Sluzki (1978) goes so far as to consider family therapy a major epistemological revolution in the behavioral sciences. Put simply, **epistemology** refers to the rules one uses to make sense out of what one is experiencing, what descriptive language one uses to conceptualize and interpret information, how one goes about gaining knowledge and drawing conclusions about the world. Gregory Bateson (1979), a cultural anthropologist with broad interests in a variety of seemingly divergent fields, provided some of the theoretical underpinnings for this new outlook, even though, essentially, he remained outside the realm of family therapy. We shall return in Chapter 4 to Bateson's seminal role in the evolution of the family therapy movement. The point we want to make here is that, in the 1950s, his interest in the application of **cybernetics** to the understanding of communication patterns within families greatly contributed to the new view of human problems we have been discussing. Bateson's work was instrumental in shifting the focus of family therapy from the single individual to the exchange of information and the process of evolving relationships between and among family members.

It was also Bateson who stressed the limitations of linear thinking in regard to living systems. In the physical world, the world of Newton, it makes sense to talk of causality in linear terms—A causes B, which acts on C, causing D. Bateson claimed that this "billiard ball" model, in which a force moves in one direction affecting the objects in its path, is inappropriate in dealing with the complexities of human relationships. He called instead for an epistemological shift—to new units of analysis, to a focus on the ongoing process, and to the use of a new descriptive language that emphasizes relationships, **feedback** information, and **circularity.** An example may help clarify the nature of this shift. "A bad mother produces sick children" is a statement that exemplifies linear thinking. The statement can be reconceptualized in terms of human relationships as follows: An unhappy middle-aged woman, struggling with an inattentive husband who feels peripheral to and excluded from the family, attaches herself to her 20-year-old son for male companionship, excluding her adolescent daughter. The daughter, in turn, feeling rejected and unloved, engages in flagrant sexually promiscuous behavior, to the considerable distress of her parents. The son, fearful of leaving home and becoming independent, insists he must remain at home because his mother needs his attention. The mother becomes depressed because her children do not seem to be like other "normal" children and blames their dysfunctional behavior on her husband, whom she labels an "absentee father." He in turn becomes angry and defensive, and their sexual relationship suffers. The children respond to the ensuing coldness between the parents in different ways: the son by withdrawing from friends completely and remaining at home with his mother as much as possible, and the daughter by having indiscriminate sexual encounters with one man after another but carefully avoiding emotional intimacy with any of them.

From this example, it should be clear to the reader that any effort to establish causality for the children's behavior by blaming the mother for victimizing them ("Look what you made us do!") is futile and naive. An explanation of their collective behavior in current relationship terms—as a network of circular causal loops in which everyone's behavior impacts on everyone else—gets closer to the truth.

The point, of course, is to speak not of causes and effects, but of living systems in which a process is taking place, a process whose units affect, and are affected by, all the others. In simple but elegant terms, Lynn Hoffman (1981)

Gregory Bateson, Ph.D.

likens the difference between the two approaches to the difference between kicking a stone and kicking a dog. In the former case, energy is transmitted by the kick, and the stone moves a specific distance determined by such factors as the force of the kick and the weight of the stone. The outcome of the latter case is far less predictable, since the dog also has energy and may respond in any number of ways, depending on the relationship between the person and the dog and how the dog interprets the kick. The dog's response offers feedback information to the person, who may need to modify his or her subsequent behavior. That circularity is even more clear in interactions between human beings.

Within a family therapy framework, problems are recast to take into consideration the fact that relationship difficulties and an individual's behavior cannot be understood without attention to the context in which that behavior occurs. Rather than seeing the source of problems or the appearance of *symptoms* as emanating from a single "sick" individual, the family therapy approach views that person simply as a symptom bearer—the **identified patient**—expressing a family's disequilibrium. As Satir (1967) contends, a disturbed person's "symptoms" may in reality be a message that he or she is distorting self-growth as a result of trying to alleviate "family pain." The person who initially seeks help, the "identified patient," does not remain the central focus of therapy for long. When the other family members, as participants, begin to understand the problems or symptoms as expressions of a dysfunctional family system, they are helped to work on their relationships—in effect, altering the system—so that each member may experience a sense of independence, uniqueness, and wholeness while remaining within the context and security of the family relationship.

HELPING TROUBLED FAMILIES: TWO CASE ILLUSTRATIONS

In the first example, an adolescent develops severe, incapacitating schizo-phrenic symptoms, leading the parents to get in touch with a therapist. Over the telephone, the therapist urges the entire family to come together, as a group, to his office.

Jerry M., a 17-year-old high school senior, living at home, suddenly began to show a dramatic change in his behavior. Formerly a friendly person, he be-came withdrawn and sometimes stayed in his room, behind a locked door, for several days at a time. He stopped attending school, refused to answer telephone calls from his friends, and demanded that his parents communi-cate with him only by passing notes under the door. When he did emerge from his room, he acted as though he were being plotted against by his fam-ily. He seemed to be hearing voices that were chastising him for his "evil" thoughts. When he finally spoke, he was incoherent and produced a jumble of words that made absolutely no sense to his dumbfounded parents.

Jerry was the only child of a traditional working-class family. The father, 54, worked on an automobile assembly line, a job he had held for over 25 years. He had a tenth-grade education, having dropped out of high school to help support his mother and younger sister when his father died. Jerry's mother, 44, had graduated from high school and attended a junior college at night for one semester before she left her clerical job and schooling to get married. Although the couple was childless for the first eight years of their marriage, Jerry's mother stayed at home as homemaker. There were times when she brought up the subject of returning to work, part-time, but her hus-band was adamant that his wife should not work.

Roles within the M. family were established early in the marriage and re-mained more or less fixed thereafter. Mr. M. earned the money, Mrs. M. took care of the house and her husband. He demanded that she keep a clean house, have meals ready on time, and be available for sexual relations when-ever he approached her. She expected him to work at a steady job and not gamble, drink, or chase other women. He controlled the money, giving her a weekly allowance for purchasing food. Mr. and Mrs. M. rarely, if ever, social-ized as a couple with other people. Generally on Sunday, Mr. M. would go with his friends to a soccer match, which his wife found boring and refused to attend. At home, he was likely to watch television nightly, especially sporting events. Mrs. M. preferred reading in another room.

When Jerry was born, he became Mrs. M.'s responsibility. Tired at night, lonely, bored, she became increasingly resentful of being neglected by her husband. In turn, her refusal of his sexual advances infuriated him, leading him to withdraw further from her. A stalemate resulted, with Mr. M. beginning to stay away from home more and more and Mrs. M. developing an increas-ingly close relationship with Jerry, whom she began to use as a substitute for her husband. As he grew up, Jerry had few friends and was considered a "mama's boy." Ashamed of the nonexistent relationship between his parents, he never invited a friend to his home. Increasingly, his schoolmates began to think of Jerry as odd, a loner.

The psychotherapist whom Jerry's parents contacted insisted that the entire family come to his office together for weekly sessions. On first impression, Mr. and Mrs. M. appeared solicitous toward Jerry—if he had a problem they would certainly try to help. However, it was clear from the first session that the parents communicated little with each other. Further sessions revealed that they had little in common, except for their concern over their "sick" child.

Slowly, the therapist helped them see that "Jerry's problem" was a family problem. It was the system that had broken down; Jerry was merely expressing that fact through his symptoms. As Mr. and Mrs. M., along with Jerry, continued seeing the therapist together, all were encouraged to express their feelings, especially their frustrations and dissatisfactions with one another. As Jerry's schizophrenic behavior was reduced and his symptoms disappeared, the fact that Mr. and Mrs. M. were in open conflict with each other became clear. The therapist decided to see them together without Jerry, who now was planning to attend college away from home after graduation.

Jerry's "symptoms" represented a desperate effort to hold his family together. Family therapy helped his parents to eventually work out a mutually satisfying relationship. Once that was accomplished, Jerry's "symptoms," no longer necessary, disappeared.

Jerry, the "identified patient," and his parents lived together in a closed, constricted system that they managed to keep in balance by making certain that all external stresses were kept to a minimum. Mrs. M., a dependent person in need of a strong male figure, made certain she did not tax herself by getting a job or making many friends, at the same time assuring herself that she was being a good wife by agreeing with her husband's wish that she stay home. Mr. M., insecure and defensive about his lack of education, needed to be the sole breadwinner so that he, his wife, and the rest of the world would see him as competent, strong, and masculine.

Together, Mr. and Mrs. M. lived a secluded and relatively joyless existence. However, it is important to emphasize that it was an existence at a level they both felt they could handle, one that was controlled, self-contained, tolerable, undemanding. They also managed to survive their first family crisis—the birth of Jerry. Within this traditional, inflexible role arrangement, the infant became Mrs. M.'s responsibility—one of the first major tasks for which she was accountable in their marriage. Mr. M., inexperienced and possibly fearful of intruding on the role already assigned to his wife, avoided responsibility for Jerry, convincing himself that women were more knowledgeable and thus better able to rear children. The stress that motherhood put on Mrs. M., and her husband's increasing resentment, served to heighten family tension considerably. Jerry's alliance with Mrs. M., although comforting to her, only made Mr. M. more bitter and more withdrawn.

As Jerry grew up, relatively friendless like his parents, he lacked the social skills necessary to cope with life outside the family. His periodic efforts to separate from the family and achieve some independence increased the strain and threatened to unbalance the precarious equilibrium the three had established. As a result, he withdrew back into the family.

Family therapy was directed at encouraging Jerry in his efforts to become a separate, autonomous person, while supporting Mr. and Mrs. M. in their efforts to let go of him. At the same time, the parents were assisted in their efforts to make friends and engage in more activities together. Ultimately, they felt their relationship was stable enough to "release" Jerry and continue to build on what they had together.

In our next example, Eric, age 9, is brought to a therapist by his parents because he is causing problems at home and at school. The parents, Laura and Mark T., are a young, upper-middle-class, well-educated couple with two other children: Lynne, age 7, and Patty, age 4. As in the previous case, and as is true in the overwhelming majority of cases seen by a family therapist, the dysfunctional behavior of the "identified patient" signals the therapist that the family is having problems.

Eric had been a difficult child as far back as his parents could remember. Bright, oversensitive, socially immature for his age, he frequently would fight with the other children in the neighborhood. At home, he was apt to cling to his parents, sometimes insisting they stay close to him before he would fall asleep at night. As he grew older, Eric began to have trouble at school; he did not like to leave his mother's side, and, once in school, he refused to study or do what the teacher requested. By way of contrast, his two younger sisters, both beautiful, were considered by relatives, friends, and teachers alike as "good little girls" and always held up to Eric as models he would do well to emulate. One additional source of family conflict was the fact that Eric was extremely unathletic, a fact his sports-minded father found difficult to accept. Eric had previously been in play therapy on a weekly basis when he was 6, although his parents terminated his sessions after two months because they believed he was making little progress for the expense involved.

When Eric came for psychotherapy this time, he was given a battery of psychological tests by the psychologist. Test results indicated he was an intelligent child, not seriously emotionally disturbed, but undergoing some current stress, probably of an **interpersonal** nature. When his parents were brought in to hear the results of the testing, they were extremely agitated, indicating they were at a loss to know how to handle Eric. They both claimed that, no matter what the test results indicated, the child was an irritant and the family would be a happy family if only he were not there.

During this discussion, with Eric not present, Mr. and Mrs. T. admitted they were having marital problems and needed counseling. The therapist suggested family therapy for the parents, Eric, and his sisters together. After two sessions, it became clear that the core problem in the family was the underlying conflict between the parents, which now was surfacing. The children were asked to stop attending, and the parents continued for 20 sessions. As the therapist had predicted, Eric's problems began to clear up at home and at school as his parents worked on their differences in therapy. In addition, the girls, Lynne and Patty, began to act like more normal children, no longer needing to show how "good" they were as compared to their "bad" brother.

The problems Mr. and Mrs. T. were having were a lot more difficult to resolve. Married right out of high school, they now found themselves ten years later at a quite different place in their lives. The mutual dependence of their early years together was gone, and they had developed very different attitudes and values. Their sexual relations, never entirely satisfactory, had deteriorated further in recent years, so that now they were almost nonexistent. Despite their efforts to make the marriage work, they drifted even further apart and finally decided to separate. After several months, they divorced. The children remained with Mrs. T.

Within two years, both Mr. and Mrs. T. had remarried, each to a partner who had children from a previous marriage. Some time after his mother's remarriage, Eric's school difficulties flared up once again. When Eric, along with his natural mother and stepfather, came to see the family therapist, all three were upset and quarreling. The therapist recognized that the old fight between Eric's natural parents had resumed, with their new spouses presumably adding fuel to the fire. True to form, Eric once again offered himself as the family scapegoat by reviving his behavior problems.

The therapist requested that all four adults—Eric's parents and stepparents—join Eric for several joint sessions. Although a great deal of quarreling went on, particularly between the two women, each assisted by her husband, some resolution of the conflict occurred, and, once again, Eric's symptomatic behavior waned. Later, the therapist was able to help Mr. T. and his new wife work out some difficulties they were having concerning their differential treatment of their children and stepchildren.

One important distinction between this family and the one in the previous example is that here we are dealing with an upper-middle-class, achievement-oriented family, and thus one that is apt to have high expectations for the children and is likely to place a high value on competition and accomplishment. (We will discuss the relationship between socioeconomic class and family functioning later in this chapter.) For the T. family, it was important that each member strive to be perfect. The therapist discovered, after meeting the entire family, just how central to their day-to-day functioning was the emphasis on winning, being successful, being on top. Not only Eric but also the other family members showed stress-related symptoms: Lynne was the top student in her class, received straight A's, and was crestfallen if she made a mistake in class; Patty, not yet in school, spent a great deal of time fishing for compliments on her appearance and was a nailbiter; Mrs. T. was preoccupied with her status in the community; her husband relished his luxury automobile and on weekends played basketball with a group ten years his junior.

The whole family, with the exception of Eric, had found socially acceptable ways of expressing competitiveness and status seeking. Although Eric was no more stressed than the others, his extreme discomfort around home and school and his antagonistic behavior toward the teacher were more obvious signs of what he must be experiencing internally. Moreover, once the boy had been identified as a family scapegoat, his sister tormented him and kept telling their parents that he was responsible for whatever was missing or broken in the house.

As their strivings for achievement, especially for social status and financial success, were fulfilled, and they felt somewhat less driven to make good, the parents looked at their marriage and found it rather empty. Mrs. T. began to realize that, to compensate for the unfulfilling relationship with her husband, she had overconnected with her son, even though she was dissatisfied with him. Mr. T. recognized he was spending more and more time away from home in order to avoid family tensions. As the parents eased up on their demands, the children relaxed more, but Mr. and Mrs. T. found less and less purpose in staying together.

This case illustrates several points about intervention and outcome. Family therapy can occur with subsections of a family and need not involve the entire group. Not all couples live happily ever after; in reality, divorce is a common consequence and often is for the better of all concerned. The family therapist tries to remain flexible, dealing with various combinations of people at different times, including new extended-family members (ex-spouses, stepparents). Finally, this case demonstrates that brief therapy at different phases of stress within a family can be helpful and effective.

CHANGING AMERICAN FAMILIES

There is no typical American "family" today. It is more accurate to speak of types of "families," with diverse organizational patterns, diverse styles of living, diverse living arrangements. The traditional family structure—the conventional intact, self-reliant, middle-class nuclear family consisting of a full-time homemaker mother with exclusive responsibility for child care, a sole wage earner (the father), and dependent children all living in the same household—is now in the minority. Although this model remains for many Americans a standard by which they judge the "normal American family," in fact fewer than one in four American families of the 1980s fit that description (Walsh, 1982). Today there are a variety of family household arrangements (see Table 1-1), attitudes toward marriage and divorce are changing, and more and more couples are accepting the idea of males and females being equally involved in parenting and in work activities.

National surveys continue to document the drop in marriage rates, the jump in divorce rates (now double what they were as recently as 1965), the significant increase in the number of unwed mothers, and the dramatic rise in the number of Americans choosing to live alone. Masnick and Bane (1980) predict that, by 1990, of the 20 million new households that will be formed during the prior 15 years, only 3–4 million will be made up of married couples. Those who are divorced, those who never married, those who live together without the formality of a wedding ceremony, **gay couples,** and those who are widowed or deserted will likely make up the remainder. As historian Hareven (1982) points out, such variations in life-styles are not necessarily new; rather, they reflect a more open society—a society more tolerant of social change, individual preferences and priorities, and alternative options. Different forms of living styles have been in existence all along, Hareven argues, but have been less visible

TABLE 1–1. Common Variations in Family Organization and Structure

Family type	Composition of family unit
Nuclear family	Husband, wife, children
Extended family	Nuclear family plus grandparents, uncles, aunts, and so on
Blended family	Husband, wife, plus children from previous marriage(s)
Common-law family	Man, woman, and possibly children living together as a family, although the former two have not gone through a formal legal marriage ceremony
Single-parent family	Household led by one parent (man or woman), possibly due to divorce, death, desertion, or to never having married
Commune family	Men, women, and children living together, sharing rights and responsibilities, and collectively owning and/or using property, sometimes abandoning traditional monogamous marriages
Serial family	Man or woman has a succession of marriages, thus acquiring several spouses and different families over a lifetime but one nuclear family at a time
Composite family	A form of polygamous marriage in which two or more nuclear families share a common husband (polygyny) or wife (polyandry), the former being more prevalent
Cohabitation	A more or less permanent relationship between two unmarried persons of the opposite sex who share a nonlegally binding living arrangement
Gay couples	Couples of the same gender who develop and maintain a homosexual relationship

than they are now. What we are witnessing is not a fragmentation of traditional family patterns but the emergence of a greater acceptance of pluralism in family living arrangements.

Even the nuclear family is undergoing dramatic changes. American women working at paying jobs—many of them mothers of young children—already outnumber those who stay at home. Two-income families are becoming more commonplace, resulting in many changes in role sharing and child rearing, in widespread use of day-care facilities and domestic help, and in relationship changes between husband and wife. A "career woman" in the past was likely to be defensive about not devoting most of her time and energies to her home, husband, and children. Today she probably is either a working wife trying to attend to her job and home (with assistance from her husband and others), a single woman who may or may not marry, a married woman who has chosen to delay or forego having children, or the head of a single-parent household. And it is the woman who describes herself as "only a housewife" who today may feel on the defensive.

One major reason for these changing family patterns is the fact that divorce has become more commonplace than ever before. Nowadays, almost four out of ten marriages end in divorce, because people with marital problems are less willing to maintain an unhappy marriage than were their counterparts in the past. Greater public acceptance of divorce, liberalized divorce laws (shorter state residence requirements, "no-fault" divorce proceedings, briefer waiting periods for the final divorce decree, efforts to arrange joint custody of the children), and the increased economic independence of women (which makes them less likely to stay in a marriage for reasons of financial security) have all contributed to this phenomenon and made divorce a realistic alternative to an unhappy marriage. Rather than representing the breakdown of the family, divorce may mean that people care enough about the quality of family life and marriage that they willingly dissolve an unsatisfactory relationship and seek alternative arrangements (Hareven, 1982).

The rising divorce rate has contributed greatly to the diversity of contemporary family life, because many people, following the dissolution of their marriage, either choose or are forced to become heads of single-parent households. The number of families led by one parent has doubled in the last decade, according to data provided by the U.S. Bureau of the Census (1982). Of these households, 90% are headed by divorced mothers and 10% by divorced fathers. It is interesting to note that the phenomenon of households led by divorced fathers was almost nonexistent a decade ago. And the proportion of single-parent families, which was only 11% of all American families barely a decade ago, has jumped to over 21%, an extraordinary leap in a single ten-year span. In 1981, fully half of all Black families with children at home were led by one parent, almost certainly the mother. Economic strain, the demand that the parent play the dual role of mother and father, parental fatigue and feelings of loneliness, and the inevitable need for children to play roles beyond their maturity level are some of the many problems that typically occur in such family arrangements.

Remarriage is also on the increase (80% of those who get divorced remarry), especially for divorced men, suggesting a commitment to family life even if a previous marriage was an unhappy experience. As a result, stepfamilies have become common, as divorced people remarry and the children from the previous marriage of each are blended into one family. Visher and Visher (1982) estimate that in the United States over 35 million adults are stepparents and that one child in six is a stepchild. In some sections of the country, the figures may be as high as one in four.

There are a wide variety of family patterns represented among stepfamilies (women with no children married to divorced men with custody of their children, or vice versa; remarriages in which each partner has children, some or all or none of whom may be living under one roof all or part of the time; stepfamilies that in addition to any of the above patterns also include children from the parents' present marriage). Endless reruns of television situation comedies such as *The Brady Bunch* to the contrary, such blending more often brings new complications and puts stresses on the family's ability to establish and redefine relationships. Stepparenting has created new extended families made up of ex-spouses, new spouses, and assorted grandparents as well as the children and their stepsiblings, making it difficult to keep track of so many new relationships. As Nass (1978) illustrates in a rather overwhelming example:

If a divorced woman with children, for instance, marries a divorced man whose children from his former marriage visit him occasionally, the new relationships include those between the new husband and wife, the wife and the husband's children, the husband and the wife's children, the two sets of children who must at least sometimes live together, the husband and the wife's ex-husband, the wife and the husband's ex-wife, the new couple and the new in-laws on either side, the spouses' parents and their stepchildren, and everybody with any new children conceived within the remarriage [p. 439].

Marital separation, divorce, and then remarriage, especially when children are involved, inevitably create dislocations within a family system. In addition to the specific problems indigenous to any particular stepfamily, we must consider the following structural problems characteristic of all stepfamilies: (1) all members have experienced important losses (such as the death of a parent, separation from a parent or sibling, life in an unfamiliar community away from old friends); (2) families come together suddenly with different (and often contradictory) experiences, traditions, values, and expectations that must be resolved; (3) parent–child bonds predate the new husband–wife relationship and often put an instant strain on a new and fragile marriage, without allowing a period of intimate time for the newlyweds to learn to strengthen their new relationship; (4) a biological parent exists, in actuality or memory, and continues to influence the formation, promotion, or building of new ties; (5) children may be members of two households simultaneously, especially under a joint-custody arrangement, and may find themselves caught up in an unfinished war between parents (Visher & Visher, 1982).

Ninety-six out of every 100 American adults marry; nearly two-thirds of these people remain married until separated by death. Of the 38% who get divorced, 75% of the women and 83% of the men remarry within three years. Clearly, marriage remains the preferred state for the majority of our population. Even those who know from bitter experience that marriage is not all harmony and satisfactions are willing to try again, accepting the fact that intimacy provides not only love and care but often tension and conflict as well. Both aspects of marriage are inseparable parts of intimate relationships. All the changing patterns described above mean that we are experiencing not the death of the family but the demystification of family life, the erosion of sentimental myths about the family. The various alternative family styles existing today (see Table 1–1) do not mean that the traditional nuclear family is obsolete; rather, that it is not the only possible living arrangement.

Our society is likely to continue to experiment with unconventional family patterns and nonfamilial living organizations. A rise in singlehood, delayed marriages, **dual-career marriages, cohabitation,** child-free marriages, blended families, single-parent (especially female-headed) families, homosexual couples, and possibly other as yet unfamiliar patterns can be anticipated. We live in a pluralistic society as well as in a period of rapid social change; together, these two aspects assure U.S. contemporary life continuing diversity and a heterogeneous culture.

THE PROCESS OF FAMILY DEVELOPMENT

Having looked at some of the structural aspects of the family today, we now turn to the family's developmental process and examine the stages through which a family passes over time. Frequently, family behavior patterns or even crises are more understandable when they are seen within the context of the family's current phase of development. Moreover, the development of an individual family member can be fully understood only with reference to the family situation in which that growth is promoted or inhibited. According to Carter and McGoldrick (1980), it is the family's life cycle "that is the major context and determinant of the development of individual family members" (p. 4). If we can identify the phase of the family's development, we will know what tasks its various members—grandparents, parents, children—are attempting to master as the family, an ongoing system, moves through time.

Before we discuss some typical sequences of the **family life cycle** for various kinds of families, we should note that all families, like individuals, pass through certain predictable events or phases (such as marriage, the birth of the first child, the onset of adolescence) but may also be confronted suddenly by unexpected events (financial reverses, teenage pregnancy, birth of a defective child). Such crises disrupt the family's normal flow of development and inevitably produce relationship changes within the family system. As Neugarten (1976) points out, the inappropriate or unanticipated timing of a major event may be particularly traumatic precisely because it upsets the sequence and disturbs the rhythm of the expected course of life. As examples, Neugarten cites the death of a parent during one's childhood, teenage marriage, first marriage postponed until late in life, or a child born to parents in mid-life.

Disruptions to family life may also occur as a result of what Hoffman (1980) calls "discontinuous changes"—changes that suddenly shake up and transform a family system so profoundly that it never returns to its former way of functioning. Hoffman notes particularly those events that affect family membership—events representing gain (children acquired through remarriage) or loss (separation, death). Even a natural transition point that produces major shifts in roles (a child entering kindergarten, a husband retiring from his lifelong work) may serve as a "discontinuous change" and have a similar effect on the family system.

Family Life Cycle[2]

As we have suggested, intact families go through more or less the same developmental process over time. They pass through the same sequences or phases, most of which are marked by a critical transition point—marriage, birth of the first child, departure from home of the youngest child, retirement. Much like

[2]The reader might assume from the following discussion that we believe that all families remain intact over the lifetimes of the parents, that all families have children, and so on. Of course this is not the case. In recent years there has been a dramatic rise in the rate of divorce and an increase in the number of single-parent families. There is a trend for young men and women to live together without being married, or to marry after some years of living together, or to marry but decide to

an individual, a family can be viewed as going through a life cycle as members age and play a variety of roles in succession. To be sure, each family has its unique and peculiar rhythms and tempos, its own disappointments and re- wards, but a longitudinal frame of reference is generally useful for looking at family life (Duvall, 1977). From a family therapy perspective, psychiatric symp- toms (anxiety, for example, or depression) are thought to appear in a family member when there is a dislocation or interruption in the naturally unfolding family life cycle. The symptom is a signal that the family is having problems mastering the tasks associated with that stage of the life cycle (Haley, 1973).

In *Uncommon Therapy* (1973), Haley presents and expands on the theories and therapeutic strategies of Milton Erickson, an extraordinarily inventive psychiatrist who contributed much of the rationale and therapeutic techniques of both family therapy and **hypnotherapy.** With the stages of the family life cycle as his frame of reference, Haley argues that the appearance of symptoms in any family member signals that the whole family is "stuck," experiencing difficulties moving on to the next phase of its cycle. Traditionally, for example, a woman who suffers a postpartum depression following the birth of a child is commonly thought to be undergoing an intense, intrapsychic conflict. The fam- ily therapy viewpoint, on the other hand, is that the entire family is having difficulty as it enters the new phase in its development marked by the baby's birth. The task for the family therapist is to help the family members resolve the immediate crisis and achieve a new balance; if therapy is successful, the family will resume its developmental course.

Traditional middle-class American families generally proceed through the life cycle in this sequence: two unattached adults marry and separate from their families of origin, learn to accommodate to each other as husband and wife, and assume new roles as father and mother with the arrival of their first child. Each addition to the family not only increases the size of the family but significantly reorganizes the family structure and way of living. We might say that no two children are ever born into the identical family situation. As the family matures, new parent–child relationships develop; the mother's and father's relationship to each other may undergo change in the process. The family that once expanded to accommodate the requirements of growing chil- dren must later contract when these children launch their own families. Duvall (1977) portrays the typical life cycle of an intact family in terms of a circle with eight sectors (Figure 1–1). No one family is apt to resemble the model in all particulars, but the circle helps us to plot the stages through which families typically pass and to predict the approximate time in the family's life cycle when each stage will be reached. Note especially that about half of an average family's life is spent with children at home, half with husband and wife alone.

---

remain childless. Despite the fact that most research on the family-life cycle pertains to conven- tional middle-class family arrangements, we will try to focus on the changes in the relationships among family members as the family matures, since such observations are broadly applicable to all family living arrangements. Later in this chapter we will consider some features of the life cycles of non-traditional families.

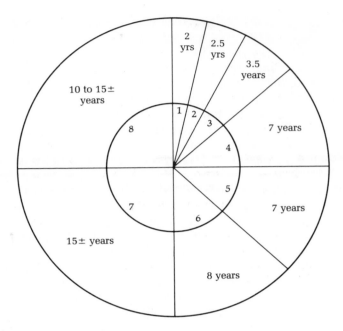

1. Married couples
   (without children)
2. Childbearing families
   (oldest child, birth—30 months)
3. Families with preschool children
   (oldest child 30 months—6 years)
4. Families with schoolchildren
   (oldest child 6—13 years)
5. Families with teenagers
   (oldest child 13—20 years)
6. Families as launching centers (first
   child gone to last child leaving home)
7. Middle-aged parents
   (empty nest to retirement)
8. Aging family members
   (retirement to death of both spouses)

Figure 1-1. The traditional family life cycle by length of time in each of the eight stages of life as proposed by Duvall (1977). The duration of each stage has implications for budgeting, housing needs, health care, recreation, education, home management, and various other family resources and services. Note especially that one-half of the marriage typically is spent as a couple after the children have grown and left the home. (Source: Duvall, 1977)

   Carter and McGoldrick (1980) provide another approach to understanding the family life cycle. In their view, a family system encompasses at least three generations; although the typical American family maintains its own two-generational household, the members of that family are bound to react to past, present, and future relationships within the three-generational family system. Life cycle transitions affect all members simultaneously as grandparents cope with the problems of old age, parents are dealing with the departure of their last child—"the empty nest"—and the children are attempting to become independent adults. The events occurring at any one stage of the life cycle have a powerful influence on relationships at another stage.

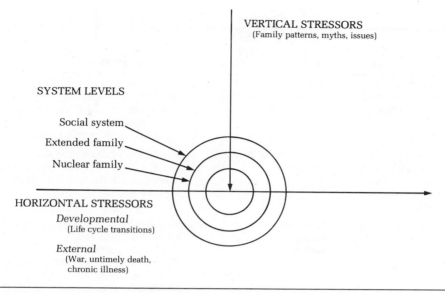

Figure 1-2. Horizontal and vertical stressors within a family system. (Source: Carter & McGoldrick, 1980, p. 10)

According to Carter and McGoldrick (1980), dysfunctional behavior in individual family members is related to "vertical" and "horizontal" stressors within the family system. The vertical stressors include patterns of relating and functioning that are transmitted down through generations—family attitudes, expectations, prejudices, and taboos. The horizontal stressors are the anxiety-producing events experienced as the family moves through its life cycle—the various maturational crises as well as unexpected, traumatic ones. Figure 1-2 depicts the impact of stress on a family extending beyond the nuclear family. With enough stress on the horizontal axis, any family will become dysfunctional. However, even a small amount of horizontal stress can cause great disruption to a family in which the vertical axis already contains intense stress. Carter and McGoldrick maintain that the family therapist must look at both vertical and horizontal stressors to predict how well a family will manage its life transitions. In addition to current life cycle stress, he or she must look at the stress "inherited" from earlier generations. The greater the anxiety experienced by previous generations at any transitional point (for instance, at the birth of the first child), the more difficult or anxiety producing or dysfunctional that point will be for this generation.

Family Developmental Tasks

Each phase of family development requires that the family face new tasks and learn new adaptational techniques; correspondingly, the family faces new risks of family dysfunction. Successful adaptation at any one phase depends

TABLE 1-2. The Stages of the Family Life Cycle

Family life cycle stage	Emotional process of transition: Key principles	Second order changes in family status required to proceed developmentally
1. Between families: the unattached young adult	Accepting parent-offspring separation	a. Differentiation of self in relation to family of origin b. Development of intimate peer relationships c. Establishment of self in work
2. The joining of families through marriage: the newly married couple	Commitment to new system	a. Formation of marital system b. Realignment of relationships with extended family and friends to include spouse
3. The family with young children	Accepting new members into the system	a. Adjusting marital system to make space for child(ren) b. Taking on parenting roles c. Realignment of relationships with extended family to include parenting and grandparenting roles
4. The family with adolescents	Increasing flexibility of family boundaries to include children's independence	a. Shifting of parent-child relationship to permit adolescent to move in and out of system b. Refocus on mid-life marital and career issues c. Beginning shift toward concerns for older generation

heavily on the family's ability to master the tasks required at the previous phase. We might ask "How well did the family do on its last assignment?" For example, a young husband and wife who have not achieved enough separation from their parents to be able to establish their own independent unit as a couple may experience considerable distress, conflict, and confusion when they enter their next phase—the birth and rearing of their own children.

Successful separation from one's family of origin is the first stage in a new family life cycle. All too often, a young adult marries prematurely as a means of disengaging from the enmeshed family system in which he or she grew up. Once the marriage has taken place—the escape made—the couple is faced with finding a sounder basis for their life together, or the relationship will flounder (Haley, 1973).

Another unsatisfactory rationale for marriage is the wish to secure an emotional refuge that will substitute for the family of origin. Partners who are thus motivated to marry are, in effect, bypassing the "unattached young adult" phase of the life cycle (see Table 1-2). Carter and McGoldrick (1980) contend

TABLE 1-2. (continued)

Family life cycle stage	Emotional process of transition: Key principles	Second order changes in family status required to proceed developmentally
5. Launching children and moving on	Accepting a multitude of exits from and entries into the family system	a. Renegotiation of marital system as a dyad b. Development of adult to adult relationships between grown children and their parents c. Realignment of relationships to include in-laws and grandchildren d. Dealing with disabilities and death of parents (grandparents)
6. The family in later life	Accepting the shifting of generational roles	a. Maintaining own and/or couple functioning and interests in face of physiological decline; exploration of new familial and social role options b. Support for a more central role for middle generation c. Making room in the system for the wisdom and experience of the elderly; supporting the older generation without overfunctioning for them d. Dealing with loss of spouse, siblings and other peers and preparation for own death. Life review and integration

Source: Carter & McGoldrick, 1980, p. 17.

that, until the present generation, few women had the opportunity to experience this stage; traditionally, the responsibility for a young woman was handed from her father to her husband. Today, both men and women have the freedom to establish identities independent of their families of origin.

Early in marriage, the partners must learn to develop new patterns of behavior that are mutually satisfying. Each mate has acquired from his or her own family a set of expectations or rules for marital interaction. Minuchin and associates (1978) call these the partners' paradigms. In the marriage, both paradigms must be retained so that each person maintains a sense of self; the two paradigms must also be reconciled in order for the couple to have a life in common. In the process of reconciling their paradigms, spouses arrive at new transactional patterns—compromises or tacit agreements to disagree—that become familiar and ultimately their preferred way of dealing with each other. In the marital coalition, the partners must not only provide for their basic physical needs but negotiate (and renegotiate over a period of time) such personal issues as when and how to sleep, eat, have sex, fight, and make up. They must decide how to celebrate holidays, plan vacations, spend money, and do household chores. The transition to becoming a functional marital couple is a difficult one; almost certainly, it is the most significant challenge the partners are likely to have faced up to this point in their young lives.

A newly married couple also has the developmental task of separating still further from their families of origin. New relationships must be negotiated with each set of parents, siblings, and in-laws. Loyalties must shift if the couple's primary commitment is to be to the marriage, and the families of origin must accept and support this break (Minuchin, 1974a). In the same way, each spouse must meet the other's friends and select those who will become the couple's friends. Together they gain new friends and lose touch with old ones.

When first married, the spouses have roles that are flexible and interchange-able. The structure of a family without children allows for a wide variety of solutions to immediate problems. For example, either or both of the partners may prepare dinner; they may choose to go out to eat; they may drop in at a friend's or parents' house for a meal; or they may eat separately. When there are children to be fed, a more formal and specific solution will have to be formulated in advance of dinnertime. The distribution of duties, the division of labor, must be more clearly defined: who will shop, cook, pick up the child at the child-care center, wash the dishes? The physical and emotional commit-ments to offspring usually change the transactional patterns between spouses. The risk at that point is that roles between husband and wife may become too fixed, too rigid, without room for the previous flexibility.

The decision to have children, then, represents another highly significant transition point in the life cycle. Hareven (1982) points out that marriage no longer inevitably leads to parenthood—as it did in earlier times—so couples today need not postpone a wedding ceremony to delay becoming parents. In many ways, the partners' lives may not change nearly as much by getting married as by having children; this is even more likely to be the case if they live together before marriage and/or have established a satisfactory sexual rela-tionship. Child rearing may take a woman away from adult social life and work activities for a period of time, and this may be personally frustrating to her and potentially damaging to the marriage.

When husband and wife become parents, both must "move up" a generation and provide care for a younger generation. Making this shift, taking and shar-ing responsibility, developing patience, setting limits, tolerating the restriction of their free time and their mobility, all these tasks must be accomplished by the couple. The most common period of crisis, according to Haley (1973), occurs when children start school; this represents the family's first step toward the realization that the children will eventually leave home. If a grandparent lives with the family, the resulting grandparent–parent–child triangle may intensify the conflict in the home over how best to deal with the growing child; single-parent households are particularly vulnerable.

When children reach adolescence, the family faces new challenges. Parents of adolescents may no longer be able to maintain complete authority but they cannot abdicate authority completely. Adolescents must strike a balance of their own: teenagers who remain too childlike and dependent or who become too isolated and independent may become problems, putting a strain on the family system. The three-generation triangle must also adjust to changing relationships between adolescents and grandparents, necessitating adjustments between parents and their own parents.

In the middle years of marriage, a husband may begin to realize that he will not fulfill his youthful ambitions; conversely, he may achieve more success than he had anticipated. In the former case, his depression may permeate the entire family; in the latter, his wife may still relate to him as he was before, causing resentment and family conflict. A wife, similarly, may discover that she has not fulfilled certain earlier ambitions for a career or realized her hopes for a particular kind of marriage relationship. As her free time increases, she may consider employment outside the home but feel insecure about her skills and abilities. Life at home may seem to have lost its purpose, now that the children are grown and need her less. Grandparents may become more dependent and needy just at the time when the last child leaves the house. The parents must work on their own relationship since they will spend more and more time alone together in the coming years. Some partners see this phase as liberating—a carefree time for travel and new hobbies—while others may need to take considerable caretaking responsibility for elderly and infirm parents of their own. The family as a whole must deal with changes in roles, the loss of older members, and the entry of new members during this transitional phase.

The retirement years mean that a husband and wife must cope with a dramatic increase in their daily time together and, usually, a significant reduction in income. A man must detach himself from his familiar occupational role, and both he and his wife must work out new arrangements with each other and find some new involvements outside the home. Enduring the loss of friends and relatives, coping with role reversal and dependence on one's children, handling relationships with grandchildren, relinquishing power and status, coming to terms with one's own illness or limitations—these are the problems of later life. With the death of one partner, the family must often assume care of the surviving parent, with all family members experiencing a new set of transitional stresses.

Alternative Families

Clearly, not all families fit the life cycle we have outlined, nor do all families face identical developmental tasks. As we noted earlier, disruptions can occur in any family because of sudden, unexpected traumatic events. In addition, not all families resemble the picture of the flourishing, intact, middle-class, nuclear family or extended family we have presented. In this section we take a look at some key exceptions: (1) families that, because of disrupting events such as marital separation, divorce, and possibly remarriage, must restabilize the family life cycle before resuming their ongoing development, and (2) families from different ethnic or socioeconomic backgrounds whose culture is an influence on family transaction patterns, behavioral rules, communication styles, and belief systems.

Single-parent families are created in a number of ways—death of a spouse, desertion, separation, divorce, or births outside of marriage. Most single-parent families result from divorce, and 90% consist of single mothers and their children. Perhaps as many as 20% of today's children will spend at least part of their childhoods with a single parent. Of all types of family structures, single-parent families are most clearly at risk of dysfunction (Lamb, 1982). Single mothers—many of whom have not worked outside the home for years and lack skills as well as recent work experience—struggle to find jobs for adequate pay. Many find themselves socially isolated from their coupled friends. **Role overload,** loneliness, lack of partner support, the strain of solo decision making, jealous reactions from children if they choose to date, the demand for children to take roles and responsibilities prematurely—all these are potential hazards. The stage of the life cycle at which the family becomes a single-parent family is often a vital factor affecting the nature and intensity of the problems to be expected and the likelihood of dealing with them successfully (whether preschool age children are involved or only late adolescents, whether education and/or work experience is recent and marketable or not, whether remarriage is being considered or not). According to the longitudinal research findings reported by Hetherington, Cox, and Cox (1982), the main areas of change and stress occur to single parents in the following order:

> first, those related to practical problems of living such as economic and occupational problems and problems in running a household; second, those associated with emotional distress and changes in self-concept and identity; and third, interpersonal problems in maintaining a social life, in the development of intimate relationships, and in interactions with the ex-spouse and child [p. 244].

According to Hetherington, Cox, and Cox (1982), mothers, fathers, and children alike continue to experience severe emotional stress a year after divorce. Divorce clearly interrupts the sequence of the traditional family life cycle, resulting in a disequilibrium that may take considerable time—perhaps two years or more—to restore (McGoldrick & Carter, 1982). In the course of separation and divorce, each partner needs to come to terms with his or her own part in the failure of the marriage; deal with custody, visitation, and financial arrangements; inform family and friends. Eventually, family members must go through a period of mourning for the loss of the intact family—and ultimately surrender their fantasies of a reunion. After the divorce, the family faces the difficult tasks of rebuilding its social networks and restructuring parent–child relationships.

Remarriage and the formation of a stepfamily not only cause further disruption in the family life cycle but initiate a new one: the "old" nuclear family life cycle persists in some form (with continuing visitation, custody, and financial arrangements; ties to old extended families) and a "new" family life cycle begins (Sager, Brown, Crohn, Engel, Rodstein & Walker, 1983).

Ethnic and Socioeconomic Considerations

Ethnicity, the unique characteristics of a cultural subgroup, is surely a fundamental determinant of how families establish and reinforce acceptable values, behavior patterns, and modes of emotional expression. Transmitted over generations by the family, ethnicity patterns surpass race, religion, or national origin in significance for the family, representing deeper psychological needs for identity and a sense of historical continuity (McGoldrick, 1982). Our ethnic backgrounds influence how we think, how we feel, how we work, how we relax, how we celebrate holidays, how we express our anxieties, how we feel about life and death. If it is superficial to try to understand an individual's behavior without some awareness of that person's family of origin, it is equally naive not to acknowledge the contribution of ethnic style and cultural tradition.

Even the definition of "family" differs in different groups. The dominant American White, Anglo-Saxon, Protestant (WASP) definition focuses on the intact nuclear family. Blacks expand their definition to include a network of kin and community. Italians think in terms of tightly knit three- or four-generation families, often including godfathers and old friends. The Chinese include all ancestors and descendants in their definition.

Similarly, family life cycle timing is influenced by ethnic considerations. For example, Mexican Americans have longer courtship periods and extend childhood beyond the dominant American pattern but shorten adolescence and hasten adulthood. Different groups also define problematic behavior differently. If WASPs are concerned about expressing emotionality, the Irish, according to McGoldrick (1982), are fearful of "making a scene," while Italians worry about family disloyalty, Greeks about an insult to their pride, Jews about their children not being successful, Puerto Ricans about not receiving respect from their children.

Although cautioning family therapists not to think in terms of stereotypes (some families, for example, are more assimilated than others to mainstream American society, some have long histories of intermarriages, and so on), McGoldrick, Pearce and Giordano (1982) provide what they describe as "paradigms" outlining common family patterns for 19 different ethnic groups. These authors wish to emphasize the importance of ethnocultural factors in behavior. Since therapists inevitably impose some of their own cultural biases on their work, they need to be more aware of their own values as well as those values influenced by the cultural backgrounds of client families. Rather than oversimplified pictures of ethnic groups to be taken at face value, the 19 profiles are intended to call attention to the rich variety of human experiences and behavior—to emphasize the fact that family therapists must consider the possible impact of cultural idiosyncrasies in assessing and treating families they might otherwise label deviant or dysfunctional.

In the same manner, therapists need to be alert to socioeconomic factors, being careful not to impose middle-class viewpoints and values when inappropriate and culturally biased. Poor families, often deprived for many generations, may evolve a family life cycle pattern at considerable odds with middle-class expectations. For example, as Colon (1980) notes, unattached young people—perhaps 10 or 11 years of age—may be virtually unaccountable to parents or older adults. Drawn by peers away from family ties and influences, many of them struggle, eventually recognize the few options available to them, and ultimately turn to illegal activity (drug traffic or prostitution). Others are more fortunate: better endowed, more determined to escape, they may succeed, but often at the expense of losing connections with cultural roots, family, and friends. Colon considers young adulthood to be the most critical of all life-cycle stages for the economically impoverished person, because many later life developments are determined by whether that person remains in or escapes from the context of poverty.

The chronic stress of poverty, the sense of defeat and helplessness, and the pervasive feelings of despair, impotence, and rage make survival a daily battle for many poor people. However, poor families are often able to call upon resources not ordinarily available to their middle-class counterparts—neighbors, large extended families, or community members who can lend a hand in times of trouble or grief periods. When several generations live in one household, a grandmother may take over the child-rearing role for a young, unmarried daughter, raising the children as her own. Although desertion or illegitimacy may be widespread, they are often viewed with a sense of tolerance and acceptance.

The family therapist, likely to be middle-class, must be careful not to regard being poor as synonymous with leading a chaotic, disorganized life. It is essential to distinguish between those families who have been poor for many generations, poor intermittently, or recently poor because of loss (such as the death of the major wage earner). It also helps to be aware that some poor people share middle-class values and others embrace the values of the working class. Some lead lives that are a series of crises, and others have forged family and social networks that are resourceful and workable. Above all, as Aponte (1976) reminds us, any efforts to equate poverty with psychological deviance first must take into account the social conditions associated with being poor.

SUMMARY

A family is a natural social system typically extending over at least three generations. The way it functions—it establishes roles, communicates, and negotiates differences between members—has numerous implications for the development and well-being of its individual members. Adopting a family perspective, a member's dysfunctional behavior may represent a system that is in disequilibrium; he or she may simply be the "identified patient," a representative of a troubled family. From a family perspective, the locus of pathology can be found in family relationships and clinical intervention involves the entire family unit. Such an approach views the family as a living system and calls for an epistemological shift in conceptualizing human transactions.

Americans today have a variety of living styles and living arrangements in addition to the traditional nuclear family. The single-parent household, the stepfamily, extended singlehood, cohabitation, child-free marriage, dual-career marriage, and gay couples all represent alternatives to the familiar nuclear family organization. A major reason for these changing family patterns is the large jump in the divorce rate in recent years.

A family undergoes a life cycle of its own, providing a context for determining the development of individual family members. Passing through expected milestones as well as dealing with unexpected crises may temporarily threaten the family's usual developmental progress, causing realignments in the family system. Each stage in the cycle calls for accepting and completing certain developmental tasks. Alternative families, such as those led by single parents and those where remarriage has created a stepfamily, may experience disruptions in the life cycle before resuming their development.

Ethnic background may help determine how many families establish values, behavior patterns, and modes of emotional expression. Although family therapists must be careful not to stereotype individuals and entire families on the basis of such ethnocultural factors, they need to be aware of their own cultural biases and to take other cultural influences into account before judging the behavior of others as deviant or dysfunctional. Similarly, they need to be alert to the strengths and weaknesses that may result from growing up and living in a poor family.

CHAPTER TWO

Functional and Dysfunctional Family Systems

We have described the family as a natural social system that can be studied in terms of its structure (the way it arranges or organizes itself at any given moment) and its processes (the ways in which it changes over time). Before continuing our exploration of how families operate as ongoing living systems, we need to discuss systems theory itself and demonstrate its relevance to family functioning. Later in the book we hope to clarify how such a theoretical framework may provide the rationale for therapeutic intervention at the family level.

SYSTEMS THEORY: SOME BASIC CONSIDERATIONS

A system may be defined as a set of interacting units with relationships among them (Miller, 1978) or as sets of elements standing in interaction (Bertalanffy, 1968). That is, a system is an entity with component parts or units that covary, with each unit constrained by or dependent on the state of other units. There are solar systems, ecosystems, systems of law, electronic systems, and so on. In each case, there are components that have some common properties. These components interact so that each influences and in turn is influenced by other component parts, together producing a whole—a system—that is larger than the sum of its interdependent parts.

As Gray, Duhl and Rizzo (1969) explain, systems theory represents a new scientific approach because it emphasizes wholeness, the interaction of component parts, and organization as unifying principles. The systems perspective deliberately rejects such traditional reductionistic concepts as the familiar stimulus/response (S/R) model, which it considers a simplistic, mechanistic, linear way of explaining behavior by means of a step-by-step cause-and-effect equation. To the systems scientist, all forms of life need to be understood as existing within a certain time and space and as organized into interacting components. The system provides the context in which relationships between component parts may be understood and, if necessary, changed.

The concept of **organization** is fundamental to systems theory (Steinglass, 1978). If a system represents a set of units or elements that stand in some consistent relationship to each other, then we can infer that the system is organized around those relationships. Furthermore, we can say that the elements of the system interact with each other in a predictable, "organized" fashion.

These elements, once combined, produce an entity that is greater than the sum of its parts. This concept of **wholeness,** deceptively simple and generally taken for granted, actually represents two fundamental principles of systems theory. First, no system can be adequately understood or fully explained once it has been broken down into its component parts or elements. Second, no element within the system can ever be understood in isolation since it never functions independently; in other words, the units within a system are so interrelated that the state of each is constrained by the state of all the others.

Boundaries represent the perimeter of a system; they hold together the components that make up the system, protect them from outside stresses and control the flow of matter, energy and information to and from the system itself (Miller, 1978). We may also think of boundaries as membranes or borders between a system and its environment. As such, they have both protective and regulating functions. Boundaries help keep the elements within the system intact and cohesive. At the same time, they can be permeable and allow the system free and easy exchange with other systems or be impermeable and restrict the system's interaction with the world outside. If boundaries are too permeable, the system loses its integrity and identity. If boundaries are too impermeable, the system is cut off and isolated.

An **open system** receives input—matter, energy, or information—from the environment and discharges output into the environment. The boundaries of an open system must be flexible enough to permit these transactions with the outside world, but not so poorly defined that the system loses the unity of its parts or its wholeness. A **closed system** has no exchanges with the environment; it operates only within the confines of its own boundaries. Open systems are said to have relative **negentropy;** they are adaptable and open to change. Closed systems tend toward **entropy;** they are disorganized and destined for eventual disorder.

All systems strive to maintain some kind of balance. **Homeostasis** refers to the inclination of a system to maintain a dynamic equilibrium around some central tendency and to undertake operations to restore that equilibrium whenever it is threatened. Typically, homeostasis is achieved with the help of what cyberneticists call servomechanisms, such as pressure gauges or thermostats. In a self-regulating system, the servomechanisms are the **feedback loops** that return information back into the system in order to activate the internal interactional processes that maintain stability within the system and ensure a dynamic but steady state of being.

SOME CHARACTERISTICS OF A FAMILY SYSTEM

A family is a system in which the member components are organized into a group, forming a whole that transcends the sum of its separate elements. When we speak of the Johnson family, for example, we are discussing a complex and recognizable entity—not just the aggregate of Mr. Johnson plus Mrs. Johnson plus the Johnson children. Within such a grouping, a variety of intricate relationships evolve; alliances and coalitions are formed; information and energy are exchanged. Each member of the family influences and is influenced by the other members; over time, their transactions become patterns that shape the behavior of all participants within the system. Some families operate as more-or-less open systems, while others tend to close themselves off from the outside world. Generally speaking, the family provides the overall context in which several subsystems (the spouse subsystem, the sibling subsystem, the parent–child subsystem) operate in some hierarchical order.

Family Rules

A family is a rule-governed system; the interaction of family members follows organized, established patterns. This idea was first proposed by psychiatrist Don Jackson (1965a); as a founder of the Mental Research Institute in Palo Alto, California, Jackson contributed many of the conceptualizations of family life that we now consider part of communication theory (see Chapter 9). Jackson observed that partners in a marriage face multiple challenges as potential collaborators in wage earning, housekeeping, socializing, love-making, and parenting. From the start, husband and wife exchange views and express feelings about the nature of their relationship. More or less explicitly, they define the rights and duties of the spouses: "You can depend on me to be logical, practical, realistic."; "In return, you can depend on me to be a feeling, sensitive, social person." Such decisions often reflect culturally-linked sex roles—in this case, male and female, respectively—but variations are frequent. If it is appropriate for the individuals involved and not too rigidly set, a division of labor helps a couple pursue the sort of life they want to lead.

Despite his psychoanalytic training and commitment to the study of intrapsychic conflict, Jackson became intrigued with the influence of family interactive patterns on individual functioning. Family rules, he noted, determine the way people pattern their behavior and thus become the governing principles of family life. Jackson adopted the concept of marital *quid pro quo* to describe a relationship with well-formulated rules in which each partner gives and receives something in return. At an elementary level, Jackson was beginning to develop a language of interaction, a way of depicting human exchanges. By means of this descriptive language, he was attempting to account for the stabilizing mechanisms in any ongoing relationship (Greenberg, 1977).

 Beyond these initial formulations, Jackson (1965b) hypothesized that a **redundancy principle** operates in family life, according to which a family interacts in repetitive behavioral sequences. Instead of utilizing the full range of behavior available to them, the members settle on certain "rules" or redundant patterns when dealing with one another. If you understand the rules—usually unstated and out of the awareness of family members—you begin to understand how the family defines its relationships. According to Jackson, it is these rules rather than individual needs, drives, or personality traits that determine behavior between the participants. Rules may be descriptive (metaphors describing patterns of interchange) or prescriptive (directing what shall or shall not occur between members) (Greenberg, 1977). As Jackson (1965b) puts it:

> A rule is . . . a formula of relationship—No one shall control anyone else, father overtly runs the show, but mother's covert authority is respected . . . [p. 11].

For example, note the "unwritten rules" that define the relationship between husband (H) and wife (W), as they are getting dressed to go out to dinner with another couple:

W: I wish you would dress better. I'd like you to pay more attention to your clothes. Why don't you take your Christmas bonus and buy yourself a new suit?

H: I just can't spend the money on myself when you and the children need so many things.

W: But we want you to have something, too.

H: I just can't put myself first.

His statements to the contrary, the one-down behavior of the husband (whereby he humbly places his needs "one down" from those of the rest of the family) is quite controlling. What sort of relationship have they worked out? The wife is allowed to complain about her husband's appearance, but he retains control over the family's expenditure of money. He apparently does not intend to follow her suggestions but cannot be faulted because he is a good person, making sacrifices for his family (and probably making them feel guilty). Caught up in a repetitive exchange that defines and redefines the nature of their relationship, this couple takes no action and finds no new solutions to their differences.

All families follow rules that enable them to carry out the tasks of daily living.[1] Sometimes these rules are stated overtly: children allow adults to speak without interrupting; children hang up their clothes; parents decide on bedtime; father chooses the television programs on Monday nights; mother makes decisions regarding purchases of new clothes.

But most family rules are unwritten and covertly stated. That is, they are inferences that all family members make in respect to the redundancies or repetitive patterns in the relationships they observe around the house. Children learn and perpetuate these rules: "Go to father when you have a problem;

[1]A small child visiting a friend for the first time is apt to be bewildered by observing a family operating under an alien set of rules. Mother and father may greet each other with a kiss, may not get into a quarrel over the dinner table, may include the children in the conversation. A visiting child is sometimes startled to learn that, according to the rules of another family, it is not necessary to finish all the food on your plate before you are allowed to have dessert!

31

he's more understanding."; "It's best to ask mother for money after dinner when she's in a good mood."; "Stay away from their bedroom on Sunday morning, they like to be alone." Parents act according to covert rules of their own: daughters help with dishes, but it isn't right to ask a son; child A can be depended on to tell the truth, but child B cannot; child C is a spendthrift and always will be. Sometimes a family rule, unstated but understood by all, is that decisions are made by the parents and handed down to the children; in other cases, all family members learn they may state their own opinions freely. In a well-functioning family, there are rules that allow for changes with changing circumstances as well as rules that maintain order and stability.

Family therapists such as Virginia Satir (1972) often try to help a family recognize its unwritten rules, especially those that involve the exchange of feelings or that cause family pain. For example, some families forbid discussion of certain topics ("Mother is becoming an alcoholic."; "Father does not come home some nights."; "Brother does not know how to read."; "Sister should be talked to about sex and contraception.") and, as a consequence, fail to take realistic steps to alleviate the problems. Other families forbid overt expressions of anger or irritation with each other ("Stop! The children will hear us."). Still others foster dependence ("Never trust anyone but your mother and father.") and thus keep children from entering the outside world. Satir argues that dysfunctional families follow dysfunctional rules. She helps such families to become aware of these unwritten rules that retard growth and maturity. Once identified, outmoded, inappropriate, or irrelevant rules can be revised or discarded as a means of improving the family's functioning.

Family Homeostasis

Physiologists have long been aware of the body's ability to operate as a self-regulating system, maintaining a steady state in the presence of drastic changes in the environment. Despite outside temperatures, body temperature varies little from its customary 98.6°; various body-regulating mechanisms (perspiration, change in water retention, "goose pimples," shivering) are ordinarily called into play to maintain the constancy of body temperature should a sudden change in outside temperature occur. This automatic tendency of the body to maintain balance or equilibrium is called homeostasis. Restated in cybernetic terms, the body may be seen as a dynamic biosocial system that exchanges information with the outside world and utilizes feedback processes to maintain internal stability.

In family terms, homeostasis refers to those internal, ongoing, sustaining interactional processes that take place within a family and help assure internal balance. Such an error-activated (or excess-activated) system usually restricts behavior to a narrow range—for example, a quarrel between two children is not permitted to escalate to the point of physical assault on each other. In such a situation, a parent is likely to do one or more of the following: scold them, lecture one or both, remind them of their family ties and responsibilities, punish one or both, hug them both and urge them to settle the argument, act as referee, or send each out of the way of the other until tempers cool. Whatever the solution, the effort is directed, at least in part, to returning the system to its previous balance or equilibrium.

In a similar manner, couples typically monitor the state of their relationships and—usually without being aware of doing so—provide input to return it to a steady state should certain errors or excesses threaten their established homeostatic balance. Jackson (1965b) noted that during the courting period most couples' behavior is characterized by wondrously varied amorous advances and flirtatious moves. In the course of a long-term relationship, however, most of these behavioral ploys are dropped from their interactional repertoire. What remains is a narrower range of behavior that may require the couple to restore the balance from time to time. Usually a private code develops, each partner learning to cue the other homeostatically, perhaps with a glance or gesture that means, for example, "I'm hurt by what you've just said and want you to reassure me that you don't mean it and that you still love me." Such cues are a signal that disequilibrium has just been created and some corrective step is required in order to return the relationship to its previous balanced state. The analogy has been made to a home heating system with the thermostat set to cause the furnace to respond if the temperature in the house dips below the desired level of warmth. Figure 2-1 demonstrates such a situation.

Homeostatic mechanisms help to maintain an ongoing arrangement between two people by activating the rules that define their relationship. If a family "rule" is that no disagreement ever gets aired, family members may act nervous, change the topic, or become physically ill when conflict arises. In the case cited in the previous chapter, Jerry M. developed severely dysfunctional behavior just before the family had to deal with separating. The parents were thus distracted, they again functioned as a unit in their concern over their emotionally disturbed child, and the family's homeostatic balance was restored, at least for the time being.[2]

What happens when a family must change or modify its rules? As children grow up, they put pressure on the family to redefine its relationships. Many adolescents expect to be given allowances to spend as they wish, to make their own decisions about a suitable bedtime, to listen to music that may be repellent to their parents' ears. They want to borrow the family car, sleep over at a friend's, pursue interests other than those traditionally cared about in the fam-

---

[2]One of the most salient controversies within the field of family therapy today is whether this concept of homeostasis and the analogy of a cybernetic machine such as a home heating system has not outlived its usefulness. A number of influential family therapists (Dell, 1982; Hoffman, 1981) have called for a new epistemology. Rather than viewing the family as a homeostatic machine with a governor (for example, a family member develops dysfunctional behavior when a family breakup is threatened), they argue that this descriptive language incorrectly assumes a dualism between one part of the system and another. More to the point, they believe, is that all parts of the system together engage in change. To think otherwise is to use a mechanical cause–effect model of closed systems feedback in the guise of a cybernetic analogy. Moreover, living systems such as families may leap to new (and often unpredictable) integrations and not simply return to old levels of equilibrium. In many cases, the task for the family therapist is to force the family to search for new solutions, in effect pushing the system out of homeostatic balance.

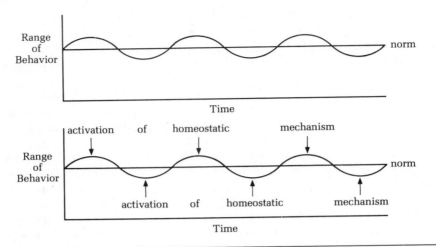

Figure 2–1. This figure demonstrates the operation of homeostatic mechanisms in the family. As in a home heating system, when the temperature deviates from a preset norm, the deviation is registered and counteracted by the homeostatic mechanisms of the thermostat system. Families utilize similar cues for achieving balance and equilibrium. (Source: Jackson, 1965b)

ily. They challenge the family's values and customs; they insist on being treated as equals. All of this causes disequilibrium within the family system, a sense of loss, and perhaps a feeling of strangeness until new transactional patterns restore family balance. As Minuchin and associates (1978) point out, the system tends to maintain itself within preferred ranges; a demand for deviation or change that is too great, too sudden, or too far beyond the system's threshold of tolerance, is likely to elicit counterdeviation responses. In **pathogenic** families, demands for even the most necessary changes may be met with increased rigidity as the family stubbornly attempts to retain familiar patterns. Unless the family is helped to remain flexible and open to change, some family members will inevitably feel trapped within a system that allows no alternatives to the *status quo*.

Feedback, Information, and Control

Speaking in systems terms, a marriage may be characterized as "a dynamic steady state in which there are built-in control mechanisms, homeostatic mechanisms, that allow change to occur in an orderly and controlled manner" (Prochaska & Prochaska, 1978, p. 20). By means of feedback loops, both positive and negative information about the state of the system can be fed back through the system, automatically triggering any necessary changes to keep that system "on track." A part of a system can alter its communications or behavior (output) based on information it receives regarding the effects of its previous outputs on other parts of the system. That is, through feedback mechanisms, part of any system's output is reintroduced into the system as information about the original output. Setting a home thermostat at 70°F programs the heating system so that it will receive instructions to activate when the temperature drops below that point. When the desired temperature is reached, feedback information will alter the ongoing state and the system will deactivate until such time as reactivation is needed to warm up the house again and keep the temperature stable.

Family members continuously exchange information—introducing new inputs, discarding unnecessary or harmful outputs, correcting errors, communicating feelings and interpreting responses, advising, notifying, problem solving. Such feedback may be either positive or negative. Positive feedback increases deviation from a steady state (in the analogy above, the furnace gets hotter and hotter). By definition, a positive feedback loop has the potential to amplify deviation to the point that the system self-destructs if it eventually drives the system beyond the limit within which it can function (Steinglass, 1978). An escalating argument between husband and wife that gets increasingly vicious, ugly, and violent and reaches the point where neither spouse can (or wants to) control the consequences is an example of such a positive feedback loop.

Negative feedback is corrective, adjusting the input so that the system may adjust homeostatically to its environment and return to its steady state (see Figure 2–2). A negative feedback loop minimizes deviation and is a critical component in the system's ability to maintain stability. In the following condensed exchange of information, note how the husband and wife provide the negative feedback each needs to modify the original position he or she has taken. Six months before this therapy session, the husband left his wife to move in with a younger woman from his office. He now lives alone in a furnished room and wants to return home but his wife resists the idea.

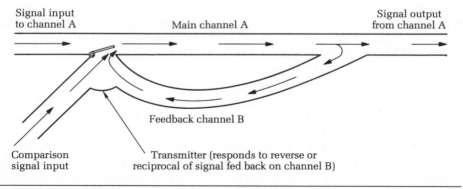

Signal input to channel A   Main channel A   Signal output from channel A

Feedback channel B

Comparison signal input   Transmitter (responds to reverse or reciprocal of signal fed back on channel B)

Figure 2–2. In this illustration of negative feedback, part of a system's output is reintroduced into the system as information about the output, thus governing and correcting the process. A negative signal from channel A, fed back to the sender through channel B, alters the signal in A. Feedback loops characterize all interpersonal relationships. (Source: Miller, 1978)

H: I don't want to move back in if you're never going to let me forget what happened earlier this year.

W: I'm afraid to let you move back. I don't trust you not to do the same thing again.

H: We can't work out anything while we're apart.

W: I wish I could believe it was me you were coming home to, and not so that you could have your meals served when you arrived home and your laundry done for you.

H: How can I prove I want to try again?

W: You could love me. . . . You could want to make love to me, which you don't seem to want to do anymore.

H: You could be more friendly yourself, not so angry at me all the time.

W: I want this to work out. It would be awful if you left again. I just don't know.

H: Let's try. I can't promise, but let's try.

W: Okay . . . but I'm still not sure.

To describe their situation in linear terms—the wife feels hurt and rejected and therefore wants to punish the husband—implies that the problem resides in one person and is imposed on the other. The systems approach emphasizes the behavior of an individual within a context in which another person or persons is present and exchanges information with that individual, each influencing the other. Within a system, a single event such as the husband leaving is both effect and cause. There is a circular movement of parts that affect each other but no beginning or end to the circle. Each person's behavior is simultaneously caused by and causative of behavior in another part of the system. It is that system that the family therapist tries to help overhaul and change.

A system is constantly changing as new input information is fed back into the system and alterations are made in response to the new input. According to Bateson's (1972) elegant definition, information is "a difference that makes a difference." A word, a gesture, a smile, a scowl—these are differences or changes in the environment, much as a temperature drop is an environmental difference or change in the heating system. These differences in turn make a difference when the receiver of the information alters perceptions of the environment and modifies behavior.

Information processing is fundamental to the operation of any system. If information processing is faulty, the system is likely to malfunction. In a sense, information is the equivalent of negentropy—it helps maintain a system by reducing uncertainty, thus avoiding disorder. The exchange of information is essential to the maintenance of a living system. How such information exchange takes place and the role that communication patterns play in defining relationships will be discussed in terms of family communication theory in Chapter 9.

How deviant does an output have to be before corrective action is initiated? Broderick and Smith (1979), pointing out the necessity for cybernetic control for stable system operation, offer this example: parents may respond to their daughter's return home from a date positively or negatively, depending on whether she conformed to family rules in the time she arrived, the condition she was in, and other factors. These authors note that the response will depend on the way the family has determined the degree of calibration—how much deviation it will allow. If the event is calibrated too narrowly, the daughter may not easily achieve a sense of independence and reliance on her own judgment. If it is calibrated too broadly, she may fail to learn limits and a sense of responsibility. Family therapists need to be aware of a family's efforts at calibrating their responses to events and help them fine-tune such responses for more effective functioning as a family unit.

Family Subsystems, Family Boundaries

A system is organized into a more or less stable set of relationships; it functions in certain characteristic ways; it is continuously in the process of evolution. Here we are principally concerned with the organization or structure of a system, especially the arrangement of its subsystems in a particular geographic space and at a given moment in time. Subsystems are units within the overall system that carry out distinctive functions in an effort to maintain themselves and sustain the system as a whole.

Every family system contains a number of coexisting subsystems. Husband and wife constitute a subsystem, mother and children another, siblings still another, and so on. Subsystems can be formed by generation, by sex, by interest, or by function (Minuchin, 1974a). In each subsystem, different levels of power are exercised and different skills learned. For example, the oldest child may have power within the sibling subsystem but must cede that power when interacting with his or her parents.

Because each family member belongs to several subsystems simultaneously, he or she enters into different complementary relationships with other members. For instance, a woman can be wife, mother, daughter, younger sister, older sister, niece, granddaughter, and so on. In each subsystem she plays a different role and can expect to engage in different transactional patterns. Consider this example: while giving her younger sister advice about finding a job, a woman is told by her husband to get off the phone and hurry up with dinner. She decides how to deal with his demand. Some moments later, she remembers not to be hurt when the children do not eat what she has cooked. She even responds diplomatically when her mother, a dinner guest, gives her advice on how to improve the table setting.

The most enduring subsystems are the spousal, the parental, and the sibling subsystems (Minuchin, Rosman, & Baker, 1978). The husband–wife subsystem is basic; any dysfunction in this subsystem reverberates through the family as children are scapegoated or co-opted into an alliance with one parent against the other because the couple are in conflict. The spousal subsystem teaches the child about the nature of intimate relationships and provides a model of transactions between a man and a woman, both of which are likely to affect the child's relationships later in life. The parental subsystem (which may include grandparents or older children assigned to parental roles) is involved with child rearing and serves such functions as nurturance, guidance, and control. Through interaction with the parental subsystem, the child learns to deal with authority, with people of greater power, before increasing his or her own capacity for decision making and self-control. The sibling subsystem contains the child's first peer group. Through participation in this subsystem, patterns of negotiating, cooperating, or competing develop. The interpersonal skills thus developed by a child will increase in significance as he or she moves beyond the family into school and later into the world of work.

As we have indicated, families may be thought of as rule-governed systems with more or less permeable boundaries[3] that permit interaction with the outside environment. Subsystems also require exchange with other subsystems for proper family functioning, allowing subsystem members to carry out their designated roles and responsibilities effectively; boundaries protect the necessary differentiation between them. A mother defines the boundaries of the parental subsystem when she tells her 15-year-old son, the oldest of three children: "Don't you decide whether your sisters are old enough to stay up to see that TV program. Your father and I will decide that." However, she temporarily redefines that boundary to include the oldest child within the parental subsystem when she announces: "I want all of you children to listen to your older brother while your father and I are away from home tomorrow evening." Or she may invite grandparents to join the parental subsystem temporarily; they can be asked to check on how the children are getting along or advise the oldest son on necessary action in case of an emergency. These examples remind us that the clarity of the subsystem boundaries is far more significant in the effectiveness of family functioning than the composition of the family's subsystems (see Figure 2–3).

According to Broderick and Smith (1979), even a social interaction as brief and tentative as a first date is concerned with boundaries. A number of "rules" are in effect. It is bad form to pay too much attention to someone other than your date, and rude and insulting to abandon your date and return home with someone else. Moreover, others are expected to respect the couple's boundaries and refrain from cutting in on another's partner. It is also understood that the arrangement—the establishment of the unit—is time-limited, and when the date is over, so is the claim, and the rules described above no longer apply. If the couple move to a more intimate relationship and see each other more regularly, they—as well as others such as their friends—behave as though the boundary is more clearly drawn and now operates between dates as well.

In a family, as in any complex system, numerous boundaries exist, all serving in some way to promote the functioning of the whole, ongoing system. We have

[3]Boundaries of a living cell, seen under a microscope, provide a useful prototype of a membrane that separates a system from its environment. Activity and interaction take place within its borders; an interchange of matter, energy, and information—input and output—occurs with the outside world; the boundary ensures strength, integrity, and a cohesive organization within, identifying the cell as a separate and unique entity, distinguishable from other (perhaps similar) entities within the environment.

Figure 2-3. The effect of stress on the subsystem boundaries of a family. In the top diagram, a father (F) and mother (M), both stressed at work, come home and criticize each other, but then detour their conflict by attacking a child. This results in less danger to the spouse subsystem, but stresses the child (C). In the lower figure, the husband criticizes the wife, who seeks a coalition with the child against the father. Note the inappropriately rigid cross-generational subsystem of mother and child in the latter case as well as the diffuse boundary between mother and child; both have the effect of excluding the father. Minuchin refers to this result as a cross-generational dysfunctional pattern. (Source: Minuchin, 1974)

emphasized the need for each subsystem to maintain its own boundaries. As the system becomes more complex, an analysis of its operations must take into account such issues as the family's ability to function as an open system, the hierarchical order of its members, how roles are distributed and assigned, and the guidelines for behavior within the family—as well as the rules that govern the boundary between the family and the outside world (Freeman, 1981).

Changing Male–Female Roles

Living systems thrive on synergy—the joint and simultaneous action of components that together produce a greater total effect than the sum of individual effects. The synergy of a family derives from the cooperative and supportive interactions of its members as they play out roles that are appropriate and realistic to their age, sex, and personality characteristics.

A family member's role defines certain expected and permitted, as well as forbidden, patterns of behavior. On the surface, such roles may appear to be biologically based and sexually stereotyped (although they need not be unchangeable). In almost all societies, men are likely to be perceived as more aggressive than women and women are apt to be viewed as more nurturant, cooperative, emotional, and tender (D'Andrade, 1974). According to tradition, men are identified with instrumental activities (making decisions, earning money, solving problems rationally) and women are associated with expressive activities (forming and maintaining emotional bonds, caring for children, creating a warm and supportive home atmosphere).

As a consequence of such sex-role programming, men often learn to inhibit emotional expressiveness, empathy, and dependency and women fail to develop their potential for assertiveness or independence. Feldman (1982) lists the characteristics typically associated with male and female roles (see Table 2–1). Feldman argues that learning to play such sex-defined roles often causes males and females to interact in mutually reinforcing ways that restrict individual psychological development and may lead to dysfunctional marital and family relationships.

TABLE 2–1. Psychological Dimensions of the Female and Male Roles

The female role. Women are expected to be (or allowed to be) the following:
1. Home-oriented, child(ren)-oriented.
2. Warm, affectionate, gentle, tender.
3. Aware of feelings of others, considerate, tactful, compassionate.
4. Moody, high-strung, temperamental, excitable, emotional, subjective, illogical.
5. Complaining, nagging.
6. Weak, helpless, fragile, easily emotionally hurt.
7. Submissive, yielding, dependent.

The male role. Men are expected to be (or allowed to be) the following:
1. Ambitious, competitive, enterprising, worldly.
2. Calm, stable, unemotional, realistic, logical.
3. Strong, tough, powerful.
4. Aggressive, forceful, decisive, dominant.
5. Independent, self-reliant.
6. Harsh, severe, stern, cruel.
7. Autocratic, rigid, arrogant.

Source: Feldman, 1982, p. 355.

Today, social scientists question whether such role distinctions are biologically determined or fixed. According to psychologist Hoffman (1977), sex differences in personality and behavior are not inborn traits but reflections of adult role expectations that females will be mothers and males will be workers. Hoffman argues that the reproductive role has been a major factor in determining the status and behavior patterns of women in all societies.

Role-playing differences between adult males and females originate in childhood. Males prepare for adult occupational roles from their earliest years, while much of the socialization experience of females is geared toward motherhood. But Hoffman (1977) notes that stereotyped differences in roles may be expected to diminish in the future, due largely to two factors: (1) motherhood is no longer the only major role open to a woman in society, with mothering now occupying only a small portion of her adult years, and (2) the trend for wives to share the breadwinner role with their husbands has led many men to participate more fully in child rearing than in previous generations. According to Hoffman's thesis, smaller family size today than in the past, higher employment rates for women (over half of all mothers with children under age 18 now work outside the home), and a longer life expectancy are some factors influencing changes in family roles that tend to blur differences between the sexes.

During the past decade, American society has undergone both a sexual revolution and a sex-role revolution (Skolnick & Skolnick, 1977). The former has liberalized attitudes toward erotic behavior and its expression; the latter has changed the roles and statuses of both men and women in the direction of greater equality. With more egalitarian relationships between many husbands and wives, there is a greater sharing and interchanging of the parenting roles. For many parents this means a joint effort to "humanize the young" (Fleck, 1976) by teaching them about themselves, making them aware of what is involved in living within a family, and emphasizing the mores and cultural values of the society.

Over the course of a lifetime, a woman tends to experience a number of changes in family and work roles; a man is more apt to play both kinds of roles at the same time throughout his adult life (Stewart and Platt, 1982). A woman's work experience outside the home is likely to be affected by her marital status, childbirth, the presence of young children at home, and so on. Increasingly, contemporary sex-role norms permit women to occupy work and family roles simultaneously or to alternate roles at different stages of the life cycle. Though men shift roles less frequently, recent social changes such as joint custody and single-parent households led by fathers have given men more role options than ever before.

One particularly noteworthy development has been the dramatic increase in the number of dual-career marriages, which Goldenberg and Goldenberg (1984) estimate at approximately 5 million by the mid-1980s. A dual-career marriage means more than two incomes; husband and wife in such a marriage seek to equalize their power and their domestic responsibilities and share a commitment to the career advancement of each partner (Pepitone-Rockwell, 1980). Spouses in a dual-career marriage are vulnerable to "role overload" (Rapoport & Rapoport, 1969), the stresses likely to appear when a person tries to play too many roles for the time and energy he or she has available. Fatigue and guilt feelings (particularly in women) over not fulfilling traditional role expectations at home are common and often increase the tension between husband and wife, especially if no domestic help or adequate childcare facilities are available. Other strains may result from social prejudice (wife stepping out of her customary role), professional slights (husband assumed to be superior, better informed), restricted job mobility (neither partner can easily move to another city for a better career opportunity), lack of leisure time, feelings of competition between spouses, and so on (Goldenberg & Goldenberg, 1984).

Despite these obstacles, the dual-career marriage offers the benefits of personal stimulation and fulfillment, increased income, and possibly a closer relationship between the father and his children as a result of his greater participation in their upbringing. However, despite the couples' egalitarian intentions, women are likely to retain the major responsibilities for the housekeeping and child rearing. A mother may try to take advantage of the opportunity to utilize her talents and skills outside the home but not without a significant shift in the roles played within the home by other family members. Clearly, a successful dual-career marriage requires major structural and functional changes in the family system.

CLASSIFYING FAMILY FUNCTIONING

Classification is an essential part of the process by which scientists seek to understand and explain the large and varied masses of data they accumulate. Furthermore, classification into categories helps scientists to direct and structure the search for new information and provides a framework that enables them to explain their discoveries to one another. In an interdisciplinary area such as family therapy, it is particularly important to develop and refine some systems of classification so that members of different scientific and professional disciplines can communicate more meaningfully.

Most family therapists today are systems-oriented. In general, they focus on patterns, relationships, and reciprocal interactions within the family unit, but their emphases vary. As we are about to see, Kantor and Lehr are particularly intent on differentiating family systems through an analysis of their structural development and transactional styles. Olson and his associates offer a family classification matrix based on underlying dimensions of family functioning. Reiss classifies families according to the way they construct reality and make sense out of their social environment. Beavers attempts to distinguish the processes occurring within families that differentiate those that function competently from those that become dysfunctional.

Kantor and Lehr's Family Typology

Based on their observations of ordinary families over a period of nearly a decade, and without attempting to distinguish "normal" from "pathological" families, Kantor and Lehr (1975) offer a comprehensive description of a variety of family structures. Working within a systems framework, they attempt to identify those basic family processes that regulate the behavior of members. In particular, they are concerned with how families process information and develop strategies for regulating distances between one another. How do family subsystems "interface" with one another, they ask, and how does the family unit subsystem communicate with the outside world? Some families, for example, scrutinize an outsider for a lengthy period of time before admission is granted, while other families, with looser boundaries, respond quickly with an invitation to come inside (White, 1978).

According to Kantor and Lehr (1975), there are three basic family types—open, closed, and random—representing different configurations for structuring the family's internal relationships and its access to, and exchange with, the outside world. No type is superior or inferior to the others; no type exists in a pure form, although the researchers believe that families cluster around the three categories. Each type has its own rules, boundary arrangements, and form of homeostatic balance.

Open family structures are neither too tightly nor too loosely bounded. Such families are essentially democratic; honest exchange is encouraged both within the family and with outsiders. Although there is a sense of order, flexibility is given high priority: negotiation is encouraged; adaptation through consensus is endorsed; the rights of individuals are taken for granted; loyalty to oneself and to the family is expected.

Within closed structures, rules and a hierarchical power structure make individual family members subordinate their needs for the benefit of the group. As White (1978) depicts such families, parents make sure that doors are locked, family reading material and television programs are screened, and children scrupulously report their comings and goings. Privacy may border on suspiciousness, and strangers are given a hard look before being allowed access to the family. Rigid daily schedules are apt to be followed. The "core purpose" of such families is stability through tradition, in contrast to open families that encourage adaptability.

Random family structures are fragmented. Each person does what he or she wishes, which may or may not be related or connected to what others are doing. There are few, if any, rules. Boundaries are blurred and easily crossed. Traffic in and out of the family is loosely regulated as everyone, strangers included, comes and goes according to some irregular pattern. Mealtimes are seldom scheduled for the family as a whole but are left up to the individual. In a random family, the "core purpose" is exploration through intuition.

As we noted, Kantor and Lehr (1975) do not assume that dysfunctional families necessarily stem from one or another of these structural types. Potentially, each type of normal homeostatic arrangement may become flawed. If closed structures become too rigid, family members may run away or otherwise rebel. Random family structures run the risk of becoming chaotic. Even open families, desirable as they appear to be, may be disposed toward schism or divorce if incompatibilities produce excessive strain and create a family impasse (Hoffman, 1981).

Olson's Circumplex Model

Research psychologist David Olson and his colleagues (Olson, Sprenkle & Russell, 1979) propose an integrative model of family functioning based on the intersection of two basic family dimensions: cohesion and adaptability. Cohesion is defined as the emotional bonding family members have with one another and the degree of individual autonomy a person experiences in the family system. Adaptability refers to the ability of a family system to change its power structure, rules, and role relationships in response to situational and developmental stress. Olson and colleagues argue that a balance between these dimensions is most desirable for effective marital and family relationships as well as optimum individual development. With too much cohesion, the family is enmeshed and its members overly entwined in each other's lives;

with too little, the members remain distant, isolated, and disengaged. Excessive adaptability leads to too much change, unpredictability, and possible chaos; too little adaptability may cause rigidity and stagnation. With a self-report instrument entitled Family Adaptability and Cohesion Evaluation Scales (FACES) that reveals individual family members' perceptions of family cohesion and adaptability, these researchers have compared a variety of family systems. Overall, results indicate that high-functioning families show moderate scores on the two dimensions, while low-functioning families reveal extreme scores.

Olson and associates' empirically developed "circumplex model" identifies 16 types of marital and family systems based on each family type's extent of cohesion and adaptability. As shown in Figure 2-4, the 16 types emerged from classifying the two dimensions into four levels (very low, low to moderate, moderate to high, and very high), thus creating a 4×4 matrix or 16 cells. The four cells in the central area (flexibly separated, flexibly connected, structurally separated, and structurally connected) reflect balanced levels of cohesion and adaptability and have been found most functional in regard to both individual and family development. Correspondingly, the four extreme types (chaotically disengaged, chaotically enmeshed, rigidly disengaged, and rigidly enmeshed) are least functional over a period of time (although they may work well temporarily, as in response to a crisis such as death in the family).

Note further that the four central types are labelled open systems and the outer rings are characterized as closed or random systems, thus linking the "circumplex model" to the typology developed by Kantor and Lehr (1975). However, unlike their predecessors, Olson, Sprenkle and Russell (1979) contend that closed and random family types are potentially dysfunctional, not simply different forms of family structure and life style.

Reiss's Family Paradigms

A psychiatrist originally intent on discovering through laboratory research how families with schizophrenic members process information (in the hope of learning more about comparable information-processing deficits in the identified patient), David Reiss has moved beyond the study of family cognitive patterns and problem-solving styles. What has emerged from his efforts—now extended to include "nonclinical" (normal) families—is a differentiation of several family perceptual and interactive patterns that goes beyond arbitrary functional/dysfunctional distinctions (Reiss, 1981; Oliveri & Reiss, 1982). Reiss's current research efforts are directed at discovering how families develop "paradigms" (in his terms, a family's shared assumptions about the social world), how such family paradigms may change, and what happens when a paradigm breaks down.

Beginning in the late 1950s, Reiss gave families a number of problem-solving tasks (puzzles or card-sorting exercises), and observed how they developed strategies, shared information, and traded ideas. Soon it became clear to him that what was most significant was not how they processed information but how they perceived the laboratory setting in which they were being tested. For

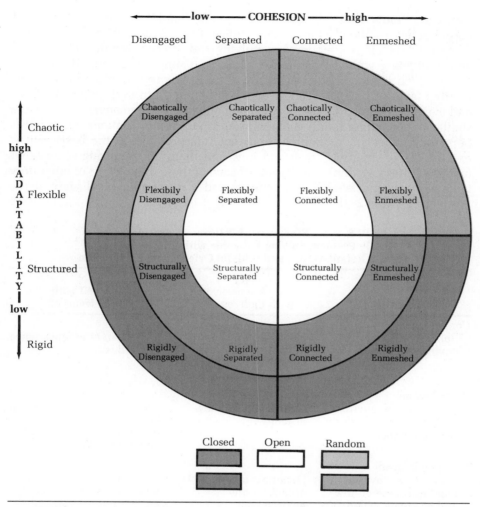

Figure 2-4. Sixteen possible types of marital and family systems derived from the circumplex model. (Source: Olson, Sprenkle, & Russell, 1979, p. 17)

example, families with schizophrenic adolescents often perceived the laboratory as dangerous and threatening to family ties; families with delinquent adolescents tended to view the laboratory as a place to demonstrate distance and independence from one another; and families with normal adolescents were apt to view the experience as an opportunity to explore and master a challenging situation together. Thus, the family's reaction to the unfamiliar experimental situation itself was the crucial determinant of their behavior as a family. Reiss then reasoned that perhaps the laboratory response reflected a general construct with which the family viewed the social world. He called this construct or blueprint for dealing with new situations the "family paradigm."

Just as an individual develops ways to comprehend the meaning of events in his or her environment, a family unit—integrating the construing styles of all its members—develops a mode of perceiving and interpreting the social world and interacting with the environment. Reiss distinguishes three dimensions along which characteristics of family paradigms vary: "configurations" (the family's level of belief that the world is inherently ordered, understandable and masterable); "coordination" (the level of belief that the environment has a similar impact on all family members); and "closure" (variations in a family's perception of events as familiar and thus interpretable on the basis of past experience, or uniquely fresh and new and therefore requiring some other means of interpretation). High levels of each of these dimensions of laboratory behavior are associated with openness and a nonstereotypical view of the family (see Table 2-2).

TABLE 2-2. Summary of Patterns of Association of Family Problem-Solving Behavior with (a) Perceptions of Social Relationships, and with (b) Orientations toward Kin

High levels of:	(a) . . . were associated with high levels of:	(b) . . . and with high levels of:
Configuration Belief in a masterable environment	Nonstereotypic view of family Openness to individuals outside the family	Child–parent independence in kin ties
Coordination Sense that the environment functions similarly for all members	Nonstereotypic view of family	Child–parent congruence in kin ties Investment in close-knit networks of kin
Closure (delayed) View of the environment as source of new and changing experience	Openness to inanimate aspects of the environment	Investment in large networks of kin

Source: Oliveri & Reiss, 1982, p. 109.

Reiss (1981) differentiates three ways of constructing reality, or three types of family paradigms. **Environment-sensitive families** believe the world is knowable and orderly and expect each member to contribute to its understanding and mastery. **Interpersonal distance-sensitive families** are composed of disengaged individuals ("loners") who strive to demonstrate their autonomy and believe that any attention paid to suggestions or observations from others is a sign of weakness. **Consensus-sensitive families** are made up of enmeshed members who perceive the world as so chaotic and confusing that they must join together, maintain agreement at all times, and thus protect themselves from danger.

Clearly, it is the environment-sensitive family that is the most problem-free. Its members are able to accept aid and advice from others, benefit from cues from the environment, act individually or jointly, and delay closure in order to make an effective response based on the consideration of a number of alternative solutions. In terms of flexibility, the environment-sensitive family resembles the open family systems described in Olson's "circumplex model." Should its paradigm be threatened as a result of family crisis, this type of family will attempt to maintain family integrity and overcome adversity together. Reiss (1981) cites the example of a family called upon to deal with the birth of a handicapped child, an event that temporarily threatened the family notion that the world was predictable and thus comprehensible. By learning all they could about the child's disability and arranging for the best available treatment, family members once again confirmed for themselves that they live in an orderly, manageable world, adding the realization that certain afflictions or adversities were inevitable but that together they were able to prevail.

Beavers's Levels of Functioning

Up to this point, we have focused on family typologies, efforts to classify and differentiate family structures and styles. Largely unanswered is the question of how families get that way and whether they are capable of changing or evolving from one pattern to another. Moreover, there is a need to look at interaction in healthy families, not simply extrapolate from dysfunctional family systems in order to infer what functional systems must be like. Beavers (1977) and his colleagues have made a contribution by observing and analyzing various forms of negotiation and other transaction patterns within competent families in an effort to shed light on how such processes evolve in healthy families.

In their research, Lewis, Beavers, Gossett, and Phillips (1976) looked beyond the strengths and weaknesses of individual family members in order to identify the interactions within a "healthy" family system that make for optimal functioning. Members of intact families (each of which had at least one adolescent and no family member identified as a psychiatric patient or receiving psychiatric treatment) were interviewed and their interactions at a variety of tasks videotaped. The study had limitations: "healthy" was defined negatively as the absence of emotional disturbance in a family member; subjects in the study were all from intact, White, middle-class, urban families; videotaped behavior is not necessarily representative of their day-to-day interaction patterns. Nevertheless, Beavers and associates' findings expand our understanding of common relationship patterns characteristic of competent families.

The research plan required several judges to rate each family's videotaped behavior along five major dimensions and according to a variety of subtopics and themes:

I. Structure of the Family
   A. Overt power (how family dealt with influence and dominance)

    B. Parental coalitions (strength of husband/wife alliance)

    C. Closeness (presence or absence of distinct boundaries and degree of interpersonal distance)

    D. Power structure (ease in determining family "pecking order")

II. Mythology (degree to which a family's concept of itself was congruent with rater's appraisal of family behavior)

III. Goal-Directed Negotiation (the effectiveness of the family's negotiations)

IV. Autonomy

    A. Communication of self-concept (degree to which family nourished or discouraged clear communication of feelings and thoughts)

    B. Responsibility (degree to which the family system reflected family members' acceptance of responsibility for their own feelings, thoughts, and actions)

    C. Invasiveness (extent to which the family system tolerated or encouraged family members to speak for one another)

    D. Permeability (degree to which the family system encouraged the acknowledgment of the stated feelings, thoughts, and behavior of its members)

V. Family Affect

    A. Expressiveness (extent to which the open communication of affect was encouraged within the family system; see Figure 2–5)

    B. Mood and tone (the family system's mood, ranging from warm and affectionate to cynical and hopeless; see Figure 2–5)

    C. Conflict (degree of family conflict and its effect on family functioning)

    D. Empathy (degree to which the family system encouraged members to be sensitive to each other's feelings and to communicate this awareness)

On the basis of these ratings, each family received a score on a Global Health–Pathology Scale. In the sample, 33 "healthy" families were distinguished from 70 families with a hospitalized adolescent; 12 families in the former group were studied intensively.

Results indicated that no single quality was unique to highly functional or competent families compared to the less functional families. A number of variables in combination accounted for family members' special style of relating to each other. Thus, family "health" was considered not as a "single thread" but a tapestry reflecting differences in degree along many dimensions. The capacity of the family to communicate thoughts and feelings and the cardinal role of the parental coalition in establishing the level of functioning of the total family stand out as the key factors. The parental coalition provides family leadership and serves as a model for interpersonal relationships.

In the highly functional families in this study, members welcome contact with each other. They expect their transactions to be caring, open, empathic,

A. *Expressiveness:* Rate the degree to which this family system is characterized by open expression of feelings.

1	1.5	2	2.5	3	3.5	4	4.5	5
Open, direct expression of feelings		Direct expression of feelings despite some discomfort		Obvious restriction in the expression of some feelings		Although some feelings are expressed, there is masking of most feelings		No expression of feelings

B. *Mood and Tone:* Rate the feeling tone of this family's interaction.

1	1.5	2	2.5	3	3.5	4	4.5	5
Unusually warm, affectionate, humorous and optimistic		Polite, without impressive warmth or affection; or frequently hostile with times of pleasure		Overtly hostile		Depressed		Cynical, hopeless and pessimistic

Figure 2–5. Two of 13 rating scales used by judges to score family interaction patterns following the viewing of the videotape of a family carrying out a variety of tasks together. The upper scale measures the degree to which the family system encourages the open communication of feelings. The lower scale asks the judge to rate the mood or feeling tone of the family interaction. (Source: Lewis et al., 1976)

and trusting. By contrast, members of dysfunctional families often are defensive, distant, or hostile. In highly functional families, members respect personal autonomy and tolerate individuality; each member feels free to agree or disagree with others, even if it leads to conflict. Family members are active and do things together. In dysfunctional families, members are more apt to feel isolated and to respond to each other in a passive, powerless, controlled fashion.

Though power resides in the parental coalition in highly functional families, it is not exercised in an authoritarian way; parents and children exchange opinions and feel free to negotiate, making power struggles unnecessary. Members of these families are close but well-differentiated; boundaries make it possible to maintain a strong sense of self within the family. Separation and loss are accepted realistically; family members are able to adapt to changes brought about by growth and development, aging and death. The most capable families express humor, tenderness, warmth, and hopefulness.

What characterizes families who function less well (for example, those who fail miserably at child rearing)? Are they different in degree or kind from the families we have just described? Beavers (1977) presents convincing evidence that families can be ordered along a continuum with respect to their effectiveness. The most flexible, adaptable, goal-achieving systems are at one end of the continuum; the most inflexible, undifferentiated, and ineffective systems are at the other end of the continuum. Beavers uses the systems concept of entropy as an aid to understanding the effectiveness of family functioning. As we noted earlier in this chapter, entropy is a term used to describe the tendency of things to go into disorder; thus "a family with low entropy" implies a high degree of orderliness. Systems, including family systems, have degrees of entropy; a system can be in a state of greater or lesser disorder. Beavers contends that the more closed family systems are doomed to increase in entropy because—lacking access to the world outside their boundaries—they cannot avoid the pull toward greater disorder. By contrast, open systems receive energy by interacting with the environment and use it to build increasingly ordered structures, low in entropy, within their boundaries.

Moderately dysfunctional families are midrange on the continuum. More entropic than those labeled highly functional or even adequate, these families tend to experience greater pain and difficulty in their day-to-day functioning. Their offspring tend not to be as seriously disturbed as children from severely dysfunctional families (who have a high incidence of schizophrenia), but they are frequently diagnosed as neurotic (experiencing marked feelings of anxiety or depression, with inadequate coping devices) or as having a behavior disorder (experiencing difficulty in following the rules of behavior expected in the world beyond the family). In terms of the general population, Beavers contends that midrange families probably constitute the largest group, larger than the family types at either end of the continuum.

The midrange families, according to Beavers, have parental coalitions but they are unstable. They maintain generational boundaries between parents and children but power issues persist unresolved and family rules are full of "shoulds" and "oughts," fostering more intimidation than negotiation when the family interacts. Members of such families do attempt to communicate but they tend to avoid taking responsibility for their own feelings, thoughts, or actions. ("You shouldn't talk that way about your teacher," declares a parent, rather than stating "I'm upset that you're unhappy about your teacher.") Family myths—shared distortions—are powerful: father is only interested in his business, mother is a saint, one child is mean and another is always kind. Family members find it hard to accept changes brought about by time; for example, a mother may compete with her teenage daughters to see who is more sexually attractive.

Competition and hidden conflicts between members of moderately dysfunctional families suggest that frustration is common and may even be a constant underlying factor in their transactions. When children grow up in an atmosphere of family friction, they learn stereotyped roles and develop constricted identities. For example, in the midrange families in a White, middle-class, urban sample it may be assumed as inevitable that men are powerful, unfeeling, rational, aggressive, and monetarily successful. By the same token, it may be assumed without question that women are ineffective, emotional, intuitive, and dependent. Such stereotyped role definitions—in combination with unchallenged family myths—may fix behavior patterns early in life, allowing little room for developing individual capabilities or loosening family bound-~~*kicked out of the family.*~~ aries in order to increase contact with the outside world.

When the time comes for adolescents to separate from the family, the family stance can be characterized as either **centripetal** or **centrifugal** (Stierlin, 1972). Centripetal refers to the tendency for family members to enmesh or cling together; centrifugal signifies the ease with which the process of disengagement takes place. These differences in style exist in all families regardless of competence level. However, in families that function well, the centripetal/centrifugal style is modified by other patterns of family interaction and the adolescent's departure is rarely dramatic or noteworthy. But in dysfunctional families with a centripetal style, according to Beavers, adolescent children view the family as holding greater promise for fulfillment of their needs than the outside world. Separation appears threatening and difficult because the family's style is binding and discouraging of experiences in the world beyond the family. Moderately dysfunctional families with a centripetal style usually produce neurotic children. (Figure 2-6 depicts the relationship between level of family functioning and centripetal or centrifugal patterns.)

On the other hand, members of centrifugal families look for gratification outside the family. They tend to distance themselves from family conflict and seek solace with peers. Rather than binding children, centrifugal families expel children, often before they are mature enough to develop anything but shallow relationships with others. Midrange families with a centrifugal style are apt to produce offspring with behavior disorders.

Even more than midrange families, those families who are seriously disturbed represent closed systems—chaotic, rigid, with little vital interaction with the outside world. Beavers believes that in severely dysfunctional families with a centripetal style there is a good chance that one or more offspring will become a process schizophrenic. (A *process schizophrenic* usually demonstrates social isolation and a lack of emotional responsiveness to others early in life, becoming progressively more withdrawn and disorganized as an adult. A *reactive schizophrenic* is more apt to have a history of adaptive behavior but, due to sudden precipitating external stresses, has an acute onset of symptoms, often in adulthood. Of the two diagnoses, the **prognosis** for the former is much poorer.) Children in severely dysfunctional families with a centrifugal style are prone to sociopathic behavior. (A *sociopath* is an antisocial person who is callous, irresponsible, egocentric, impulsive, fails to learn from experience or punishment, and is without remorse or shame. Many criminals probably come under this heading.)

Centripetal families who are severely dysfunctional have fragile parental coalitions; they lack leadership and it is often difficult to tell who is the parent and who is the child. Individuality is discouraged and family closeness is defined as everyone thinking and feeling alike. As a result, offspring often fail to establish a coherent identity or to develop a clear sense of their own boundaries as distinct from those of other family members. At the same time, the

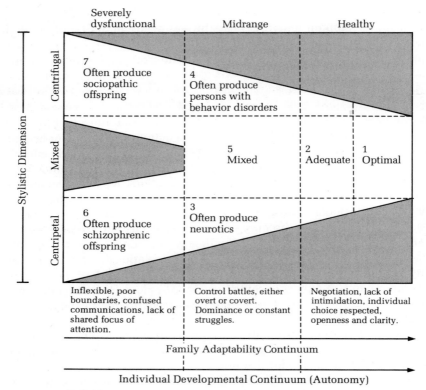

Severely dysfunctional | Midrange | Healthy

Stylistic Dimension

Centrifugal

7
Often produce sociopathic offspring

4
Often produce persons with behavior disorders

Mixed

5
Mixed

2
Adequate

1
Optimal

Centripetal

6
Often produce schizophrenic offspring

3
Often produce neurotics

Inflexible, poor boundaries, confused communications, lack of shared focus of attention.

Control battles, either overt or covert. Dominance or constant struggles.

Negotiation, lack of intimidation, individual choice respected, openness and clarity.

Family Adaptability Continuum

Individual Developmental Continuum (Autonomy)

Definitions

Autonomy: A continuous or infinite dimension, related to the capacity of individuals within a system to function competently in defining themselves, assuming responsibility for themselves, and negotiating with others.

Adaptability: A continuous or infinite dimension, related to the capacity of a family to function competently in effecting change and tolerating differentiation of members.

Centripetal/centrifugal: A curvilinear stylistic dimension; the extreme styles are associated with severely disturbed families, and the most competent families avoid either extreme.

Inflexibility: The inability to change. The most chaotic families are the most inflexible, due to their lack of a shared focus of attention.

Severely dysfunctional: the lowest level of functioning along the adaptiveness continuum, indicated by poorly defined subsystem boundaries and by confusion due to nonautonomous members' having little tolerance for clear, responsible communication.

Figure 2-6. Beavers's cross-sectional process model, in the form of sidewise A, with each leg representing either centripetal or centrifugal families. In severely dysfunctional families, the centrifugal group is likely to produce sociopathic behavior and the centripetal group schizophrenic disorders. Both show poor or unclear boundaries and confused communication. In midrange families, both groups are less discrepant, although one tends to behavior disorders and the other to neurosis. Some effort is being made to achieve autonomy, adaptability and a power hierarchy. Within the healthy category, extremes are rare and the structure aids effective functioning for individuals as well as the family as a whole. (Source: Beavers, 1982, p. 58.)

impermeability of the family boundary handicaps them from engaging in relationships outside the family. Needless to say, communication within the family is poor and confused, making the negotiation of differences between members all but impossible. The absence of warmth is striking—participants look on every encounter within the family as inevitably destructive. The passage of time is denied so that the myth persists that everything and everyone will always remain the same. Any thought of change—increased competence in children, for example, or failing abilities in parents—is too upsetting to consider. It is hardly surprising that Beavers describes the process schizophrenic as someone who has suffered a profound deficiency of human relationships.

Interaction in families with centrifugal styles who are severely dysfunctional is often marked by open discord or teasing manipulation. In such an unstable family structure, no one (including the parents) has a clear idea of what his or her role should be and leadership shifts from moment to moment or is nonexistent. Bickering, blaming, attempting to gain control through intimidation—all of these make for chaos and incoherent communication. In such a family it seems as if no two people are talking on the same topic or responding to what has just been said. Children are apt to escape from such family environments as soon as they can, even by running away or engaging in antisocial behavior that brings them in conflict with the law and leads to placement in a detention home.

The lack of warmth or tenderness, the inconsistent rules, the shifting power structure, the disjointed pattern of communication—these factors in the life of an entropic family provide little incentive for closeness or caring. A child in such a family may develop a facade of indifference and appear to be without guilt but, according to Beavers, he or she is actually feeling hopeless. Experiences in such families lead to the conclusion that one's feelings, impulses, and needs are unacceptable. The antisocial person's self-defeating behavior, seen in a family light, may be an expression of rage at an uncaring world.

SUMMARY

A system is made up of units or elements that interact with one another. Wholeness, the relationship between the component parts, and organization are its unifying principles. The units within a system are related to one another in such a way that the state of each is constrained by the state of all of the others. Boundaries delineate the elements belonging to the system or may separate the various subsystems that together form the overall system. Living systems tend to be open systems, exchanging matter, energy and information with the outside environment. Closed systems are doomed to entropy, the tendency to become disorganized and go into disorder. All systems strive to maintain a dynamic equilibrium or homeostasis.

Families may be thought of as living systems with multiple, intricate, long-standing relationships, alliances, and coalitions, in which information and energy get exchanged and the behavior of each member influences, and in turn is influenced by, the behavior of all others. The systems characteristics of a family include: its rules, implicit or explicit, for behavior; its homeostatic mechanisms for maintaining internal stability; its subsystem arrangements; and its boundary operations. Changing male–female role relationships are characteristic of the contemporary family system.

Family functioning has been classified by a number of researchers. Kantor and Lehr distinguish three basic family types—open, closed, random—each representing unique ways of structuring the family's internal relationships and its access to, and exchange with, the outside world. Olson offers a "circumplex model" of 16 types of marital and family systems based upon the family's degree of cohesion and adaptability. Reiss concerns himself with "family paradigms"—shared ways of perceiving and interpreting the social world and interacting with the environment—and distinguishes between environment-sensitive, interpersonal distance-sensitive, and consensus-sensitive families. Beavers is interested in the processes that make for a competent, functional, "healthy" family and how such families differ from midrange or severely dysfunctional families.

Expressions of Family Dysfunction

Having looked at some systems principles of family life and the possible causes of dysfunction within a family, we can be more specific about the ways dysfunction manifests itself in a family's transactional patterns. Once again, it should be noted that all families have faulty transactions at one time or another; in dysfunctional families, a distinctive interactional pattern is likely to persist over time and become the members' characteristic way of dealing with each other.

In this chapter we look first at ways in which families respond to various crises during their life cycles. Times of crisis can provide the opportunity for growth, with a family emerging better equipped to meet future challenges. On the other hand, a family may fail to cope or gain a sense of competence and its members will continue to deal with one another in ways that retard growth. We then examine some common expressions of dysfunctional behavior in a family: pathological communication patterns, **enmeshment** and **disengagement,** scapegoating, family violence, the family's role in substance abuse, and, finally, the persistence of family myths.

LIFE STRESS AND FAMILY CRISES

Stress, tension, frustration, and anxiety—these are all too often the by-products of modern living. Families rarely experience life without complication, strain, and the experience of failure at one time or another. Even the most tranquil family must occasionally deal with major or minor disruptive events (such as deaths or accidents) or threats to their safety, gratification, and well-being; to quote Menninger (1963), at times life seems like "one damned thing after another," a succession of irritations, changes, traumas, or emergencies.

Many families experience more than their share of prolonged stress. For some families, living from crisis to crisis becomes an acceptable if unwelcome way of life. In others, an unexpected, unpredictable crisis—the birth of a severely handicapped infant, accidental death of a young parent, the discovery of a terminal illness in a young child—is a stimulus for coping, mobilizing family resources, and reorganizing family functioning.

A family crisis is provoked when members face an obstacle to their goals that, at least for some period of time, appears insurmountable by means of their customary problem-solving strategies. Since its ordinary coping behavior is inadequate, the family restructures itself in some way. Typically, the moment of crisis is followed by a period of disorganization and emotional upheaval during which the family makes various abortive attempts to solve their problems. Ultimately, some adaptation is achieved, for better or worse; the outcome is frequently governed by the way in which the family organizes itself and by its interaction during the crisis period (Goldenberg, 1983).

Crisis theory is based on the concept of homeostatic balance discussed in Chapter 2. It assumes that families are ordinarily in a state of relative equilibrium. As a group, family members have evolved a set of coping techniques that permit them to deal successfully with most common, everyday problems. Even if certain situations prove to be somewhat less manageable and generate frustration or temporary emotional upset, members can generally rely on their usual approaches to tolerate the stress, resolve the problems, and successfully discharge the accumulated tension. However, when problems persist, when they touch significant vulnerable areas of their lives—or when several problems impinge at once—family members find themselves in a crisis situation for which they must seek resolution and relief.

Developmental Crises

As we indicated above, there are some families for whom life seems to be an uninterrupted series of disasters but such families are, fortunately, relatively rare. More likely, family crises are tied rather specifically to the tasks current to the family's developmental phase. Thus, a childless couple who appear content may face considerable marital stress when a baby is born and they experience changes in their roles, freedom of movement, and economic status. Another set of parents may do an excellent job when nurturing behavior is called for but fail to provide support and encouragement when the child needs to separate from the family in order to enter school. In another family, one or both parents may enjoy being playful with a child, acting like a pal, but cannot behave like an adult and offer the necessary leadership and guidance when the child reaches adolescence.

Similarly, an older adolescent may provoke a family crisis with his or her departure from home and separation from the family (for example, a student's first year away at college). Shapiro (1967) studied young people and their families in both individual and family therapy and found that the early parent–child relationship contributes to the adolescent's consolidated or confused sense of identity; this identity was an important determinant of the adolescent's (and consequently the family's) disturbance. Specifically, he found that in families where there is evidence of distortion, inconsistency, and contradiction in the way the parents view and treat their child, the adolescent is likely to react by showing serious psychological disturbance. In such families, Shapiro found repeated evidence of anxiety in the parents over an adolescent's expression of his or her developing potential.

Crises continue throughout the family life cycle as family members (not just the aging individual) make accommodations to retirement, grandparenthood, illness, the process of dying, and widowhood. Elderly parents, once accustomed to power and decision-making privileges within a family, may relinquish such perquisites only with great reluctance or under duress. To change roles with one's children—become dependent on those previously considered one's dependents—calls for considerable reorganization and rarely occurs without stress felt throughout the family system.

The death of a grandparent may be the young child's first encounter with separation and loss and, at the same time, be a reminder to the parents of their own mortality. How the family copes with the dying process has implications for several generations as all move inevitably toward the aging phase of the family life cycle (Brody, 1974).

Situational Crises

In addition to the maturational or developmental crises that are predictably part of the family life cycle, certain situational crises may occur suddenly and abruptly at any point in the family's development. In the course of a family's career, one or more of the following may precipitate a crisis:

Miscarriage	Prolonged unemployment of major
Abortion	wage earner
Rape	Major role shifts (for example,
Adoption	mother returns to work
Separation	outside home)
Death of a family member	Divorce
Single parenthood	Career changes
Birth of a handicapped child	Physical abuse
Serious accident	Runaway adolescent
Suicide	Teenage pregnancy
Substance abuse	Desertion
Medical hospitalization	Jail
Mental hospitalization	Severe financial pressures
(for example, schizophrenia,	Incest
brain damage)	Sexual molestation
Geographic moves	

Each crisis calls for the family members to develop new styles of coping. Although the stress may cause the family's regression to ineffective behavior patterns, the crisis also presents the family with an opportunity to grow through adaptive strategies (for example, role realignment or reestablishment of

boundaries can lead to a more equitable distribution of power, greater independence of family members, a greater sense of family loyalty). In the following case, a father and his adolescent daughter constitute a subsystem operating
within the family system. Although such an alliance need not necessarily
threaten overall family functioning, in this case it does. (In dysfunctional
families, subsystems are often formed by a parent who, unable to communicate
with the marital partner, makes a close emotional alliance with one or more of
the children.) Notice how the crisis situation provides an opportunity for positive change, as the mother challenges the father–daughter subsystem.

> A domineering, stubborn husband; his meek, childlike wife; and their 16-
> year-old daughter Joyce were approaching the point in Joyce's therapy
> where they were becoming aware that the 16-year-old's repeated behavior
> of running away and sexually acting-out often occurred after father and
> daughter had had a particularly intense encounter with one another. In their
> encounters each usually tried to convince the other of the "rightness" of his or
> her point of view by means of shouting arguments. When all three came to
> the therapist's office after a crisis phone call, they began by relating that two
> days ago Joyce had met a former boyfriend and spent the night with him at
> the beach without letting her parents know where she was, and had been
> "raped" by him. The next morning, that is, yesterday, Joyce had come home
> sobbing to tell her parents of the outrage that had befallen her. The father
> was incensed. He didn't believe Joyce's cry of rape; he accused her of being
> a slut. Predictably, this triggered Joyce, and the father and daughter were
> into a shouting match. The meek wife spoke up, addressing her husband,
> "Why object now, it's happened many times before. I don't like it either; but I
> like it even less that she is getting between you and me again. I had begun to
> think recently that maybe I was more to you than just the 'child-mother' of
> your daughter. I don't want her to ruin that" [McPherson, Brackelmanns &
> Newman, 1974, p. 83].

PATHOLOGICAL COMMUNICATION PATTERNS

Flawed Communication: The Concept of Communication Deviance

For a family to function effectively, it must develop ways and means of establishing and maintaining clear communication channels. Researchers Wynne,
Jones, and Al-Khayyal (1982) emphasize the role of "healthy communication"
on the part of parents in promoting adaptive behavior in their offspring. In
particular, they have found that such communication patterns provide children
with a model for developing the essential cognitive capacities of attending,
focusing, and remaining task-oriented as well as a model for communicating
ideas and feelings clearly and directly. (Previous research by Wynne and his
colleagues has shown that the cognitive capacities of attending and transactional focusing are consistently impaired in parents of schizophrenics.)

"Healthy communication" calls for two or more people to attempt to share
the same focus of attention and to derive shared meaning during this effort. In

order to study what they called **communication deviance,** Singer and Wynne (1966) at the National Institute of Mental Health examined the **Rorschach test** protocols of parents of young adult schizophrenics and discovered numerous examples of confused, contradictory and diverting responses. In complementary research at UCLA, Goldstein, Rodnick, Jones, McPherson, and West (1978) used the **Thematic Apperception Test (TAT)** as well as other test and interview devices and also found that parents' high communication deviance increased the risk of schizophrenia in their offspring. Particularly prominent in the TAT test responses were contorted or peculiar use of language, misperceptions of the stimulus pictures, and difficulty with task instruction. The UCLA Family Project Study also found that people with high communication deviance tended to overly personalize problems (for example, worrying about the people depicted in the cards).

In all families the spoken word is the most effective means for exchanging factual information, but a great deal of the emotional interaction is expressed through nonverbal messages—gestures, tones of voice, facial expressions, even the amount of physical distance between the members. Sometimes silence is a powerful message (for example, when one marital partner, hurt and angry, stops talking to the other for a period of time). In dysfunctional families, it is common for members to make speeches at each other in place of conversation or to turn away and avoid eye contact when someone is speaking. Some families engage in other activities (for example, watching TV, walking in and out of the room) while allegedly conversing, once again interfering with clear and direct communication.

As we have seen, from a systems viewpoint each participant contributes to the behavior of the other; their interaction reflects this joint influence. According to a survey conducted by Beck and Jones (1973), poor communication is by far the most frequent problem reported by couples seeking family counseling (see Figure 3-1).

Paradoxical Communication: The Double-Bind Concept

A **paradoxical communication** is one that moves in two opposite or internally inconsistent directions at the same time (Steinglass, 1978). Although a feature at times of any family's interaction, and tolerable in moderate doses, paradoxical communication used at time of crisis, as a characteristic way of dealing with family conflicts, or as a major model for child rearing can lead to pathological transactions. If you claim you are interested in what someone is saying while never looking up from the newspaper, you convey two contradictory messages, leaving the other person confused about how to proceed. Every reasonable move made in response to you would inevitably be proven wrong and would lead to increasing frustration and, depending on the importance of the issue at hand, eventual despair.

The **double-bind message** is a particularly destructive form of paradoxical communication. One person issues a statement to another that simultaneously

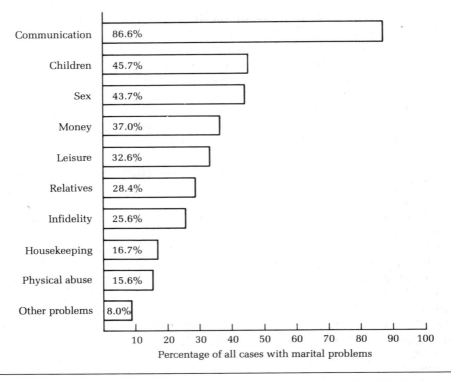

Figure 3-1. Ranking of marital problems reported in the case loads of 266 U.S. family counseling agencies that participated in this survey. Note that almost nine out of ten couples complained of difficulties communicating with each other. Communication problems in this sample are almost twice as common as the next highest set of family problems involving relationships with children. (Beck and Jones, 1973)

contains two messages or <u>demands</u> that are logically inconsistent and contra-dictory. Moreover, there is a third message: an injunction that the receiver of the message must not comment about the inconsistency. Thus, the person re-ceiving the message is called on to make a response but is doomed to failure with whatever response he or she makes since to respond positively to one message is automatically to respond negatively to the other—a no-win situa-tion. For example, a young woman, having been taught by her parents to be careful of men's advances, becomes anxious whenever her husband gets phys-ically close to her. If he approaches her affectionately, she stiffens and recoils. At the same time, the woman finds the image of herself as "frigid" or a prude to be repugnant, so as the husband begins to withdraw in response to her with-drawal from him, she simulates affectionate and seductive behavior and asks in a hurt manner why he is so unresponsive tonight. The husband is caught in a double-bind, a situation without alternatives. Whichever message he obeys— "go away" or "come closer"—he is disobeying the other. His dilemma becomes

No matter what you are doing wrong.

"Trapped between a rock + a hard place"

"If I like her, I must not show her affection, but if I do not show her affection then I will lose her."

The "double-bind" concept grew out of the work of Bateson, Jackson, Haley, and Weakland (1956) at Palo Alto, California; the Bateson group attempted to describe psychiatric problems such as schizophrenia in terms of family and interaction patterns rather than as disease entities residing within the individual. (For discussion of the pivotal role of this work in the history of family therapy, see Chapter 4.)

Originally a linear concept involving a two-person arrangement, in which the victim is penalized for whatever move he or she makes, "double-bind" is now used in describing the circular pattern of relating in an unstable family in which such communication is customary. In such a family, confusion arises not only because of contradictions and inconsistencies in the messages the members exchange but because there are deeper, more pervasive contradictions and inconsistencies in their relationships.

Disguised Communication: Mystification

Closely related to the "double-bind" concept, the term **mystification** is used by Laing (1965) to describe how some families deal with conflict and contradictory viewpoints by befuddling, obscuring, or masking whatever is going on between members. Masking devices do not deter conflict but they cloud over what the conflict is all about. In everyday family life, one person may mystify another by confirming the content of the experience the second person is having but disconfirming that person's interpretation of the experience. Suppose a young, ambitious husband—moonlighting at a second job after a day's work—comes home to find his wife sitting in front of the TV set, a six-pack of beer nearby, still wearing the dirty jeans he left her in early in the morning. The breakfast dishes are still unwashed in the kitchen sink. Harassed by her three preschool children all day and frustrated by the responsibility of raising them by herself since her husband is rarely home before 10 P.M., the wife barely manages a smile when he arrives. He looks grim.

W: Are you angry?
H: No—just tired.
W: How come you look angry?
H: It's just your imagination.
W: Why don't you admit it? I know you well enough to know when you are pissed with me.
H: I don't know where you dream up these ideas.

In actuality, the husband is furious but he is afraid to have an angry confrontation with his wife. Instead, he tries to mystify her by telling her she has misperceived the situation. However, his avoidance behavior—intended to avoid conflict—only causes greater internal conflict for her. If she believes her husband, she thinks she must be "crazy" to imagine he is angry but their relationship is preserved; if she believes her own senses, she retains a firm grip on reality but must deal with their deteriorating relationship.

The prime function of mystification is to maintain the status quo. It is brought into play when one or more family members threatens that status quo by expressing feelings. A child who complains of being unhappy is told by his or her parents that such a thing is not possible: "You have no right to feel that way. Haven't we given you everything you want? How could you be so ungrateful?" Through mystification, the parents simply deny or negate what the child is feeling or experiencing as though whatever he or she reports as taking place does not really exist. They know better what the child is experiencing; his or her perceptions have no validity. After admitting to her parents that she had sexual thoughts and sometimes masturbated, an adolescent girl was flatly told by her parents that she did not. As this pattern was repeated, she began to doubt the validity of her own feelings and thoughts and slowly withdrew into schizophrenia (Laing & Esterson, 1970). According to the authors describing her case, the girl was behaving adaptively, making a logical response to an illogical situation.

Patterned Communication:
Symmetrical and Complementary Relationships

As we can see from the exchange just described, therapists are interested in far more than the verbal content of any communication between two or more people. In most cases, how the participants define their relationship is at least as important. Who has the right to say what to—and about—the other? Patterns of communication and relationships between people may be symmetrical or complementary. In **symmetrical relationships,** participants mirror each other's behavior; if A boasts, B boasts more grandly, which causes A to boast still further and so on in this "one-upsmanship" game. In **complementary relationships,** one partner's behavior complements the other; that is, if A is assertive, B becomes submissive, which encourages A to greater assertiveness, demanding still more submissiveness from B, and so on (Bateson, 1958).

As an example of a symmetrical relationship, read the following exchange between a husband (H) and his wife (W). The couple has sought help from the interviewer (I) because they feared their constant bickering might hurt their children.

Transcript	*Comments*
I: How, of all the millions of people in the world, did the two of you get together?	
H: We ... both worked in the same place. My wife ran a comptometer, and I repaired comptometers, and ...	H speaks first, offering a unilateral summary of the whole story, thereby defining his right to do so.

W: We worked in the same building.

W restates the same information in her own words, not simply agreeing with him, but instead establishing symmetry in regard to their discussion of this topic.

H: She worked for a firm which had a large installation, and I worked there most of the time because it was a large installation. And so this is where we met.

H adds no new information, but simply rephrases the same tautological sentence with which he began. Thus, he symmetrically matches her behavior of insisting on his right to give information; on the relationship level they are sparring for the "last word." H attempts to achieve this by the finality of his second sentence.

W: We were introduced by some of the other girls up there.
(Pause)

W does not let it drop; she modifies his statement, reasserting her right to participate equally in this discussion. Though this new twist is just as passive an interpretation as their "working in the same building" (in that neither is defined as having taken the initiative), she establishes herself as "a little more equal" by referring to "the other girls," a group in which she was obviously the insider, not H. This pause ends the first cycle of symmetrical exchange with no closure.

H: Actually, we met at a party, I mean we first started going together at a party that one of the employees had. But we'd seen each other before, at work.

Though somewhat softened and compromising, this is a restatement which does not let her definition stand.

W: We never met till that night.
(Slight laugh)
(Pause)

This is a direct negation, not merely a rephrasing, of his statement, indicating perhaps that the dispute is beginning to escalate. (Notice however that "met" is quite an ambiguous term in this context—it could mean several things from "laid eyes on each other" to "were formally introduced"—so that her contradiction of him is disqualified; that is, she could not, if queried, be pinned down to it. Her laugh also enables her to "say something without really saying it.")

H: (Very softly) Mhm.
(Long pause)

H puts himself one-down by agreeing with her—overtly: but "mhm" has a variety of possible meanings and is here uttered almost inaudibly, without any conviction or emphasis, so the result is quite vague. Even more, the previous statement is so vague that it is not clear what an agreement with it might mean. In any case, he does not go further, nor does he assert still another version of his own. So they reach the end of another round, again marked by a pause that seems to signal that they have reached the danger point (of open contradiction and conflict) and are prepared to end the discussion even without closure of the content aspect.

I: But still, I have an image of dozens of people, or maybe more, floating around; so how was it that the two of you, of all these people, got together?

Interviewer intervenes to keep the discussion going.

H: She was one of the prettier ones up there. (Slight laugh)
(Pause)

H makes a strong "one-up" move; this dubious compliment places her in comparison with the others, with him as the judge.

W: (Faster): I don't know, the main reason I started going with him is because the girls—he had talked to some of the other girls before he talked to me, and told them he was interested in me, and they more or less planned this party, and that's where we met.

She matches his condescension with her own version: she was only interested in him because he was initially interested in her. (The subject around which their symmetry is defined has shifted from whose version of their meeting will be told and allowed to stand to who got the trophy, so to speak, in their courtship.)

H: Actually the party wasn't planned for that purpose—

A straightforward rejection of her definition.

W: (Interrupting): No, but it was planned for us to meet at the party.

After agreeing with his correction, W repeats what she has just said. Her

Meet formally, you might say. In person. (Slight laugh) We'd worked together, but I didn't make a habit of—

H: (Overlapping) She was certainly a backward-bashful type of worker as far as associating with uh, uh strange men on the place, yeah, but the women knew it. (Pause) And I was flirtin' with lots of 'em up there. (Slight laugh) Nothing meant by it I guess, but just . . . (Sigh) just my nature I guess.

nonpersonal formulation has been weakened, but she now relies on a straight self-definition ("I am this kind of person . . ."), an unassailable way to establish equality.

H gives a symmetrical answer based on his "nature," and another round ends.

[Watzlawick, Beavin, & Jackson, 1967, pp. 111–113]

As this excerpt illustrates, a symmetrical relationship may be characterized by equality and the minimization of differences between the participants. A symmetrical relationship may also be competitive, with each partner's actions influencing the reactions of his or her partner in a spiraling effect called **symmetrical escalation.** Quarrels may get out of hand and become increasingly vicious as a nasty jibe from one person is met by a nastier response from the other which prompts the first person to become even more mean and ill-tempered, and so on.

Complementary interaction is based on inequality and the maximization of differences. In this form of reciprocal interaction, one partner (traditionally the male) takes the dominant "one-up" position and the spouse (traditionally the female) assumes the submissive "one-down" position. However, despite appearances, these positions need not be taken as an indication of their relative strength or weakness. Each partner behaves in a manner that presupposes— and at the same time provides a rationale for—the behavior of the other. In a complementary relationship, dissimilar but apt responses evoke each other in an interlocking pattern (Watzlawick, Beavin, & Jackson, 1967).

The following transcript is from an interview with a couple who have a complementary relationship, the husband in the "one-up" position and the wife "one-down." The spouses are emotionally distant from one another and the wife is depressed. After the interviewer has asked the standard opening question about the way the couple met, the husband responds first:

H: And—see, when'd you start there?
W: W—I haven't any i—
H: (Interrupting)—seems to me it was about, I came in October, the year before . . . and you probably started about . . . February uh, January or February—probably February or March 'cause your birthday was in December, that same year.

W: Mm, I don't even remember . . .

H: (Interrupting): So I happened to send her some flowers, you see, when—our first date out. And that never—we'd never gone anywhere had we?

W: (With short laugh): No, I was very surprised.

H: And we just went from there. It was about a year later I guess we got married. Little over a year.

I: What did you . . .

H: (Interrupting): Although Jane left the company very shortly after that. Mm, I don't think you worked there over a couple of months, did you?

W: You know, I'm sorry, I don't remember a thing about (Slight laugh) how long it was or when I went—

H: (Interrupting): Yeah, a couple of months, and then you went back into teaching. (*W:* Mhm, mhm) 'Cause we—she found I guess that this war work was not contributing as much to the war effort as she thought it was, when she went out there.

I: So you—you went to a school?

W: Yes, I'd been working in it, before (*Int:* Mhm) I went to work there.

I: And you continued the contact without interruption. (*H:* Oh yeah) What, uh, beside the fact that your wife is obviously attractive, what else do you think you have in common?

H: Absolutely nothing. (Laughing) We never have had—'r we—(Sharp breath). (Pause)

[Watzlawick, Beavin, & Jackson, 1967, pp. 114–115]

This is a good illustration of the reciprocal roles each partner plays in the complementary interaction pattern. The wife's apparent amnesia and helplessness make it possible for the husband to appear to be the strong, realistic partner and, at the same time, serve as the very factors against which his strength and realism are quite powerless. In this kind of relationship, the outward appearance of who is weak and who is strong may be quite misleading.

Every communication reflects a struggle for control of a relationship (Haley, 1963). While each exchange between two persons may be defined by both as either symmetrical or complementary, their overall relationship may alternate from one style to the other, depending on the situation. The way partners define their relationship in a restaurant (symmetrically exchanging ideas about what sounds good on the menu) may differ drastically from how they define it in the bedroom (as a complementary relationship in which one controls and the other submits). Neither pattern is necessarily more or less effective. However, the communication pattern that characterizes most of a couple's transactions plays a large part in determining the roles and power structure of their relationship.

Symmetrical and complementary relationships are, of course, common enough in family life and under ordinary circumstances are not considered pathological. However, each pattern runs the risk of getting out of control—in systems terms, of introducing positive feedback loops that amplify deviation and have the potential to destroy or seriously damage the system. For example, symmetrical escalations can transform a conversation to an ugly exchange that leaves each participant physically and emotionally drained. Complementary sequences, should they become rigid and characteristic of a couple's interaction, can turn a dominant–submissive pattern into a series of **sadomasochistic** exchanges that are inevitably destructive to the self-esteem of both partners.

ENMESHMENT AND DISENGAGEMENT

In a highly functional family, clear boundaries between people give each family member a sense of "I-ness" along with an ingroup sense of "we" or "us." That is, each member retains his or her individuality but not at the expense of losing the feeling of belonging to a family. The boundaries of subsystems also remain clear and well-defined for proper family functioning. Most family systems fall somewhere along the continuum between enmeshment (boundaries are blurred) and disengagement (boundaries are rigid and communication across subsystems is difficult).

word for "closed" family.

— pathway to schizophrenia.

Enmeshment refers to an extreme form of proximity and intensity in family interactions in which members are overconcerned and overinvolved in each other's lives. In extreme cases, the family's lack of differentiation makes any separation from the family an act of betrayal (Minuchin, 1974a). Belonging to the family dominates all experiences at the expense of each member developing a separate sense of self. Whatever is happening to one family member reverberates throughout the system. A child sneezes, his sister runs for the tissue, his mother for a thermometer, and his father starts worrying.

Subsystem boundaries in enmeshed families are poorly differentiated, weak, and easily crossed (Minuchin & Associates, 1978). Children may act like parents and parental control may be ineffective. Excessive togetherness and sharing may lead to a lack of privacy; members, overly alert and responsive to signs of distress, intrude on each other's thoughts and feelings. Members of enmeshed families place too high a value on family cohesion to the extent that they yield autonomy and have little inclination to explore and master problems outside the family.

In the following case, a woman seeks psychotherapy to obtain relief from her acute depression. Closer examination reveals that her symptoms are related and secondary to a basic family entanglement or enmeshment. Contrary to appearances, it is the adolescent son in the family, not the mother, who is most at risk.

Helen Turner, a 48-year-old housewife, was seriously depressed following the death of her eldest child, a daughter of 22. Her depression persisted beyond the expected bereavement period, and reached the point where she had difficulty eating and sleeping. Her waking hours were filled with gloomy thoughts, frequent crying spells, and a sense of hopelessness regarding the future.

Helen's husband as well as her remaining three children (2 daughters and a son) seemed unable to console her, no matter how hard they tried. Her family physician thought that perhaps the lingering depression might be related to hormonal changes during the menopause, which she was undergoing, but that proved to be a false lead. The antidepressant medication he prescribed helped some, but Helen's symptoms of depression continued.

Mrs. Turner finally decided to seek help at a neuropsychiatric hospital outpatient clinic. It had been five weeks since her daughter's death; sad as it was, it may have triggered some deeper family disturbance, and the intake worker, after interviewing Mrs. Turner, concluded that her depression was related primarily to that family's difficulty in resuming their life cycle. Family therapy was decided upon on a weekly basis; thereafter, Mr. and Mrs. Turner, their son Barry, and their daughters Barbara and Tracy, all the children in their late adolescence (18-21), were seen together by co-therapists over a six-month period.

During the first family session, all of the family members expressed their grief over Katherine's strange death. What seemed to emerge, heretofore covered over, was the suspicion each had in varying degrees that Katherine had committed suicide, if not intentionally then subintentionally (i.e. by excessive risk-taking). (Katherine had actually fallen from the rooftop of their house, although it was never clear why she had climbed onto the roof in the first place.) This, and data accumulated over subsequent sessions, led the therapists to speculate: first, that Katherine may have seen death as her only way to separate from her parents and family; and second, that this same pattern is being reenacted with Barry, who is now the oldest child. A straight A student, president of his student body and a tennis champ in high school, Barry never went to college or work, but was at home unable to make a decision about the right school to attend.

(In an enmeshed family, such as the Turners, a member may view suicide as the only way to make a statement that will finally be heard. To such a desperate and despairing person, the suicidal act may be attempted as the only way to separate from the family. Ironically, the successful suicide may leave the family even more enmeshed than before. Moreover, the act may increase the likelihood of further suicides among the surviving family members. Working with such a post-suicidal family, therapists must help its members to develop alternate methods for gaining autonomy.)

Apparently, for some time prior to her death, Katherine served as a bridge between her parents. Because of their widening marital rift, it was her family function to keep them together. One consequence of that family role, however, was her own inability to leave the home to form an identity of her own. Unable to resolve the conflicts that the parents had and unable to leave, as she felt her mother could not manage without her, she became more and more confused about her own competency and identity and increasingly desperate about her own feelings of powerlessness and inadequacy, ultimately killing herself. Piecing the story together, the two therapists helped the family accept the reality of the suicide, along with its attendant rush of anger, blame, and guilt. At the same time, the therapists helped each member work through the usual grief process at the loss of a loved one. Barry, in particular, needed to understand his own behavior, especially the danger that he might follow in Katherine's footsteps unless he could emancipate himself from the family without excessive guilt. While the conflict between mother and father did not prevent the children from growing up and becoming individuals, it did make it extremely difficult for the children to separate from the parents. As the marital discord was brought into the open and slowly resolved, the children, and especially Barry, felt free to step out into the world [Goldenberg & Goldenberg, 1977].

At the other extreme, members of disengaged families may function separately and autonomously but with little sense of family loyalty. They frequently lack the capacity for interdependence or for requesting support from others when needed. Communication is difficult and the family's protective functions are limited. When an individual family member is under stress, the enmeshed family responds with excessive speed and intensity while the disengaged family hardly seems to respond at all. Minuchin (1974a) offers this graphic illustration: The parents in an enmeshed family may become enormously upset if a child does not eat dessert. In a disengaged family, the parents may feel unconcerned about the child's hatred of school.

In disengaged families, the boundaries are so inappropriately rigid that only a high level of individual stress can reverberate strongly enough to activate support from other family members. In their isolation, members of disengaged families tend not to respond to each other even when a response is indicated. Such individuals are rarely able to form caring relationships outside of the family because they have not had the experience within the family.

Delinquency-Producing Families

In a landmark study of poor, disadvantaged, unstable families that produce **delinquent** children (Minuchin, Montalvo, Guerney, Rosman, & Schumer, 1967), the extremes of enmeshment or disengagement (or alternation between the two) were found to characterize family interaction. In such families, largely without fathers or stable father-figures, the responsibility for rearing and educating the children is left almost entirely to the mother. She tends to nurture them adequately but becomes anxious when called on to provide guidance or exercise control. Mothers at the extreme of enmeshment feel absolutely responsible for their children's behavior. If a child steals,[1] the mother reacts as if she were a failure. This evokes a complementary response in her child: "If I steal, I hurt my mother," rather than, "If I steal, I am a thief." The child does not learn responsibility for his actions because there is no clear demarcation between his own and his mother's behavior. Disengaged mothers, at the other extreme, rarely inquire about what is happening in the day-to-day life of the child, thus abdicating their supervisory role. Neither extreme prepares the child for dealing with stress and conflict or for focusing attention on solutions to problems in the outside world.

[1]Families for this study were drawn from the Wiltwyck School for Boys, a residential treatment center serving the most disadvantaged ghetto areas in New York City. All resident children have been in trouble with the law.

The alternation between enmeshment and disengagement in some families is depicted in Figure 3-2. Generally speaking, the enmeshment period (lower portion of figure) takes place before the family reaches the attention of social service agencies; the disengagement period (upper portion) usually occurs with the relinquishment of parental authority.

Minuchin and his co-researchers gathered behavioral data on family interaction patterns by observing how the families under study (12 families with a child at the residential treatment center and 11 matched non-treatment-center control families) went about solving tasks together. Families were also assessed by analyzing the content of members' stories told in response to the Family Interaction Apperception Technique, a **projective technique** consisting of a series of cards depicting various aspects of family functioning. From the analysis of this data, Minuchin developed a family therapy approach that was practical, action-oriented and directed at solving immediate and tangible here-and-now problems, always mindful of the social environment or context in which the problems emerged and were maintained. Post-therapy assessments of families generally showed a shift away from extreme enmeshment or disengagement positions. A forerunner of Minuchin's **structural family therapy** (which we discuss more fully in Chapter 8), the therapeutic intervention helped most families develop clearer and less rigid boundaries between the parent and child subsystems.

Psychosomatic Families

In families where asthma, diabetes, or **anorexia nervosa** (self-starving) threaten a child's life, the locus of pathology may be in the family itself rather than in the medical problem of the affected individual. Although the **etiology** of the disease may be physical and not psychological, the **psychosomatic** element of the disease lies in the exacerbation of the underlying symptoms triggered by emotional stress. For example, an allergy-prone child may react to emotional arousal within the family (for example, marital problems between the parents) by having an asthmatic attack. That attack may, in turn, obscure or deflect the parental conflict. Seen in this light, the asthma reaction may be considered an expression of family stress within an enmeshed group; the detouring maneuver (the child's acute symptomatology) is the mechanism by which the family diffuses the stress between the parents, designates another family member as having "the problem," and allows attention now to be paid to the needy child.

Minuchin and Associates (1978) indicate that families of children who manifest these psychosomatic problems are characterized by certain transactional patterns that encourage somatization (see related discussion in Chapter 8). Enmeshment is common, subsystems function poorly, individual boundaries are too weak to allow for individual autonomy. A psychosomatic family tends to be overprotective, inhibiting the child from developing a sense of independence, competence, or interest in activities outside the safety of the family. The child, in turn, feels great responsibility for protecting the family. Sometimes the

The Enmeshment-Disengagement System

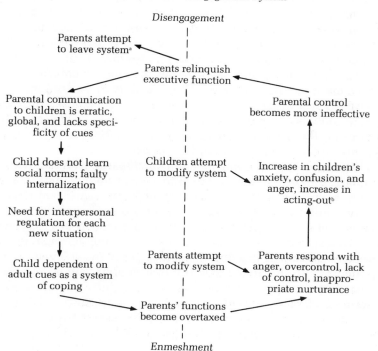

Disengagement

Parents attempt
to leave system[a]

Parents relinquish
executive function

Parental communication
to children is erratic,
global, and lacks speci-
ficity of cues

Parental control
becomes more ineffective

Child does not learn
social norms; faulty
internalization

Children attempt
to modify system

Increase in children's
anxiety, confusion, and
anger, increase in
acting-out[b]

Need for interpersonal
regulation for each
new situation

Child dependent on
adult cues as a system
of coping

Parents attempt
to modify system

Parents respond with
anger, overcontrol, lack
of control, inappro-
priate nurturance

Parents' functions
become overtaxed

Enmeshment

[a]When parental control becomes ineffective and parents relinquish executive functions, they may abandon the family altogether, but most of the time they segment the family by institutionalizing a child or children, acting-out (in illness, promiscuity, alcoholism, and so on), or allowing a sibling substructure to take over parental functions.

[b]At the point of increase in the children's anxiety and acting-out as an attempt to modify the system, children may turn to siblings for control, guidance, or identification (delinquent or not); they may abandon the family, that is, run away; or they may join a delinquent gang.

Figure 3–2. Alternations between enmeshment and disengagement found in some disorganized and disadvantaged families. (Minuchin et al., 1967)

physiologically vulnerable child protects family members by manifesting symptoms over which they all may then become concerned. Any external stress, such as a father changing jobs or a mother going to work outside the home, overloads the family's already dysfunctional coping mechanisms and precipitates illness in the child. This is especially true in rigid families with a commitment to maintaining the status quo. Such families typically have a very low threshold for conflict, which they feel they must avoid or diffuse for the sake of harmony and consensus. Unable to permit disagreement among themselves, members refuse to confront differences and negotiate their resolution.

The child's psychosomatic symptoms have a regulating effect on the family system. Parents who cannot deal with each other directly unite in protective concern over their sick child, avoiding their underlying marital conflict through this detouring maneuver. The sick child is thus defined as the family problem, and the other children join the parents in worrying or being exasperated over the burden. In such cases, as concern for the child's health absorbs the family, marital strife is ignored. The sick child in an enmeshed psychosomatic family is easily cast in the role of family conflict defuser. By returning the family to its previous homeostatic condition, he or she receives reinforcement for manifesting the symptoms, increasing the probability of their reappearance whenever a similar threat to the family occurs.

From the study of psychosomatic families compared with families of anorexics, diabetics, and asthmatics in which there was no evidence of a psychosomatic link, Minuchin and Associates (1978) found significant differences in how family conflicts were handled. Unable to define issues clearly or consider alternative solutions, the psychosomatic families tended to leave conflicts unresolved, leading ultimately to some denouement only through psychosomatically-induced symptoms in a family member. As in the Wiltwyck School studies reported in the previous section, family therapy aimed at changing the structure of relationships within the family was effective in most cases, alleviating the medical crisis as well as improving the psychosocial functioning of family members. (For discussion of the issues in respect to the effectiveness of this and other family therapy approaches, see Chapter 13.)

Boundary-Violating Families

The concept of boundaries is central to understanding enmeshed or disengaged behavior in families. We need to address questions of differentiation, permeability and rigidity of boundaries among and between individuals and subgroups within a family, and between the family with its subsystems and its social environment (Aponte & Van Deusen, 1981). As we noted in Chapter 2, members of families who function with poorly defined boundaries run the risk of overinvolvement with one another and the subsequent loss of autonomy and diminished potential for individual mastery of problems. Families whose boundaries are firmly delineated, impermeable and rigid tend to have members who go their own ways. Families are said to violate functional boundaries when members, crossing generations and subsystems, intrude upon functions that are properly the domain of other members. For example, children may be assigned long-term roles that are inappropriate, inflexible and ill-fitting; in some cases, children and their parents may even exchange family roles.

A harmonious dyadic relationship does not necessarily assure that a happy couple will be involved and caring parents. Unless they develop a strong parental coalition, the opposite is often the case: the arrival of a child is seen as a threat to the closeness between man and wife (one or both of whom are immature and self-centered), an intrusion that jeopardizes the dependency gratification sought by one or the other (or both). On the other hand, it is possible for husband and wife to be good parents but have a poor marriage; this situation may put children at even greater risk. Instead of forming a workable coalition, each parent may openly deprecate the other or become a rival for the child's attention and affection. In severe cases, a parent equates loyalty to the other parent with being rejected by the child. Such parents frequently remind the child that some undesirable behavior is "just like your mother" or "just like your father" and therefore unacceptable. Inevitably, destructive parent–child coalitions develop.

Some families become governed by these secret cross-generational coalitions that polarize the members (males versus females, hardliners versus softliners, dominators versus submitters, achievers versus nonachievers, "givers" versus "takers"). Children caught up in these field forces may be forced to choose sides, inevitably disengaging from the parent not chosen. Sometimes, as we saw in the case of Helen Turner, children may become so caught up in the family vise that they become immobilized or can escape only through suicide.

Children inevitably acquire labels in the process of growing up. Billy is lazy, Joey is handsome, Elizabeth is bright, Amy tells lies. Some children make a determined effort to play the pleasing "good child"; their rooms are neat, their homework turned in on time, their library books never overdue. Others, more defiant, may be scapegoated as the "bad child"—incorrigible, destructive, unmanageable. For every child who pays the price of being a "bad" child there is probably a sibling who pays the price of posing as a "good child" (who may devote a lifetime to seeking other people's approval and love at the expense of self-actualization).

In pathogenic families—families that produce dysfunctional behavior—one or both adults and any of the children may be assigned roles inappropriately or be treated as if they have only a single personality characteristic (laziness or selfishness, for example) instead of a wide range of human feelings and attitudes. In some cases, parents who are uncomfortable in accepting the dependence of their child (possibly because they themselves are immature and needy) reverse roles with that child; in extreme cases, the child is overburdened with demands that he or she take care of infantile parents (to say nothing of younger siblings) and is never given a chance to be a child in his or her own right. Boszormenyi-Nagy and Spark (1973) refer to this process as the **parentification** of the child. They believe that such a child—usually one who is quiet, conforming, and good—is frequently part of a family in which there is depression, despair, and rage, although these feelings may not get expressed. Sometimes, the childlike adults who abdicate their leadership responsibilities to the child try to justify their inadequacies under the guise of permissiveness or being democratic and nonauthoritative, thus "allowing" the child adult responsibilities.[2]

---

[2]Parentification of a child may occur under a variety of circumstances. More and more commonly we see the phenomenon when a parent deserts the family; becomes ill or incapacitated; dies; drinks too heavily; and so on. In each case, the parent is unavailable and the child is expected to fill the parent role, physically as well as psychologically.

The assignment of the scapegoat role—bad, always in trouble, uncontrolla-ble, the cause of "the mess" the family is in—to a child usually occurs through the collusive action of several family members. They validate each other's impression that the family must punish, restrain, or in some way get rid of this bad influence. Closer observation of the family reveals that the members have no intention of letting the scapegoat leave because they need that person to blame for any signs of family disharmony or dysfunction.

Some pathogenic families maneuver their children into playing out sexual-ized roles. Seductive, almost incestuous relationships or overt incest may be found in many severely disturbed families. In these cases, sexual relations between the parents occur infrequently or have stopped completely. As a consequence, the angry or rejected parent seeks gratification with his or her child. This may result in incest but more likely it means showering special attention or gifts on the child, overinvolving oneself in the child's social life, perhaps taking the child regularly to places (restaurants, the theater, parties) one would normally go with a spouse. Boszormenyi-Nagy and Spark (1973) point out that the child is not seen by the offending parent as a child but as an object; the object is used to satisfy parental dependency needs or to retaliate and gain revenge against the rejecting or indifferent marital partner.

Finally, Boszormenyi-Nagy and Spark (1973) describe the family pet, a role in which a family casts one of its children as perfect or ideal. Such children rarely cause overt trouble and are allowed to act silly or clownlike. If the parentified child is the family "healer" or caretaker and the scapegoated child is the family troublemaker, the family pet is the good, carefree, affectionate, undemanding "model child." Unfortunately, "pets" are rarely taken seriously; they seem to exist merely to bring laughter and lightness to the family. Yet there may be considerable sadness and depression underneath the surface playfulness and good citizenship. One reason is that the family pet, frequently the youngest child, is treated in a sense as a nonperson; without position or status in the family, the child suffers a loss of self-esteem. The cute, adorable, "darling" facade may hide inner feelings of emptiness.

As Aponte and Van Deusen (1981) point out, "the ability of a family to func-tion well depends on the degree to which the family structure is well defined, elaborated, flexible and cohesive" (p. 315). To violate clearly demarcated fam-ily boundaries on a regular basis (it may happen in all families on occasion) is to upset the family structure. If the family system lacks the ability to negotiate a new structure more in harmony with the requirements of its members and its social environment, it may persist in unsuitable but unyielding role assign-ments that ultimately damage all family members.

SCAPEGOATING

As we pointed out in the previous section, children in particular are often selected for and inducted into specific family roles. Commonly, some chance characteristic that distinguishes the child from other family members (it need not be an obnoxious trait; it need only differentiate the person) is singled out and focused on by the others, emphasizing the differences between that child and the rest of them. Bell (1975) contends that such roles are externally imposed because the family has discovered that this structuring is the best way to handle the complex interrelationships that exist within the group. Once the roles become fixed—and especially if they are labeled or **typecast** as **pathological**—the basis for chronic behavioral disturbance is established. Bell argues, as do most family therapists, that a family with a disturbed child is generally motivated to preserve that disturbance by seeking to perpetuate the child's pathology. It follows that individual therapy with that child—the traditional route to alleviating his or her symptoms—is doomed to failure since the family will very likely reinstitute the disturbance. Intervention at the family level offers the best chance to change the interactions out of which the disturbance in the one person emerged. The following is a case in point.

Larry S., by the time he was 14 years old, was failing at school and had been apprehended by the school authorities for vandalism on more than one occasion. A bright youngster according to the school counselor who had given him an intelligence test, Larry nevertheless was receiving Ds and Fs in all his classes. He was habitually late to school and almost invariably turned in assignments at least a week late. On numerous occasions he overslept and missed school, complained of being ill, or left home in the morning but went to a movie or video parlor for the day. Invariably, these actions resulted in shouting matches with his mother.

Life at home for Larry was a series of struggles with his parents (especially his mother) and his two younger brothers, Bill, age 12, and John, age 7. He felt blamed by his parents for everything that went wrong. By contrast, his brothers were held up to him by his parents as good children. Bill was a straight-A student (although probably no more intelligent than Larry), helped out at home after school, and never caused his parents any trouble. John was the family "pet," cute and playful; any deviation in his behavior from what his parents expected was quickly dismissed as insignificant, something he would grow out of soon enough.

Scapegoated as the family deviant, Larry proceeded to show the family just how deviant he could be. He stole money from his mother's purse, became a drug user and dealer, sometimes sold family possessions to raise more money. He destroyed some kitchen chairs in a rage one day, even wrote obscene words on the living room wall using a spray can of paint. He refused to bathe or clean his room. More and more, he stayed in his room listening to his portable radio. His ability to tolerate frustration was so low that one day, when he discovered the battery was dead, he hurled the radio through the closed bedroom window.

Distraught over their son's behavior, Larry's parents finally sought professional help for him. Larry consented reluctantly, although his behavior with the psychologist repeated his pattern at home: he frequently missed sessions without notifying the therapist or, if he attended, did destructive things in the office, such as dropping a lighted cigarette on the sofa. After several months, Larry seemed more trusting of the psychologist but little progress was being made. Finally, the psychologist suggested family therapy.

In family therapy, the following family portrait began to emerge: Mr. S. was a passive, dependent man, overwhelmed by pressures from his business and family. Chronically frustrated and angry at his wife for presenting him with problems (usually involving Larry) when he arrived home in the evening, he nevertheless suppressed his anger because he worried that she might leave him. However, he secretly got some satisfaction from Larry fighting with Mrs. S., since Larry was acting out something Mr. S. was feeling but was afraid to express. Mrs. S., on the other hand, was an insecure woman filled with a multitude of self-doubts. Unsure of her own judgment in almost all situations, she looked to her husband for family leadership or counsel, neither of which he seemed willing to give. Her anger at Larry was at least in part a displacement of her rage at her husband, with whom she appeared to get along beautifully on the surface. Both parents thus had a stake in perpetuating Larry's deviant behavior, since it allowed them to gain some satisfactions without risking open hostility toward each other.

What of the children? Bill, suffering under the strain of being a model child, ultimately complained that he was merely trying to keep his parents together but was building up resentment over losing out on being a child. He no longer wished to be compared with Larry. John found being a "pet" harder to give up but realized that he was losing out on the privileges associated with greater maturity. Larry sensed the underlying strain between his parents; his acting-out behavior was a smoke screen to distract the family from facing their problems of leadership, cohesiveness, and respect for each other's individuality. The parents were the most resistant to change. After six months of therapy with the entire family, all of the children felt ready to terminate, including Larry, whose deviant behavior had ceased almost entirely. Mr. and Mrs. S. joined a couples group with four other couples and continued treatment for several months longer.

The scapegoat who develops symptoms is usually the identified patient who is carrying the pathology for the entire family. Note, however, that scapegoating is a mutual causal process, not a matter of the victimization of one person by others. All members, including the scapegoat, participate in the process. As we have just seen, by displacing their conflict onto a child, parents frequently maintain harmonious relationships at the expense of the child's emotional development. The child, in turn, struggles to keep the family intact even if it means sacrificing himself or herself. Scapegoating may take a variety of forms, depending on how the family typecasts its deviant members. Some common guises are "the mascot, the clown, the sad sack, the erratic genius, the black sheep, the wise guy, the saint, the idiot, the fool, the imposter, the malingerer, the boaster, the villain" (Hoffman, 1971, p. 296). Different family members may switch roles during the family life cycle as needs change, crises come and go, and different persons offer themselves for scapegoating purposes.

FAMILY VIOLENCE

Wife beating, child battering, the sexual abuse of children, the physical mistreatment of the elderly by their children or grandchildren, and spousal rape are persistent forms of family violence; the public disclosure of such happenings is a recent phenomenon. Victims today are less apt to feel they must bury their shame and humiliation and, at all cost, keep the information behind closed doors. Although the precise number of victims of "private violence" is open to dispute (estimates of wife beating, for example, range from 2 million to 6 million annually; see "Private Violence," 1983), it is an uncontested fact that the family—potentially a source of strength and comfort without rival—may also be the context for the expression of rage and brutality.

From their analysis of FBI data, Anthony and Rizzo (1973) concluded that murders of one family member by another constitute about one-third of all homicides committed in the United States every year. Most of the cases involved one spouse killing the other (53%), but the numbers of murders of children by parents (17%) and parents by children (6%) were also significant. These authors describe a family's "aggressive climate" as well as its "sexual climate" as conducive to family violence. They cite the case of a father, the dominant figure in his household, who typically became violent when drunk. (There is a large body of evidence linking the effects of alcohol with the expression of violence.) He had a long history of beating his wife regularly but had stopped several years earlier; in a drunken episode, he had slapped her in the abdomen and his wife, pregnant, had drawn a gun and threatened to kill him. Thereafter, he physically and/or sexually abused his three daughters and a son. Once he flew into a violent rage and began to strangle one of his daughters; his 15-year-old daughter ran for a gun she had hidden and, when he ignored her threats to shoot if he did not stop, she killed him. She later expressed surprise that the family responded angrily after the fact since she thought everyone was in agreement at the time she took action. Describing herself as nervous and impulsive, she believed the family always used her when it wanted some "dirty business" carried out.

Painful as it may be, most family violence fortunately falls short of murder. Nevertheless, a pattern of physical abuse may have repercussions throughout a family. A wife, beaten by her husband, may herself get out of control and brutalize the children. Older siblings observe that family business is often transacted by brute force and may use such force upon younger children. Battered children are likely to grow up predisposed to batter their own offspring. Sexually abused children may turn to prostitution or sexually deviant behavior as adults or may themselves become sexual abusers of children.

In episodes of family violence, the passion, the intensity, the rivalry, and the loss of control (in systems terms, the failure to introduce error-activated mechanisms to help return the relationship to its previous homeostatic state) all suggest that we are dealing with more than personal immaturity or unresolved aggression on the part of an individual perpetrator (Goldenberg & Goldenberg, 1982). Why are some families able to argue or fight, temporarily destabilize themselves, but impose limits on their members when they go too far (provide negative feedback), while other families escalate their conflicts to the point of mayhem or even murder (provide only positive, deviation-amplifying feedback)?

The circularity of violent behavior patterns in many couples (brutality → separation → despair → remorse → reunion → love → brutality) suggests a basic disturbance in the family's relationship system. A wide variety of factors are associated with family violence and aggression: childhood experiences with violence; current situational stresses; poor impulse control; inner rage; the effects of alcohol and other drugs; living in a society that tends to seek violent solutions to immediate problems; jealousy; sexual conflicts; poor communication skills; panic over imminent loss; displacement of aggression from a stronger person apt to retaliate onto a weaker spouse or child; overcompensation for feelings of inadequacy; fear of intimacy (Gelles, 1972; Justice & Justice, 1976; Martin, 1978). Various combinations of these factors are probably present in each case to some degree. The primary condition for family violence appears to be a potentially (and periodically) unstable family relationship in which certain internal, external, or interpersonal stresses trigger a family crisis that ends in psychological and/or physical damage and destruction.

FAMILIES AND SUBSTANCE ABUSE

Systems theory assumes that every family member plays a part in the dysfunctional behavior of a disturbed member. In the case of alcohol and drug dependence, it is clear that an individual's symptomatic behavior soon reverberates throughout the family. The "identified patient" may be signaling that the family is in distress; acting as family scapegoat; helping to close the family's boundaries and isolate it from the surrounding community; or promoting family homeostasis by providing the system with a central organizing principle and purpose. Substance abuse is an expression of family dysfunction that goes far beyond the personal woes of the individual heavy drinker or drug user.

Family therapists working with an "alcoholic system" focus their attention on the characteristic pattern of relationships between family members that emerges when alcohol is present (Steinglass, 1979). Of special interest is the contrast between "sober" and "intoxicated" interaction in the family. For example, drinking may allow a person to violate family rules and express otherwise forbidden feelings (such as resentment or even rage) or engage in prohibited behavior (menacing or even assaultive). Moreover, the intoxicated person—temporarily in a position of power and control—may escape the logical consequences of an emotional outburst, since presumably it was not he or she but "the alcohol" that was at fault. Thus the drinking episode allows the individual to play a dominant, one-upsmanship role and at the same time to deny responsibility for doing so (Gorod, McCourt, & Cobb, 1971).

Because of its cultural and societal significance and profound physical and behavioral consequences, alcohol can take a central place in the life of a family. With one or more members in a state of intoxication, drinking may be the single most important variable determining family interactional behavior. Although ostensibly disruptive, alcohol abuse may actually produce "extremely patterned, predictable, and rigid sets of interactions which dramatically reduce uncertainties about the family's internal life and its relationship to the external society" (Steinglass, 1979, p. 163). Thus, alcohol may serve a homeostatic, system-maintaining function. Consequently, effective therapeutic intervention calls for helping the family redefine their problems in family rather than individual terms as well as encouraging more open communication about conflicts and better problem-solving approaches. In contrast to the traditional treatment objective of simply reducing an individual family member's alcohol consumption, family therapy of alcoholism attempts to improve the functioning of the entire family.

As in the case of the "alcoholic system," we need to examine the structure, communication style, and transactional patterns of the families of drug abusers in order to more fully comprehend the problem and initiate therapeutic intervention. Kaufman and Kaufman (1979) identify a number of interrelated factors—individual, family, community, society—that influence the addict and his or her family. Drug abuse typically begins in adolescence; its etiology is difficult to distinguish from the usual process of seeking independence, experimenting with new behavior, becoming self-assertive, developing close relationships outside the family, and leaving home. However, male addicts' mothers are often described as enmeshed, indulgent, overprotective, and overly permissive with their sons; fathers tend to be disengaged, weak, and uninvolved, sometimes absent, sometimes with drinking problems of their own (Stanton, Todd, & Associates, 1982).

In a family system, the substance-abusing child has many functions. He or she is likely to: (1) be the symptom carrier of family dysfunction; (2) help maintain family homeostasis; (3) reinforce the parental need to control and continue parenting, inadequate as such parenting might be; (4) provide a displaced family battleground so that parental conflict can continue to be denied; (5) imitate parental drug and/or alcohol abuse; (6) form alliances across generations, dividing the parental coalition (Kaufman & Kaufman, 1979). Problems of addiction may persist over several generations of a family, each family unit interacting as the one before it. Double-bind communications are relatively overt; the adolescent who seeks an escape route from the family often finds it through drugs. It is common for the addict to be the family's youngest child, the addiction helping to maintain his or her infantile status. Family therapy usually attempts to restructure the family, encourage more appropriate family interaction, reinforce generational boundaries between parents and their children, and help the substance-abuser achieve greater self-sufficiency and autonomy (Ziegler-Driscoll, 1979).

PERSISTENT FAMILY MYTHS

Individuals as well as families have their myths. Conceivably ill-founded or self-deceptive, and almost certainly well-systematized, these are the beliefs they hold uncritically about themselves. Within families, these myths, shared by all members, help to shape interaction, assign complementary roles and partly determine the nature of intrafamilial relationships. Glick and Kessler (1980) have outlined some common myths regarding marriage held by people seeking family therapy (Table 3–1).

Mutual make-believe as well as elements of distortion and denial of reality play a part in the myths that are subscribed to by a family and convincingly presented to the outside world (Ferreira, 1966). Sometimes these myths infer general family characteristics: "Our family is easygoing and happy-go-lucky. Our neighbors are stuffy and uptight"; "We are good, responsible parents; our friends are too casual and indifferent about the welfare of their children." Sometimes these myths differentiate family members: "My side of the family has humor and is fun-loving, yours are a bunch of sourpusses"; "The males in this family are intellectually superior to the females, who are too emotional." To an outsider these may appear to be blatant misstatements but the myths are shared and supported by all family members as if their truth were beyond challenge.

The importance of these myths, as Ferreira (1966) points out, is that they organize the beliefs in the name of which the family initiates, maintains, and justifies many interactional patterns. Ferreira offers the following examples to illustrate how a family operates under rules that are not openly stated:

> In Family A, the husband has to drive the wife wherever she may need to go, oftentimes to the detriment of his business activities, since she does not know how to drive a car, nor does she care to learn. Although this pattern has been in operation since they were married some sixteen years ago, she explains it in terms of not being "mechanically inclined," a statement that the husband immediately endorses and corroborates.
>
> In Family B, no friend is ever invited to the house since no one quite knows when father is going to be drunk. The mother, who pointedly "does not drink," not only provides most of the family income (part of which goes, of course, for the father's liquor), but also stands vigil over who comes in the house lest someone think that "he is almost an alcoholic."
>
> In Family C, the delinquency of a teenage son is becoming the increasing concern of the local Juvenile Authorities. The parents profess total bewilderment on how to direct their son on a less troublesome path. They consider themselves a "very happy" family, with a "happiness" marred only by their son's encounters with the law. In this regard, the parents claim that they are constantly out-argued by their son, who happens to be, in the mother's proud and public statement, "the legal mind in the family" [Ferreira, 1966, p. 86].

Note how certain family patterns and rules are translated into family myths, beliefs, and expectations about each other that lead automatically to action without further thought. In Family A, for example, the myth about the wife who is not "mechanically inclined" influences the behavior of the husband. The reason is that if both husband and wife agree that she is nonmechanical, there is the implied statement that he is mechanical. Therefore, he is prepared to carry out a complementary role vis-à-vis the wife. The myth helps define the nature of the relationship.

Similarly, in Family B, defining the husband as an alcoholic or near-alcoholic clearly establishes that the wife, a teetotaler, plays a counter-role: stable, responsible, dependable, protective. These complementary roles influence much, if not all, of their interaction. The "legal mind" delinquent in Family C is undoubtedly part of a family with members who do not have legal minds (but who take some satisfaction from the fact that he does). Despite their protests, they may have a vested interest in maintaining the situation just as it is.

All of this is significant because a family, by labeling one of its members as "sick," "crazy," or a "patient," is making a statement that the other family members are all well! This myth, once it becomes operational, may become an integral part of the family's transactions, a buffer against sudden change, the basis for explaining all interactions involving the labeled person; it may even be passed from generation to generation. Because of its usefulness as a homeostatic mechanism, the myth is resistant to change. Despite efforts by the family to seek help for the "sick" person, family members are likely to fight to maintain the status quo. To abandon the myth is to open up the issue of their own disturbances or dysfunction as a family.

Pseudomutuality and Pseudohostility

Dysfunctional families are often distinguished by the number of myths they hold. Wynne, one of the first researchers to study the family organization of schizophrenics, suggests that members of dysfunctional families, overburdened by their own mythology, relate to one another by **pseudomutuality** (Wynne, Ryckoff, Day, & Hirsch, 1958). They make a strong attempt to maintain the appearance of a relationship, the illusion that they have an open and mutually empathic way of interacting, when in reality they maintain great distance between one another. What they do have in common is a shared maneuver designed to defend against pervasive feelings of meaninglessness and emptiness among all the family members. Pseudomutuality is thought to be characteristic of family settings in which schizophrenia develops. Anxious about separating from an established and familiar relationship, family members together pretend that there is a perfect fit between their own behavior and expectations and those of the other members. Divergence in viewpoint is intolerable; the illusion of family unity must be maintained. Any potential for growth or autonomy is sacrificed to the cause of holding the group together.

According to Wynne, mutuality describes relationships in which each member forms a separate and unique identity while respecting and appreciating the individuality of each of the other members; nonmutuality characterizes casual contact with others for a specific purpose rather than for personal involvement (for example, an encounter between a customer and sales clerk). In pseudomutuality, participants are determined to fit together according to stereotyped roles at the expense of losing their individual identities. Divergence in viewpoint, interest, or attitude could disrupt the family relationships, and thus is forbidden. As a consequence, members fail to separate from one another or to fulfill their own potentialities. A strong sense of personal identity, which requires honest and meaningful feedback information from others in order to

[handwritten margin note: pretending everyone gets along when they really don't.]

TABLE 3-1. Some Common Myths Concerning Ways to Achieve Marital Happiness

Common marital myths	*Family systems perspective*
1. Marriage and families should be totally happy; each member should expect all or certainly most gratifications to come from the family unit.	A romantic myth; overlooks fact that many of life's satisfactions are commonly found outside family setting.
2. "Togetherness" through close physical proximity or joint activities leads to satisfactory family life and individual gratification.	Varies greatly from one family to another; cannot be considered ideal pattern for all families under all conditions.
3. Marital partners should be totally honest with one another at all times.	While openness and frankness are usually desirable, especially in the service of a constructive, problem-solving approach, they may also be damaging if used in the service of hostile, destructive feelings.
4. In happy marriages there are no disagreements; when family members fight it means they hate each other.	Differences between family members are inevitable and often lead to arguments; if these clarify feelings and are not personal attacks, they may be constructive and preferable to covering up differences by always appearing to agree.
5. Marital partners should see eye to eye on every issue and work toward identical outlook.	Differences in background, experiences, personality make this impossible to achieve; actually different outlooks, if used constructively, may provide family with more options in carrying out developmental tasks.
6. Marital partners should be unselfish and not think of their individual needs.	Extremes of self-absorption or selflessness are undesirable; satisfactions are needed as an individual, not merely appendage to others (for example, mother lives only to serve family).
7. Whenever something goes wrong in the family, it is important to determine who is at fault.	Rather than blaming a single individual, dysfunction in the family interactions should be examined so that all members accept responsibilities.
8. Rehashing the past is helpful when things are not going well at present.	Endless recriminations about past errors usually escalate present problems, not reduce them, since they usually invite retaliation from the partner.
9. In a marital argument, one partner is right and the other wrong, with the goal of seeing who can score the most "points."	Marriages generally suffer when competition rather than cooperation characterizes marital interactions.
10. A good sexual relationship inevitably leads to a good marriage.	Good sexual relationship is an important component of a satisfactory marriage, but it does not preclude presence of interpersonal difficulties in other areas.

TABLE 3-1. (continued)

Common marital myths	Family systems perspective
11. In a satisfactory marriage, the sexual aspect will more or less take care of itself.	Not necessarily; sexual difficulties may be brought into marriage or related to stresses outside of the marriage.
12. Marital partners understand each other's nonverbal communications and therefore do not need to check things out with one another verbally.	Less likely to be true in dysfunctional families, where misperceptions and misinterpretations of each other's meanings and intent are common.
13. Positive feedback is not as necessary in marriage as negative feedback.	Positive feedback (attention, compliments) increases the likelihood that desirable behavior will reoccur, rather than taking for granted that it will and focusing on what's wrong with the other's behavior.
14. Good marriages simply happen spontaneously, and require no effort.	Another romantic myth; good marriages require daily input by both partners, with constant negotiation, communication, and mutual problem solving.
15. Any spouse can (and often should) be reformed and remodeled into the shape desired by the partner.	A poor premise in marriage, and one likely to lead to frustration, anger, and disillusionment. Working on improving the relationship should make partners more compatible and sensitive to each other's needs.
16. In a stable marriage, things do not change and there are no problems.	All living systems change, grow, and develop over time. Fixed systems sooner or later are out of phase with current needs and developments.
17. Everyone knows what a husband should be like and what a wife should be like.	Untrue, especially in modern society, where new roles are being explored.
18. If a marriage is not working properly, having children will rescue it.	On the contrary, children usually become the victims of marital disharmony.
19. No matter how bad a marriage, it should be kept together for the sake of the children.	Not necessarily true that children thrive better in an unhappy marriage than with a relatively satisfied divorced parent. In marriages where partners stay together as "martyrs" for the children's sake, children usually bear the brunt of resentment partners feel for one another.
20. If marriage does not work out, an extramarital affair, or divorce and marriage to another spouse will cure the situation.	Occasionally true, but without gaining insight similar choices will be made and the same nongratifying patterns repeated.

Based on information in Glick and Kessler, 1980.

Lyman C. Wynne, M.D.

develop, cannot be formed under such circumstances. Moreover, efforts to assert such individuality are likely to be perceived as a threat to the facade of mutuality.

Particularly in families with a schizophrenic member (but not only in those families), people become locked into fixed roles from which it becomes extremely difficult to escape. Wynne (1961) observed a strangely unreal quality to the expression of both positive and negative emotions in such families. No long-term or stable alignments of members developed (pseudomutuality); even their apparent disagreements and splits seemed superficial, unreal and meaningless (pseudohostility). (In Wynne's usage, alignments are experienced as shared values, attitudes and interests, while splits reflect the opposite—conflict and estrangement.)

Within a normal family, each person develops a sense of personal identity and also learns to relate to others meaningfully. Such a balance allows closeness to others without any subsequent loss of identity. By contrast, growing up in a pseudomutual setting means belonging to a self-sufficient social unit that has a flexible, expanding and contracting boundary with the outside world. Wynne describes such a boundary as a **rubber fence** that stretches itself to include whatever can be interpreted as complementary to its structure and contracts to extrude that which it considers alien. As a result, life is neither stable nor predictable; one's own perceptions cannot be trusted; escape is impossible. The rubber fence may appear to yield but is actually a barrier that shields the family from outsiders, from new information, from the possibility of change— while helping the family maintain the illusion that it is united and protected.

In a family that values uniformity and allegiance to the family above all else, the preschizophrenic person learns a prescribed role but fails to develop a personal identity or to become equipped to deal with life outside the family circle. A common family myth in such a situation is that open divergence from the family or departure from one's assigned role will lead to catastrophe or personal disaster. According to Wynne (1961), an acute schizophrenic episode is most likely to occur when the individual must leave the confines of the family, struggle for autonomy and learn to relate to others in unfamiliar surroundings and unrehearsed ways. The schizophrenic behavior is a reaction to an identity crisis caused by the threat of separation from the familiar pseudomutuality of the family.

SUMMARY

Stress related to expected developmental events and transitions throughout the family life cycle or sudden and abrupt changes of circumstance can lead to a family crisis that severely threatens family stability. Pathological communication patterns within a family may cause serious disruption in functioning. Such patterns may derive from cognitively flawed communication deviance; from paradoxical forms of communication such as double-bind messages; from disguised communication (mystification); or from exaggerated forms of communication (symmetrical or complementary relationships).

Enmeshment (blurred family boundaries) and disengagement (rigid boundaries) are other expressions of family dysfunction, represented most prominently by delinquency-producing, psychosomatic, or boundary-violating families. Scapegoating (labeling as pathological) is another common phenomenon in dysfunctional families. Family violence—long concealed as "private violence," now more openly revealed—has many determinants. In systems terms, family violence results when a potentially unstable family system is triggered by a crisis and goes into a deviation-amplifying, runaway state. Alcohol and drug abuse also represent family dysfunction. In some cases, the symptomatic behavior of a family member signals that the family is in distress and in others it helps the family maintain its homeostatic balance.

Through the use of persistent family myths, some families initiate, maintain, and justify many of their dysfunctional interactional patterns. Pseudomutuality—the myth that the family has an open, mutually empathic way of interacting when in reality it does not—is thought to be characteristic of family settings in which schizophrenia develops.

PART TWO

Historical and Theoretical Foundations

CHAPTER FOUR

Origins and Growth of Family Therapy

In Part One we conceptualized the family as a living system, documented its changing nature over time, and considered some current alternate living arrangements in addition to the traditional nuclear family. We offered various ways to classify family functioning and described some of the ways families manifest dysfunction. We emphasized interpersonal relationships rather than intrapsychic functioning, the process of family interaction rather than its content, the sequential acts of a network of people rather than the behavior patterns of separate individuals. Above all, we strove to establish that family relationships are complex and enduring; and thus they demand to be understood in terms of constructs that stress circularity rather than linear thinking.

In Part Two we explore the historical as well as theoretical foundations of the family therapy movement. In this chapter, we will examine some scientific and clinical developments that coalesced in the late 1940s and early 1950s to give birth to that movement, before discussing in detail its evolution over the last three decades. In subsequent chapters in this section we will offer a variety of contemporary theoretical models for conceptualizing how and why certain families establish—or fail to establish—successful adaptational skills and competencies.

HISTORICAL ROOTS: SOME INTERDISCIPLINARY CONSIDERATIONS

It is never easy or entirely accurate to pinpoint the beginning of a scientific endeavor. But most authorities point to the decade following World War II as the period when researchers, followed by practitioners, turned their attention to the family's role in creating and maintaining psychological disturbance in one or more family members. The sudden reuniting of families in the aftermath of the war created a number of problems (social, interpersonal, cultural, situational) for which the public sought solutions by turning to mental health specialists. Accustomed to working with individuals, these professionals were now expected to deal effectively with an array of problems within the family. Family members experienced the stress associated with delayed marriages and hasty wartime marriages; the baby boom brought pressures of its own. Changing sexual mores and increasing acceptance of divorce brought new freedoms—and conflicts. Transitions to new jobs, new educational opportunities, and new homes with mortgages meant new tensions within the family. Most significant of all, the family had entered the nuclear age: the atom bomb had challenged its basic security.

In general, psychological intervention became acceptable to people from a broader range of social and educational backgrounds than had been the case in pre-war days. Practitioners from many disciplines—clinical psychologists, psychiatric social workers, marriage counselors, pastoral counselors—began to offer such aid as well as psychiatrists, the primary pre-war providers of psychotherapy. The definition of problems considered amenable to psychotherapy also expanded to include marital discord, separation and divorce, delinquency, problems with in-laws, and various forms of emotional disturbance not requiring hospitalization. Although many clinicians continued to offer individual treatment only, others began to look at family relationships, the transactions between members that needed modification if individual well-being was to be achieved. Eventually, more and more clinicians began to recognize that it was necessary to alter the family's structure and interaction patterns in order for adaptive behavior to replace problematic, dysfunctional or maladaptive behavior. In the last three decades, representatives from a wide variety of behavioral sciences and professional disciplines have become involved in examining and better understanding family functioning (see Table 4–1).

Goldenberg and Goldenberg (1983) draw attention to five seemingly independent scientific and clinical developments that together set the stage for the emergence of family therapy. These include: (1) the extension of psychoanalytic treatment to a full range of emotional problems, eventually including work with whole families; (2) the introduction of general systems theory, with its emphasis on exploring relationships between parts that make up an interrelated whole; (3) the investigation of the family's role in the development of schizophrenia in one of its members; (4) the evolution of the fields of child guidance and marital counseling; and (5) the increased interest in new clinical techniques such as **group therapy.**

Psychoanalysis

Psychoanalysis, the theory and set of therapeutic techniques advanced by Sigmund Freud, had become the dominant ideology in American psychiatry after World War II. Shortly before the war, a large migration of European psychologists and psychiatrists, psychoanalytic in their orientation, had come to this country to escape the Nazi regime. The American public had been receptive to Freud's ideas since early in this century. With the arrival of these clinicians, psychoanalysis began to gain greater acceptance among medical

TABLE 4–1. Behavioral Sciences and
Disciplines Involved in the Study of the Family

Disciplines	Illustrative studies	Representative researchers*

Anthropology
  Cultural anthropology
  Social anthropology
  Ethnology
	Cultural and subcultural family forms and functions
	Cross-cultural comparative family patterns
	Ethnic, racial, and social status family differences
	Families in primitive, developing, and industrial societies
		Ruth Benedict
		Allison Davis
		Clyde Kluckhohn
		Oscar Lewis
		Ralph Linton
		Helen and Robert Lynd
		Margaret Mead
		George Murdock
		W. Lloyd Warner

Counseling
  Counseling theory
  Clinical practice
  Evaluation
	Dynamics of interpersonal relationships in marriage and family
	Methods and results of individual, marriage, and family counseling
		Rollo May
		Emily Hartshorne Mudd
		James A. Peterson
		Carl Rogers

Demography	Census and vital statistics on many facets of family life Cross-sectional, longitudinal, and record-linkage surveys Differential birth rates Family planning and population control	Donald Bogue Hugh Carter Harold Christensen Ronald Freedman Paul Glick Philip Hauser P. K. Whelpton
Economics	Consumer behavior, marketing, and motivation research Insurance, pensions, and welfare needs of families Standards of living, wage scales, socioeconomic status	Robert C. Angell Howard Bigelow Milton Friedman John Kenneth Galbraith John Morgan Margaret Reid

Education
  Early childhood
  Early elementary
  Secondary
  College
  Parent
  Professional
	Child-rearing methods
	Developmental patterns
	Educational methods and evaluation
	Family-life education
	Motivation and learning
	Preparation for marriage
	Sex education
		Orville Brim
		Catherine Chilman
		Cyril Houle
		Harold Lief
		Nevitt Sanford
		Ralph Tyler
		James Walters

History	Historical roots of modern family Origins of family patterns Predictions of the future of families Social influences on the family Social trends and adaptations	Arthur Calhoun Franklin Frazier Bernard Stern Edward Westermarck Carle Zimmerman

TABLE 4-1. (continued)

Disciplines	Illustrative studies	Representative researchers*

Home economics
  Family relationships
  Home-economics
    education
  Home management
  Nutrition
	Evaluation of practices and
	  measurement of educa-
	  tional results
	Family food habits and
	  nutrition
	Home management practices
	Relationships between family
	  members
		Muriel Brown
		Irma Gross
		Paulena Nickell
		Evelyn Spindler
		Alice Thorpe

Human development
  Child development
  Adolescent
    development
  Middle age and aging
	Character development
	Child growth and
	  development
	Developmental norms and
	  differences
	Nature of cognitive learning
	Cross-cultural variations
	Personality development
	Social roles of aging
		Nancy Bayley
		Urie Bronfenbrenner
		Erik Erikson
		Dale Harris
		Robert Havighurst
		Lois Barclay Murphy
		Bernice Neugarten
		Jean Piaget

Law	Adoption and child protection
	Child care and welfare
	Divorce and marital
	  dissolution
	Marriage and family law
	Parental rights and
	  responsibilities
	Sexual controls and behavior
		Paul Alexander
		John Bradway
		Harriet Daggett
		Marie Kargman
		Harriet Pilpel
		Max Rheinstein

Psychoanalysis	Abnormal and normal
	  behavior
	Clinical diagnosis and
	  therapy
	Foundations of personality
	Stages of development
	Treatment of mental illness
		Nathan Ackerman
		Erik Erikson
		John Flugel
		Irene Josselyn
		Harry Stack Sullivan

Psychology
  Clinical
  Developmental
  Social
	Aspirations and self-concepts
	Drives, needs, and hungers
	Dynamics of interpersonal
	  interaction
	Learning theory
	Mental health
	Therapeutic intervention
		Rosalind Dymond
		Gerald Gurin
		Robert Hess
		Eleanore Luckey
		Frederick Stodtbeck
		John Whiting

Public health	Epidemiology and
	  immunization
	Family health and preventive
	  medicine
	Maternal and infant health
	Noxious materials research
	Pediatric health education
	Venereal disease
		Cecelia Deschin
		Nicholson Eastman
		Earl L. Koos
		Niles Newton
		Clark Vincent

TABLE 4-1. (continued)

Disciplines	Illustrative studies	Representative researchers*
Religion	Church policies on marriage and family Families of various religions Interfaith marriage Love, sex, marriage, divorce, and family in religious contexts	Stanley Brav Roy Fairchild Seward Hiltner John L. Thomas John C. Wynn
Social work Family casework Group work Social welfare	Appraising family need Devising constructive pro- grams for family assistance Measuring family functioning	Dorothy F. Beck L. L. Geismar James Hardy Charlotte Towle
Sociology	Courtship and mate selection Family formation and functioning Effects of social change on families Family crises and dissolution Prediction of family success Social class influence on families	Ernest W. Burgess Ruth S. Cavan Harold Christensen Reuben Hill Judson Landis Marvin Sussman

*Illustrative of those research workers whose published findings may be available to students of the family in various disciplines; not an all-inclusive listing. (Duvall, 1977)

specialists, academicians, and clinicians in the psychology community, as well as among sociologists and psychiatric social workers.

Freud had been aware of the impact of family relationships on the individual's character formation, particularly in the development of symptomatic behavior. For example, in his famous case of Little Hans, a child who refused to go out into the street for fear that a horse might bite him, Freud hypothesized that Hans was displacing anxiety that was associated with his Oedipus complex. That is, Freud believed Hans unconsciously desired his mother sexually but felt competitive with, and hostile toward, his father, as well as fearful of his father's reaction to his hostility. Hans had witnessed a horse falling down in the street, and Freud speculated that he unconsciously associated the scene with his father, since he wanted his father hurt too. According to Freud, Hans unconsciously changed his intense fear of castration by his father into a **phobia** about being bitten by the horse, whom Hans had previously seen as innocuous. Having substituted the horse for his father, Hans was able to turn an internal danger into an external one. The fear was displaced onto a substitute object, a prototype of what takes place in the development of a phobia. In this celebrated 1909 case (Freud, 1955), the boy was actually treated by the father, under Freud's guidance.

Historically, the case of Little Hans, a 5-year-old boy, has conceptual as well as technical significance. Conceptually, it enabled Freud to elaborate on his earlier formulations regarding psychosexual development in children and the use of **defense mechanisms** (such as displacement) as unconscious **ego** devices a person calls on as protection against being overwhelmed by anxiety. Moreover, the case supported Freud's developing belief that inadequate resolution of a particular phase of psychosexual development can lead to neurotic behavior such as phobias. Technically, as Bloch and LaPerriere (1973) point out, "Little Hans" represents the first case in the history both of child analysis and of family therapy. Note, however, that Freud chose not to work with either the child or the family but encouraged Hans's father, a physician, to treat his own son under Freud's supervision.[1] The clinical intervention remained individually focused; ultimately, Hans was relieved of his phobic symptom.

From the case of Little Hans and similar examples from among Freud's published papers, we can appreciate how family relationships came to provide a rich diagnostic aid to Freud's psychoanalytic thinking. Four years earlier, in 1905, he had written that psychoanalysts were

> obliged to pay as much attention . . . to purely human and social circumstances of our patients as to the somatic data and the symptoms of the disorder. Above all, our interest will be directed toward their family circumstances (pp. 25–26).

In practice, however, Freud preferred working therapeutically with individuals; both his theories and techniques stress the resolution of intrapsychic conflicts. So strongly was he opposed to working with more than one family member at a time that his negative assessment became virtually a doctrine among psychoanalysts who, for many years, accepted the prohibition against analyzing members of the same family (Broderick & Schrader, 1981).

In fact, as Bowen (1975) notes, one psychoanalytic principle that may have retarded earlier growth of the family therapy movement was the isolation of the therapist/patient relationship and the related concern that contact with the patient's relatives would "contaminate" the therapist. Bowen reports that some hospitals went so far as to have one therapist deal with the patient's intrapsychic processes while another handled practical matters and administrative procedures and a third team member, the social worker, talked to relatives. According to Bowen's early experiences, failure to respect these boundaries was considered "inept psychotherapy." It was only in the 1950s that this principle began to be violated—more often for research than for clinical purposes—and that family members began to be seen therapeutically as a group.[2]

---

[1]Unwittingly Freud was anticipating a technique used by many of today's family therapists, particularly those with a behavioral approach, of using family members, especially parents, as agents of change.

[2]Just how much change in attitude has taken place in the last 30 years may be gleaned from the fact that family therapists are willing to demonstrate their work with families quite openly, even before a large professional audience, without benefit of one-way mirrors or other devices to shield participants from viewers. Families typically report that any initial self-consciousness is quickly overcome.

Nathan Ackerman, a psychoanalyst and child psychiatrist, is generally credited with adapting psychoanalytic formulations to the study of the family. In what may have been the first paper to deal specifically with family therapy, published as the lead article in the *Bulletin of the Kansas Mental Hygiene Society*, Ackerman (1937) emphasized the role of the family as a dynamic psychosocial unit in and of itself. The constant interaction between the biologically-driven person (a psychoanalytic concept) and the social environment (a systems concept) was to preoccupy him for more than three decades, as he attempted to apply an intrapsychic vocabulary to systems phenomena he observed in the family and in society at large. As he summed it up in a paper that was published shortly after his death (Ackerman, 1972):

> Over a period of some thirty-five years, I have extended my orientation to the problems of behavior, step-by-step, from the inner life of the person, to the person within family, to the family within community, and most recently, to the social community itself (p. 449).

Considered by many to be the "grandfather" of the family therapy movement, Ackerman's contribution to both theory and practice will be discussed in Chapter 5.

Another psychoanalytic influence on family therapy is the work of Alfred Adler, an early associate of Freud's; among other accomplishments, Adler is credited with helping to found the child guidance movement in Vienna in the early 1900s. Adler insisted that an individual's conscious personal and social goals as well as subsequent goal-directed behavior could be fully understood only by comprehending the environment or social context in which that behavior was displayed. Adlerian concepts such as sibling rivalry, family constellation, and style of life attest to Adler's awareness of the key role of family experiences in influencing adult behavior. Like Freud, Adler did not himself work therapeutically with entire families but he did influence one of his associates, Rudolf Dreikurs, to expand child guidance centers in the United States into family counseling centers (Lowe, 1982). Classes for teachers, parent education study groups, single-parent groups, even groups for grandparents have been organized in these centers in an effort to facilitate adult–child understanding and cooperation (Dinkmeyer & McKay, 1976).

Finally, the American psychiatrist Harry Stack Sullivan was psychoanalytically trained but was also influenced by sociology and social psychology. Throughout a career that began in the late 1920s, he stressed the role of interpersonal relationships in personality development. Sullivan argued that people are essentially products of their social interactions; to understand how people function, he urged the study of their "relatively enduring patterns of recurrent interpersonal situations" (Sullivan, 1953, p. 110). Working mostly with schizophrenics, Sullivan noted that the disorder frequently manifested itself during the transitional period of adolescence, leading him to speculate about the possibly critical effects of the patient's ongoing family life in producing the confusion that might lead ultimately to schizophrenia (Perry, 1982).

Don Jackson and Murray Bowen, both of whom were later to become out-standing figures in the emerging field of family therapy, trained under Sullivan and his colleague Frieda Fromm-Reichmann. Jackson's work (see Chapter 2) was clearly influenced by Sullivan's early notion of redundant family interactive patterns. Bowen's theories (see Chapter 7), especially those that pertain to individual pathology emerging from a faulty multigenerational fam-ily system, can be traced to Sullivan's influence.

General Systems Theory

First proposed by the biologist Ludwig von Bertalanffy in the 1940s, **general systems theory** represents an effort to provide a comprehensive theoretical model embracing all living systems, a model relevant to all the behavioral sciences. Bertalanffy's major contribution is in providing a framework for looking at seemingly unrelated phenomena and understanding how together they represent interrelated components of a larger system (Bertalanffy, 1968).

A system is a complex of component parts that are in mutual interaction. Rather than viewing each part as isolated and simply adding the parts to make up an entity, this theory stresses the relationships between the parts; the var-ious components are best understood as functions of the total system. (The application of the theory to a family, made up of members, each of whom influences and, in turn, is influenced by all other members, has been discussed in Chapter 2.) According to Bertalanffy, to understand how something works, we must study the transactional process taking place between the components of a system, not merely add up what each part contributes.

General systems theory seeks to classify systems by the manner in which they are organized and by the interdependence of their parts. It thus represents a new approach to scientific knowledge, a new, holistic way of thinking. The traditional reductionistic view of a system (derived from the physical sciences) explains complex phenomena by breaking them down into series of less com-plex cause-and-effect reactions, by analyzing in a linear fashion how A causes B, B causes C, C causes D, and so on. By contrast, general systems theory presents a new epistemology in which it is not the structure that defines an object but its organization as defined by the interactive pattern of its parts. That is, the component parts of a system are less important than their interrelations (Segal & Bavelas, 1983). A may cause B, but B also affects A, which affects B, and so on in circular causality. Moreover, patterns form and persist over time, since we are dealing with a process as well as a structure.

As we noted in Chapter 2, a family system is not a list of family members; rather, it is a set of enduring relationships between and among family mem-bers. To understand the family, we must do more than analyze each individual member. (That would be analogous to understanding a rectangle by making a separate study of each of its four unassembled lines.) How the parts connect to form a whole, the way the system is organized, the structure and interaction of the various units—these are some of the factors to consider in studying the complexities of a family's relationships.

Families are open systems in the sense that they belong to larger systems; in turn, they contain their own subsystems (the spouses, the children, and so forth). A behavioral scientist, Miller (1978) views all living systems as special subsets of open systems. According to his set of principles, all phenomena described by the biological and social sciences can be arranged according to a comprehensive schema with seven hierarchical levels (see Figure 4-1). In increasing order of complexity, the levels are: cells; organs (composed of cells); organisms (independent life forms); groups (families, committees); organizations (universities, multinational corporations, cities); societies or nations; and supranational systems. Each higher-level system encompasses all lower-level ones and provides the environment for the systems on the level directly below it. Miller's thesis holds that ever since cells evolved about 3 billion years ago, the general direction of evolution has been toward ever-greater complexity.

Nothing and nobody exists in isolation; the world is made up of systems within systems. The emotionally disturbed person is just one part of a subsystem in the family system, but the entire family system is influenced by and influences the disturbed person. Dysfunctional families who seek treatment at a social agency are components in that agency's organizational system. They, in turn, affect disbursement of government funds, training grants for research on family life or educating family counselors, and so on. A human being is a system of many organ subsystems and, as we have shown, is an organism that is part of a larger scheme. Consider an example offered by Bloch and LaPerriere (1973) of a woman who becomes depressed. At what level would her symptomatic behavior be best understood and intervention be most effective? At the organ system level her depression might be related to hormonal changes during her menstrual cycle; at the organism level, to her way of handling aggressive impulses; at the group level, to her way of dealing with her family; at the society level, to the socialization process that teaches females to suppress assertive impulses. Family therapists take the position that intervention at the family level addresses many of this woman's problem areas and offers an effective method for expediting change.

Although systems thinking permeates all aspects of family therapy—its theories, its assessment techniques, its therapeutic approaches—we want to emphasize the historical significance of systems theory to the emerging family therapy movement. In contrast to psychoanalysis, with its psychopathological orientation, general systems theory views an individual as a complex being operating within a system where concepts such as "sick" or "well" are irrelevant; a symptom developing in one person merely means that the system (that is, the family, community, or society at large) has become dysfunctional. In contrast to the psychoanalyst who remains distant from the patient, a family therapist is apt to intervene more directly and even become a participant in the family system. In family therapy, the emphasis is on multiple causality at various levels rather than on defining an individual's unresolved intrapsychic conflicts; on dealing with the present rather than the past. Watzlawick, Beavin and Jackson (1967) point out that when we focus on an emotionally disturbed

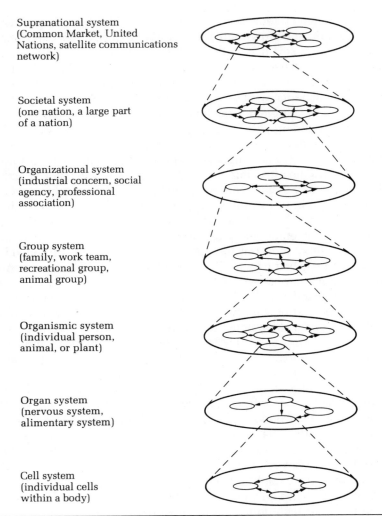

Supranational system
(Common Market, United
Nations, satellite communications
network)

Societal system
(one nation, a large part
of a nation)

Organizational system
(industrial concern, social
agency, professional
association)

Group system
(family, work team,
recreational group,
animal group)

Organismic system
(individual person,
animal, or plant)

Organ system
(nervous system,
alimentary system)

Cell system
(individual cells
within a body)

Figure 4-1. Living systems exist in a hierarchy of levels. Each level is made up of subsystems that have a relationship with other parts of their own system and to systems at other levels. Behavior at an individual (organismic) level is different than that individual's behavior at a group or family level, because of characteristics of that higher level (family rules, roles, power structure, ways of communicating). Family members relate to each other with greater intensity than they do to others outside the family boundary, but they also relate to others in society, a higher system. (Sundberg, Tyler, and Taplin, 1973)

individual we are inevitably led to speculate on the nature of that person's mind (what must be going on inside the mysterious "black box"). However, when we look at the effects of the individual's disturbed behavior, the way others react to it, and the context in which this interaction transpires, the focus shifts to a consideration of relationships between system parts. Perhaps even more significant for family therapists, the shift represents a change of course from inferential studies of the mind to the study of the observable manifestations and behavioral consequences of interpersonal relationships. As we shall see in the next six chapters, these are the phenomena to which family therapists such as Jackson, Bowen, Minuchin, Watzlawick, Stuart, and Liberman have paid attention.

Schizophrenia and the Family

What role does a disturbed family environment play in the development of schizophrenia in a family member? Lidz and Lidz (1949), among the first to investigate the characteristics of mothers of schizophrenic patients, found serious inadequacies and psychological disturbances in the mother–child relationship. Fromm-Reichmann (1948) introduced the term **schizophrenogenic mother** to denote a domineering, cold, rejecting, possessive, guilt-producing person who, in combination with a passive, detached, and ineffectual father, causes her male offspring to feel confused and inadequate and ultimately to become schizophrenic. These family pathology studies, extending into the 1950s, sought to establish a linear cause-and-effect relationship between a pathogenic mother, an inadequate father, and schizophrenia in the male child. This psychological analysis of the family was soon complemented by a broader and more systematic psychosocial approach to the family as a group of individuals influencing each other and by a sociological perspective in which the family is perceived as a dysfunctional system supporting the disturbed person (Waxler, 1975); the study of family environment and the development of schizophrenia was launched.

During the mid-1950s, the major impetus for family research in the area of schizophrenia came from Gregory Bateson in Palo Alto, California; Theodore Lidz at Yale; Murray Bowen (and later, Lyman Wynne) at the National Institute of Mental Health. Working independently at first, the investigators did not become fully aware of each other's research until later in the decade. Guerin (1976) maintains that family research on schizophrenia was the primary focus of the majority of the family therapy pioneers.

In 1952, Bateson—then affiliated with the Palo Alto Veterans Administration Hospital—received a grant to study patterns and paradoxes of communication in animals as well as in human beings. Soon he was joined by Jay Haley, then a graduate student studying communication, John Weakland, a former chemical engineer with training in cultural anthropology, and Don Jackson, a psychiatrist experienced in working with schizophrenics. Among other communications phenomena, they began to study the relationship between "pathological" communication patterns within a family and the emergence and maintenance of schizophrenic behavior in a family member. More specifically, they hypothesized that the family might have shaped the strange and irrational behavior of a schizophrenic by means of its contradictory, and thus impossible, communication requirements.

Four years later, Bateson, Jackson, Haley, and Weakland published a land-mark paper (1956) introducing the "double-bind" concept to account for the development of schizophrenia in a family member. According to their thesis, a double-bind situation occurs when an individual (often a child) habitually receives contradictory messages from the same person, who forbids comment on the contradiction; the individual, perceiving the threat to his or her survival, feels compelled to make some response, but feels doomed to failure whatever response he or she chooses. Their paper reports the following poignant example:

> A young man who had fairly well recovered from an acute schizophrenic episode was visited in the hospital by his mother. He was glad to see her and impulsively put his arm around her shoulders, whereupon she stiffened. He withdrew his arm and she asked, "Don't you love me anymore?" He then blushed, and she said, "Dear, you must not be so easily embarrassed and afraid of your feelings" (p. 259).

Note the sequence of the mother's underlying messages: "Don't touch me" ("Go away"); "Don't trust your feelings in regard to how I respond" ("Come closer"); "Don't challenge the contradictions in my behavior"; "You can't survive without my love"; "You're wrong and at fault no matter how you interpret my messages." The authors report that the distressed patient promptly became violent and assaultive when he returned to the ward.

Confronted by expressions of love and hate, with an invitation to approach and an injunction to stay away issued by the same important figure—a person is forced into an impossible situation of trying to discriminate correctly between the messages. Unable to form a satisfactory response (and in the case of a child, unable to escape) and unable to comment on the dilemma without being punished further, such a person becomes confused. Response leads to rejection and failure to respond leads to the loss of potential love, the classic "damned if you do and damned if you don't." If the important figure (a parent, for example) then denies sending simultaneous and contradictory messages, this only adds to the confusion. Once the pattern is established, only a hint of or initial step in the original sequence is enough to set off a panic or rage reaction. Bateson and his colleagues suggested that the typical result of repeated and prolonged exposure to this kind of impossible situation is that the child learns to escape hurt and punishment by responding with equally incongruent messages. As a means of self-protection, he or she learns to deal with all relationships in this distorted manner and finally loses the ability to understand the true meaning of his or her own or others' communications. At this point the child begins to manifest schizophrenic behavior. The group led by Bateson thus focused on schizophrenia as a prototype of the consequences of failure in a family's communication system.

The double-bind hypothesis has become one of the most scientifically respectable theories relating to schizophrenia and family interaction (Sluzki & Ransom, 1976). However, more recent research (Hirsch & Leff, 1975) demonstrates that double-bind communication patterns sometimes occur in "normal" families and thus are not unique to parents of schizophrenics. Rather, as Shean (1978) concludes, such communication patterns are only one aspect of a more complex family interaction pattern frequently associated with the development of schizophrenic disorders.

At about the same time that Bateson and his colleagues were doing family research with schizophrenia on the West Coast, Theodore Lidz on the East Coast (in Baltimore and later in New Haven, Connecticut) began publishing his research on the family's role in schizophrenic development of one or more of its children. These studies (Lidz, Cornelison, Fleck, & Terry, 1957) represented an extension of psychoanalytic concepts to the family, although these concepts are broadened somewhat in the transition. For example, Lidz and his coworkers at the Yale Psychiatric Institute recognized oral fixation—which orthodox psychoanalytic formulations consider a primary factor in the development of schizophrenia—as only one aspect of the disorder. To these researchers, schizophrenia was a "deficiency disease" resulting from the family's failure to provide the essentials for integrated personality development. More specifically, they suggested that a parent's (usually the mother's) own arrested personality development leads to an inability to meet the child's nurturance needs; the child is likely to grow up with profound insecurity and be unable to achieve autonomy. They also postulated that an unstable marriage in which there is considerable conflict between husband and wife provides poor role models for children. As a consequence, a child may fail to acquire the coping skills that are necessary for interaction with others outside the family and, ultimately, for independent adult living. You can see from this brief description that to Lidz, it was the **psychodynamics** of the parents, rather than the family as a social system, that was primarily responsible for the development of schizophrenic behavior in the child.

Lidz and Associates (1957) described two patterns of chronic marital discord that are particularly characteristic of families of schizophrenics (although each may exist in "normal" families to a lesser extent). **Marital schism** refers to a disharmonious situation in which each parent, preoccupied with his or her own problems, fails to create a satisfactory role in the family that is compatible with and reciprocal to the other spouse's role. Each parent tends to undermine the worth of the other, especially to the children, and they seem to compete for the loyalty, affection, sympathy, and support of the children. Neither valuing nor respecting each other, each parent may fear that a particular child (or children) will grow up behaving like the other parent. Threats of separation or divorce are common; it is usual in such families for the father to become ostracized, a virtual nonentity if he remains in the home. In the pattern of **marital skew,** which these researchers have also observed in families with a schizophrenic offspring, the continuity of the marriage is not threatened, but mutually destructive patterns nevertheless exist. The serious psychological disturbance of one parent (such as psychosis) usually dominates this type of home. The other parent, who is often dependent and weak, accepts the situation and goes so far as to imply to the children that the home situation is normal. Such a denial of what they are actually living through may lead to further denials and distortions of reality by the children. Lidz and Associates (1957) conclude that male schizophrenics usually come from skewed families in which there is a dominant, emotionally disturbed mother, impervious to the needs of other family members but nevertheless intrusive in her child's life. At the same time, a skewed family usually has a father who can neither counter the mother's child-rearing practices nor provide an adequate male role model.

If marital skew is often an antecedent of schizophrenia in a son, marital schism often precedes schizophrenia in a daughter. Here there is open marital discord and each parent particularly wants the daughter's support. However, the father's disparagement of the mother (or perhaps all women) together with his seductive efforts to gain the daughter's love and support lead to the daughter's confusion about her identity as a woman, as well as to doubt her eventual ability to carry out an adult role as wife and mother. Pleasing one parent means rejection by the other. In some cases, as Shean (1978) notes, such a child may become a family scapegoat, causing problems that mask and divert attention from parental incompatibility. Unfortunately, the diversion is at the expense of the child's own developmental needs.

First at the Menninger Foundation in Topeka, Kansas, in the early 1950s, and later at the National Institute of Mental Health (NIMH) near Washington, D.C., Murray Bowen arranged for family members to move in with hospitalized schizophrenic patients in order to study the family as a unit; Bowen was especially interested in identifying symbiotic mother–child interactions. As he later reported (Bowen, 1960) in a book edited by Don Jackson that brought together for the first time various family theories related to the etiology of schizophrenia, families of schizophrenics often demonstrate interaction patterns resembling Lidz's findings about marital schism. Bowen termed the striking emotional distance between parents in such a situation **emotional divorce.** He described relationships of this kind as vacillating between periods of overcloseness and overdistance. Eventually the relationship becomes fixed at a point of sufficient emotional distance between the parents to avoid anxiety; they settle for "peace at any price." One area of joint activity—and, commonly, conflicting view—is the rearing of their children, particularly of children who show signs of psychological disturbance. It is as if the parents maintain contact with each other (and therefore a semblance of emotional equilibrium) by keeping the disturbed child helpless and needy. Thus adolescence, the period in which the child usually strives for a measure of autonomy, becomes especially stormy and stressful. This is typically the time when schizophrenic behavior first appears. Bowen proposed the intriguing notion that schizophrenia is a process that spans at least three generations before it is manifested in the behavior of a family member. He suggested that one or both parents of schizophrenic are troubled, immature individuals who, having experienced serious emotional conflict with their own parents, are now subjecting their offspring to similar conflict situations (for further discussion of Bowen's theories, see Chapter 7).

Succeeding Bowen as head of the Family Studies Section at NIMH, Lyman Wynne focused his research on the blurred, ambiguous, and confused communication patterns in families with schizophrenic members. In a series of papers (Wynne, Ryckoff, Day, & Hirsch, 1958; Wynne & Singer, 1963), he and his colleagues addressed themselves to the social organization of such families. For example, if schizophrenics interpret the meaning of what is happening around them in unusual and idiosyncratic ways, these researchers viewed the family's recurrent and characteristic fragmented and irrational style of communication as contributing to their vulnerability. As noted in Chapter 3, Wynne offered the term pseudomutuality—giving the appearance of a mutual, open, and understanding relationship without really having one—to describe how such families conceal an underlying distance between members. Pseudo-mutuality is a shared maneuver designed to defend all of the family members against pervasive feelings of meaninglessness and emptiness.

A person who grows up in a pseudomutual family setting fails to develop a strong sense of personal identity. This lack of identity handicaps the person from engaging in successful interactions outside the family and makes involvement within one's own family system all-important. According to Wynne et al. (1958), the preschizophrenic doubts his or her capacity to accurately derive meaning from a personal experience outside the family, preferring instead to return to the familiar, self-sufficient family system with its enclosed (but safe) boundaries.

By 1950, the Group for the Advancement of Psychiatry formed a committee to look into the subject of family behavior (Spiegel, 1971). Within a few years, a number of schizophrenic-family researchers met together for the first time at the 1957 national convention of the interdisciplinary American Orthopsychiatric Association. Although no separate organization was formed by this still-small group, considerable enthusiasm was aroused for the new field of "family therapy" research with schizophrenics. During subsequent national meetings, Bowen (1976) reports presentations by dozens of new therapists (rather than researchers) eager to describe clinical intervention techniques that involved entire families. Boszormenyi-Nagy and Framo edited *Intensive Family Therapy* in 1965, bringing together the reports of 15 authorities on their clinical work with schizophrenics and their families. The researchers of a decade earlier, studying the relationship between family processes and the development of schizophrenia, had laid the groundwork for the emerging field of family therapy.

Marital Counseling and Child Guidance

The fields of marital counseling and child guidance, precursors of family therapy, are based on the concept that psychological disturbances arise from conflicts between persons as well as from conflict within a person. Effective intervention requires the therapist to work simultaneously with the troubled marital partners or parent–child pair.

If we assume that people have always been ready to advise or seek advice from others, informal marriage counseling has certainly existed for as long as the institution of marriage. On the other hand, formal counseling by a professional marriage counselor probably began somewhat over 50 years ago in the United States when the physicians Abraham and Hannah Stone opened the Marriage Consultation Center in New York in 1929. A year later, Paul Popenoe (a biologist specializing in human heredity) founded the American Institute of Family Relations in Los Angeles, offering premarital guidance as well as aid in promoting marital adjustment. Family educator Emily Mudd started the Marriage Council of Philadelphia in 1932 and later wrote what is thought to be the first textbook in the field (Mudd, 1951). By 1942, largely through Mudd's prodding, the American Association of Marriage Counselors (AAMC) was formed, bringing together various professionals (primarily physicians, educators, lawyers and social workers, but also psychologists, sociologists and clergymen) concerned with the new interdisciplinary field of marriage counseling. This organization has led the way in developing standards for training and practice, certifying marriage counseling centers, and establishing a professional code of ethics (Broderick & Schrader, 1981).

TABLE 4-2. Nature of Personal Problems
for Which People Sought Professional Help (N = 345)

Problem area	Percent*
Spouse; marriage	42
Child; relationship with child	12
Other family relationships—parents, in-laws	5
Other relationship problems; type of relationship problem unspecified	4
Job or school problems; vocational choice	6
Nonjob adjustment problems in the self (general adjustment, specific symptoms)	18
Situational problems involving other people (that is, death or illness of a loved one) causing extreme psychological reaction	6
Nonpsychological situational problems	8
Nothing specific; a lot of little things; can't remember	2
Not ascertained	1

*Total is more than 100% because some respondents gave more than one response. (Gurin, Veroff, and Feld, 1960)

When Gurin, Veroff, and Feld (1960) conducted a nationwide survey on the nature of personal problems for which people seek professional help (as part of the ground-breaking work of the Joint Commission on Mental Illness and Health), they found that, in their sample of 2460 individuals, only one person in seven had ever sought such help. However, as indicated in Table 4-2, marriage and family problems together were by far the most common reasons given for seeking such help. Nevertheless, by the mid-1960s, it was still possible to characterize marriage counseling as a set of practices in search of a theory (Manus, 1966). Little ground-breaking research was being carried out, no dominant theories had emerged, no major figure had gained recognition. The

AAMC published no journal of its own; if practitioners published at all, they apparently preferred to submit articles to journals of their own professions. By the 1970s, however, the situation began to change. Olson (1970) urged an integration of marriage counseling and the emerging field of family therapy, since both focused on the marital relationship and not simply individuals in the relationship. By 1970, the AAMC, bowing to increased interest by its members in family therapy, changed its name to the American Association of Marriage and Family Counselors (in 1978, it became the present American Association for Marriage and Family Therapy). In 1975, the organization launched the *Journal of Marriage and Family Counseling* (renamed the *Journal of Marital and Family Therapy* in 1979). In 1977, the American Family Therapy Association, a smaller group of senior members working specifically in the field of family therapy, was formed.

What exactly is marriage counseling or, as it is called more and more frequently, marital therapy? According to Silverman (1972), marriage counseling differs from individual treatment in that it centers primarily on the married couple and the problems arising from their relationship. It is concerned not only with the growth of two individuals as separate persons but with their growth as they relate to each other in an intimate emotional and sexual relationship. Unlike psychotherapy that probes into inner meanings, marital counseling addresses reality issues and attempts to facilitate the couple's conscious decision-making process.

Most people who seek marriage counseling are coping with a crisis (such as infidelity, threat of divorce, disagreements regarding child rearing, money problems, conflict with in-laws, sexual incompatibility) that has caused an imbalance in the family equilibrium. Each partner enters counseling with different experiences, expectations and goals and with different degrees of commitment to the marriage. Both partners are probably somewhat invested in staying married or they would not seek professional marriage counseling, but the strength of the determination to stay together may vary greatly between them. Most marriage counseling is brief, problem-focused, and pragmatic. In treating the relationship the marriage counselor considers each individual's personality, role perceptions, and expectations as husband or wife (and how each perceives the partner's counter-role), patterns of communication (including sexual patterns), disruptive and inconsistent patterns of verbal communication, and the couple's ability to function together as a working unit in dealing with problems and reaching decisions (Cromwell, Olson, & Fournier, 1976).

As traditionally practiced, marriage counseling was likely to involve a collaborative approach: each spouse was seen by a separate therapist. By collaborating with one another, each counselor could then compare how his or her client saw a conflict situation with how the spouse reported the same situation to another counselor. Martin and Bird (1963) called it "stereoscopic therapy" to emphasize that each counselor got a double view of each client. While such an approach overcomes some of the pitfalls inherent in seeing a single individual about his or her marital problem, first-hand observation of the ongoing relationship is forfeited. No matter how well briefed by the collaborating colleague, each counselor has a necessarily limited view of the marriage and no view whatsoever of the marital interaction (Bodin, 1983).

In concurrent counseling, a less common approach, a counselor works with both spouses, but sees each one separately. The counselor must piece together how the couple functions by hearing two sides of the same event or transaction. Mittelman (1948), a psychoanalyst, was an early advocate of this procedure but he cautioned therapists to remain impartial and to remember what information had been learned from which partner. The counselor also faced the problem of keeping confidential the secrets one spouse wished not to reveal to the other. Although Sager (1966) reports that the concurrent-but-separate rule was occasionally broken (for example, with a couple seeking a divorce), for the most part the spouses were treated separately.

As the focus of marital counseling turned more and more to changing the marital relationship as such, it became clear that couples should be seen together in joint therapy sessions. Jackson (1959) introduced the term **conjoint** therapy to describe the situation where a couple (or perhaps the entire family) worked with the same therapist in the same room at the same time. By the end of the 1960s, Olson (1970) was able to state that marital therapists as a group could be distinguished by their primary emphasis on understanding and modifying the marital relationship and their preference for conjoint treatment.

Turning to historical developments in the child guidance movement, note that the systematic study of early childhood simply did not begin anywhere until early in this century (Kanner, 1962). In a careful survey of the child psychiatry literature before 1900, Rubenstein (1948) found no references to the psychological or developmental aspects of normal childhood. With the exception of some studies of the "mentally defective" child of subnormal intelligence, little if anything that is known today in the fields of child psychology and psychiatry was published before 1900.

Early in this century, major social reforms and changes in the legal status of children occurred, leading to universal compulsory education, restrictions on child labor, and a greater respect for children's rights. Inevitably, interest grew in establishing groups of experts who might work as a team to help emotionally disturbed children—the child guidance movement was launched (Rosenblatt, 1971). (Earlier in this chapter, we acknowledged Adler's contribution to the development of this movement in Europe and later, through his followers, in the United States.) By 1909 the psychiatrist William Healy had founded the Juvenile Psychopathic Institute in Chicago, a forerunner among child guidance clinics (now known as the Institute for Juvenile Research). Healy was specifically concerned with treating (and if possible, discovering ways of preventing) juvenile delinquency. By 1917 Healy had moved to Boston and established the Judge Baker Guidance Center devoted to diagnostic evaluation and treatment of delinquent children (Goldenberg, 1983). In 1924 the American Orthopsychiatric Association, largely devoted to the prevention of emotional disorders in children, was organized. Although they remained few in number until after

World War II, child guidance clinics now exist in almost every city in the United States.

An important innovation introduced by Healy was the formation of a team of professionals from different disciplines to assess both the child and his or her family. The practice of utilizing a team made up of a psychiatrist, a clinical psychologist, and a psychiatric social worker to examine the child through interviews, psychological tests, and history taking, respectively, became standard in child guidance clinics. The same may be said for involving one or both parents in the treatment. The psychiatrist was generally responsible for making most clinical decisions and conducting psychotherapy, the psychologist for developing educational and remedial programs, and the social worker for casework with the parents and liaison with other agencies in order to help improve the family's social environment. If therapy was undertaken with the child, it was common for the parents (particularly the more available mother) to visit the clinic regularly for therapy also, usually seeing a different therapist from the one working with the child. This collaborative approach, with the two therapists presumably consulting each other frequently, became traditional in child guidance clinics. According to Cooper (1974), direct work with the parents of emotionally disturbed children had three basic aims: (1) to establish an alliance with the parents that would support the child's growth in therapy; (2) to secure pertinent information about the child's experiences and the family situation; and (3) to help change the environment, thus aiding the child's growth and development. This type of intervention implies that the child's disturbance may very likely arise from interaction with one or both parents and that therapeutic change is best brought about by changing the nature of that interaction. Moreover, child guidance clinics function on the principle of early intervention in a child's—family's—emotional problems in order to avert the later development of more serious disabilities.

Group Therapy

Group therapy has been practiced in one form or another since the beginning of the 20th century but the impetus for its major expansion came from the need for clinical services during and immediately after World War II. The earliest use of the group process in psychotherapy can be credited to the Austrian psychiatrist Jacob Moreno who, around 1910, combined dramatic and therapeutic techniques to create **psychodrama.** Moreno, whose psychodramatic techniques are still used today, believed that it is necessary to recreate in the therapeutic process the various interpersonal situations that may have led to the patient's psychological difficulties. Since this was difficult to accomplish in the one-to-one therapist–patient situation, Moreno, in the role of therapist/ director, utilized a stage in which the patient could act out his or her significant life events in front of an audience. In these psychodramas, various people (frequently, but not necessarily, other patients) represented key persons ("auxiliary egos") in the patient's life. At certain junctures, the director might instruct the patient to reverse roles with one of the players so that he or she could gain a greater awareness of how another person saw him or her. In 1925 Moreno introduced psychodrama into the United States; in 1931 he coined the term "group therapy" (Gazda, 1975).

Stimulated largely by the theories developed by British psychoanalyst Melanie Klein, considerable interest in group processes developed during the 1930s at the Tavistock Institute in London. Several therapists began experimenting with group intervention techniques (Bion, 1961). In particular they emphasized dealing with current problems ("here and now") rather than searching for past causes and explanations or reconstructing possibly traumatic early experiences. Samuel Slavson, an engineer by training, began to do group work at the Jewish Board of Guardians in New York City at about the same time; from this work emerged his activity-group therapy technique, in which a group setting encourages disturbed children or adolescents to interact, thereby acting out their conflicts, impulses, and typical behavior patterns (Slavson, 1964). Slavson's approach was based on concepts derived from psychoanalysis, group work, and progressive education. In 1943 the American Group Psychotherapy Association was formed, largely through Slavson's efforts.

The sudden influx of psychiatric casualties during World War II, along with a shortage of trained therapists to work with these individuals, led to increased interest in briefer and more efficient therapeutic techniques such as group therapy. Shortly after the war, human-relations-training groups (T-groups)— sometimes referred to as "therapy for normals"—originated at the National Training Laboratory (NTL) at Bethel, Maine. Here the focus was on group discussion and role-playing techniques; these groups were part of an educational effort to provide interpersonal feedback information to the participants so that they could gain a better understanding of the group process, examine their attitudes and values, and become more sensitive to others. (T-groups were sometimes referred to as sensitivity-training groups on the West Coast.) In the 1960s, stimulated by the emergence of various growth centers around the United States, particularly the Esalen Institute in Big Sur, California, the **encounter group** (part of the **human-potential movement**) made a dramatic impact on the therapy scene and seemed to gain the immediate approval of large numbers of people, mostly from the upper-middle social classes. Today that enthusiasm has waned considerably, although traditional group therapies, NTL groups, and, to a lesser extent, encounter groups continue to exist side by side (Goldenberg, 1983).

Fundamental to the practice of group therapy is the principle that a small group can act as a carrier of change and strongly influence those who choose to be considered its members. A therapy group is a meaningful and real unit in and of itself, more than a collection of individuals, more than the sum of its parts. Another way of putting it is that the group is a collection of positions and roles and not of individuals (Back, 1974). The Tavistock version of group therapy is a good illustration: the group is treated as if it were a disturbed patient who is hurting because certain functions are not being carried out successfully. In a Tavistock group, the leader helps the group to function in a more balanced, coordinated, and mutually reinforcing way so that the group may accomplish productive work more efficiently. The implications for family therapy with a dysfunctional family are obvious.

As group therapy is practiced today (Yalom, 1975), most groups consist of between five and ten members plus a leader, meet at least once a week in $1\frac{1}{2}$- to 2-hour sessions, and sit in a circular arrangement so that each member can see and readily talk to every other member including the therapist. The groups are usually heterogeneous although, under certain circumstances, homogeneous groups are formed (for example, women's consciousness raising groups, groups composed of rape victims, groups of child-abusing parents). NTL groups, in which participants generally meet over a two-week period away from home, tend to focus on training community, business, and government leaders in organizational development; these laboratories have expanded from their beginnings in Bethel in 1946 to various parts of the world today. Encounter groups are still available in many large cities, although they no longer attract the large numbers of people they did a decade or more ago. Goldenberg (1983) summarizes some of the unique advantages of group therapy (see Table 4–3).

TABLE 4–3. Some Special Advantages of Group Therapy over Individual Therapy

Principle	*Elaboration*
Resembles everyday reality more closely	Therapist sees patient interacting with others, rather than hearing about it from the patient and possibly getting a biased or distorted picture; adds another informational dimension regarding his or her customary way of dealing with people.
Reduces social isolation	Patient learns that he or she is not unique by listening to others; thus he or she may be encouraged to give up feelings of isolation and self-consciousness.
Greater feelings of support and caring from others	Group cohesiveness ("we-ness") leads to increased trust; self-acceptance is likely to increase when patient is bolstered by acceptance by strangers.
Imitation of successful coping styles	New group members have the opportunity to observe older members and their more successful adaptational skills.
Greater exchange of feelings through feedback	Group situation demands expression of feelings, both positive and negative, directed at other members who evoke love, frustration, tears, or rage; patient thus gains relief while also learning from responses of others that intense affect does not destroy anyone, as he or she may have feared or fantasized.
Increases self-esteem through helping others	Patient has the opportunity to reciprocate help, to offer others empathy, warmth, acceptance, support, and genuineness, thereby increasing his or her own feelings of self-worth.
Greater insight	Patients become more attuned to understanding human motives and behavior, not only in themselves but also in others.

DEVELOPMENTS IN FAMILY THERAPY

The 1950s: From Family Research to Family Treatment

Most historical surveys of the family therapy movement (Guerin, 1976; Broderick & Schrader, 1981; Goldenberg & Goldenberg, 1983) agree that the 1950s was its founding decade. It was then that the theories and approaches we have been describing seemed to coalesce. Those ideas, to be sure, pertained more to clinical research than to clinical practice. Observation of a family—particularly one with a symptomatic member—could be justified only if it was presented as a research strategy. Observation of a family as a basis for treatment would have been a direct challenge to the prevailing sanction against a therapist's contact with anyone in the family other than one's own patient.

Family therapy therefore owes its initial legitimacy to the fact that (1) it was being carried out for scientifically defensible research purposes; and (2) the "research" was being done on clinical problems such as schizophrenia that did not respond well to the established psychotherapies of that time (Segal & Bavelas, 1983). As Wynne (1983) notes, Bateson's "Schizophrenia Communication Research Project" in Palo Alto, the work of Lidz and his co-researchers in New Haven, and Bowen's ambitious effort to hospitalize parents of schizophrenics for residential treatment with their disturbed offspring were all initially research-motivated and research-oriented. Wynne's own work at NIMH with schizophrenics was based on the use of therapy as a source of experimental data. It was the apparent success of the family research that helped give the stamp of approval to the development of therapeutic techniques.

At the 1952 American Psychiatric Association convention, Christian Midelfort presented a paper that was probably the first to report on the treatment of psychiatric patients and their families. Later expanded into a book (Midelfort, 1957), he described his experiences and results with family therapy working with relatives and patients in and out of mental hospitals. Unfortunately, Midelfort's pioneering efforts are all but forgotten by most family therapists today since his geographic location (Lutheran Hospital in La Crosse, Wisconsin) isolated him from the mainstream of activity and the exchange of ideas and techniques then taking place.

John Bell, an academic psychologist at Clark University in Worcester, Massachusetts, was another major architect of family therapy who receives little recognition for his contributions; as an inductive, action-oriented researcher and innovator, Bell was more interested in new ideas and practices than in establishing a reputation. Bell (1975) recalls that a casual remark overheard while he was visiting the Tavistock Clinic in London in 1951—to the effect that Dr. John Bowlby was experimenting with group therapy with families—stimulated his interest in applying the technique to treat behavior problems in children. Bell assumed that Bowlby, a distinguished British psychiatrist, was treating the entire family, although this later proved to be an erroneous assumption; actually Bowlby only occasionally held a family conference as an adjunct to working with the problem child. On the basis of this misinformation,

John Bell, Ed.D.

Bell began to think through the technical implications of meeting with an entire family on a regular basis. Once back in the United States, a case came to his attention that gave him the opportunity to try out this method as a therapeutic device, although Bell's description of his work did not receive widespread dissemination until a decade later (Bell, 1961). That ground-breaking monograph is often thought, along with Ackerman's text (Ackerman, 1958), to represent the founding of family therapy as practiced today. Unlike most of their colleagues in the 1950s, both Bell and Ackerman worked with nonschizophrenic families.

Meanwhile, the Palo Alto group led by Bateson was influenced greatly by the clinical wisdom of Milton Erickson, a Phoenix psychiatrist whose extraordinary powers of observation and therapeutic "wizardry" were becoming renowned among psychotherapists and hypnotherapists alike. (They would become even more celebrated after Haley's 1973 exposition of Erickson's work.) Erickson's gifts were his spontaneity, his quick and intuitive reading of a client's uniqueness, his tactical skills in reaching a resistant person, his artful use of persuasive communication at several simultaneous levels. His use of paradoxical instruction was to have an impact in general on the "communication" approach to family therapy and specifically on Haley's later "strategic" techniques (see Chapter 9).

Carl Whitaker, a psychiatrist, worked at Oak Ridge, Tennessee, during World War II. There he developed many of his innovative techniques: the use of a co-therapist; the inclusion of intergenerational family members in a patient's therapy; a highly active style with patients (including physical interaction such as arm wrestling); and what he later described (Whitaker, 1975) as the

111

"psychotherapy of the absurd." Lovingly carried out by Whitaker, this was a tongue-in-cheek procedure of escalating the incongruity of a symptom or bit of patient behavior to the point that the absurdity was easily apparent to the patient, sometimes by means of the therapist exposing his own absurd behavior or "creative craziness." Whitaker's use of self (stemming largely from his **experiential** view of psychotherapy) is not incidental to the treatment process but consciously intended to help the family achieve a looser, more caring, more intimate set of relationships among its members. Working at Emory University in Atlanta and later the University of Wisconsin at Madison, Whitaker—in spite of his deliberately irreverent style—was considered a key figure in family therapy by the late 1950s. He achieved further recognition for including extended family members in the family therapy process.

By 1957 the family movement surfaced nationally (Guerin, 1976) as family researchers and clinicians in various parts of the country began to learn of each other's work. At professional meetings, interest focused on families with a hospitalized schizophrenic member; and as noted earlier in this chapter, a number of family-related studies of the etiology of schizophrenia were published together in a volume edited by Jackson (1960). By this time, schizophrenia as well as a number of other severely incapacitating disorders were seen as resulting from a destructive family environment, the so-called "pathogenic" family (Zuk & Rubinstein, 1965).

By the decade's end in 1959, Don Jackson had founded the Mental Research Institute (MRI) in Palo Alto; Virginia Satir, Jay Haley, John Weakland, Paul Watzlawick and Richard Fisch would soon join the staff. A year later, Ackerman organized the Family Institute in New York (renamed the Ackerman Institute for Family Therapy after the death of its founder in 1971). Representing East and West coasts, both institutes have played seminal roles in the family therapy field.

The 1960s: The Rush to Practice

The early 1960s was a time of greatly heightened curiosity regarding family therapy. An increasing number of clinical practitioners began to think of family therapy as a new way of conceptualizing the origins of mental disorders and their amelioration, not simply one more method of treatment. A number of therapists began working with whole families. Those with an individual orientation recognized that the "identified patient" was the victim of family strife but preferred to work with each family member separately in a family group setting. Largely oblivious to any of the results of the theoretical research of the 1950s, these therapists simply extended their familiar and primarily psychodynamic techniques and concepts to family settings and situations. The more family-oriented therapists did more than treat individuals in a family context; they began to realize that it was the dysfunctional family patterns that needed to be transformed. For this latter group, as Haley (1971b) points out, the focus of treatment was on a family's structure and its members' interaction, not on an individual's perception, affect, or behavior as such. For these therapists, the goal of therapy shifted from changing the person to changing the sequences of behavior between intimates. At the same time, family therapy programs were established in new outpatient settings (such as community mental health centers) and were directed at new kinds of families (for example, poor families and minority families); family therapy was no longer restricted to the treatment of hospitalized schizophrenics and their families (Zuk, 1981).

Several significant developments in the early 1960s indicate the momentum that the field of family therapy was gathering. In 1962, Ackerman and Jackson founded the first—and still the most influential—journal in the field, *Family Process*, with Jay Haley as its editor. From its beginnings, the journal has enabled researchers and practitioners alike to exchange ideas and identify with the field. In addition, several important national conferences were organized. A meeting in 1964 dealt with the application of systems theory to understanding dysfunctional families (Zuk & Boszormenyi-Nagy, 1967); in 1967 a conference organized by psychologist James Framo was held to stimulate and maintain an ongoing dialogue between family researchers, theorists, and family therapists (Framo, 1972).

Family therapy, gaining professional respectability, was becoming a familiar topic at most psychiatric and psychological meetings. As Bowen (1976) later recalled, dozens of therapists were eager to present their newly minted intervention techniques with whole families. In nearly all cases, this "rush to practice" precluded the development of procedures that were adequately grounded in research or based on sound conceptual formulations. In their clinical zeal— Bowen refers to it as "therapeutic evangelism"—many therapists attempted solutions to family dilemmas using familiar concepts borrowed from individual psychotherapy.

One notable exception to the emphasis on practice over theory and research during this period was Minuchin's (Minuchin, Montalvo, Guerney, Rosman, & Schumer, 1967) pioneering study of urban slum families and his development of appropriate clinical techniques for successful intervention (see discussion in Chapter 3). By 1965 Minuchin was director of the Philadelphia Child Guidance Center. His staff included Braulio Montalvo and Bernice Rosman from the Wiltwyck School Project and in 1967 he invited Jay Haley from Palo Alto to join them. (The Bateson research group had officially disbanded in 1962 when Bateson, an anthropologist more interested in theoretical ideas regarding communication than in their clinical application to troubled families, moved to the Oceanic Institute in Hawaii to observe patterns of communication among dolphins.) The Philadelphia center was soon transformed from a traditional child guidance clinic into a family-oriented treatment center. Minuchin and his associates developed a structural family therapy approach and established a program to train poor workers to treat families (Stanton, 1981). By the late 1960s, the Philadelphia group had begun working with psychosomatic families (with particular attention to families of anorexia nervosa patients), applying some of Minuchin's earlier concepts of boundaries and the interplay of a family's subsystems to problems of somatic dysfunction (see Chapter 3).

During this highly productive period, the MRI on the West Coast extended its earlier studies to include families with expressions of dysfunctional behavior other than schizophrenia: delinquency, school underachievement, psychosomatic disorders, marital conflict (Bodin, 1981). The 1964 publication of *Conjoint Family Therapy* by Virginia Satir, then at MRI, did much to popularize the family therapy approach, as did Satir's demonstrations at professional meetings and workshops in many parts of the world. Toward the end of the decade, the character of the work at the MRI changed as the result of Satir's departure to become the director of training of Esalen Institute, a growth center at Big Sur, California, Haley's move to Philadelphia, and especially Jackson's untimely death in 1968. Although the MRI has continued to focus on family interactional patterns (particularly communication), the Brief Therapy Project, begun in 1967, became its major thrust. In this pragmatic, short-term, team approach to working with families (see Chapter 12), a primary therapist consults with other therapists observing the session from behind a one-way mirror. Geared toward problem resolution, brief therapy helps family members to change the kinds of responses they make to problems since the solutions they have persistently chosen in the past have only served to reinforce their problematic behavior (Watzlawick, Weakland, & Fisch, 1974).

During the 1960s there were corresponding developments in family therapy outside of the United States. At the Institute of Family Therapy in London, psychoanalytic in orientation, Robin Skynner contributed a brief version of psychodynamic family therapy (Skynner, 1981). The British psychiatrist John Howells (1975) devised a system for family diagnosis as a necessary step in planning therapeutic intervention. In West Germany, Helm Stierlin (1972) called attention to patterns of separation in adolescence and related these patterns to family characteristics.

In Italy, Mara Selvini-Palazzoli (1978), trained in child psychoanalysis but discouraged by her results with anorexic children, was attracted to the new epistemology proposed by Bateson and the Palo Alto group. Shifting to a systems approach that stressed circularity, she was more successful with resistant cases. In 1967 Selvini-Palazzoli formed the Institute for Family Studies in Milan; the Institute would eventually have a worldwide impact on the field of family therapy particularly for its use of "long" brief therapy in which ten sessions are held at monthly intervals. We will return to the work of the Milan Associates (Luigi Boscolo, Giuliana Prata, Gianfranco Cecchin and Selvini-Palazzoli) in Chapter 9.

The 1970s: Innovative Techniques and Self-Examination

For the most part, technique continued to outdistance theory and research well into the 1970s. The early part of the decade saw a proliferation of family therapy approaches: treating several families simultaneously in **multiple family therapy** (Laqueur, 1976); bringing families together for an intensive, crisis-focused two-day period of continuing interaction with a team of mental health professionals, in **multiple impact therapy** (MacGregor, Ritchie, Serrano, & Schuster, 1964); working in the home with an extended family group including friends, neighbors, and employers, in **network therapy** (Speck & Attneave, 1973); treating a family on an outpatient basis in **family crisis therapy** instead of hospitalizing a disturbed, scapegoated family member (Langsley, Pittman, Machotka & Flomenhaft, 1968). Behavioral psychologists began to turn their attention to issues related to family matters, such as teaching parents "behavior management skills" to facilitate effective child rearing (Patterson, 1971), and to propose therapeutic strategies for working with marital discord (Jacobson & Martin, 1976) and family dysfunction (Liberman, 1970). The newly available technology of videotape allowed family therapists to tape ongoing sessions either for immediate playback to the family, for later study by the therapist, or for training purposes (Alger, 1976a).

In the 1970s the relatively new field of family therapy engaged in its first efforts at self-examination. The so-called GAP report (Group for the Advancement of Psychiatry, 1970) acknowledged clinicians' increasing awareness of the family's role in symptom and conflict formation as well as of the limitations of the traditional psychoanalytic emphasis on intrapsychic processes. The GAP survey of a sample of family therapists found that they belonged largely to three disciplines (psychiatry, psychology, and social work) although practitioners also included marriage counselors, clergymen, nonpsychiatric physicians, child psychiatrists, nurses, sociologists, and others. Most family therapists were young, reported dissatisfaction with the results of individual treatment, and were looking for a more efficient method of therapeutic intervention. When asked to select their primary and secondary goals from among eight categories, over 90% of the 290 respondents listed "improved communication" within the family as their primary goal; not a single respondent said it was rarely or never a goal. All eight of the goals described in the questionnaire were chosen as primary goals (with all or with certain families) by over half of the respondents (see Table 4–4). However, improvement in individual task performance or individual symptomatic improvement was more likely to be a secondary goal (see Table 4–5). This indicates that these objectives had by no means been abandoned but that change in only part of a family was given less emphasis than a family-wide change such as improved communication.

The 1970 GAP report also presented the results of a survey of practicing family therapists asked to rank the major figures in the field according to their influence at that time. The practitioners placed them in this order: Satir, Ackerman, Jackson, Haley, Bowen, Wynne, Bateson, Bell, Boszormenyi-Nagy.

In another kind of effort to bring order and self-awareness to the developing field, Beels and Ferber (1969) observed a number of leading therapists conducting family sessions and studied videotapes and films of their work with families. Beels and Ferber then distinguished two types of family therapists based on the therapist's relationship to the family group, **conductors** and **reactors.** Conductor therapists are active, aggressive, and colorful leaders who place themselves in the center of the family group. They are likely to initiate rather than respond, to propound ideas vigorously, to make their value systems explicit. Ackerman, Satir, Bowen and Minuchin are models for this type. Reactor therapists are less theatrical personalities, more subtle and indirect.

Take the one that fits your personality the best.

**TABLE 4-4. Primary Goals Stated
by Therapists with Families Actually in Treatment (N = 290)**

Primary goals	Percent of all families	Percent of certain families	Total percent
1. Improved communication	85	5	90
2. Improved autonomy and individuation	56	31	87
3. Improved empathy	56	15	71
4. More flexible leadership	34	32	66
5. Improved role agreement	32	32	64
6. Reduced conflict	23	37	60
7. Individual symptomatic improvement	23	33	56
8. Improved individual task performance	12	38	50

**TABLE 4-5. Secondary Goals Stated
by Therapists with Families Actually in Treatment (N = 290)**

Secondary goals	Percent of all families	Percent of certain families	Total percent
1. Improved individual task performance	16	29	45
2. Individual symptomatic improvement	23	15	38
3. Reduced conflict	17	18	35
4. Improved role agreement	17	15	32
5. More flexible leadership	11	19	30
6. Improved empathy	17	8	25
7. Improved autonomy and individuation	7	5	12
8. Improved communication	8	1	9

They observe and clarify the family group process, responding to what the family presents to them, negotiating differences among family members. Beels and Ferber further divided reactors into analysts (who tend to conceptualize what is taking place in psychoanalytic terms such as **transference, counter-transference,** or **acting out**) and systems purists (who view families as rule-governed systems). The authors cite Whitaker, Wynne, Boszormenyi-Nagy, and Framo as analyst reactors; Haley, Jackson, Watzlawick, and Zuk as systems purist reactors.

Beels and Ferber (1979) contended that each type of therapist was effective in directing and controlling the family sessions and in providing family members with possible new ways of relating to each other; the conductors were more direct in their methods but not necessarily more successful in helping to create a new family experience as the basis for changing its members' interactive behavior patterns.

Another kind of analysis of therapist intervention was initiated in the early 1970s at the University of California at Santa Cruz when mathematician Richard Bandler and linguist John Grinder set out to determine just how master clinicians consistently achieve their desired therapeutic outcomes. They based their inquiry on **neuro-linguistic programming** (NLP), hypothesizing that all behavior results from neurological processes ("neuro"), that these neural processes are represented, ordered and sequenced into models and strategies through language ("linguistic") and that the process of organizing the system's components determines specific outcomes ("programming") (Dilts, Grinder, Bandler, Cameron-Bandler, & DeLozier, 1980). In the effort to detect how language produces change in people, Bandler and Grinder studied the linguistic patterns of Virginia Satir, Fritz Perls, and later Milton Erickson in order to provide a more systematic explanation for how these therapists work and how their intervention strategies help clients reprogram their behavior. The work of Bandler and Grinder (1975) was especially useful in helping to clarify and systematize previously unanalyzed patterns of therapist communication and in discovering how clients reveal what they are thinking and feeling through sensory based statements ("I *see* what you mean"; "I'm *touched* by your offer"; "I like it when you *tell* me you appreciate what I've done") and behavioral cues (for example, eye movements). NLP practitioners learn to scan word patterns and body language for cues regarding a person's emotional state, preliminary to helping to change his or her behavior. In recent years NLP has developed into an all-purpose self-improvement program for salesmen and executives as well as a technique used by hypnotherapists and family therapists.

Finally, self-examination took the form of outcome research on the effectiveness of family therapy. By the late 1970s the need for such studies was generally acknowledged. Nevertheless, Wells and Dezen (1978) pointed out after surveying the outcome literature that most family therapy approaches, some of them identified with major figures in the field, "have never submitted their methods to empirical testing and, indeed, seem oblivious to such a need" (p. 266). By the end of the decade there had been some improvement (Gurman & Kniskern, 1981a) but the effectiveness of family therapy still required continuing and systematic evaluation. (For further discussion of this topic, see Chapter 13.)

The 1980s: Growth and Professionalization

A number of signs document the phenomenal growth of the field now in its "over thirty" adult years. Whereas barely a decade ago the field had one professional journal of its own, *Family Process*, there are today approximately two dozen family therapy journals, one-half of that number published in English. Once family therapy centers could be counted on the fingers of one hand; there now exist more than 300 free-standing family therapy institutes in the United States alone. Two professional organizations represent the interests of family therapy. The American Association for Marriage and Family Therapy, which grew from fewer than 1000 members in 1970 to over 7500 by 1979, has authority to accredit graduate programs and training centers and to issue credentials for qualified members; it publishes a code of professional ethics and is active in pursuing state licensing and certification for marriage and family therapists. The American Family Therapy Association, a younger and smaller group, has deliberately remained selective in its membership and restricted itself to being an interest group concerned exclusively with family therapy as distinct from marriage counseling or marital therapy.

Family therapy is clearly an international phenomenon, with active programs and congresses held regularly in Canada, England, Israel, Holland, Italy, Australia, West Germany and elsewhere. Training in family therapy is by now an integral part of most university clinical graduate programs, with students also seeking out family therapy institutes for more advanced study. Dozens of workshops are held each month in various parts of the United States and are usually heavily attended. The profession has established superstars (such as Satir, Minuchin, Whitaker, or Haley) who offer demonstrations of their work in different parts of the country throughout the year.

—Still around

No longer the radical movement it was considered barely three decades ago, family therapy has established itself as a distinctive and important mental health field. Family therapy has become the treatment of choice for a wide range of problems; public awareness of and demand for relationship-oriented services has increased dramatically. Truly, as Olson, Russell, and Sprenkle (1980) observe, marital and family therapy reflect the **Zeitgeist.**

Olson, Russell, and Sprenkle (1980) also note the important consequences for the entire mental health profession that have followed from the growth and acceptance of this new field: (1) the traditional distinction between marriage counseling and family therapy has faded so that it is now more accurate to describe marital and family therapy as one not-quite-unified field; (2) the field has achieved sufficient integrity and stature that workers in the field today are apt to think of themselves as family therapists as much or more than they identify themselves with their professional disciplines; (3) there is a trend toward treating relationships, whether the intervention be with married couples, cohabiting couples, stepfamilies, gay couples, parent-adolescent conficts, or elsewhere; (4) all stages of a relationship are now considered appropriate for intervention, from premarital counseling to divorce counseling to custody resolution counseling.

This emphasis on treating problems within a relationship context characterizes the field of family therapy today. The practice has been buttressed theoretically by the acceptance of systems theory, as well as by the renewed coherence of family therapy and family research. For example, the revival of interest in family theory (including the current debate within the field regarding the "new epistemology") is largely stimulated by clinical research observations of the type favored during family therapy's earliest days in the 1950s (Wynne, 1983).

Many of the first-generation family therapists remain active and continue to have authority in the field. In reviewing the last three decades, Thaxton and L'Abate (1982) named the following figures (not in order of importance) as having had the greatest impact: Ackerman, Boszormenyi-Nagy, Bowen, Framo, Haley, Jackson, Minuchin, Satir, Whitaker and Zuk.

Many other theorists, researchers, and therapists have made contributions and are likely to continue to be influential in the decade ahead. Prominent among these are: Gerald Patterson, Neil Jacobson, and Robert Liberman (behavioral approaches); Paul Watzlawick and Mara Selvini-Palazzoli (communication and strategic approaches); Alan Gurman, Lyman Wynne and David Olson (research approaches) (Textor, 1983). In the following chapters we intend to look more closely at the work of each of these second-generation leaders as well as the work of the early pioneers.

SUMMARY

We have discussed the diverse roots of contemporary family therapy. Psychoanalysis, as conceived by Freud, acknowledged the role of family relationships in personality development but its techniques of treatment were individual-oriented. Ackerman is generally credited with adapting psychoanalytic formulations to the study of the family and is thus considered a founder of family therapy; Adler and Sullivan also influenced the developing field. General systems theory, as proposed by the biologist Bertalanffy, described seemingly unrelated phenomena as components of a self-regulating total system with feedback mechanisms to govern the process; applied to the family, the focus is on how the parts form a whole, how they are organized, and how they interact. In schizophrenia research, Bateson and associates' work on double-bind interactions, Lidz's on marital schism and marital skew, Bowen's on symbiotic mother–child relationships, and Wynne's on pseudomutuality helped establish the role of the dysfunctional family in the etiology of schizophrenia and set the stage for studying interaction patterns in other kinds of families. The fields of marital counseling and child guidance brought pairs of family members (such as husband–wife, parent–child) into treatment, thus modifying the traditional emphasis on treating individual patients. Group therapy utilized small-group processes for therapeutic gain and provided a model for therapy with whole families.

Stimulated by the research-oriented study of families with schizophrenic members, the family therapy movement gained momentum and national visibility in the 1950s. The pioneering family therapists of that decade were joined in the 1960s by more individual-oriented therapists who were attracted to this new way of conceptualizing and treating dysfunctional behavior. Largely oblivious to the findings of earlier research on the family, clinicians during this era simply rushed into practice; in the process, they created many new strategies for intervention with whole families. Corresponding developments were taking place in various parts of the world, particularly in Europe. Selvini-Palazzoli's systems-based work with anorexic children in Milan, Italy, is particularly noteworthy.

Technique continued to outpace theory and research well into the 1970s. Additional innovative therapeutic techniques were introduced, including behavioral approaches to family-related problems. The field was growing at a rapid rate and a number of efforts aimed at self-awareness and self-evaluation were undertaken. In the 1980s marital therapy and family therapy are an all-but-unified field. Practitioners from a variety of disciplines make "family therapist" their primary professional identification. The emphasis today is on treating problems within a relationship context rather than working separately with individuals. There is a revival of interest in family theory and the linking of clinical family research and family therapy practice.

CHAPTER FIVE

Theoretical Perspectives: Psychodynamic and Related Models

Family therapists share a common view of the family as the context of and for relationships. There are, however, significant differences in the theoretical assumptions they make about the nature and origin of psychological dysfunction, in the way they understand family interactions, and in their strategies for therapeutic intervention. Although their positions do not represent rigid adherence to particular "schools," distinct differences in viewpoint and emphasis are apparent. In this and the following five chapters, we look at approaches to family theory and clinical practice from six perspectives, grouping those that are primarily psychodynamic in orientation; those that are experiential or humanistic in emphasis; those that pay special attention to the family as a system—the Bowenian, structural and communication models; and those that are behavioral in their approach.

Before explaining our reasons for such a classification scheme, let us emphasize our belief that the theoretical foundation of the field of family therapy demands to be strengthened lest it become merely a set of clever, even flashy, empirically-derived intervention techniques. Important and effective as some of these techniques may be, they require the kind of rationale or justification that only a coherent, unified theory can provide. All theories, of course, are inevitably speculations or unsubstantiated hypotheses that are offered in the hope of shedding light or providing fresh perspectives on the causes of family dysfunction. They are never, in and of themselves, true or false; rather, some are more useful than others, particularly in generating research hypotheses that can be verified through testing. All of these theories are tentative; all are expendable in the sense that useful theories lead to new ways of looking at behavior and to the discovery of new relationships that in turn lead to new sets of theoretical proposals.

At this stage in the development of family therapy—still a considerable distance from a comprehensive theory—we need to examine the usefulness of the various contributions that have already been made to our understanding of family development and functioning. Some models have come from the research laboratory, others from the consultation room of a clinician working with seriously disturbed or merely temporarily troubled families. In evaluating each of the models presented in this chapter, as well as Chapters 6 through 10, the reader would do well to keep in mind the following criteria of a sound theory:

1. Is it *comprehensive?* Does it deal with understanding family functioning rather than being trivial or oversimplified? Is it generalizable to all families as they behave in all situations (not, for example, only to White, middle-class families or only to the ways families behave in special psychotherapeutic situations)?

2. Is it *parsimonious?* Does it make as few assumptions as necessary to account for the phenomena under study? If two competing theoretical systems both predict the same behavior, is it the one with fewer assumptions and constructs?

3. Is it *verifiable?* Does it generate predictions about behavior that are confirmed when the relevant empirical data are collected?

4. Is it *precise?* Does it define concepts explicitly and relate them to each other and to data (avoiding figurative, metaphorical or analogical language)?

5. Is it *empirically valid?* Do systematic empirical tests of the predictions made by the theory confirm the theory?

6. Is it *stimulating?* Does it provoke response and further investigation to enhance the theory or even to demonstrate its inadequacies?

CLASSIFYING THEORIES IN FAMILY THERAPY

A decade ago, Gerald Zuk (1976), himself a leading figure in the field, questioned whether family therapy was a "clinical hodge podge" (of numerous techniques and incomplete theories) rather than a true clinical science. Unfortunately, the question remains almost as relevant today, although a number of scientifically-designed efforts are being made to expand theory and to conduct more research that is relevant to family assessment as well as to therapy.

One scientific endeavor involves classification of therapist styles and/or theoretical stances into groupings that are based on significant similarities. The first and necessary step in such a procedure is selecting the dimensions according to which the different therapists will be aligned. In surveying practitioners in the late 1960s, the Group for the Advancement of Psychiatry (1970) classified therapists from A to Z based on their theoretical orientation. According to this scheme:

> Position A will locate those one-to-one therapists who occasionally see families but retain a primary focus upon the individual system and Position Z those who use exclusively a family system orientation (p. 48).

According to the GAP findings, Position A therapists were likely to be psychodynamically oriented individual therapists for whom family therapy was but one method of treatment among many. If on occasion these therapists worked with entire families, they kept the focus on their individual patient; the other family members might be included to clarify some interpersonal conflict or facilitate the individual's treatment. History taking, differential diagnosis, and the noting of positive or negative affect constituted a major portion of their initial clinical activity. Position Z therapists were likely to think "systems." These therapists viewed the "identified patient" as part of a dysfunctional family and thus the family's "symptom bearer"; they held conjoint family sessions focusing on the here-and-now family interaction rather than on the past; they directed treatment at resolving relationship problems rather than holding family sessions for the purpose of uncovering affect or toward making a careful psychiatric diagnosis of the "identified patient." Although readers of the survey may have concluded that the field of psychotherapy was becoming polarized (in many ways, of course, it was), the GAP Report did acknowledge that some therapists occupied Position N; these therapists gave the individual and the systems approach equal validity and felt free to use either or both ways of conceptualizing dysfunction and planning treatment.

Rather than classifying therapists by theoretical orientation, Beels and Ferber (1969) focused on personal style; they made the distinction between "conductors" (who are active, direct, dominating, and even charismatic) and "reactors" (who are less active and directive and who prefer to observe and clarify family interaction) (see fuller discussion in Chapter 4). In Beels and Ferber's system of classification, the distinctions between psychodynamicists and systems theorists was blurred. A Positon A therapist (or a Position Z) might be a conductor or reactor, depending more on the therapist's individual personality than on his or her theoretical suppositions. For example, Ackerman (psychoanalytic in viewpoint) and Satir (then primarily a communication advocate) were both characterized as conductors; so were Minuchin (structural theory) and Bowen (family systems). Conversely, Framo (psychodynamic) and Whitaker (experiential) were identified as reactors, as were Haley and Jackson (communication approach). The reader should bear in mind that both groups—conductors and reactors—exercised control over what went on in therapy, the former in more direct and obvious but not necessarily more influential ways.

Philip Guerin (1976) made a later attempt at classification, in part as a reaction to the antitheoretical trend he saw developing in the field. Returning to the central issue of theoretical stance, he again divided family therapists into two basic groups, psychodynamic and systems. The psychodynamic category included: (1) individual approaches (similar to Position A in the GAP Report) taken by therapists, mostly psychoanalytic in orientation, who might occasionally see families for consultation or informational purposes regarding their individual patient; (2) group approaches (for example, Bell, Wynne) taken by therapists who define the family as a natural group with the therapist adopting an observer position and directing, clarifying or interpreting what is taking place during the session; (3) the Ackerman-style approach taken by a therapist who is aggressive, directive and crafty and who operates from a psychoanalytic orientation; and (4) experiential approaches (such as those developed during the late 1960s) taken by therapists who attempt to engage the family in a "therapeutic happening" or growth experience by having the members interact in an open, "gut-level," emotionally charged way. Guerin divided the systems group into the following four subgroups: communication-strategic (Haley, Satir, Erickson); structural (Minuchin); Bowen's system theory and technique (probably the most comprehensive of all theoretical formulations); and general systems (a theory-based model without direct clinical application at the time).

More recent classification proposals have come from Gurman (1979), Kaslow (1980), L'Abate and Frey (1981), and Zimmerman and Sims (1983). Gurman's three-part division—psychoanalytically oriented family therapy, systems therapy of the communication and Bowenian types, and behavioral family therapy—was supplemented by Kaslow's suggestion that Boszormenyi-Nagy's intergenerational-contextual approach be added and other, finer distinctions be made. L'Abate and Frey offered what they called an E-R-A model (Emotionality, Rationality, Activity), arguing that the differences in therapist approaches are ones of emphasis along these dimensions. That is, family therapists of the E-school, such as Satir or Whitaker, pay a great deal of attention to how feelings are felt, expressed and translated within family transactions; R-school advocates such as Bowen or Framo value cognitive activity, rational and relatively unemotional discussion, problem solving; A-school adherents such as Haley, Minuchin, Selvini-Palazzoli, and the behaviorists invite active change outside the therapy sessions by issuing directives and prescribing schedules to be followed. L'Abate and Frey's intriguing typology of family therapy theories is presented in Table 5-1.

Zimmerman and Sims (1983) devised a continuum with psychoanalytically oriented family therapy on one end and behaviorally oriented family therapy on the other, making the major distinction a psychodynamic or systems perspective. In our opinion, a system of classification that discriminates according to a single variable cannot do justice to the intricacies of the many theoretical positions formulated and utilized by family therapists. All of these efforts at classification have limitations; most important, they fail to deal adequately, if at all, with two issues. First, the systems neglect the sizeable number of family therapists, largely influenced by the **existential, phenomenological,** and human-potential movement outlooks, who were particularly prominent during the 1960s and early 1970s. Intuitive and insistently antitheoretical, they deserve a separate grouping of their own. We have labeled them experiential/humanistic to provide a broad enough rubric to embrace several approaches; Satir, Whitaker, and Kempler are key figures among this group. Second, any serious attempt at classification must acknowledge that no theory or therapist can be compared adequately with any other theory or therapist along one dimension alone.

As presented in Table 5-2, we propose seven variables according to which existing—and future—theoretical viewpoints in family therapy can be com-

TABLE 5-1. Classification of Family Therapy Theories for an E-R-A Model

Characteristic modalities	Emotionality	Rationality	Activity
Historical Background Schools of Thought	Humanism, Existential, Gestalt, Experiential	Psychoanalytic-Cognitive	Behavioral-Systems
Temporal Perspective	Present	Past	Future
Representative Theorists	Satir, Bandler & Grinder, Napier & Whitaker	Boszormenyi-Nagy & Spark, Stierlin, Bowen & Associates, Framo	Adlerians Palo Alto Group Milano Group Behaviorism Minuchin Haley
Preferred Therapeutic Interventions	Sculpture, Nonverbal role-playing	History, Genograms	Task Assignment Prescriptions
Locus of Change	Family feelings and immediacy	Family of origin Inside individuals	Family Relationships and problem solving
Predicted Length of Therapy	Variable, Intermediate	Long	Short-Fixed
Activity Level	Mostly inside office	Least active	Mostly outside office

(L'Abate & Frey, 1981)

pared. These variables include: the time frame (emphasis on the past or present); the role that unconscious processes play; the extent to which insight into past causes or action in the form of changed behavior is emphasized; the role of the therapist; the unit of analysis (individual, dyad, triad or whole group); the major theoretical underpinnings; and the goals of treatment.

Thus we offer our own system for organizing the different approaches to family therapy, not to minimize the complexities of the field, but to provide a comprehensive frame of reference for understanding the similarities and differences within it. Our model comprises six theoretical viewpoints: psychodynamic, experiential/humanistic, Bowenian, structural, communication, and behavioral.

THE PSYCHODYNAMIC OUTLOOK

The psychodynamic view of individual behavior, based largely on a psychoanalytic model, focuses on the interplay of opposing forces within a person as the basis for understanding that person's motivation and sources of discomfort and

TABLE 5-2. A Comparison of Six Theoretical Viewpoints in Family Therapy

Dimension	Psychodynamic	Experiential/ Humanistic	Bowenian	Structural	Communication	Behavioral
1. Major time frame	Past; history of early experiences needs to be uncovered.	Present; here-and-now data from immediate experience observed.	Primarily the present, although attention also paid to one's family of origin.	Present and past; family's current structure carried over from earlier transactional patterns.	Present; current problems or symptoms maintained by ongoing, repetitive sequences between persons.	Present; focus on interpersonal environments that maintain and perpetuate current behavior patterns.
2. Role of unconscious processes	Unresolved conflicts from the past, largely out of the person's awareness, continue to attach themselves to current objects and situations.	Free choice and conscious self-determination more important than unconscious motivation.	Earlier concepts suggested unconscious conflicts, although now recast in interactive terms.	Unconscious motivation less important than repetition of learned habits and role assignments by which the family carries out its tasks.	Family rules, homeostatic balance, and feedback loops determine behavior, not unconscious processes.	Problematic behavior is learned and maintained by its consequences; unconscious processes rejected as too inferential and unquantifiable.
3. Insight vs. action	Insight leads to understanding, conflict reduction, and ultimately intrapsychic and interpersonal change.	Self-awareness of one's immediate existence leads to choice, responsibility and change.	Rational processes used to gain self-awareness into current relationships as well as intergenerational experiences.	Action precedes understanding; change in transactional patterns more important than insight in producing new behaviors.	Action oriented; behavior change and symptom reduction brought about through directives rather than interpretations.	Actions prescribed to modify specific behavior patterns.
4. Role of therapist	Neutral; makes interpretations of individual and family behavior patterns.	Active facilitator of potential for growth; provides family with new experiences.	Direct but nonconfrontational; detriangulated from family fusion.	Stage director; manipulates family structure in order to change dysfunctional sets.	Active; manipulative; problem-focused; prescriptive, paradoxical.	Directive; teacher, trainer or model of desired behavior; contract negotiator.

TABLE 5-2. (continued)

Dimension	Psychodynamic	Experiential/ Humanistic	Bowenian	Structural	Communication	Behavioral
5. Unit of study	Focus on individual; emphasis on how family members feel about one another and deal with each other.	Dyad; problems arise from interaction between two members (for example, husband and wife).	Entire family over several generations; may work with one partner (or one dyad) for a period of time.	Triads; coalitions, subsystems, boundaries, power.	Dyads and triads; problems and symptoms viewed as interpersonal communications between two or more family members.	Dyads; effect of one person's behavior on another; linear view of causality.
6. Major theoretical underpinnings	Psychoanalysis.	Existentialism; humanistic psychology; phenomenology.	Family systems theory.	Structural family theory; systems.	Communication theory; systems, behaviorism.	Behaviorism; social learning theory.
7. Major theorists and/or practitioners	Ackerman, Framo, Boszormenyi-Nagy, Stierlin, Skynner, Bell	Whitaker, Kempler, Satir	Bowen	Minuchin	Jackson, Erickson, Haley, Madanes, Selvini-Palazzoli	Patterson, Stuart, Liberman, Jacobson, Margolin
8. Goals of treatment	Insight, psychosexual maturity, strengthening of ego functioning; reduction in interlocking pathologies; more satisfying object relations.	Growth, more fulfilling interaction patterns; clearer communication; expanded awareness; authenticity.	Maximization of self-differentiation for each family member.	Change in relationship context in order to restructure family organization and change dysfunctional transactional patterns.	Change dysfunctional, redundant behavioral sequences ("games") between family members in order to eliminate presenting problem or symptom.	Change in behavioral consequences between persons leads to elimination of maladaptive or problematic behavior.

anxiety. The neurotic individual, for example, may be seen as someone torn by inner conflict between his or her sexual wishes or urges and a punitive, guilt-producing conscience. Extrapolated to the family level, advocates of this view seek to discover how the inner lives and conflicts of family members interlock and how the binding together affects disturbances in family members.

According to advocates of the psychodynamic view, the two individuals joined by marriage each bring to the relationship a separate and unique psychological heritage. Inevitably the dyadic relationship bears resemblances to the parent–child relationships the partners experienced in their families of origin. As Meissner (1978, p. 26) observes, "the capacity to successfully function as a spouse is largely a consequence of the spouse's childhood relationships to his (or her) own parents." The relative success that marital partners experience, as well as the manner in which they approach and accomplish developmental tasks throughout the life cycle, is largely determined by the extent to which they are free from excessive negative attachments to the past. Troubled marriages, then, are seen as contaminated by the pathogenic **introjects** (imprints or memories of the parents or other figures) from past relationships with members of the previous generation residing in each partner. Moreover, the partners' unresolved intrapsychic problems not only prevent them from enjoying a productive and fulfilling marital experience but the conflicts are passed along to their children, who eventually bring psychic disturbances into their own marriages. Only by gaining insight, and thus freedom, into such burdensome attachments to the past can individuals—or couples—learn to develop adult-to-adult relationships in the present with members of their families of origin.

As we present various approaches that belong to the psychodynamic perspective, keep in mind that each one addresses two levels of understanding and intervention simultaneously: the motives, fantasies, unconscious conflicts and repressed memories of each family member and the more complex world of family interaction and family dynamics.

Psychoanalysis and Family Dynamics (Ackerman)

As early as the 1930s, Nathan Ackerman was writing about family dynamics and by the late 1940s he was making clinical assessments of entire families (Green & Framo, 1981). One of the earliest pioneers in studying and treating families, Ackerman remained throughout his long career a bold, confrontive therapist. He also represents early efforts to integrate a psychoanalytic stance (with its intrapsychic orientation) with the then-emerging systems approach (emphasizing interpersonal relationships).

Ackerman (1970b) saw the family as a system of interacting personalities; each individual was an important subsystem within the family, just as the family was a subsystem within the community. Understanding family functioning called for acknowledging input from several sources: the unique personality of each member; the dynamics of family role adaptations; the family's commitment to a set of human values; the behavior of the family as a social unit. At the individual level, the process of symptom formation may be understood in terms of intrapsychic conflict, a defense against anxiety aroused by the conflict, and the resulting development of a neurotic symptom (a classical psychoanalytic explanation); at the family level, the symptom is viewed as part of a recurring, predictable, interactional pattern intended to assure equilibrium for the individual, but actually impairing family homeostasis by producing distortions in family role relationships. In family terms, an individual's symptom becomes a unit of interpersonal behavior reflected within a context of shared family conflict, anxiety, and defenses. Conceptualizing behavior in this way, Ackerman was beginning to build a bridge between psychoanalysis and systems theory.

To Ackerman, homeostasis signifies the capacity of the family system to adapt to change; it means much more than restoring the system to a previous balance or accustomed level of functioning. A disturbed individual's symptomatic behavior unbalances the family homeostasis and at the same time reflects emotional distortions within the entire family. A "failure of **complementarity**" to use Ackerman's term, characterizes the roles played by various family members in respect to each other. Change and growth within the system become constricted. Roles become rigid, narrowly defined, or stereotyped—or shift rapidly, causing confusion. According to Ackerman, the family in which this occurs must be helped to "accommodate to new experiences, to cultivate new levels of complementarity in family role relationships, to find avenues for the solution of conflict, to build a favorable self-image, to buttress critical forms of defense against anxiety, and to provide support for further creative development" (Ackerman, 1966, pp. 90–91).

Family difficulties arise, Ackerman (1966) noted, not only when family roles are not "complementary" but also when there is stalemated or otherwise unresolved "conflict" and when a family engages in "prejudicial scapegoating." For a family's behavior to be stable, flexibility and adaptability of roles is essential; roles within the family, which change over time, must allow for maturing children to gain an appropriate degree of autonomy. Conflict may occur at several levels—within an individual family member, between members of the nuclear family, between generations including the extended family, between the family and the surrounding community. Inevitably, according to Ackerman's observations, conflict at any level reverberates through the family system. What begins as a breakdown of role complementarity may lead to interpersonal conflict within the family and ultimately to intrapsychic conflict in one or more individual members; the individual's conflict deepens if the internalized family conflicts are persistent and pathogenic in form. One of Ackerman's therapeutic goals was to interrupt this sequence by extrapolating intrapsychic conflict to the broader area of family interaction.

Should the conflict between members become chronic, the family is at risk of reorganization into competing factions. The process often gets underway when one individual—often noticeably different from the others—becomes the family scapegoat or "whipping post." As that individual is singled out and punished for causing family disunity, various realignments of roles follow

Nathan Ackerman, M.D.

within the family. One member becomes "persecutor," another may take the role of "healer" or "rescuer" of the "victim" of such "prejudicial scapegoating." Families are thus split into factions and different members may even play different roles at different times, depending upon what Ackerman considers the shared unconscious processes going on within the family at any particular period of time. Typically, observed Ackerman, such family alliances and interpersonal conflicts begin with a failure of complementarity within the marital dyad; the family is precluded from functioning as a cooperative, supportive, integrated whole. In cases such as these, Ackerman's therapeutic mission was to shift a family's concern from the scapegoated person's behavior to the basic disorder of the marital relationship.

In an early paper, Ackerman (1956) presented a conceptual model of **interlocking pathology**[1] in family relationships, arguing for family sessions in which such entanglements could be pointed out to the family members as they occurred so they could begin to work toward eliminating them. Concerned with the impact of the family environment on the development of childhood disorders, Ackerman was one of the first to note the constant interchange of unconscious processes taking place between family members as they are bound

[1]The pattern of interlocking pathology had long been known to therapists, many of whom had made the disquieting observation that sometimes when a patient improved, his or her marriage failed (Walrond-Skinner, 1976). This seemed to suggest that, prior to treatment, the patient had felt locked into a neurotic relationship; after treatment, he or she was no longer willing to take part in the dysfunctional interaction and felt free—and able—to leave the marriage. If in the course of psychoanalytic treatment a spouse became upset in response to the changes occurring in the patient, individual therapy with another therapist was the usual recommendation. It is not surprising that under this approach, a patient's "improvement" was viewed as a threat to other family members who might proceed to subtly undermine the therapeutic progress. It was not until family therapy began to be practiced that all of the persons involved in a family were treated together.

together in a particular interpersonal pattern. Accordingly, any single member's behavior can be a symptomatic reflection of possible confusion and distortion occurring in the entire family. With notions such as "interlocking pathology," Ackerman—by training a Freudian but personally inclined to attend to social interaction—was able to wed many of the psychoanalytic concepts of intrapsychic dynamics to the psychosocial dynamics of family life.

Ackerman's broadly based therapeutic approach utilized principles from biology, psychoanalysis, social psychology, and child psychiatry. Unaffected and deceptively casual in manner, Ackerman tried through a series of office interviews and home visits to obtain a firsthand diagnostic impression of the dynamic relationships among family members. Hearty, confident, unafraid to be himself or to disclose his own feelings, he was apt to bring out these same qualities in the family. Soon the family was dealing with sex, aggression, and dependency, the issues it previously avoided as too threatening and dangerous.

To watch Ackerman on film or videotape is to see an honest, warm, straightforward, provocative, charismatic person at work in the very midst of the family, challenging a prejudice, coming to the aid of a scapegoated child, helping expose a family myth or hypocrisy, vigorously supplying the emotional ingredients necessary to galvanize a previously subdued family. No topic is taboo or off limits, no family rules so sacred they cannot be broken, nothing so shameful as to be unmentionable. Labeled as a "conductor" type of family therapist by Beels and Ferber (1969), Ackerman is said to lend the family "his pleasure in life, jokes, good sex and limited aggression."

The following brief excerpt is from a therapy session with a family whose crisis was brought on when the 11-year-old daughter threatened to stab her 16-year-old brother and both parents with a kitchen knife. This explosive attack was precipitated by the girl's discovery of a conspiracy among the family members to say that her dog had died when in reality the mother had taken him to the dog pound. Members of the family indulge in many small lies, then cover up and deny their feelings. Note how Ackerman will have none of this charade. He reveals his own feelings in order to cut through the denial and open up the family encounter. The left-hand column is the verbatim account, the right-hand column is Ackerman's analysis of what is taking place:

Dr. A.: Bill, you heaved a sigh as you sat down tonight.

Therapist instantly fastens on a piece of nonverbal behavior, the father's sigh.

Father: Just physical, not mental.

Dr. A.: Who are you kidding?

Therapist challenges father's evasive response.

Father: I'm kidding no one.

Dr. A.: Hmmm . . .

Therapist registers disbelief, a further pressure for a more honest response.

Father: Really not . . . . Really physical. I'm tired because I put in a full day today.

Dr. A.: Well, I'm very tired every day, and when I sigh it's never purely physical.

An example of therapist's use of his own emotions to counter an insincere denial.

Father: Really?

Dr. A.: What's the matter?

Father: Nothing. Really!

Dr. A.: Well, your own son doesn't believe that.

Therapist now exploits son's gesture, a knowing grin, to penetrate father's denial and evoke a deeper sharing of feelings.

Father: Well, I mean, nothing . . . nothing could cause me to sigh especially today or tonight.

Dr. A.: Well, maybe it isn't so special, but . . . . How about it, John?

Therapist stirs son to unmask father.

Son: I wouldn't know.

Now son wipes grin off his face and turns evasive, like father.

Dr. A.: You wouldn't know? How come all of a sudden you put on a poker face? A moment ago you were grinning very knowingly.

Therapist counters by challenging son, who took pot shot from sidelines and then backed away.

Son: I really wouldn't know.

Dr. A.: You . . . . Do you know anything about your pop?

Son: Yeah.

Dr. A.: What do you know about him?

Son: Well, I don't know, except that I know some stuff.

Dr. A.: Well, let's hear.

(Ackerman, 1966, pp. 3–4)[2]

---

[2]From *Treating the Troubled Family,* by N. W. Ackerman. Copyright 1966 by Basic Books, Inc. Reprinted by permission.

Trained as a psychoanalyst, Ackerman retained his interest in each family member's personality dynamics. However, influenced by social psychology, he was impressed by how personality is shaped by the particular social roles people are expected to play. In his approach to families, Ackerman was always interested in how people define their own roles ("What does it mean to you to be a father?") and what they expect from other family members ("How would you like your daughter to react to this situation?"). When all members delineate their roles clearly, family interactions proceed more smoothly. They can rework alignments, engage in new family transactions and cultivate new levels of complementarity in their role relationships.

Ackerman (1966) described a troubled, perplexed, frightened family coming for family therapy; everyone knows something is wrong but they don't know how or why or what to do about it. By tradition they push one individual forward as "sick," although several if not all of the members are disturbed in various ways and to varying degrees. They are in the office because their previous equilibrium or homeostasis has been upset. The therapist tries to nourish hope, to keep them from feeling defeated. Generally speaking, Ackerman sees the therapist's purpose as offering *reeducation, reorganization* through a change in the pattern of communication, and *resolution* of pathogenic conflict as an avenue for inducing change and growth as a family.

Diagnosis and treatment are interwoven in Ackerman's approach. Rather than follow a formal intake procedure, the therapist watches as the family becomes engaged in the therapeutic struggle and listens as relevant historical facts emerge (for example, mental hospitalization of a member, a daughter's abortion never disclosed outside the family circle before, a suicide). The therapist is aware of the family's outer protective mask, the secret pacts to avoid discussing certain subjects, the personalities of each member and their adaptation to family roles, the family emotional climate. Families are usually seen once a week for about an hour each session. According to Ackerman (1966), therapeutic change is often achieved within a period of six months to two years.

Ackerman believed the family therapist's principal job is that of a catalyst who, moving into the "living space" of the family, stirs up interaction, helps the family have a meaningful emotional exchange and at the same time nurtures and encourages the members to understand themselves better through their contact with the therapist. As a catalyst, the therapist must play a wide range of roles from activator, challenger, and confronter to supporter, interpreter, and integrator. Unlike the orthodox psychoanalyst who chooses to remain a neutral, distant, mysterious **blank screen,** Ackerman as family therapist was a vigorous person who engaged a family in the here-and-now and made his presence felt. He moved directly into the path of family conflict, influenced the interactional process, supported positive forces and counteracted negative ones and withdrew as the family began to deal more constructively with its problems.

Diagnostically, Ackerman attempted to fathom a family's deeper emotional currents—fears and suspicions, feelings of despair, the urge for vengeance. Using his personal emotional responses as well as his psychodynamic insights, he gauged what the family was experiencing, discerned its patterns of role complementarity, and probed the deeper, more pervasive family conflicts. By "tickling the defenses," he caught members off guard and exposed their self-justifying rationalizations. In due course, he was able to trace significant connections between the family dysfunction and the intrapsychic anxieties of various family members. Finally, when the members were more in touch with what they were feeling, thinking, and doing individually, Ackerman helped them expand their awareness of alternate patterns of family relationships through which they might discover new levels of intimacy, sharing, and identification.

Object Relations and Families of Origin (Framo)

Another first-generation family therapist whose training and early orientation, like Ackerman's, was psychoanalytic, James Framo (1981) stresses the relationship between the intrapsychic and the interpersonal. Not wishing to disregard the significant contributions made by psychoanalysis to our understanding of an individual's intrapsychic world, Framo nevertheless believes psychoanalytic theory has not paid sufficient attention to the social context of a person's life, particularly the crucial role played by family relationships in shaping individual behavior. Rather than polarize the intrapsychic and the interactional, Framo maintains that both are essential to understanding the dynamic aspects of family life. As he points out in the introduction to a recent collection of his papers (Framo, 1982), his orientation to marital and family theory and therapy emphasizes:

> the psychology of intimate relationships, the interlocking of multi-person motivational systems, the relationship between the intrapsychic and the transactional, and the hidden transgenerational and historical forces that exercise their powerful influences on current intimate relationships (p. IX).

Framo believes that insoluble intrapsychic conflicts derived from one's family of origin continue to be acted out or replicated with current intimates, such as a spouse or children. Indeed, Framo (1981) contends that efforts at the interpersonal resolution of inner conflict (for example, criticizing a spouse harshly for failing to live up to one's wildly inappropriate expectations) are at the very heart of the kinds of distress found in troubled couples and families. By exploring such phenomena, Framo makes use of both dynamic and systems concepts, embracing the personal as well as the social.

Basic to Framo's outlook is the work of Fairbairn (1954) and Dicks (1967) on **object-relations theory.** Fairbairn, an English psychiatrist, postulated that human beings are object-seeking in the sense that they require relationships. He argued that it was a person's need for a satisfying object relationship—not, as Freud had maintained, the gratification of instinctual drives—that constituted the fundamental motive of life. Extrapolating from Fairbairn's proposals, Framo (1976) theorized that a young child who interprets parental behavior as rejection, desertion or persecution is in a dilemma: the child cannot give up the sought-after object (the parents) nor can he or she change that object. Typically, the ensuing frustration is dealt with by internalizing aspects of the "loved-hated"parents in order to control the objects in the child's inner world. These internalized objects, having both good and bad characteristics, are retained as introjects, the psychological representations of external objects.

According to Fairbairn (1954), these internalized objects undergo splits and become part of one's personality structure: good-object introjects remain as pleasing memories, bad-object introjects cause intrapsychic distress. That is, current life situations are unconsciously interpreted in light of one's inner object world of good-bad images. As a result, the person grows up with distorted expectations of others, unconsciously forcing intimates into fitting the internal role models. As Fairbairn illustrates, the earlier the split (resulting, for example, from an early loss of a parent), the more likely that the person will yearn for merger with loved ones so that they become a part of him or her. At the same time, he or she may also yearn for independence and separation, a normal part of growing up, although too much distance may lead to feelings of loneliness and depression. As Framo (1976) confirmed, the more psychologically painful the early life experience, the greater the investment in internal objects, the more an adult will engage in an unconscious effort to make all close relationships fit the internal role models.

Dicks (1967) expanded Fairbairn's object-relations conceptualizations to include the interaction between husband and wife. He proposed that in a disturbed marriage each partner relates to the other in terms of unconscious needs; together they function as a joint personality. In this way each partner attempts to rediscover, through the other, the lost aspects of his or her primary object relations that had split off earlier in life. As Dicks (1967) states:

> The sense of belonging can be understood on the hypothesis that at deeper levels there are perceptions of the partner and consequent attitudes toward him or her *as if* the other was part of oneself. The partner is then treated according to how this aspect of oneself was valued: spoilt and cherished, or denigrated and persecuted (p. 69).

Framo extends object-relations theory even further to include several generations of a single family. A person's current intimates, spouse and children, become shadowy stand-ins for old ghosts, the embodiments of old (parental) introjects (Framo, 1981). These introjects are reprojected onto current family members in the adult's effort to achieve satisfaction by compensating for unsatisfactory early object relations in childhood. As Framo illustrates, one major source of marital disharmony results from spouses who project disowned aspects of themselves onto their mates and then fight these characteristics in the mate. Similarly, he notes, children may be assigned inappropriate family roles based on parental introjects. In some cases, observes Framo, such roles may

James L. Framo, Ph.D.

even be chosen for them before they are born (for example, conceiving a baby in the belief that the offspring will save a shaky marriage).

Therapeutically, Framo begins by treating the entire family, especially when the presenting problem involves the children. However, symptomatic behavior in a child may simply be a means of deflecting attention from a more basic marital conflict. In such cases, once the child's role as identified patient is made clear and the child detriangulated from the parents, Framo (1976) will dismiss the children and proceed to work with the marital dyad. Frequently working with a female co-therapist, Framo insists that couples be seen together. According to his reasoning (Framo, 1981), any advantage to individual meetings (disclosure of secrets, for example) is outweighed by the suspicions aroused in the absent partner or the conflicts of loyalty and confidentiality aroused in the therapist. Conjoint sessions help maintain the integrity of the marital unit.

Framo's unique contribution to family therapy technique is his process of guiding a couple through several treatment stages:[3] couples therapy, couples group therapy, and, finally, family of origin (intergenerational) conferences. The couples group, in which many couples participate soon after they begin treatment, allows Framo to utilize many of the positive aspects of group therapy (see discussion in Chapter 4). That is, he takes advantage of the group process, especially the therapeutic feedback from other couples, to assist his efforts as therapist. In many cases it is far more enlightening and potent for a couple to see its own interaction patterns acted out by another couple than to

[3]For a detailed account of Framo's treatment of a couple, see "In-laws and Out-laws: A Marital Case of Kinship Confusion" in *Family Therapy: Full Length Case Studies*, edited by P. Papp. New York: Gardner Press, 1978.

[handwritten margin note: — Intergenerational therapy: (includes grandparents.)]

hear a therapist merely comment on the same behavior, with no one else present. The group experience has a secondary function of reducing the individual's resistance to the next stage of treatment, which involves a number of family members meeting together.

In a daring therapeutic maneuver, Framo (1976) involves each individual (without the partner present) in sessions with his or her family of origin. Two major goals are involved—to discover what issues or agendas from the family of origin might be projected onto the current family and to have a corrective experience with parents and siblings. Framo (1976) reasons that if adults are able to go back and deal directly with both past and present issues with their original families—in a sense, to come to terms with parents before they die—then they are liberated to make constructive changes in their present family. Usually held toward the end of therapy, family of origin conferences enable individuals to gain insight into the inappropriateness of old attachments, rid themselves of the "ghosts" and respond to spouses and children as individuals in their own right—not as figures on whom they project unresolved issues and introjects from the past.

The Intergenerational-Contextual Approach and The Family Ledger (Boszormenyi-Nagy)

Another family therapy approach that respects transgenerational legacies and influences is the work of Ivan Boszormenyi-Nagy and his associates (Boszormenyi-Nagy & Spark, 1973; Boszormenyi-Nagy & Krasner, 1981; Boszormenyi-Nagy & Ulrich, 1981; Ulrich, 1983). Strongly psychoanalytic in flavor but conceived from the point of view (and written in the language of) existentialism, the approach emphasizes such issues in family relationships as fairness, equitability, trustworthiness and loyalty.

Intergenerational-contextual family therapy was developed by Boszormenyi-Nagy, a psychiatrist who emigrated to the United States from Hungary in 1948, and Geraldine Spark, a psychiatric social worker with an extensive psychoanalytic background and experience in child guidance clinics. Joining together in the mid-1950s and working with families with a wide variety of problems and socioeconomic backgrounds, they slowly advanced a theory and a set of therapeutic techniques that pertained to uncovering and resolving family "obligations" and "debts" incurred over time. They introduced such new (nonpsychoanalytic) terms as "legacy" and "loyalty" to emphasize that family members inevitably acquire a set of expectations and responsibilities toward each other. Figuratively speaking, each person has a sense of unsettled accounts, how much he or she has invested in relationships within the family, and whether there has been a fair balance between what has been given and received. Hardly a strict bookkeeping system, and seldom if ever perfectly balanced, Ulrich (1983) maintains that confronting and redressing imbalances is essential if a marriage is to be kept alive. As an example, Ulrich cites a temporary imbalance: a wife works at an unsatisfying job so her husband can finish law school—but with the expectation that what she has invested in the common fund will eventually be replaced, for their mutual enrichment. Boszormenyi-Nagy and Spark entitled their 1973 book *Invisible Loyalties: Reciprocity in Intergenerational Family Therapy* to emphasize that obligations rooted in past generations need not be explicitly recognized or acknowledged to influence the behavior of family members in the present.

More recently, Boszormenyi-Nagy has chosen the name "contextual therapy" for an expanded therapeutic approach that takes into account the various personality dynamics of individual members as well as the relational dynamics between members over several generations. Basic to this approach is the therapeutic utilization of the ethical dimension of relationships, particularly the emphasis on responsible, trustworthy actions that consider the fair interests of others as well as self-interests. Boszormenyi-Nagy and his colleagues insist that the welfare and entitlements of all parties in all generations of a family be respected; an individual would not be counseled to "do your own thing."

In a sense, every family maintains a "family ledger," a multigenerational account system of who, psychologically speaking, owes what to whom. Whenever injustices occur there is the expectation of some later repayment or restitution. Problems in relationships develop when justice comes too slowly or in an amount too small to satisfy the other person. From this perspective, dysfunctional behavior in any individual cannot be fully understood without looking at the history of the problem, the family ledger, and examining unsettled or unredressed accounts.[4] A symptom that develops might represent an accumulation of feelings of injustice that has grown too large.

Being born into a family binds each person to multigenerational imperatives of what is expected, what he or she will owe, what he or she is owed. The family legacy, then, dictates debts and entitlements. One son may be slated to be successful ("We expect you'll be good at anything you try"), another to become a failure ("We don't think you'll ever amount to much"). A son may be entitled to approval, the daughter only to shame. Because of such family imperatives, as Boszormenyi-Nagy and Ulrich (1981) point out, the children are ethically bound to accommodate their lives somehow to their legacies. Ulrich (1983) gives the following graphic example:

> a son whose familial legacy is one of mistrust among family members, angrily confronts his wife every time she spends any money without his prior approval. He is convinced, and he tries to convince her, that her untrustworthy, spendthrift behavior is going to bankrupt them (p. 193).

In fact, the wife, who works full-time as well as tending to their child, may temporarily unbalance the week's budget but her overall efforts contribute to her husband's solvency. If her response to his anger is fear—a legacy she carries from her own family—she may hide her purchases. His discovery of such concealment reinforces his mistrust; his subsequent anger strengthens her

---

[4]This notion of relational patterns, expectations of entitlement, and family problems transmitted to current families from earlier generations is similar to what Carter and McGoldrick (1980) call "vertical stressors." The concept is discussed more fully in Chapter 1.

Ivan Boszormenyi-Nagy, M.D.

fears. Together their legacies have had a corrosive effect on their marriage. In classical psychoanalytic terms, the husband may be labeled as having a penurious character disorder and the wife as a hysteric. In ledger terms, he is still making payment to his mother's injunction that a wife is not to be trusted. By "overpaying" his mother, he is robbing his wife. She, in turn, may be paying off similar debts. Contextual therapy would direct them to reassess all their relationships, pay off legitimate filial debts, and free themselves from oppressive obligations.

Contextual therapy sorts relationships into four dimensions: (1) facts (race, ethnic background, religion, nationality, plus such historical facts as early death of a parent, divorce, major illness); (2) psychology (what takes place within the person, how one reacts to his or her life's facts by accepting or distorting or denying them); (3) transactions (power alignments within the family, coalitions, triangles, family communication patterns); (4) ethics (justice, fairness, consideration of welfare and survival interests of all family members).

The ethical dimension gives contextual therapy its uniqueness. Insisting that they are not moralizing or taking a judgmental position, practitioners of this approach contend that they offer a realistic strategy for preventing individual and relational imbalance and eventual breakdown. They argue that effective therapeutic intervention must be grounded in the therapist's conviction that trustworthiness is a necessary condition for reworking legacy assessments and allowing family members to feel they are entitled to more satisfying relationships (Boszormenyi-Nagy & Krasner, 1981). They maintain that families cannot be fully understood without an explicit awareness of family loyalty—who is bound to whom, what is expected of all family members, how is loyalty expressed, what happens when loyalty accounts are uneven ("We were there for you when you were growing up and now we, your aging parents, are entitled to help from you").

Contextual therapy helps rebalance the obligations kept in the invisible family ledgers. Once these imbalances are identified, efforts can be directed at settling old family accounts (for example, mothers and daughters "stuck" in lifelong conflict), "exonerating" alleged culprits, transforming unproductive patterns of relating that may have existed throughout the family over many past generations. The major therapeutic thrust is to establish or restore trustworthiness in family relationships. Grandparents may be brought into therapy sessions to redress old injustices. Parental behavior may be reassessed (and forgiven) in light of its roots in the past. Overall, each family member is viewed as someone who is a part of a multigenerational pattern. Each is guided to move in the direction of greater trust. Boszormenyi-Nagy and his co-workers believe it is the ethical dimension of trust within a family that is the invisible thread of both individual freedom and interindividual balance.

Redefining symptomatic behavior as evidence of family loyalty or as the sacrifice of self-development in the interest of the family led Boszormenyi-Nagy and Spark (1973) to describe how certain children in dysfunctional families are delegated to play such age-inappropriate, growth-retarding family roles as "parent," pet, scapegoat, or sexual object (see discussion in Chapter 3). Helm Stierlin, a German psychoanalyst and family therapist, has been particularly interested in how the processes of victimization and sacrifice and of exploitation and counter-exploitation between generations are evident in the development of schizophrenia in a family member. Stierlin (1977) views all members as participating in a system of "invisible accounts" in which

> massive guilt, an immense though thwarted need for repair work as well as revenge, a deeply felt sense of justice or injustice, and of loyalty confirmed or betrayed—all operating largely outside of awareness—become here formidable dynamic forces, influencing the members' every move. And the stakes in this "morality play" are high. On the one side, we find parents who, exploited and crippled by their own parents, attempt to survive by living through their children, crippling them in turn; and, on the other side, we find children who, as self-sacrificing, lifelong victims, gain the power to devastate their parents by inducing deep guilt. The power of loyalty-bound victims presents perhaps the most difficult single problem in the treatment of schizophrenia (p. 228).

Stierlin's concept of the schizophrenic as a delegate, ostensibly permitted to move out of the parental orbit but remaining tied and beholden, bound to his or her parents through "invisible loyalties," meshes nicely with Boszormenyi-Nagy's outlook, particularly the transgenerational influences on individual growth and development. Both theorists advocate a three-generational therapeutic effort, whenever possible, in which breaking through relationship deadlocks, gaining insight, balancing of accounts, and a final reconciliation across generations are the goals.

The Open-Systems, Group-Analytic Approach (Skynner)

According to English psychoanalyst Robin Skynner (1981), families evolving over several generations have important developmental milestones similar to the psychosexual stages in Freud's developmental scheme. A mother who lacked adequate mothering or a father who lacked satisfactory fathering is likely to behave inappropriately when called upon to play a role for which he or she has no internal model. When such a family faces stresses that correspond to repeated failures at parenting over several generations, they are likely to break down and decompensate in their functioning. Since poor relationship skills are likely to be passed along to children, developmental failures and deficits will probably occur over generations.

Skynner believes that adults with relationship difficulties (due to poor role models or other learning deficits) develop unrealistic attitudes toward others because they still carry expectations—Skynner calls them **projective systems**—left over from childhood deficiencies. When such persons select spouses, they base the choice at least in part on the mutual "fit" of the potential partners' projective systems. That is, each partner comes equipped with projections corresponding to the stage at which some aspect of his or her development was blocked; each partner seeks to create through marriage a situation in which the missing experience can be supplied. The danger, of course, is that since each wants the other to fulfill a parental role (and both wish to play the child), the partners are likely to manipulate, fight for control, and become frustrated. One consequence of this struggle between incompatible projective systems may be the diversion of some aspect of the projections onto the couple's offspring—saving the marriage at the expense of a child. In many cases, says Skynner, the child colludes in the process out of a deep, if unconscious, wish to preserve the marriage or the family.

As Skynner practices it, family therapy requires identification of the projective systems as well as removing the projections from the symptomatic child, who is likely to be the identified patient. These projections are returned to the marriage where more constructive resolutions are sought. Clarifying communication, gaining insight into inappropriate expectations, modifying the family structure, teaching new parenting skills are all part of Skynner's therapeutic efforts. In many cases, short-term tactics produce sufficient relief of discomfort and distress; in other situations, longer-term psychoanalytically oriented marital and family therapy (Skynner, 1976) is indicated for those families who can manage the conflict, pain and disruption. In the latter cases, the goal is to facilitate differentiation of the marital partners to the point that they are separate, independent persons enjoying, but no longer simply needing, each other.

Skynner (1981) refers to his therapeutic technique as an "open-systems, group-analytic" approach. He genuinely engages with the family system through a "semipermeable interface" permitting the exchange of personal information between the family members and himself. In order to understand the family "from inside," Skynner believes he must open himself up to its projective system, internalize each member separately through identification and experience personally the suffering and struggles of the family. For Skynner, the key requirement is that the therapist retain a deep awareness of his own identity, strong enough to sustain him in the face of the overwhelming (if transient) emotional arousal in the family as the result of the therapeutic encounter; arousal is particularly intense in therapy with profoundly disturbed families who seek to externalize their pathology.

To Skynner, the therapeutic encounter is an opportunity for growth for both the family and the therapist.[5] The therapist, by being receptive and responsive to the presenting problems of the family and its individual members, learns about their transactions and projective systems. In the process, the family is introduced to the family systems viewpoint and begins to look at symptomatic behavior within a family context. As Skynner becomes aware of emotional responses and fantasies in himself, he slowly responds to the family conflict. Gradually he discloses his own emotions; now he is putting his finger on the "real" family problem—what is *not* communicated, what is missing from the content of the session. In some cases, he may act upon his understanding of the family dynamic, even taking the role of scapegoat. In such instances, he consciously personifies the very emotions the family disowns. Although such a maneuver is carried out cautiously—and only after Skynner and the family have established a good therapeutic alliance—the effect may nevertheless be shocking to the family. As Skynner (1981) explains:

> It is as if the family members have been fleeing from a monster and finally find refuge in the safety of the therapist's room only to discover, as they begin to feel secure and to trust him, that he turns into the monster himself! (p. 61).

By expressing the collusively denied or repressed emotions and by absorbing the projective system of a disturbed family, Skynner experiences its dilemma firsthand; by working out for himself a way of escape, he develops a route the family can follow. In his highly responsive approach to therapy, Skynner combines the principles and techniques of psychoanalysis, group analysis, and social learning (modeling) while retaining an overall view of the family as an ongoing system in need of restructuring.

FAMILY GROUP THERAPY

Related to the psychodynamic outlook is the view, particularly prevalent in the 1960s, that family therapy is a special subset of group therapy. Many of the early pioneers—practitioners and researchers alike—took the position that families are essentially natural groups and that the task of the therapist is to

---

[5]We will return to this interesting idea of the forces and counterforces at work in the interpersonal encounter between families and therapists in Chapter 6, when we consider the viewpoints and practices of experiential/humanistic family therapists, especially Carl Whitaker.

promote interaction, facilitate communication, clarify the group processes, and interpret interpersonal dynamics—much as any group therapy leader would do. John Bell, Lyman Wynne, and Christian Beels are probably the clinicians most closely identified with this psychodynamic group therapy orientation. Bell (1975, 1983) has written most extensively about this approach and we consider his contribution to be representative of the genre.

Social Psychology and Small-Group Behavior (Bell)

John Bell, one of the founding fathers of family therapy, has continued to practice and refine his techniques for over thirty years. A California psychologist affiliated in recent years with the Palo Alto Veterans Administration Hospital and Stanford University, Bell calls his form of intervention **family group therapy** in order to emphasize that he is applying the social-psychological theories of small-group behavior to the natural group that is a family. His practical and simple purpose is to aid the family group (ultimately independent of the therapist) to function more effectively, with fewer constraints binding the members into nonfunctional activities and dysfunctional interactions, with less tension, with more skillful problem solving, and with more (and better) communications. To do this, Bell encourages the family to structure itself into a conference in which unsatisfactory relationships between members are confronted, family goals are clarified, methods for achieving those goals are agreed upon, and the proposed methods are tried until the outcome is mutually satisfactory. Bell remains the facilitator, the process leader, staying outside the family rather than joining it; he helps the family to determine its own goals and move toward them as a group.

To achieve his objectives, Bell (1976) works on process interventions that have the effect of engaging the family and moving it through the natural stages of small, task-oriented group development. Initially, the family group is helped to explore the expectations of its members as they begin to relate to the therapist, who carefully defines the rules of group participation. Even if members decide to proceed as a group, they inevitably test the limits of the rules and question the commitments each member has made and the ways in which each member will participate. Inevitably, a power struggle charged with hostility begins to develop as individuals and coalitions within the family fight to protect their own interests and compete for dominance. Rather than serving as an end in itself—exorcising family demons—the struggle is instrumental to group development and consolidation and to the ultimate emergence of consensus within the family about the problems on which to work. In Bell's view, the family members then constitute a group that has become functional. In the next stage, the family group concentrates its energies on selecting a common task to undertake (for example, getting rid of a particular family annoyance or dealing with an acute family crisis). Bell keeps everyone engaged as they struggle toward a resolution that will accommodate the respective goals of each group member or family subgroup. This is the heart of the treatment: releasing the creativity of each member, overcoming lassitude or the urge to withdraw, resolving impasses, expanding communication, redefining expectations and holding a splintering family together. The goals of therapy are reached when conciliation is achieved among the group participants, pressing problems are resolved and the group separates from the therapist. In Bell's experience, family members then typically tighten the boundaries around their family "by accentuating the strengths and importance of family initiatives, communication, decisions, and other actions" (Bell, 1976, pp. 138–139). Throughout all stages of his work with a family, Bell continues to stress that the locus of the problems amenable to family therapy is in the family and not in the individual members; similarly, outcomes must be evaluated in terms of family well-being.

Bell as process leader provides a model of himself as a listener for others to emulate. He makes opportunities for family members to participate and mirrors back to them the behavior he is observing in the group. He confines the content to family-related subjects, refusing to allow a member to escape by introducing extraneous matters. He adapts to a particular family's pace of development as a group. He encourages exploring and trying out new ways of interacting. Bell insists that the entire family be present for each session, even postponing meetings if any one member cannot attend. After the initial contact he refuses to see or talk by telephone with any one member individually. His purpose is to emphasize that family members are dealing with a family problem and the group as a whole cannot resolve a family problem unless all work together.

Bell's leadership is gentle, sympathetic, respectful, and unemotional. He does not join in or intrude on a family but affirms the ability of its members to develop strategies to solve their own problems and attain their own goals. By remaining outside the family, Bell does not take over another person's role or authority (for example, play father to a child) or make decisions for the family on how it should function. Bell works with a family as a natural group, persons who have shared experiences in the past and who will continue to live together after family therapy is terminated. He sees the family group therapist as an agent of change whose role is to help initiate and monitor the process of change as the family transforms itself into a more perfectly functioning group.

Bell readily admits that his therapy cannot solve all family problems. In recent years (Bell, 1983) he has concentrated his attention on developing methods to help families cope with problems that lie beyond the realm of family interaction. The targets of intervention might be families that include a hospitalized member; families affected adversely by unemployment and poverty, alienated from the mainstream of society, or deprived of adequate support networks; families disturbed by psychosis, character disorders, developmental problems, or physical or mental deterioration. In this work he is moving to create family-enhancing environments—a treatment program he calls **family context therapy.** Rather than treating the family directly, Bell attempts to modify the family's environment (for example, changing the circumstances of a patient's hospitalization so that the family is more closely involved or reorganizing clinical and social services at a hospital or other large institution) toward the goal of improved family functioning.

SUMMARY

Approaches to family therapy can be divided into six groupings—psychodynamic, existential/humanistic, Bowenian, structural, communication, and behavioral. Among the major distinctions, in addition to theoretical orientation, are: whether the emphasis in intervention is on the past or the present; the role unconscious processes play; whether insight or action is stressed; the primary functions of the therapist; the unit of analysis (individual, dyad, triad); and the goals of treatment.

The psychodynamic viewpoint, based largely on a psychoanalytic model, pays attention to the backgrounds and experiences of each family member as much as to the family unit itself. These therapists are concerned with the extent to which individuals are still attached to the past; in their model, a couple's marital distress is related to the pathogenic introjects each partner brings to the relationship.

Nathan Ackerman, a family therapy pioneer, attempts to integrate psychoanalytic theory (with its intrapsychic orientation) and systems theory (emphasizing interpersonal relationships). He views family dysfunction as a failure in role complementarity between members and as the product of persistent unresolved conflict (within and between individuals in a family) and prejudicial scapegoating. His therapeutic efforts are aimed at disentangling such interlocking pathologies. James Framo, another first-generation family therapist, believes that insoluble intrapsychic conflict, derived from the family of origin, is perpetuated in the form of projections onto current intimates such as a spouse or children. Using an object-relations approach, Framo concerns himself with working through and ultimately removing these introjects; in the process he sees couples alone, then in a couples group, and finally holds separate sessions with each partner and the members of his or her family of origin.

Ivan Boszormenyi-Nagy and his associates focus on transgenerational legacies and how influences from the past have a bearing on present-day functioning in all family members. In this view, families have invisible loyalties—obligations rooted in past generations—and unsettled accounts that must be balanced. Boszormenyi-Nagy's contextual therapeutic approach attempts to rebuild responsible, trustworthy behavior, taking into account the entitlements of all concerned. Helm Stierlin, in a related approach, is concerned with how families of schizophrenics maintain such invisible accounts, delegating the identified patient to work out their underlying problems.

Robin Skynner contends that adults with relationship difficulties have developed unrealistic expectations of others in the form of projective systems that are related to childhood deficiencies. Marital partners, often with incompatible projective systems, attempt to create in the marriage a situation where the missing experience can be supplied, the deficiency remediated by the other

partner. Inevitably frustrated, the couple may direct or transmit these projections onto a child, who becomes symptomatic. Skynner's therapeutic efforts,
particularly the extended version, attempt to facilitate differentiation between
marital partners so that each may become more separate and independent.

John Bell, a founder of family therapy, bases his approach on social-psychological theories of small-group behavior. His family group therapy approach
promotes interaction; he facilitates communication, clarifies and interprets,
much as any group therapy leader would do. In recent years, Bell has directed
his attention to helping create family-enhancing environments by means of an
intervention technique he calls family context therapy.

CHAPTER SIX

Theoretical Perspectives: Experiential/ Humanistic Models

Experience, encounter, confrontation, intuition, process, growth, existence, spontaneity, action, the here-and-now moment—these are the concepts used by those family therapists who, in general, shun theory (and especially theorizing) as a hindrance, an artificial academic effort to make the unknowable knowable. They argue that therapeutic change resides in a growth experience and not merely intellectual reflection or insight into the origins of problems. It is the immediacy of the relationship between the family and an involved therapist and the process in which they engage together that catalyzes the growth of the individual family members as well as the family system as a whole.

THE EXPERIENTIAL MODEL

By definition, experiential practitioners tailor their approach to the unique conflicts and behavior patterns of each family with whom they work. There are probably as many ways to provide an experience for accelerating growth as there are variations in family dysfunction. Moreover, there are some differences among therapists. The work of some experiential therapists such as Carl Whitaker (1976b) clearly reflects the psychodynamic orientation of their training and background, though they are careful not to impose any preconceived theoretical suppositions upon families. Others such as Kempler (1981) show evidence of their training in Gestalt therapy under Fritz Perls. Many experiential therapists such as Kaplan and Kaplan (1978) attend to the "individual in context" in the manner of the systems theorists we have discussed in Part I of this book.

All experiential therapists deal with the present rather than the uncovering of the past. Their emphasis is on the here-and-now, the situation as it unfolds from moment to moment between an active and caring therapist and a family.

The interactions among family members and with the therapist are confronted in an effort to help everyone involved in the encounter develop more growth-enhancing behavior. Rather than offer insight or interpretation, the therapist provides an experience—an opportunity for family members to open themselves to spontaneity, freedom of expression, and personal growth. The interpersonal experience is, in itself, the primary stimulus to growth in this approach to psychotherapy.

Experiential/Symbolic Family Therapy (Whitaker)

Carl Whitaker has made outstanding contributions to the field of family therapy. He first made his influence felt with his innovative work in individual psychotherapy, especially his trailblazing efforts to redefine a schizophrenic's symptoms as signs that an individual was "stuck" in the process of growth and was attempting to apply "creative" solutions to vexing interpersonal problems. Co-author of a landmark book, *The Roots of Psychotherapy* (Whitaker and Malone, 1953), Whitaker even then was beginning to be an active therapist providing an experience for growth and maturity for his patients and not simply offering insight to facilitate "adjustment" to society. Whitaker took the daring position, never before espoused, that each participant in therapy is, to some degree, simultaneously patient and therapist to the other. Both invest emotion in the process, both regress, both grow from the experience. The therapist must be committed to his own growth, personally as well as professionally, if he is to catalyze growth in others. As Neill and Kniskern (1982) observed recently, the thesis that a therapist should avoid technique and somehow draw on his own pathology to effect a cure was particularly unsettling to most traditional practitioners at the time.

As Whitaker pursued his unorthodox approach to treating schizophrenics, he became increasingly aware of the key role played by the family in the etiology of the disorder. Broadening his earlier perspective, he began to conceptualize schizophrenia as both an intrapsychic and interpersonal dilemma and to treat his schizophrenic patients along with their families. The multiple-therapist team—an extension of Whitaker's earlier reliance on **co-therapy**—was an innovation that helped to prevent a single therapist from becoming entangled in what Whitaker found to be a powerful, enmeshing family system. Two or more therapists working together afforded this protection and at the same time provided a model for desirable interpersonal behavior for the entire family.

By the mid-1960s Whitaker had moved from Emory University in Atlanta to the University of Wisconsin in Madison and had begun to elaborate his ideas about experiential therapy with families. In particular, he was starting to pay closer attention to what he personally was experiencing in the treatment process; he saw the potential for using that awareness to press for changes in his patients at the same time that he himself continued to benefit by investing in the therapeutic encounter. As Whitaker's students and colleagues Neill and Kniskern (1982) describe it, his thought processes over several decades have evolved from the intrapsychic to the interpersonal, from the individual to the family, from "psyche to system."

Carl Whitaker, M.D.

Whitaker now refers to his therapeutic approach as **experiential/symbolic family therapy** (Keith and Whitaker, 1982). The basic assumption is that families are changed as a result of their experiences, not through education. Because most of our experiences occur outside of our awareness or consciousness, we can only gain access to them nonverbally or symbolically, through unstated but impactful processes occurring within the family. However, Whitaker insists that both real and symbolic curative factors operate in therapy. As we have noted, Whitaker takes a nontheoretical approach to psychotherapy. He actually likens himself to a garage mechanic, presumably indicating that he listens, observes, stays in touch with what he is experiencing and actively intervenes to repair damage, without being concerned over why the breakdown occurred. He makes an effort to depathologize human experience, as suggested by his view of schizophrenia. He believes "psychopathology" arises from the same mechanisms that produce "normal" behavior.

For Whitaker, the focus of therapy is on the process—what occurs during the family session—and how each participant (himself included) experiences feelings and changes in behavior. Whenever an individual or family system seeks to grow, the therapist (or co-therapists) can take advantage of this inherent drive toward fulfillment and maturity to engage that person or group in an existential encounter free from the usual social restraints and the role playing that customarily characterizes doctor–patient or therapist–client relationships. The encounter is intended to shake up old ways of feeling and behaving and thus to provide an upsetting experience in order to reactivate the seemingly dormant but innate process of growth.

Whitaker, iconoclastic in view and creative—sometimes outrageous—in dealing with families, has been described by Minuchin (1982) as using "humor, indirection, seduction, indignation, primary process, boredom, and even falling asleep as equally powerful instruments of contact and challenge (p. ix)." Though they may appear to be chosen at random and though Whitaker himself may not always consciously know why he did or said something (he claims his therapy is controlled by his unconscious), his interventions consistently challenge the symbolic meaning that people give to events. In response to such challenges, creative solutions to problems and new arrangements among family members may arise. His provocative "psychotherapy of the absurd" is intended to shock, mystify, confuse, and induce chaos; in systems terms, the therapist is using positive feedback to activate a stalled system and accelerate disruption, believing that in the reconstitution the symptoms will disappear. In a certain sense, Whitaker is the Zen master offering *koans*—riddles or puzzles for the novice to contemplate—and in the process stimulating a nonlinear and nonlogical way of thinking that will bring enlightenment.

Whitaker (1975) has likened the use of the absurd to the Leaning Tower of Pisa. If someone comes in offering an absurd statement, he will accept it, build on it, escalate it until the tower becomes so high and so tilted that it crashes. If a woman tells Whitaker "I can't stand my husband," he will agree that men are difficult but then ask "Why haven't you divorced him?" or "Why not try an interim boyfriend?" If she answers that she loves her husband, Whitaker will respond "Of course, that's why you'd have an affair—to prove your love and to stimulate his love until it equals yours." Should she respond with "But I love my kids," the therapist will say "Well, if you do, then you should make a sacrifice by leaving them so they'll learn that father also loves them." Her answer "He'll neglect them" is met with the rejoinder "Then you can prove your love of them by suing him for child neglect." Ultimately the tower of absurdity comes crashing down, frequently with the woman saying something like "Carl, you're crazy, but I think I see what you're talking about. I really couldn't stand my husband, the rat. I would have left him long ago, but there must be something about him that makes me go on loving him." In this manner Whitaker provides an enlightenment experience; the patient develops a deeper awareness of the absurdity of certain aspects of her view of the marriage.

Family therapy (Whitaker, 1977) occurs in stages[1]: (1) a *pre-treatment phase* in which the entire nuclear family is expected to participate; the co-therapists establish that they are in charge during the sessions but that the family must make its own life decisions outside of these office visits (the latter is intended to convey the message that a therapist does not have better ideas for how family members should run their lives than they themselves do); (2) a *mid-phase* in which increased involvement between both therapists and the family develops; care is taken by the therapist not to be absorbed by the family system; symptoms are relabeled as efforts toward growth; the family is incited to change by means of confrontation, exaggeration, anecdote, or absurdity; (3) a

---

[1]Napier and Whitaker provide an intriguing full account of family therapy with the Brice family (two parents, a suicidal, runaway, teenage daughter, an adolescent son, and a 6-year-old daughter) in their book, *The Family Crucible*. New York: Harper & Row, 1978.

late phase in which increased flexibility in the family necessitates only minimal intervention from the therapy team; and (4) a *separation phase* in which the therapists and family part, but with the acknowledgement of mutual interdependence and loss.

Whitaker's change-producing interventions have a covert, implicit quality. Symptoms are rarely attacked directly. Insight seems to follow changes in feelings and behavior, not precede such changes. History taking is occasionally important but not carried out routinely; in any case, it must not be allowed to impede Whitaker's major therapeutic thrust—forming a close and personal alliance with the family as a whole and providing an experience that is symbolic to the family but does not reinforce its distress (Keith & Whitaker, 1982). What the family therapist has most to offer, believes Whitaker, is his or her personal maturity; the stage of the therapist's personal development has an influence on the kind of support or assistance provided to the family. Whitaker maintains that the therapist who does not derive benefit, therapeutically, from his or her work has little to give, therapeutically speaking, to client families. The use of co-therapists adds another dimension; the ability of both therapists to join together, have fun together, disagree or even fight with each other, perhaps go off on different tangents—one acting "crazy" and the other providing stability—is a model for spontaneous and productive interaction.

In recent years, Whitaker has included grandparents or other extended family members in his therapeutic endeavors with families. In part an effort to help a family come to grips with its continuity over time, in part an effort by Whitaker to expand his own personal growth, the participation of members of three generations may be especially effective when family therapy has reached an impasse. In such situations grandparents may be invited as assistants to the therapist, not as patients. Whitaker may even say to the family, "We want your grandparents in to help us; we are failing" (Whitaker, 1976a). Typically a part of the mid-phase of treatment, Whitaker uses this maneuver to overcome an "impotence impasse" in which the therapist feels stymied and in need of outside help. Symbolically, grandparents are apt to be seen more as real people than as threatening authority figures. Their acknowledgement that their children are in fact adults may have therapeutic value for the members of all generations. Similarly, the discovery that elderly parents are capable of running their own lives may have many liberating consequences for their children.

Throughout his work with individuals and families, Whitaker has stressed his personal need to "stay alive" as a human being and as a therapist. Toward that goal, he has offered the following set of rules:

1. Relegate every significant other to second place.
2. Learn how to love. Flirt with any infant available. Unconditional positive regard probably isn't present after the baby is three years old.
3. Develop a reverence for your own impulses, and be suspicious of your behavior sequences.

4. Enjoy your mate more than your kids, and be childish with your mate.
5. Fracture role structures at will and repeatedly.
6. Learn to retreat and advance from every position that you take.
7. Guard your impotence as one of your most valuable weapons.
8. Build long-term relations so you can be free to hate safely.
9. Face the fact that you must grow until you die. Develop a sense of the benign absurdity of life—yours and those around you—and thus learn to transcend the world of experience. If we can abandon our missionary zeal we have less chance of being eaten by cannibals.
10. Develop your primary process living. Evolve a joint craziness with some-one you are safe with. Structure a professional cuddle group so you won't abuse your mate with the garbage left over from the day's work.
11. As Plato said, "practice dying." (Whitaker, 1976b, p. 164)

Gestalt Family Therapy (Kempler)

All of the family therapy approaches we are considering in this chapter are, to a greater or lesser extent, existential in character. More an orientation to understanding human behavior than a formal school of psychotherapy, exis-tentially influenced therapies are concerned with entering and comprehend-ing the world as it is being experienced by the individual family members as well as the family as a functioning whole. The therapies have in common an emphasis on the meaning the patient gives to existence, to being. Because people define themselves through their current choices and decisions, action in the present, not reflection on the past, is the key to understanding for the existentialist. Even the future—what people choose to become—is charged with more influence than the past and the conflicts associated with the past. In existential therapies, patients examine and take responsibility for their lives. Unconscious material may be brought forth but is not automatically assumed to be any more meaningful than the conscious data of life.

Psychotherapy in this framework is an encounter between two or more persons who are constantly developing, evolving, and fulfilling their inner potential. Technique is deemphasized to preclude one person seeing the other as an object to be analyzed. In contrast to the common therapeutic belief that understanding stems from technique, existentialist therapists believe that tech-nique follows understanding. Formal and conventional doctor–patient roles are replaced by a more egalitarian and open arrangement in which each par-ticipant opens his or her world to the other as an existential partner. The emphasis is on *presence*; in a real, immediate, ongoing relationship between two or more persons, each tries to understand and experience as far as possible the *being* of the other(s).

If existentialism is concerned with how humans experience their immediate existence, Gestalt psychology focuses on how they perceive it. Having accepted the therapeutic implications of existentialism along with much of the rhetoric of Gestalt psychology, Frederick (Fritz) Perls is generally credited with launch-ing the Gestalt-therapy movement in the United States. An earthy and char-ismatic person, Perls spent the last decade of his life holding numerous dem-

Walter Kempler, M.D.

onstration workshops throughout the country in addition to making tape recordings and films demonstrating his Gestalt techniques; he died in 1970 at age 77. His book *Gestalt Therapy Verbatim* (Perls, 1969) is an edited version of his seminars at Esalen, a growth center in the Big Sur region of California. Although the practice of Gestalt therapy is for most students synonymous with the techniques developed by Perls, this is not always the case. As a matter of fact, the approach assumes that each therapist will discover his or her own unique style and utilize his or her "I"-ness as an essential part of the working relationship. According to the Gestalt approach, the organized whole of a person—his or her Gestalt—must be maintained in an integrated rather than fragmented state. In the process of attaining this wholeness, aspects of the personality that once were disowned are identified and reclaimed. Self-awareness is the means by which change is accomplished. Self-defeating tendencies must be recognized; emotional blocks to self-understanding removed; moment-to-moment feelings expressed. As self-awareness increases, so does a sense of self-direction. The Gestalt approach holds that through life experiences and observations of others a person internalizes the values by which he or she wants to live. Once a person's inner resources are mobilized, they are assumed to be more than adequate for coping with life's problems.

The therapist's role in Gestalt therapy is to help clients become aware of *how* they use their resources ineffectively and to point out *what* they do to block achievement of their goals, not to tell clients *why* they act in certain ways. Explanations and interpretations of self-defeating behavior based on the recovery of past memories or on historical reports are considered irrelevant to learning to change ineffective behavior patterns. As Walter Kempler (1982) insists, the focus must remain on the immediate moment: "what people say, how they say it, what happens when it is said, how it corresponds with what they are doing, and what they are attempting to achieve (p. 141)." Therapeutic intervention, addressed to current conflict, consists of bringing discordant elements into the open and confronting the incongruence.

Gestalt therapy, historically speaking, has dealt primarily with intrapersonal issues and responsibilities. In recent years a number of Gestaltists such as Hatcher (1978), Kaplan and Kaplan (1978), and especially Kempler (1974, 1981, 1982) have urged that more attention be paid to interpersonal processing. Kempler (1982), a California psychiatrist, has gone so far as to declare that in a dynamic sense there is no such thing as an "individual"—our existence and survival are derived from and wholly dependent upon our mutual connections and relations.

Gestalt family therapy represents an effort to blend some of the principles and procedures of family and Gestalt therapies in order to help people reach beyond their customary self-deceptive games, defenses, and facades. The goal here is to guide them, frequently by the therapist's own forthright behavior, to become aware of and release feelings; ideally, family members become aware of their reciprocal influence on each other, the identified patient's symptoms are ameliorated, and the family learns new ways of working and living together.

Kempler's (1981) therapeutic efforts are provocative, highly personal, uncompromisingly honest, and powerful. Kempler presses for self-disclosure by family members, expecting that the wish or need to resolve their problems or improve relationships will give them the courage to expose their vulnerabilities. He actively and directly insists that everyone, therapist included, become more intensely aware of what they are doing or saying or feeling. Like the mechanic who would rather listen to a troublesome engine than hear a description of it, Kempler first starts up a family conversation:

Transcript	*Comments*
Mother: Our 15-year-old son Jim has been making a lot of trouble for us lately.	The healthier the family, the more readily they talk to each other. For instance, should Jim respond immediately to his mother's charge with, "That's not true!", it would indicate that he has both self-confidence and the hope of being heard. Let's assume Jim doesn't leap in.
Therapist (to Jim evocatively): Do you agree that the number one problem in this family is that you are a troublemaker?	
Jim: Not really.	

Therapist: Tell her what you think it is.

Jim: It's no use.

Therapist (to Mother): Do you have anything to say to his hopelessness?

Mother: I think we've said all there is to say.

Family members are often reluctant to engage one another, particularly initially. The therapist perseveres by offering himself, if necessary.

Therapist (to Jim): I'd like to know what you think is the problem, Jim.

Jim: They're too rigid.

The battlelines often have both parents on one side. It is better when it is a free-for-all.

Therapist: Both of them identical?

Jim: Mother more than Father.

Therapist: Then, maybe you can get some help from him.

Jim: He's too weak. He always gives in to her.

Therapist (to Father): Do you agree with Jim?

Father: Of course not.

Therapist: You didn't tell him.

(Kempler, 1974, pp. 27–28)

Kempler is interested in what each person wants and from whom, expressed in the most specific terms possible. Participants are forced to talk to each other. If a wife complains to Kempler that her husband lacks understanding or sensitivity, Kempler directs her to tell that to her husband, not the therapist, and to be specific in her complaint. If she argues that it will do no good, Kempler insists she tell *that* to her husband. If she then breaks down, admits her feelings of hopelessness and begins to cry—all without provoking a response from her husband—Kempler will point out his silence and invite him to answer her. From the initial interview through the subsequent sessions, the focus remains the immediate present. Self-disclosure and open, honest exchanges with others are basic ground rules for family members to follow if they are to untangle a family problem or overcome an impasse.

✳ Viewing the individual within his or her functional context—the family—
Gestalt family therapists attempt to help each family member achieve maximum individuation at the same time as they promote more vital relationships
among the various members. Thus, the traditional goals of the Gestalt therapist
working with an individual client (growth of the individual and the development of a distinct sense of self) are combined with objectives for the family
group as a whole. First helping family members to explore how their awareness is blocked, the therapist then channels the increased awareness so that
they may engage in more productive and fulfilling processes with one another
(Kaplan & Kaplan, 1978).

The Gestalt therapist facilitates self-exploration, risk-taking, spontaneity.
Since such undertakings are all but impossible if an individual or family fears
that self-discovery could be harmful, it is essential that the therapist provide an
unchecked and unequivocal model for self-disclosure. To strike the familiar
pose as a benevolent and accepting therapist only plays into the client's fantasies that disapproval is dangerous, according to Kempler (1982). By contrast,
Kempler is emotionally intense, assertive, genuine, challenging, sometimes
brutally (if refreshingly) frank; in short, he expresses whatever he is feeling at
the moment in the hope of making an impact on the family. As the following
excerpt from a couple's therapy session begins, Kempler has just completed a
moving exchange with the wife, during which the husband remained silent.
Kempler now turns to the husband because he wants his participation:

Transcript	Comments

Therapist: Where are you?

He: I don't know (pause) I was thinking of something else (pause) I don't
understand what is going on. I
guess that's it (pause) partly thinking what I had to do today.

He was always inarticulate, always
speaking haltingly and tentatively.
His eyes blinked nervously as if he
were being buffeted. I had mentioned
this before. On past occasions I had
confronted him with his inarticulate-
ness and his blinking, but we had
made no progress with it. It seemed
that I had tried everything I knew to
no avail.

Therapist: Damn that makes me angry. You're a clod. That's the word I
want to buffet you with. Damn you.
So insensitive. No wonder you've
got problems in your marriage.
(Then, cooling down enough to
make an "I" statement instead of
the "you" accusations, I continued) I
want you to hear; I want you to join

in; I want you to at least acknowledge our presence some way other than leaving. At best, I'd want you to appreciate us in what happened, at worst, to tell us you don't like us for being inane, but not just to abandon us.

He: (Thoughtful) Earlier I was aware of something like envy (pause) resentment (pause) I don't know.

Therapist: (Still angry) You never know. That's your standard answer. Now I don't know. I don't know what the hell to do with you to get in touch with you.

He: I'm sorry. (pause) I always say I'm sorry. I guess I'm sorry. I was envious. (pause) I felt angry 'cause I was envious.

He was trying to be with me now, and I wanted to try harder myself. I decided to try clarifying and/or intensifying his statement.

Therapist: Try on: "I long to be close to both of you, but I never learned how."

I felt my own sadness when I said that and knew I was on target—or else I would not have been so angry with him. His tears were confirmation as he choked up trying to say the sentence.

Therapist: You don't have to, but I wish you could talk to us now.

He: I can't. It's too sad.

Therapist: It?

He: I'm too sad every time I think of it.

Therapist: It?

He: The sentence . . .

Therapist: Then try to include all the words "I'm so sad when I think of how I long to be close and can't because I never learned."

I kept wanting to return to this key phrase and yet I did not want my urging to become more central for him than his experiencing his longing. He sat thoughtfully, still tearing and saying nothing. Several minutes passed.

Therapist: I'm suddenly aware of my own difficulty in speaking about longing. I could debate with you more easily than I can speak of feeling the longing to be close. I realize I still haven't spoken of mine and can only hesitantly speak about yours.

This feels better than debating or idly chatting but it sure is sad.

I feel closer to you in our sadness.

He: (Finally) I can do it with my car—feeling close by racing people . . . I'm so safe that way. I can't just be close.

Therapist: (I seemed finished with me for the moment and was free to turn once again to him. I offered the sentence again—modified.) "I long to be close but never learned how, but now I'm learning finally."

I began to cry. He was now trying harder to look at me through his tears. I found myself smiling through my tears.

"It," I thought. How clever.

He nodded, still unable to speak.

He began to cry more heavily as he nodded his head and turned inward again, looking down. His wife reached out warmly, "This reminds me of the time that you . . ." I interrupted her, "Leave him alone now. You can talk to him later." She grasped, or at least readily accepted, my command. I wanted him to be wherever he was with his feelings, not diverted to some other time and place. Her comment sounded like an "aha" announcement and I felt no compunction to honor it. She could keep it to and for herself.

I left them and was visiting my father, fluttering through historical scenes like a hummingbird. His lovingly tousling my hair—the only times he ever touched me that I could recall. His angrily shouting at me. His intellectual lectures to teach me something. I became painfully aware of his absent touch and never being spoken to affectionately by him. He never told me he loved me or even that he liked me. I recalled the surprise I once felt when I overheard him admiring me to one of his friends. I am sad. Of course, I long.

I came back to our session and was aware of this couple once again. They were both looking at me. I shared my thoughts. Then he related clearly, articulately his own longings, recalling, smiling through his fresh tears, his father teaching him to drive, the only closeness he knew with his father. To intensify his experience, I suggested that he envision his father. He couldn't. He just cried. "Tell him," I suggested, "how you longed to be close to him but just didn't know how because you never learned." After a long pause, he replied: "I used to feel angry and frustrated. I realize now he never learned either."

He was integrating and I was pleased. I became vacant, and we all sat silently, alone and close (Kempler, 1981, pp. 11–13).

THE HUMANISTIC MODEL

Humanistically oriented clinicians conceptualize dysfunctional behavior as the result of a deficit in growth. They point to an arrest in self-development (or somewhat more specifically, in self-awareness or self-direction) or to a failure to actualize one's inherent potential as the explanation for all current psychological problems. In general, they define a mature person as a rational being (rather than one driven by irrational forces) who is capable of making conscious choices on the basis of his or her intentions (rather than being directed by unresolved unconscious conflicts) and who is able to plan for the future (and not simply fall victim, as an adult, to problems from the past). From the humanistic viewpoint, growth is a natural and spontaneous process occurring in all human beings, given an environment that encourages it; psychological disorders represent a failure to fulfill potential for growth.

The theories presented in this section may be considered phenomenological. The philosophy of phenomenology contends that understanding another person requires an understanding of that individual's perception of a situation, not simply the physical reality of the situation. Phenomenologists insist that behavior is determined by personal experience and by individual perception rather than by external reality. Thus, behavior that appears irrational and confused to an outside observer may seem reasonable and purposeful to the person experiencing the situation; the action may seem to the actor to be the most appropriate and effective behavior he or she can muster under the circumstances, although it seems to others to be based on faulty perceptions. With such an orientation, all behavior makes sense; it reflects the client's perception of reality, the only reality he or she can know. The humanistic family therapist takes on the task of enriching a family's experiences and enlarging the possibilities for each family member to realize his or her unique and extraordinary potential.

The Process/Communication Approach (Satir)

Virginia Satir's central place in the history of the family therapy movement has been noted several times earlier in this book. In 1959 Satir, a psychiatric social worker, launched at the MRI what was probably the first formal training program in family therapy (Satir, 1982); in 1964 Satir wrote the first significant description of the conjoint approach (Satir, 1964). Along with Ackerman, Satir is usually named as one of the earliest and most charismatic leaders of the field (Beels & Ferber, 1969). Over a 30-year span, she has continued to be a prolific writer and is especially celebrated for her inspiring family therapy demonstrations (often billed as "the Satir experience") around the world. Although linked to the communication approach because of her MRI affiliation, Satir's later work at Esalen, a growth center, encouraged her to emphasize feelings and to

Virginia Satir, M.S.W.

adopt a humanistic framework for her efforts at clarifying family communication patterns. In her latest writing, Satir (1982) identifies her approach as a "process model" in which the therapist and family join forces to stimulate a health-promoting process in the family.

Satir concerns herself with the family as a balanced system. In particular, she wants to determine "the price" each part of the system "pays" to keep the overall unit balanced. That is, she views any symptom in an individual member as signaling a blockage in growth, and as having a homeostatic connection to a family system that requires blockage and distortion of growth in some form in all of its members to keep its balance. To Satir (1982), the rules that govern a family system are related to how the parents go about achieving and maintaining their own self-esteem; these rules, in turn, shape the context within which the children grow and develop their own sense of self-esteem. Building self-esteem, promoting self-worth, exposing and correcting discrepancies in how the family communicates—these are the issues Satir tackles as she attempts to help each member of the family develop "wellness" and become as "whole" as possible. The humanistic influence of the human-potential movement on these goals is unmistakable.

One of Satir's contributions is her classification of styles of communication. Under stress, a person in a relationship with another person communicates in one of five ways, according to Satir's scheme (Satir, Stachowiak, and Taschman, 1975). The *placater* always agrees, apologizes, tries to please; the *blamer* dominates, finds fault, and accuses; the *super-reasonable* person remains detached, calm, cool, not emotionally involved; the *irrelevant* person distracts others and seems unable to relate to anything going on; only the *congruent* communicator seems real, genuinely expressive, responsible for sending straight (not double-binding or other confusing) messages. Various combinations of these styles exist in most families. For example, take the case of a blaming wife, a blaming husband and a placating child triad: "It's the school, they don't teach anything anymore"; "It's the child down the street, that's where she's learned those bad words"; "It's the way you've raised her, she's just like you"; "I'll try to do better, Daddy, you're absolutely right. I'll stop watching TV tomorrow, go to the library . . . leave the dishes and I'll do them tomorrow after school." In a blamer/super-reasonable couple, the wife might complain bitterly "We hardly ever make love anymore, don't you have any feelings for me?" The husband might respond coldly "Of course I do or I wouldn't be married to you. Perhaps we define the word 'love' differently." In the case of a conversation between a super-reasonable parent ("Let's discuss precisely why you seem to be having difficulties with your math problems tonight") and the irrelevant child ("It's time for my shower now"), nothing gets settled or resolved and the tension is maintained if not increased. Table 6–1 illustrates Satir's four-stance model of dysfunctional family communication.

Satir maintains that these roles are essentially poses that keep distressed people from exposing their true feelings because they lack the self-esteem that would allow them to be themselves. Placaters are afraid to risk disapproval if they speak up or disagree or act in any way independent of a parent or spouse. Blamers also feel endangered and react by attacking in order to cover up feeling empty and unloved themselves. Super-reasonable people only feel safe at a distance and rely on their intellect to keep from acknowledging that they too have feelings and are vulnerable. Irrelevant people (often a youngest child in a family or a family pet) gain approval only by acting cute and harmless.

Satir tends to work with families in terms of their members' day-to-day functioning and their emotional experiences with each other. She teaches people congruent ways of communicating by helping to restore the use of their senses and the ability to get in touch with and accept what they are really feeling. Thus, she helps individuals (and families) build their sense of self-worth; she opens up possibilities for making choices and bringing about changes in relationships (Bandler, Grinder, & Satir, 1976).

Because Satir believes human beings have within them all the resources that they need in order to flourish, Satir directs her interventions at helping families gain access to their nourishing potentials—and then learn to use them. This is a growth-producing approach in which she encourages people to take whatever risks are necessary in order to take charge of their own lives. Early in the treatment process, Satir presents herself as a teacher introducing the family to a new language, helping them to understand their communication "discrepancies," blocking the kinds of repetitive sequences that end with members falling into the family roles discussed above.

A presenting symptom in a family member gives Satir the initial clues for "unraveling the net of distorted, ignored, denied, projected, unnourished, and untapped parts of each person so that they can connect with their ability to

TABLE 6-1. Four Dysfunctional Communication Stances Adopted under Stress (Satir)

Category	Caricature	Typical verbal expression	Body posture	Inner feeling
Placater	Service	"Whatever you want is okay. I'm just here to make you happy."	Grateful, bootlicking, begging, self-flagellating	"I am like a nothing. Without you I am dead. I am worthless."
Blamer	Power	"You never do anything right. What is the matter with you?"	Finger pointing, loud, tyrannical, enraged	"I am lonely and unsuccessful."
Super-Reasonable	Intellect	"If one were to observe carefully, one might notice the workworn hands of someone present here."	Monotone voice, stiff, machine-like, computer-like	"I feel vulnerable."
Irrelevant	Spontaneity	Words unrelated to what others are saying. For example, in midst of family dispute: "What are we having for dinner?"	In constant movement, constant chatter, distracting	"Nobody cares. There is no place for me."

Adapted from R. Bandler, J. Grinder, and V. Satir, *Changing with Families*, Palo Alto, Calif.: Science and Behavior Books, 1976.

cope functionally, healthily, and joyously" (Satir, 1982, p. 41). What she offers is acceptance and a non-judgmental attitude, believing that as a consequence family members will begin to explore their patterns and change the destructive (for example, blamer–placater) transactions that leave no one happy or satisfied. To tap the individuals' nourishing potentials, Satir works at eight different levels: physical, intellectual, emotional, sensual, interactional, contextual, nutritional, spiritual. Each approach is important, from the tactile contact with one needy family member to the spiritual experience required by another.

Satir's primary talent is as a therapist with a remarkable ability to communicate clearly and perceptively. She is a vigorous, down-to-earth person who engages a family authoritatively from the first session onward. She speaks simply and directly, keeps up a running account of what she is doing with the family, tries to pass along her communication skills to family members, then arranges encounters between members according to the rules she has taught them. In the following example from an early family session (Satir, 1967) the parents and their children, Johnny, age 10, and Patty, age 7, are being seen together; Johnny, the identified patient, is having behavior problems at school. Satir wants to clarify what ideas each member has about what to expect from therapy and why each is there. Note how she tries to help the family members: (1) to recognize individual differences among them by having each member speak for himself or herself; (2) to accept disagreements and differing perceptions of the same situation; and, most important, (3) to say what they see, think, and feel in order to bring disagreements out into the open.

Patty: Mother said we were going to talk about family problems.
Therapist: What about Dad? Did he tell you the same thing?
Patty: No.
Therapist: What did Dad say?
Patty: He said we were going for a ride.
Therapist: I see. So you got some information from Mother and some information from Dad. What about you, Johnny. Where did you get your information?
Johnny: I don't remember.
Therapist: You don't remember who told you?
Mother: I don't think I said anything to him, come to think of it. He wasn't around at the time, I guess.
Therapist: How about you, Dad? Did you say anything to Johnny?
Father: No, I thought Mary had told him.
Therapist: (to Johnny) Well, then, how could you remember if nothing was said.
Johnny: Patty said we were going to see a lady about the family.
Therapist: I see. So you got your information from your sister, whereas Patty got a clear message from both Mother and Dad.
   (Shortly, she asks the parents what they remember saying.)
Therapist: How about that, Mother? Were you and Dad able to work this out together—what you would tell the children?

Mother: Well, you know, I think this is one of our problems. He does things with them and I do another.

Father: I think this is a pretty unimportant thing to worry about.

Therapist: Of course it is, in one sense. But then we can use it, you know, to see how messages get across in the family. One of the things we work on in families is how family members communicate—how clearly they get their messages across. We will have to see how Mother and Dad can get together so that Johnny and Patty can get a clear message.

(Later, she explains to the children why the family is there.)

Therapist: Well, then, I'll tell you why Mother and Dad have come here. They have come here because they were unhappy about how things were going in the family and they want to work out ways so that everyone can get more pleasure from family life.

(Satir, 1967, pp. 143–145.)

In this brief excerpt we also see Satir's effort to build self-esteem in each family member and to emphasize that each person is unique and has the right to express his or her own views without another person (for example, a parent) answering for him or her. Warm and caring herself, with a strong set of **humanistic** values, Satir stresses the role of intimacy in family relationships as a vehicle for growth among all family members. A healthy family is a place where members can ask for what they need, a place where needs are met and individuality is allowed to flourish. Dysfunctional families do not permit individuality and members fail to develop a sense of self-worth.

In some cases, Satir initiates a family's treatment by compiling a **family life chronology** to understand the history of the family's development. More often, she gathers information in order to ascertain the way the family members themselves want their family experience to be. What do they seek and what resources have they already developed to achieve it? For the therapist, this information is a key to the process of opening up the family system to the possibilities of growth and change and preparing the members for active participation in creating a new state of existence. As the work progresses, the information gathered early in therapy is discussed openly so that the members understand more clearly the process that brought them to where they are now and what steps are in order to make the changes they desire. As they learn to understand and trust each other, past miscommunications can be uncovered and corrected. The verbal communication among family members begins to accord with the nonverbal behavior. In this respect, the therapist's chief role is to be a model for the desired change. The therapist's messages must be congruent; gestures and tone of voice must match the words.

If parents are models of confused and ambiguous communication, Satir believes the therapist must show them how to change, how to get in touch with their own feelings, how to listen to others, how to ask for clarification if they do not understand another person's message, and so on. Through her gentle, matter-of-fact questioning, Satir enables parents to listen to their children's statements and opinions for the first time and the children to understand their parents' views and behavior. In time, with the feedback process flowing in both directions, congruent communication replaces the blaming, placating, super-reasonable, even irrelevant family communication styles described earlier.

In the final phase of treatment, the therapist assists the family to solidify its changes and gains. In effect, a new family history gives the family the confidence to take further risks toward growth.

In recent years, Satir has been working to supply a systematic rationale for her interventions. With two colleagues who have analyzed and devised a model of Satir's linguistic style with families (Bandler, Grinder, & Satir, 1976), she has begun to identify the key elements in her therapeutic approach: challenging the built-in expectations in the family's existing communication patterns; helping the family members work together to understand what they want in terms of change; preparing the family for a new growth experience; helping the members learn a new family process for coping; and providing the tools they will need to continue the change process after therapy. Most important, she teaches the actual skills necessary to communicate differently as a family. Having learned these skills, family members will be able to cope more creatively and effectively with any new problem or crisis using the strategies they themselves developed during family therapy. In her most recent writings, Satir (1982) discusses specific techniques; for example, directing family members to pose in the way they normally relate to each other—a living sculpture of the family.

SUMMARY

Experiential/humanistic family therapists utilize the immediacy of the therapeutic encounter with family members to help catalyze the family's natural drive toward growth and the fulfillment of the individuals' potentials. Essentially nontheoretical and nonhistorical, the approach stresses action over insight or interpretation, primarily by providing a growth-enhancing experience through family–therapist interactions.

Major practitioners of the experiential approach are Carl Whitaker and Walter Kempler. Whitaker, who some thirty years ago began redefining a schizophrenic's symptoms as signs of arrested growth, has continued in his work with families to stress both intrapsychic and interpersonal barriers to development and maturity. His family therapy approach, often involving a cotherapist, is designed to capitalize on both the real and symbolic experiences that arise from the therapeutic process and is aimed at bringing enlightenment. Claiming that his interventions are largely controlled by his unconscious, Whitaker promotes a "psychotherapy of the absurd" designed to shock, confuse, and ultimately activate a stalled or disrupted family system. In the process he seeks a growth-producing experience for himself, believing that a therapist who does not personally benefit, therapeutically speaking, from the encounter has little to give to client families.

Kempler, a practitioner of Gestalt family therapy, is adamant in dealing only with the "now"—the moment-to-moment immediacy shared by the therapist and the family members. Like most Gestalt therapists, Kempler guides individuals to reach beyond their customary self-deceptive games, defenses, and facades. Uncompromisingly honest himself, he confronts and challenges all family members to explore how their self-awareness is blocked and to channel their increased awareness into more productive and fulfilling relationships with each other.

The most celebrated humanistically oriented family therapist is Virginia Satir. Over a thirty-year period, Satir has been at the forefront of the family therapy movement. Her demonstrations with families—"the Satir experience"—are known around the world. Her approach to families combines her early interest in clarifying communication "discrepancies" between family members with humanistically oriented efforts to build self-esteem and self-worth in all the members. Believing that human beings have within themselves the resources they need in order to flourish, Satir views her task as one of helping people gain access to their nourishing potentials and teaching people to use them effectively.

CHAPTER SEVEN

Theoretical Perspectives: The Bowenian Model

In this and the following three chapters, we examine a number of theories (and corresponding therapeutic techniques) that have in common their view of the family as an ongoing system. Murray Bowen's work can be considered a bridge between the psychodynamically oriented approaches that emphasize self-development, intergenerational issues, and significance of the past and the systems approaches that restrict their attention to the family unit as it is presently constituted and currently interacting. The structuralists (Chapter 8) and strategic therapists (Chapter 9) attend specifically to the family's present organization and alignments and, in general, direct their clinical interventions to problematic situations rather than to the people in them (Madanes & Haley, 1977). The behavior therapists (Chapter 10) also focus on issues of the here-and-now such as interpersonal environments that maintain and perpetuate functional or dysfunctional family patterns.

Family therapists who adopt systems thinking describe the dysfunctional family as a family whose members are caught up in repetitive, destructive games or sequences; no one is able to get "unstuck" from the rules and expectations that govern their relationships. For the family therapist with such an outlook, intervention requires reordering the family system, changing its structure and ways of functioning, removing or rearranging the elements that perpetuate problematic behavior.

FAMILY SYSTEMS THEORY

A key figure in the development of family therapy, Murray Bowen remains today its major theoretician. Since his early clinical work with schizophrenics and their families at the Menninger Foundation as well as at NIMH (see Chapter 4 for details), Bowen has stressed the importance of theory for research, for teaching purposes, and as a blueprint for guiding a clinician's actions during psychotherapy. He is concerned with what he considers the field's lack of a coherent and comprehensive theory of either family development or therapeutic intervention and its all-too-tenuous connections between theory and practice. In particular, Bowen (1978) decries efforts to dismiss theory in favor of an intuitive "seat of one's pants" approach, which he considers to be especially stressful for a novice therapist coping with an intensely emotional, problem-laden family. The contrast between Bowen's cerebral, deliberate, theoretical approach and Satir's or Whitaker's spontaneous, emotional, nontheoretical way of working with families will surely not be lost on the reader.

By educational background and training, Bowen was imbued with the individual focus of psychoanalysis, a fact that is reflected in some of his early (1957–1963) theoretical formulations (Bowen, 1976). However, as Bowen moved toward developing the theory that emotional disturbance arises from, and is maintained by, relationships with others, he adopted the language of systems science and its broader view of human functioning. At Georgetown University in Washington, D.C., Bowen continues his clinical research and theory building and conducts a family therapy practice with families with a wide range of problems. An extremely influential family therapy leader, Bowen numbers among his students and colleagues such currently well-known family therapists as Philip Guerin, Elizabeth Carter, Monica McGoldrick, Thomas Fogarty and Michael Kerr.

Eight Interlocking Theoretical Concepts

In its present state of refinement, Bowen's theory of the family as an emotional relationship system consists of eight interlocking concepts. The first six concepts, formulated before 1963, address emotional processes taking place in the nuclear and extended families. The two later concepts, emotional cutoff and societal regression, added in 1975, speak to the emotional process across generations in a family and in society (Papero, 1983). The eight forces shaping family functioning include:

1. Differentiation of self
2. Triangles
3. Nuclear family emotional system
4. Family projection process
5. Emotional cutoff
6. Multigenerational transmission process
7. Sibling positions
8. Societal regression

The cornerstone of Bowen's carefully worked out theory is his notion of the forces within the family that make for togetherness and the opposing forces that lead to individuality. To Bowen, the degree to which a **differentiation of self** occurs in an individual reflects the extent to which that person is able to discriminate intellectual from emotional functioning. Those individuals with the greatest **fusion** between the two function most poorly; they are likely to be at the mercy of involuntary emotional reactions and tend to become dysfunctional even under low levels of stress. Just as they are unable to differentiate thought from feeling, such persons have trouble differentiating themselves from others and thus fuse easily with whatever emotions dominate the family.

Bowen introduced the concept of **undifferentiated family ego mass,** derived from psychoanalysis, to convey the idea of a family emotionally "stuck together," one where "a conglomerate emotional oneness . . . exists in all levels of intensity" (1966, p. 171). For example, the symbiotic relationship of interdependency between mother and child may represent the most intense version of this concept; a father's detachment may be the least intense. The degree to which any one member is involved in the family from moment to moment depends on that person's basic level of involvement in the family ego mass. Sometimes the emotional closeness can be so intense that family members know each other's feelings, thoughts, fantasies, and dreams. This intimacy may lead to uncomfortable "overcloseness," according to Bowen, and ultimately to a phase of mutual rejection between two members. In other words, within a family system, emotional tensions shift over time (sometimes slowly, sometimes rapidly) in a series of alliances and rejections. What Bowen had initially characterized in psychoanalytic terms—undifferentiated family ego mass—he later recast in systems language as fusion/differentiation. Both sets of terms underscore Bowen's insistence that maturity and self-actualization demand that an individual become free of unresolved emotional attachments to his or her family of origin.

For illustrative purposes, Bowen (1966) proposed a theoretical scale (not an actual psychometric instrument) for evaluating an individual's differentiation level. As noted in Figure 7-1, the greater the degree of undifferentiation (no sense of self or a weak or unstable personal identity), the greater the emotional fusion into a common self with others (the undifferentiated family ego mass). A person with a strong sense of self ("these are my opinions . . . this is who I am . . . this is what I will do, but not this . . .") does not compromise that self for the sake of marital bliss or to please parents or achieve family harmony, although fusion of self occurs to some degree between husband and wife as well as between and among all family members.

People at the low extreme are those whose emotions and intellect are so fused that their lives are dominated by the feelings of those around them. As a consequence, they are easily stressed into dysfunction. Those far fewer individuals at the high end are emotionally mature; because their intellectual functioning remains relatively (although not completely) dominant during stressful periods, they can take action independent of the emotionality around them. In the midrange are persons with relative degrees of fusion or differentiation. Note that the scale eliminates the need for the concept of normality. It is entirely possible for people at the low end of the scale to keep their lives in emotional equilibrium and stay free of symptoms, thus appearing to satisfy the

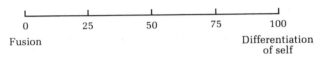

Figure 7–1. The theoretical Differentiation of Self Scale, according to Bowen's conception, distinguishing people according to the degree of fusion or differentiation between their emotional and intellectual functioning. Those at the lowest level of differentiation (0–25) are emotionally fused to the family and others and lead lives in which their thinking is submerged and their feelings dominate. The lives of those in the 25–50 range are still guided by their emotional system and the reactions of others; goal-directed behavior is present but carried out in order to seek the approval of others. In the 50–75 range, thinking is sufficiently developed so as not to be dominated by feeling when stress occurs, and there is a reasonably developed sense of self. Those rare people functioning between 75–100 routinely separate their thinking from their feelings; they base decisions on the former but are free to lose themselves in the intimacy of a close relationship. Bowen (1978) considers someone at 75 to have a very high level of differentiation and all those over 60 to constitute a small percentage of society.

popular criteria for being "normal." However, these people are not only more vulnerable to stress than those higher on the scale but, under stress, are apt to develop symptoms from which they recover far more slowly than those at the high end of the scale. According to Bowen, any person's level of differentiation reflects that individual's level of differentiation from the family as well as from others outside the family group. A moderate to high level of differentiation permits interaction with others without fear of fusion (losing one's sense of self in the relationship).

In addition to his interest in the degree of integration of self, Bowen's theory also emphasizes anxiety or emotional tension within the person or in his or her relationships. The basic building block in a family's emotional system is the **triangle,** according to Bowen. During periods when anxiety is low and external conditions are calm, two persons may engage in a comfortable back-and-forth exchange of feelings. However, the stability of this situation is threatened if one or both participants gets upset or anxious, either because of internal stress or from stress external to the twosome. When a certain intensity level is reached, one or both partners will involve a vulnerable third person. According to Bowen (1978), the twosome may "reach out" and pull in the other person, the emotions may "overflow" to the third person, or that person may be emotionally "programmed" to initiate involvement. This triangle dilutes the anxiety; it is both more stable and more flexible than the twosome and has a higher tolerance for dealing with stress. When anxiety in the triangle subsides, the emotional configuration returns to the peaceful twosome plus the lone outsider. However, should anxiety in the triangle increase, one person in the triangle may involve another outsider, and so forth. Sometimes such triangulation can reach beyond the family, involving social agencies or the courts.

Generally speaking, the higher the degree of family fusion, the more intense and insistent the triangling efforts; the least well-differentiated person is particularly vulnerable to being drawn in to reduce tension. Beyond seeking relief of discomfort, the family's reliance on triangles helps maintain an optimum level of closeness and distance between members while permitting them the greatest freedom from anxiety (Papero, 1983).

By definition, a two-person system is unstable (Bowen, 1975) and forms itself into a three-person system or triad under stress. As more people become involved, the system becomes a series of interlocking triangles. As an example, note that conflict between siblings quickly attracts a parent's attention. Let us assume that the parent has positive feelings toward both children who, at the moment, are in conflict with each other. If the parent can control his or her emotional responsiveness and manage not to take sides while staying in contact with both children, the emotional intensity between the original twosome, the siblings, will diminish. (A parallel situation exists when parents quarrel and a child is drawn into the triangle in an attempt to dilute and thus reduce the strain between the combatants.) Generally speaking, the probability of triangulation within a family is heightened by poor differentiation of family members; conversely, the reliance on triangulation to solve problems helps maintain the poor differentiation of certain family members.

As we discuss later in this chapter when we describe Bowen's therapeutic technique, a similar situation exists when a couple visits a marital/family therapist. Following from his theory, Bowen contends that if the therapist—the third person in the system—can remain involved with both spouses without siding with one or the other, the spouses may learn to view themselves as individual, differentiated selves as well as marital partners. However, if the third person loses emotional contact with the spouses, the twosome will proceed to triangulate with someone else.

Bowen also believes people choose mates with equivalent levels of differentiation to their own. Not surprisingly, then, the relatively undifferentiated person will select a spouse who is equally fused to his or her family of origin. It is probable, moreover, that these poorly differentiated people, now a marital couple, will themselves become highly fused and will produce a family with the same characteristics. According to Bowen, the resulting **nuclear family emotional system** will be unstable and will seek various ways to reduce tension and maintain stability. The greater the nuclear family's fusion, chronic anxiety and potential instability, the greater the family's propensity for: (1) increased emotional distance between the spouses; (2) physical or emotional dysfunction in a spouse; (3) overt, chronic, unresolved marital conflict; (4) psychological impairment in a child. According to Kerr (1981), some families select one of these mechanisms to preserve equilibrium in a system and others rely upon several.

A parent does not respond in the same way to each child in a family, despite claims to the contrary. Differences in parental behavior, however, do make for significant differences in how each child functions. Children who are the object of parental focus tend in general to develop greater fusion to the family than their siblings and consequently remain more vulnerable to emotional

Murray Bowen, M.D.

stresses within the family (Papero, 1983). The fusion-prone, focused-on child is the one most sensitive to disturbances and incipient signs of instability within the family. Bowen (1976) believes that the parents, themselves immature, select as the object of their attention the most infantile of all their children, regardless of his or her birth order in the family. Bowen stresses the sibling positions of the parents in their families of origin as clues to which child will be chosen in the next generation; Bowen calls this the **family projection process.** As the child most emotionally attached to the parents of all the children within a family, he or she will have the lowest level of differentiation of self and the most difficulty in separating from the family. Moreover, Kerr (1981) believes that the greater the level of undifferentiation of the parents and the more they rely on the projection process to stabilize the system, the more likely that several children will be emotionally impaired. This process of projecting or transmitting parental undifferentiation may begin as early as the initial mother–infant bonding.

Children less involved in the projection process are apt to emerge with a greater ability to withstand fusion, to separate thinking and feeling. Those who are more involved try various strategies upon reaching adulthood, or even before. They may attempt to insulate themselves from the family by geographic separation, through the use of psychological barriers, by the self-deception that they are "free" of family ties because actual contact has been broken off. Bowen (1976) considers such supposed freedom an **emotional cutoff,** a flight from unresolved emotional ties, not true emancipation. Avoidance of attachments may simply mask unexamined fusion. Kerr (1981) contends that emotional cutoff *reflects* a problem (underlying fusion between generations), *solves* a problem (reducing anxiety associated with making contact) and *creates* a problem (isolating people who might benefit from closer contact).

Bowen insists that adults must resolve their emotional attachments to their families of origin. In a very revealing paper about his own family Bowen delivered in 1967 to a national conference of family researchers and therapists ("Towards," 1972), he openly described his personal struggles to achieve a differentiation of self from his own family of origin. Without this differentiation, Bowen argues, family therapists may unknowingly be triangulated into conflicts in their client families (much as they were as children in their own families), perhaps overidentifying with one family member or projecting onto another their own unresolved difficulties. In general, the therapist is vulnerable to the client family's effort to resist change and retain homeostasis. Family therapists need to get in touch with and be free of their own "internalized" family so that unfinished business from the past does not intrude on current dealings with client families.

Guerin and Fogarty (1972), former students of Bowen now supervising and training family therapists themselves, openly share with students information about current relationships with their own families. Their efforts to achieve their own differentiation serve as a model for trainees to study their own families and to be equally self-disclosing in the supervisory relationship. Fogarty, in particular, sees no difference between treatment, teaching, living in one's own family, or conducting one's professional life; triangles, fusions, distances, and so on occur in each context. The therapist who understands the way these concepts operate in his or her family has a solid grounding for work with client families.

In perhaps his most intriguing formulation, Bowen (1976) proposed the concept of **multigenerational transmission process,** in which severe dysfunction is conceptualized as the result of the operation of the family's emotional system over several generations. Two earlier concepts are crucial here—the selection of a spouse with a similar differentiation level as one's own and the family projection process that results in lower levels of self-differentiation for certain offspring.

Assume for a moment that the least well-differentiated members of two families marry—as Bowen's theory would predict—and that at least one of their children, as the result of the projection process, will have an even lower differentiation level. The eventual marriage of this person—again, to someone with a similarly poor differentiation of self—passes along the increasingly lowered level of differentiation to the members of the next generation, who in turn pass it along to the next, and so forth. As each generation produces individuals with progressively poorer differentiation, those people are increasingly vulnerable to anxiety and fusion. Although the process may slow down or remain static over a generation or two, ultimately—it may take as many as eight or ten generations—a level of impairment is reached that is consistent with schizophrenia. If the family encounters severe stress and anxiety, however, schizophrenia may develop in an earlier generation. In some less stressful cases or under favorable life circumstances, Bowen believes poorly differ-entiated people may keep their relationship system in relatively symptom-free equilibrium for several generations longer. This process may be re-versed, of course, should someone in this lineage marry a person considerably higher on the differentiation-of-self scale. However, as noted earlier, Bowen observes that most persons choose mates at more or less their own level of differentiation.

Two more concepts round out Bowen's theorizings to date. Bowen credits Toman's (1961) work on the relationship between birth order and personality with clarifying his own thinking regarding the influence of **sibling position** in the family emotional process. Bowen realized that some interactive patterns between marital partners may be related to the position of each partner, based on order of birth, in his or her family of origin. Thus, an oldest child who marries a youngest may expect to take responsibility, make decisions, and so on; this behavior is also expected by the mate on the basis of his or her expe-riences as the youngest in the family. Two youngest children who marry may both feel overburdened by responsibility and decision making; the marriage of two oldest children may be overly competitive because each spouse is accus-tomed to being in charge (Kerr, 1981). Note, however, that it is a person's func-tional position in the family system, not necessarily the actual order of birth, that shapes future expectations and behavior.

In a final concept, **societal regression,** Bowen extended his thinking to so-ciety's emotional functioning. In the least well developed of his theoretical formulations, Bowen argues that society, like the family, contains within it opposing forces toward undifferentiation and toward individuation. Under conditions of chronic stress (population growth, depletion of natural resources) and thus continual anxiety, there is likely to be an erosion of the forces intent on achieving individuation. It is Bowen's (1977) pessimistic view that society's functional level of differentiation has decreased over the last several decades.

Like Ackerman, Bowen began his professional career with a psychoanalytic orientation, and, as we have noted, many of his early theoretical concepts (for example, undifferentiated family ego mass) reflect that viewpoint. Unlike Ackerman, Bowen moved more steadily toward systems thinking (Bowen, 1975) and many of his later concepts (for example, interlocking triangles, multi-generational transmission of dysfunction) reflect this later direction.

A recent collection in one volume of papers by Bowen (1978) affords the reader an opportunity to study the evolution of Bowen's theories and tech-niques over 20 years, from his initial concern with families with a schizo-phrenic member to the development of a broader family theory of emotional disorders and a method of family intervention developed from that theory.

Bowen's Family Intervention Techniques

Bowen's standard method of conducting family therapy is to work with a system consisting of two adults and himself. Even when the identified patient is a symptomatic child, Bowen asks the parents to accept the premise that the basic problem is between the two of them. In such a situation, Bowen may never see the child at all. As Kerr (1981), one of Bowen's associates, explains:

> a theoretical system that thinks in terms of family, with a therapeutic method that works toward improvement of the family system, is "family" regardless of the number of people in the sessions (p. 232).

Bowen presents himself as a researcher helping the family members become researchers into their own ways of functioning. The term he prefers is *coach* (having moved during his career, in his own words, from "couch" to "coach")— an active expert who helps individual players and the team (family) perform to the best of their abilities.

Bowen (1976) takes the position that the successful addition of a significant other person (a friend, teacher, minister) to an anxious or disturbed relationship system can modify all relationships within the family. The family therapist can play this role as long as he or she manages to stay in emotional contact with the two most significant family members (usually the parents) but remains uninvested in (triangled into) the family conflict. Bowen's insistence that the therapist not engage with the family system is dramatically different from the "total immersion" approach of family therapists such as Ackerman, Satir, Kempler, or Whitaker. In the Bowen approach, the therapist remains unsusceptible, calm, detriangulated from the emotional entanglements between the spouses. If the therapist can maintain that kind of stance—despite pressures to be triangled into the conflict—tension between the couple will subside, the "fusion" between them will slowly resolve, and other family members will feel the repercussions in terms of changes in their own lives. Bowen's overall objective is for each family member to maximize his or her self-differentiation.

Bowen frequently chooses one partner, usually the one who is more mature and better differentiated, and works with that individual for a period of time. This person is assumed to be the member of the family most capable of breaking through the old emotionally entangling patterns of interaction. When that person succeeds in taking an "I"-stand, the others will shortly be motivated to do the same, subsequently moving off in their own directions. A stormy period may follow before a new equilibrium is reached but the former pathological ties are broken and each person has achieved a greater sense of individuality.

Family therapy sessions as directed by Bowen (1975) are controlled and cerebral. Each partner talks to the therapist rather than talking directly to the other. Confrontation between the partners is avoided to minimize the tensions between them. Instead, what each partner is thinking is externalized in the presence of the other. Interpretations are avoided. Calm questioning defuses emotion and forces the partners to think about the issues causing their difficulties. Rather than blaming the other or ignoring their differences in a rush of intimacy, Bowen insists that each partner focus on the part he or she plays in the relationship problems.

In Bowen's experience, some families need as few as 5–10 sessions to achieve good results. Other families may require 20–40 sessions until symptoms subside. Bowen (1975) claims that no other approach to family therapy has been as effective in producing good long-term changes in family functioning.

Because Bowen is particularly concerned that his clients develop the ability to differentiate themselves from their families of origin, the focus of much of his work is on extended families. In this respect Bowen resembles Framo (1981), although Bowen sends clients home for frequent visits (and self-observations) after coaching them in their differentiating efforts, while Framo brings origin family members into the final phases of therapy with his clients (see Chapter 5). Reestablishing contact with the family of origin is a critical step in reducing a client's residual anxiety, in detriangulating from members of that family, and in ultimately achieving self-differentiation, free of crippling entanglements from the past or present.

SUMMARY

Murray Bowen's approach, called family systems theory, may be considered a bridge between psychodynamically oriented views and more strictly systems perspectives. The major theoretician in the field, Bowen conceptualizes the family as an emotional relationship system and offers eight interlocking concepts to explain the emotional processes taking place in the nuclear and extended families.

The cornerstone of Bowen's theory is the concept of the differentiation of self, the extent to which a family member can discriminate his or her intellectual and emotional functioning and thus avoid fusion with whatever emotions dominate the family. Under stress, participants in a two-person relationship have a tendency to recruit or triangle in a third member in order to lower the intensity and regain stability. The nuclear family emotional system is usually founded by marital partners with similar differentiation levels; if the system is unstable, the partners seek ways to reduce tension and preserve equilibrium, sometimes at the expense of particularly vulnerable, fusion-prone offspring. The sibling position of the parents in their families of origin offers clues as to which child will be chosen in this family projection process.

Bowen uses the concept of emotional cutoff to describe how some family members, usually upon reaching adulthood, attempt to break off contact with their families in the mistaken notion that they can insulate themselves from fusion. However, as progressively lower levels of differentiation-of-self occur over several generations, symptoms of severe dysfunction may eventually appear as a result of a multigenerational transmission process. The sibling position of each of the marital partners influences their interaction. In extending his theory to society at large, Bowen believes that chronic external pressures and stresses lower society's functional level of differentiation, resulting in societal regression.

Therapeutically, Bowen works with marital partners in a calm and carefully detriangulated way, attempting to resolve the fusion between them; his goals are to maximize each person's self-differentiation within the nuclear family system—and from the family of origin.

CHAPTER EIGHT

Theoretical Perspectives: The Structural Model

Many of the concepts of the structural approach to family therapy are already familiar to the reader: subsystems, boundaries, alignments, enmeshment and disengagement. The very fact that these words are part of the everyday vocabulary of family therapy—and so readily come to mind in thinking of family relationships and transactional patterns—underscores the prominence of this model. The writings of Salvador Minuchin (Minuchin, 1974a, 1974b; Minuchin, Rosman, & Baker, 1978), particularly during the 1970s, helped insure that a legion of family therapists would adopt the structural view of family organization and utilize the therapeutic techniques of the structural approach.

STRUCTURAL FAMILY THEORY

More strictly systems-oriented than Bowen's theory, the structural approach is usually associated with Salvador Minuchin and his colleagues (at one time or another including such notable family therapists as Edgar Auerswald, Braulio Montalvo, Harry Aponte, Jay Haley, and Lynn Hoffman). Born in Argentina, Minuchin received his medical training there and set out to practice pediatrics. When Israel declared itself a state in 1948, Minuchin volunteered his services as an army doctor in the war with the Arab nations. After subsequent training as a child psychiatrist in the United States, he returned to Israel to work with displaced children from the Holocaust and then with Jewish immigrants from the Arab countries. It was at this point that Minuchin became interested in working with entire families. Back in the United States, he started developing a theory and set of special techniques for working with urgently needy, under-organized poor families at the Wiltwyck School where many delinquent Black and Puerto Rican children from New York City were sent. It was there that Minuchin devised many of the brief, direct, action-oriented intervention procedures for restructuring the family that he later brought to the Philadelphia

Child Guidance Clinic, where he was director from 1965 to 1975. Originally a small clinic with a staff of ten located in the heart of the Black ghetto, the Philadelphia Child Guidance Clinic blossomed under Minuchin's boldly imaginative leadership until it grew into the largest facility of its kind ever established. The clinic now occupies an elaborate modern complex, has close to 300 people on its staff and is affiliated with Children's Hospital on the campus of the University of Pennsylvania. It remains one of the few clinics in the United States where ghetto families are in the majority. In recent years, Minuchin has spent most of his professional time teaching, consulting, supervising, writing and demonstrating his dramatic techniques in front of professional audiences around the world.

Using a number of the systems principles we discussed in Chapter 2, Minuchin (1974a) emphasizes the active, organized wholeness of the family unit. More specifically, he addresses the rigid, repetitive sequences and habits by which some families organize themselves and then, by deliberately "unfreezing" these patterns, creates an opportunity for the family to reorganize itself and substitute new structures and transactional patterns. Generally, this therapeutic effort involves a push for clearer boundaries, increased flexibility in family interactions, and most important, modification of the dysfunctional structure. As Minuchin (1974a) describes his viewpoint:

> In essence, the structural approach to families is based on the concept that a family is more than the individual biopsychodynamics of its members. Family members relate according to certain arrangements, which govern their transactions. These arrangements, though usually not explicitly stated or even recognized, form a whole—the structure of the family. The reality of the structure is of a different order from the reality of the individual members (p. 89).

Like most systems theorists, the structuralists are interested in how the components of a system interact, how balance or homeostasis is achieved, how family feedback mechanisms operate, how dysfunctional communication patterns develop, and so forth. Beyond that, they are especially attentive to family transaction patterns because these offer clues to the family's organization, the permeability of the family's subsystem boundaries, the existence of alignments or coalitions. Rosenberg (1983) summarizes this position succinctly when he concludes that "when a family runs into difficulty, one can assume that it is operating within a dysfunctional structure (p. 160)." Perhaps the family, functioning along normal developmental lines, has hit a snag in entering a new developmental stage or in negotiating a particular life cycle crisis such as the birth of another child, children leaving home, or retirement. Perhaps the family members have become overinvolved or enmeshed with each other (parental behavior that seems supportive and loving to a preadolescent is experienced as suffocating and intrusive by a teenager). Or perhaps we are dealing with, at the other end of the continuum, the dilemma of disengagement (parents' detachment permits growth and encourages children's resourceful-

Salvador Minuchin, M.D.

ness, but at the same time represents parents' unavailability and lack of support in time of crisis). Dysfunctional structures suggest that the covert rules that govern family transactions have become (temporarily) inoperative or inappropriate and require renegotiation.

Although Minuchin does not define a broad theory base for his clinical interventions, he has offered some useful concepts for analyzing the mechanisms by which families organize themselves, cope with transitional issues, and adapt to new developmental stages (1974a, 1981). Theoretically, Minuchin perceives the family as a differentiated social system that develops identifiable transactional patterns for how, when, and to whom each member relates. To Minuchin, repeated operations (for example, who has the right to say what to whom in which way) build patterns over time and these patterns become the familiar, even preferred ways for family members to interact. Basically, the family system is structured by its transactional patterns. The system maintains itself within a more or less narrow range; deviations trigger homeostatic mechanisms to reestablish the accustomed range.

Subsystems, Boundaries, and Alignments

Family systems carry out their tasks through subsystems. An individual is a subsystem; dyads such as husband and wife or larger subgroupings determined by generation, by gender, by assigned tasks, or by common interests are subsystems. Each person participates in a variety of subsystems within the family and may play different roles in each. As Minuchin (1981) illustrates, a child has to act like a son so his father can act like a father, but he may take on executive powers when he is alone with his younger brother.

Figure 8–1. According to Minuchin, family coalitions frequently introduce stress into a family system, handicapping the functioning of individual members as well as the family as a whole. In this simulated family scene, the mother and younger daughter sit separately from the father and older daughter, suggesting a division within the family. Mother's whispered secret further strengthens her alliance with one child, while the other members appear to be out of touch with what is going on. Successful structural family therapy may produce role changes, clearer communication patterns, and a restructuring of the family organization.

Aponte and Van Deusen (1981) believe that every stroke of a family transaction makes a statement about boundaries, alignments and power. The *boundaries* of a subsystem are the rules defining who participates and what roles they will play in the transactions or operations necessary to carry out a particular function (for example, should the sex education of young children be carried out by father, mother, older siblings or be a shared responsibility? Or should the task be left to the schools?). *Alignments* refer to the joining or opposition of one member of a system to another in carrying out an operation (for example, does father agree or disagree with his wife's disciplinary actions with the children?). *Power*, the relative influence of each family member on an operation's outcome, is seldom absolute but is related to the context or situation (for example, the mother may have considerable influence on her adolescent daughter's behavior at home but minimal influence over the daughter's social contacts outside the home). Power is also related to the way family members actively or passively combine forces (for example, mother's authority depends on her husband's support and backing as well as on the acquiescence of her children).

For parents to achieve a desired outcome in the family, there must be: (1) clearly defined generational boundaries so that parents together form a subsystem with executive power; (2) alignments between the parents on key issues, such as discipline; and (3) rules related to power and authority, indicating which of the parents will prevail if they disagree and whether the parents are capable of carrying out their wishes when they do agree. Note that strong generational boundaries also prohibit interference from grandparents as much as they prevent children from taking over parenting functions. In addition, alignments must function properly or individuals will cross generational boundaries—go to Father for permission if Mother says no—to get what they want.

Some families respond to developmental changes by making their transactional patterns more rigid. As the family becomes a more closed than open system, family members narrow their choices and develop stereotyped responses to each other and to the outside world. In certain cases, the stereotyping may lead to a member being labeled as deviant (the so-called identified patient). Minuchin (1981) makes it clear that a family's difficulties in carrying out its tasks in modern society may be real and intense; distress in the family system, particularly at times of transition, is not in and of itself a sign of abnormality or dysfunction. However, Minuchin is concerned that a family not become so rigid and resistant to change that it avoids or fights the idea of exploring alternative patterns. The families whose adaptive coping mechanisms have been exhausted, who are conflict-ridden as a result, and who see no alternatives may require therapeutic intervention if its members are to experience reality in a new way, alter their transactional patterns, modify their family structure (perhaps reactivating dormant but functional structures) and accommodate to the possibilities of change.

STRUCTURAL FAMILY THERAPY

Minuchin's therapeutic efforts are geared to the present and are based on the principle of action preceding understanding (Minuchin & Fishman, 1981). That is, action leads to new experiences, to insight and understanding, to rearranged structures. (The sequence is reversed for Bowen.) Minuchin's approach is to challenge the family's patterns of interaction, forcing the members to look beyond the symptoms of the identified patient in order to view all of their behavior within the context of family structures (the covert rules that govern the family's transactional patterns). He offers the family leadership, direction and encouragement to examine and discard rigid structures that no longer are functional. For example, changes in the relative positions of family members may be in order, such as more proximity between husband and wife or more distance between mother and son. Hierarchical relationships in which the parents customarily exercise authority may be redefined and made more flexible in some cases and reinforced in others. Alignments and coalitions may be explored, embedded conflicts acknowledged, alternative rules considered. To use an example offered by Colapinto (1982), a mother may be urged to abstain from intervening automatically whenever the interaction between her husband and son reaches a certain pitch, while father and son should not automatically abort an argument just because it upsets Mom. For Minuchin and his colleagues, the most effective way to alter dysfunctional behavior and eliminate symptoms is to change the family's transactional patterns that maintain them.

Minuchin himself is a compelling presence, a colorful and somehow larger-than-life therapist who enters a family, adapts to the family organization, refuses to be ignored and forces the family members to accommodate to him in the ways he chooses to facilitate movement toward the goals of treatment. He adopts the family's affective style; in a constricted family he is undemonstrative; in an expansive family he is jovial and uses expressive movements. He quickly assimilates the family's language patterns and commonly used terms. He tells anecdotes about his own experiences when he feels they are relevant to the family discussion. As a therapist, he describes himself (Minuchin, 1974a) as acting like a distant relative, *joining* a family system and *accommodating* to its style. As Minuchin blends into the family and begins to understand family themes and family myths, to sense a member's pain at being excluded or scapegoated, to distinguish which persons have open communication pathways between them and which closed, he intuitively obtains a picture of the family structure in operation.

Restructuring Dysfunctional Sets

Minuchin (1974b) conceives of family pathology as resulting from the development of dysfunctional **sets.** Dysfunctional sets are the family reactions, developed in response to stress, that are repeated without modification whenever there is family conflict. A husband experiencing stress at work comes home and shouts at the wife. The wife counterattacks, escalating the conflict that continues without change until one partner abandons the field. Both parties experience a sense of nonresolution. In another example, a mother verbally attacks an adolescent son, the father takes his side, the younger children seize the opportunity to join in and pick on their older brother. All family members become involved and various coalitions develop but the family organization remains the same and the dysfunctional sets will be repeated in the next trying situation.

Minuchin assumes that any family seeking treatment is experiencing some stress that has overloaded the system's adaptive and coping mechanisms, handicapping the optimum functioning of its members in the process. Minuchin sets himself the task of rearranging the family organization—restructuring the system that governs its transactions—so that the family will function more effectively and the growth potential of each member will be maximized (Minuchin, 1974b). Restructuring involves changes in family rules and realignments, changes in the patterns that support certain undesirable behaviors, changes in the sequences of interaction.

Minuchin's therapeutic approach is innovative and deliberately manipulative, following a carefully calculated set of plans and intervention procedures. Minuchin generally advises that the therapist begin by affiliating with the family in order to experience firsthand the pressures of the family system. Once Minuchin has gained entrance, he begins to probe the family structure, looking for areas of flexibility and possible change. For example, if a family has come for therapy because the teenage daughter is shy, withdrawn, and has difficulties in her social life, he may observe for diagnostic purposes how the family enters the therapy room: the girl sits next to her mother and they move their two chairs close together. When the therapist asks what the problem is, the mother answers, ignoring her daughter's attempts to add her thoughts on the matter. The mother makes comments that suggest she has too intimate a knowledge of her adolescent daughter's personal life, more knowledge than is usual. Within a few minutes after starting, Minuchin makes his first intervention, asking the mother and father to change chairs. Structural therapy has begun: as the father is brought into the picture, the family flexibility is being tested; with the implication of pathology in the mother–daughter dyad, the family's reason for seeking therapy for the teenager is already being reframed or relabeled as a problem with a larger focus (Minuchin, 1974b).

Structural Intervention Techniques

Minuchin, primarily a clinician, developed his theory of family structures as a result of his therapeutic work with the underorganized families of delinquent youngsters at Wiltwyck as well as the overconcerned families of psychosomatic children, especially anorexics, at the Philadelphia Child Guidance Center (for discussion of both studies, see Chapter 3). He is most at home as a practicing family therapist, however, and from his clinical experiences he has developed certain intervention strategies that form the basis for the structural approach. Simple, practical, calculated to have certain effects, these strategies have made structural family therapy a popular and influential form of treatment. We alluded to some of these tactics in the previous section: joining and accommodating to the family, confronting the family transactional patterns, attempting to rearrange or restructure the members' patterns of behavior.

Several other clinical tactics deserve special note. **Mimesis** refers to the process of joining the family by imitating the manner, style, affective range, or content of its communications. Through **tracking,** the structural therapist adopts symbols of the family's life gathered from members' communication (such as life themes, values, significant historical events) and deliberately uses them in conversation with the family. This effort to confirm that the therapist values what family members say is also a way of influencing their later transactional patterns; Minuchin (1974a) calls this "leading by following."

Enactments are efforts by the therapist to bring an outside family conflict into the session so that the family members can demonstrate how they deal with it and the therapist can begin to map out a way to modify their interaction and create structural changes. To use an example offered by Rosenberg (1983), a mother complained that her 2½-year-old daughter has tantrums and embarrasses her in front of grandparents, on buses, in other situations. The daughter remained well-behaved during the early sessions despite (or maybe because of) her mother's insistence that she engages in this awful behavior away from the therapist. During the third or fourth session, when the child asked for gum, Rosenberg saw his chance: he asked mother not to give her the gum because lunchtime was approaching. As the child's whimper turned to crying, to begging, and finally to falling on the floor and undressing herself—and the mother considered giving in—Rosenberg encouraged the mother to hold firm, despite the by-now deafening noise. More than a half hour later, the child came to a whimpering stop; she seemed fine although both mother and therapist were exhausted! However, the mother had asserted her control as a result of the enactment. In structural terms, the generational boundaries were reestablished, mother was again in charge, and her daughter, whose tantrums at home ceased shortly thereafter, was comfortable in knowing that her mother could handle her.

Enactments are often useful for **reframing** purposes. In such instances, the structural family therapist redefines a problem (for example, an adolescent daughter's self-starvation) as a function of the family's structure. An anorexic girl is labelled as "stubborn" and not "sick," forcing the family members to reconsider their view of what is occurring and ultimately change their transactional patterns. The "fact" of the daughter not eating has not changed, only the "meaning" attributed to that behavior. Reframing is used by many family therapists (especially the "communication" advocates) to change family perspectives and, ultimately, to change family behavior patterns on the basis of the new options and alternatives.

Minuchin's interventions very likely increase the stress on the family system—perhaps even create a family crisis that unbalances family homeostasis—but they open the way for transformation of the family structure. Minuchin recognizes that in an enmeshed family system, for example, members often believe the family as a whole can neither withstand change nor adapt to it; as a consequence, the system demands that certain members change (develop symptoms) in order to maintain the dysfunctional homeostasis. When the danger level of family stress is approached, the symptom bearer is activated as part of a conflict avoidance maneuver; the family system reinforces the continuance of the symptoms that help maintain the system's balance and status quo. It is the therapist's job to make everyone aware, often through reframing, that the problem belongs and pertains to the family, not an individual; that the implementation of new functional sets must replace the habitual repetition of the dysfunctional ones.

The therapeutic tactics employed by Minuchin are often dramatic and at times theatrical. Like a stage director, he enjoys setting up a situation, creating a scenario, assigning a task to the family and requiring the members to function according to the new sets he has imposed. For example, in treating an anorexic child, self-starving but refusing to eat, Minuchin arranges to meet the family at lunch for the first session (Minuchin, Rosman, & Baker, 1978). He creates such an enactment deliberately, in order to foster a crisis around eating and experience what the family members are experiencing. He observes the parents plead, demand, cajole, become desperate and feel defeat. He watches the adolescent girl demonstrate hopelessness and helplessness, pathetically asserting through her refusal to eat that she has always given in to her parents at the expense of her self, but will do so no longer. While the daughter is usually labeled as the problem, Minuchin, reframing, helps them see that anorexia nervosa is a diagnosis of a family system, not simply the adolescent's symptomatic behavior. All the family members are locked into a futile pattern of interaction that has become the center of their lives; each member has a stake in maintaining the disorder. A particular type of enmeshed family organization in which a daughter learns to subordinate her sense of self has been found by Minuchin and his colleagues to be related to the development and maintenance of psychosomatic syndromes in adolescent girls (Minuchin, Rosman, & Baker, 1978). In turn, the syndrome plays an important role in maintaining family homeostasis. Structural family therapy helps each person in the family to recognize the syndrome and take responsibility for contributing to it. By creating a family crisis, Minuchin forces the family to change the system, substituting more functional interactions.

The following is typical of Minuchin's manipulative, unyielding, crisis-provoking approach. Demonstrating his technique with a family with an anorexic adolescent daughter, Minuchin insists that the parents force the emaciated girl to eat or she will die. They coax, cajole, threaten, yell, and finally stuff food down her throat until their daughter collapses in tears. Minuchin believes she will now eat. As he later explains it:

> "The anoretic is obsessed with her hopelessness, inadequacy, wickedness, ugliness. I incite an interpersonal conflict that makes her stop thinking about how terrible she is and start thinking about what bastards her parents are. At that demonstration, I said to the parents, "Make her eat," and when they did she had to deal with them as people. Previously, the parents had been saying "We control you because we love you." In the position I put them in, they were finally saying "Goddam it, you eat!" That freed her. She could then eat or not eat; she could be angry at them as clearly delineated figures" (Malcolm, 1978, p. 78).

With this approach, Minuchin has been able to show that the anorexic symptom is embedded in the faulty family organization. Changing that organization eliminated the potentially fatal symptom.

Psychosomatic disorders represent a type of illness where cure can be scientifically measured, not merely assumed or implied. Minuchin's data indicate an 86% success rate for the treatment of anorexics with structural therapy. Minuchin's success in this area suggests the desirability of further research to see if this form of highly calculated intervention may be similarly effective with other family problems.

SUMMARY

The structural approach in family therapy, prominent during the 1970s, is associated with Salvador Minuchin and his colleagues at the Philadelphia Child Guidance Center. Systems-based, structural family theory focuses on the active, organized wholeness of the family unit and the ways in which the family organizes itself through its transactional patterns. In particular, the family's subsystems, boundaries, coalitions and alignments are studied in an effort to understand its structure. Dysfunctional structures point to the covert rules governing family transactions that have become inoperative or in need of re-negotiation.

Structural family therapy is geared to present-day transactions and gives higher priority to action than insight or understanding. All behavior, including symptoms in the identified patient, is viewed within the context of family structure. Minuchin's interventions are active, carefully calculated, even manipulative efforts to alter rigid, outmoded or unworkable structures. By joining the family and accommodating to its style, he gains an understanding of the members' way of dealing with problems and with each other, ultimately helping them to change dysfunctional sets and rearrange or realign the family organization.

Enactments (the family demonstrating typical conflict situations in the therapy session) and reframing (the therapist relabeling or redefining a problem as a function of the family's structure) are therapeutic techniques frequently used to bring about a transformation of the family structure. Minuchin's approach has been particularly effective with psychosomatic disorders such as anorexia nervosa.

CHAPTER NINE

Theoretical Perspectives: The Communication Model

Enormously influential in the founding of the family therapy movement, the communication model as it first took form in the late 1950s offered an intriguing alternative to the established ways of conceptualizing psychopathology. For example, the traditional psychoanalytic or psychodynamic view of conflict between a mother and adolescent daughter holds that the mother is overidentifying with her child and perhaps projecting unresolved problems from her own adolescence onto her. The daughter, rebellious and with an incompletely formed sense of personal identity, may be introjecting many of her mother's characteristics but undergoing an "identity crisis" at the same time. However, it is entirely possible, argued people like Gregory Bateson, Don Jackson, Jay Haley, and Virginia Satir, to understand this conflict not in terms of two persons, each of whom has "problems," but as a dysfunctional relationship that manifests itself, among other ways, in faulty communication. If we adopt the latter view, notice how the emphasis has shifted—from the past to here-and-now, from analyzing the inner dynamics of each individual to studying their pattern of interaction and communication, from seeing pathology in one or both members of a family to understanding how each has defined her role and adapted to the other. Their recurring struggle becomes circular: "I nag because you defy me." "No, Mom, it's the other way around; I defy you because you nag." In the new way of conceptualizing, attention is paid to the ongoing process between and among people and the ways in which they interact, define and redefine their relationships. Communication patterns—as much as the content of what is communicated—help determine those relationships.

The major impact of this new epistemology was to recast human problems as interactional and situational (specific to a particular time and place). In shifting the locus of pathology from the individual to the social context and the interchange between individuals, Jackson and his co-workers were not denying that intrapsychic mechanisms influence individual functioning. Rather, they were giving greater credence to the power of family rules to govern interactive behavior; to them, a breakdown in individual or family functioning followed from a breakdown in rules. The shift in Jackson's thinking led inevitably to redefining the appropriate unit of study for the therapist; the observation of exchanges between people became more relevant than the process of drawing difficult to validate inferences regarding the character or personality deficits of an individual (Greenberg, 1977). In the situation described in the previous paragraph, for example, the attempt to determine cause and effect is irrelevant and, indeed, incorrect. The mother is not the cause of her daughter's behavior nor is the daughter causing her mother's behavior. Both are caught up in a circular or reverberating system, a chain reaction that feeds back on itself. This circular interaction continues because each participant imposes her own **punctuation;** each arbitrarily believes that what she says is caused by what the other person says. In a sense, such serial punctuations between family members resemble the dialogue of children quarreling: "You started it!" ("I'm only reacting to what you did.") "No, you started it first!" and so on. As Weakland (1976), a longtime proponent of the communication view, contends, it is meaningless to search for a starting point to a conflict between two people because it is a complex repetitive interaction, not a simple, linear, cause-and-effect situation.

Once considered iconoclastic if not radical, the communication/interactional view has had an influence on all subsequent approaches to family therapy and has undergone considerable revision as it has evolved over three decades. Consequently, we have chosen to divide this presentation into three parts: the original Mental Research Institute (MRI) interactional view, the strategic therapy refinements advanced primarily by Jay Haley and Cloë Madanes, and the systemic outlook as advocated by Mara Selvini-Palazzoli and her associates in Milan, Italy.

THE MRI INTERACTIONAL VIEW (JACKSON, HALEY, SATIR)

We have already noted the role played by the prestigious MRI in Palo Alto in originating many of the ideas regarding family communication patterns now considered axiomatic to the field. Gregory Bateson, Don Jackson, Jay Haley, Virginia Satir, John Weakland, Jules Riskin, Paul Watzlawick and Richard Fisch are just some of the prominent family therapy figures who have been closely affiliated with the Institute over the years. In the decade ending not long after Jackson's death in 1968, the theoretical foundation for a communication/interaction approach to the family was laid, based largely on ideas derived from general systems theory, cybernetics and information theory. The concepts of family rules, family homeostasis, marital quid pro quo, the redundancy principle (according to which a family interacts within a limited range of repetitive behavioral sequences), punctuation, symmetrical and complementary relationships, and circular causality are all attributable to the seminal thinking of MRI researchers, in addition, of course, to prototypic work on the double-bind in schizophrenia.

To communication/interaction theorists, all behavior is communication; just as it is impossible not to behave, so communication cannot be avoided. The wife who complains in utter frustration that her husband "refuses to communicate" with her but instead stares at the television set all evening is responding too literally to his failure to "talk" to her. On a nonverbal level, she is receiving a loud and clear message that he is rejecting her, withdrawing from her, may be angry or bored with her, wants distance from her, and so on. Communication occurs at many levels—gesture, body language, tone of voice, posture, intensity—in addition to the content of what is said. Sometimes, as discussed in Chapter 3, a message is sent in the form of a double-bind, containing an implicit contradiction:

| IGNORE THESE INSTRUCTIONS |

To follow instructions, one must not follow instructions, which becomes very confusing.

There is, of course, no such thing as a simple message. People continually send and receive a multiplicity of messages by both verbal and nonverbal channels and every message is qualified and modified by another message on another level of abstraction (Weakland, 1976). People can say one thing and mean another, modifying, reinforcing, or contradicting what they have just said. In other words, they are both communicating ("How are you?") and communicating *about* their communication ("I do not really expect you to answer, nor do I especially want to know the answer, unless you say you are fine."). All communication takes place at two levels—the surface or content level and a second level called **metacommunication** that qualifies what is said on the first level (Watzlawick, Beavin, & Jackson, 1967). Problems may arise when a message at the first level ("Nice to see you") is contradicted by a facial expression or voice tone ("How can I make a quick getaway from this boring person?") that communicates at the second level. As we have seen, communication theorists, following the original research of Bateson and his co-workers, propose that such contradictions are common in families that produce schizophrenic children: we love you (hate you), we want you close by (go away), and so on. In effect, the parent is saying "I order you to disobey me" to a confused child to whom the relationship is important; the child cannot escape but must respond to the incongruent messages. In that situation he or she may develop a similarly incongruent way of communicating back, sometimes in a schizophrenic manner.[1]

[1]Although the communication theorists did their early work at the Mental Research Institute in Palo Alto, primarily with families with schizophrenic members, they have since affiliated themselves with many other family therapy centers around the country and expanded their interests to other aspects of family functioning. In the meantime, the MRI has continued as a research, training, and family therapy center, emphasizing the interactional view of behavior (Watzlawick & Weakland, 1977) and developing new therapeutic techniques (such as brief family therapy, a time-

Every communication has a content "report" and a relationship "command" aspect. That is, every communication does more than convey information; it also defines the relationship between communicants. For example, the husband who announces "I'm hungry" is offering information but, more important, is telling his wife that he expects her to do something about it by preparing dinner. He is thus making a statement of his perceived rights in the relationship; he expects his wife to take action based on his statement. The way his wife responds tells him whether she is willing to go along with his definition of the relationship or wants to engage in what could be a struggle to redefine it ("Why don't you make the dinner tonight?" or "I'd like to go out to a restaurant tonight." or "I'm not hungry yet.").

Relationships are defined by command messages. These messages constitute regulating patterns for stabilizing relationships and defining family "rules." In operation, the "rules" preserve family homeostasis. The notion of the family attempting to maintain a homeostatic balance is central to Jackson's thinking. You will recall from Chapter 2 that Jackson (1965b) likened the family's operations to those of a home heating system, in which a sudden change in temperature initiates a number of events designed to reestablish the equilibrium. In a family, when a teenager announces she is pregnant, or a grandmother moves in with her children and grandchildren, or there is a divorce between parents, or the onset of chronic illness in a child, or a family member becomes schizophrenic, it has an effect similar to flinging open a window when the house has been warmed to the desired temperature. The family goes to work to reestablish its balance; ironically, a family that was disintegrating and disunited has a sudden impetus to become functional again in order to cope with the crisis.

In a family, a communication pattern reveals much about the sender's and receiver's relationship. If it is a relationship based on equality, the pattern is symmetrical; if not, the pattern is complementary. (These concepts, illustrated by a transcript of a husband and wife talking to a therapist, are presented in Chapter 3.) Symmetrical communication may be a simple open exchange of views or perhaps highly competitive, but it takes place between peers, while complementary communication inevitably involves one person assuming a superior position and the other an inferior one. In this respect, Jackson's thinking resembles that of Haley (1963), who underscores the struggle for power and control in every relationship that is inherent in the messages that sender and receiver exchange with each other. Who will define the relationship? Will that person turn it into a symmetrical or complementary one? Who decides who decides? Observe a couple discussing how to allocate expenditures, for example, or what television program to watch, or who will answer the telephone, balance the checkbook, go out to buy some ice cream, or pick up the dirty socks

---

limited, pragmatic approach intended to help families cope with the changes in their relationships associated with the various stages of family development) (Watzlawick, Weakland, & Fisch, 1974). We include the MRI's Brief Therapy Center work among the innovative techniques discussed in Chapter 12.

and underwear from the floor and see if you do not learn a great deal about how the partners define their relationship.

Haley believes that a symptom is a strategy for controlling a relationship when all other strategies have failed; moreover, the symptomatic person denies any intent to control by claiming the symptom is involuntary. As an example, Haley cites the case of a woman who insists her husband be home every night because she suffers anxiety attacks if left alone. However, she refuses to acknowledge her demand as a means of controlling his behavior, but blames it on the anxiety attacks over which she presumably has no control. The husband faces a dilemma: he cannot acknowledge that she is controlling his behavior (the anxiety attacks are at fault for that) but he cannot refuse to let her control his behavior (after all, she has anxiety attacks). He is in a double-bind situation.

Haley, therefore, focuses on the power struggles within a family and how each family member constantly seeks to define or redefine his or her relationships. ("You can't boss me around anymore; I'm not a baby" is a familiar taunt heard from a teenager trying to change old family "rules.") Jockeying for control, according to Haley, occurs in all families and in every relationship between two or more people. Most couples develop suitable means of dealing with issues of control; people who present symptoms are resorting to subtle, indirect methods. Haley's (1976) therapeutic approach is to treat individual problems as symptoms of an improperly functioning family organization. He seeks to provoke a change in the patient's behavior that will alleviate the symptom. (In the following section of this chapter, we present Haley's more recent work, particularly his contributions to strategic family therapy.)

In addition to Jackson and Haley, Satir became known during the 1960s as an open, direct, caring person intent on teaching families more honest and effective communication patterns. At the time, it was thought that a therapist, simply by assuming the role of educator and pointing out communication problems within a family, could make a family's implicit rules more explicit to them and thus help them to change. Satir's approach epitomized this view, now largely abandoned as too simplistic a strategy by all but a few novice family therapists. Satir herself, as we saw in Chapter 6, has since modified her position and now, as a humanistically oriented family therapist, concerns herself more with such issues as self-awareness, self-expression and self-esteem in families.

The interactional view continues to be represented by the therapeutic interventions of Don Jackson and associates such as Paul Watzlawick. One direct outgrowth of the research on the pathological double-bind was the notion of the **therapeutic double-bind,** a general term used to describe a variety of paradoxical techniques. Jackson and Watzlawick (who extended Jackson's work after his death) assume that the therapist, as an outsider, is the one to provide the family with an experience that will enable them to change their rules, something they are powerless to do without an external stimulus. Therapeutic double-binds, interventions that mirror paradoxical communication within a family, were proposed as a powerful strategy for implementing change.

A paradox, you will recall, can be defined as a "contradiction that follows correct deduction from consistent premises" (Watzlawick, Beavin & Jackson, 1967). In a pathogenic double-bind situation, the recipient is placed in a position where no solution is possible. Applied therapeutically to a family, a symptomatic member is told not to change (for example, a paranoid patient is encouraged to become more suspicious) in a context where the family has come expecting to be helped to change. The family member is caught in a trap: if the person resists the injunction, it constitutes change; if the person does not change, it represents a choice; a person who makes a choice is exercising control. Since symptoms, by definition, are beyond control, the family member is no longer behaving symptomatically.

Technically, Watzlawick, Beavin, and Jackson (1967, p. 241) outline the structure of the therapeutic double-bind as follows:

1. It presupposes an intense relationship, in this case the psychotherapeutic situation, which has a high degree of survival value and of expectation for the patient.
2. In this context, an injunction is given which is so structured that it:
   a) reinforces the behavior the patient expects to be changed;
   b) implies that this reinforcement is the vehicle of change; and
   c) thereby creates paradox because the patient is told to change by remaining unchanged. He is put in an untenable situation with regard to his pathology. If he complies, he no longer "can't help it"; he does "it," and this, as we have tried to show, makes "it" impossible, which is the purpose of therapy. If he resists the injunction, he can do so only by *not* behaving symptomatically, which is the purpose of therapy. If in a pathogenic double-bind the patient is "damned if he does and damned if he doesn't," in a therapeutic double-bind he is "changed if he does and changed if he doesn't."
3. The therapeutic situation prevents the patient from withdrawing or otherwise dissolving the paradox by commenting on it. Therefore, even though the injunction is logically absurd, it is a pragmatic reality: the patient cannot *not* react to it, but neither can he react to it in his usual, symptomatic way.

In a form of therapeutic double-bind called **prescribing the symptom,** Jackson tried to produce a runaway system (positive feedback) by urging the family *not* to change—to keep things, including symptoms, as they are, at least for the present time. The family is instructed to continue or even exaggerate what it is already doing (for example, the mother and daughter described at the beginning of this chapter might be directed to have a fight on a regular basis). Since the family has come for help from the therapist (who does not seem to be stupid, crazy or incompetent) and since the directive is easy to follow because the symptomatic behavior is occurring anyway, the family complies. The therapist, asked to help them change, appears to be asking for no change at all! Such an assignment, however, undermines family members' resistance to change by rendering it unnecessary. Confronted with the idea of fighting regularly, the mother and daughter begin to interact in a different manner. The unstated rules by which they operated before become more obvious to them, as does the notion that their previous quarreling did not "just happen" involuntarily but can be brought under voluntary control.[2]

Another form of therapeutic bind, **relabeling** (similar to what was described in Chapter 8 as reframing), attempts to alter the meaning of a situation by altering its conceptual and/or emotional context in such a way that the entire situation is perceived differently. The situation remains unchanged, but the meaning attributed to it, and thus its consequences, is altered. The classic example involves Tom Sawyer, who relabeled as pleasurable the drudgery of whitewashing a fence and thus was in a position to ask other boys to pay for the privilege of helping him. Relabeling typically emphasizes the positive ("Mother's not being overprotective; she merely is trying to be helpful") and helps the family redefine disturbing behavior in more sympathetic or optimistic terms. Relabeling provides a new framework for looking at interaction; as the rules by which the family operates become more explicit, the family members become aware that old patterns are not necessarily unchangeable. Like the other binding techniques, the goal of relabeling is to change the structure of family relationships and interactions.

STRATEGIC FAMILY THERAPY (HALEY, MADANES)

If the communication/interaction approach, the MRI model, drew the greatest attention from professionals in the 1960s and Minuchin's structural model was the most consistently studied and emulated in the 1970s, then it is fair to say that the strategic approach has taken center stage in the 1980s. As its leading advocates Madanes and Haley (1977) contend, the main characteristic of this therapeutic approach is that the therapist devises a strategy for solving the client's presenting problems. Goals are clearly set; therapy is carefully planned, in stages, to achieve these goals; problems are defined as involving at least two and usually three people. The thrust of the intervention is to shift the family organization so that the presenting problem no longer serves a function. To the strategic therapist, change occurs not through insight and understanding but through the process of the family carrying out directives issued by the therapist.

The career of Jay Haley plays an important part in the development of the strategic approach to family therapy. Haley was an early worker in family

---

[2]Maurizio Andolfi (1979), Director of the Family Therapy Institute in Rome, is particularly adept at unbalancing rigid family systems, often through effective use of "prescribing the symptom." In a family in which an anorexic adolescent girl controls family communication and defines all relations, including the relationship between her parents, Andolfi will *forbid* the girl from eating during a lunch session when the therapist and family eat together normally. Since her symptom (non-eating) is now involuntary, it no longer serves as a means of controlling family interactions. At the same time, the family can no longer use its typical incongruent message: "Eat, but don't eat." The prescription interrupts the family game based on the daughter's eating problem and helps expose the rules of the anorexic system.

Milton Erickson, M.D.

research who had a significant role in developing the "double-bind" concept to account for the effect of a family's pathological communication patterns on the development of schizophrenia in a family member (Bateson, Jackson, Haley & Weakland, 1956). As a pioneer in family therapy, Haley became a student and interpreter of Milton Erickson, whose hypnotic techniques typically required the therapist to assume full charge of the treatment and to issue directives (however subtle) as a way of gaining leverage with patients and, ultimately, manipulating them to change. Erickson's extraordinary feats of observation and uncanny ability to tap unrecognized resources in his clients (usually individuals rather than families) have been chronicled by Haley (1973) and more recently by Zeig (1980). Erickson was particularly skilled at "encouraging resistance." That is, he was able to encourage patients to maintain a symptom (by not fighting it, or insisting the client work at giving it up) and then subtly introduce directions to induce change. Thus, he was able to avoid direct confrontation with the symptom, a tactic likely to have been met with resistance, and to utilize the client's own momentum to force symptom abandonment. This common hypnotic technique became the basis for the development of the paradoxical directive, a hallmark of the strategic approach (Hoffman, 1981).

Haley was also influenced by his long association as trainer and theory-builder with Salvador Minuchin and Braulio Montalvo at the Philadelphia Child Guidance Center. Hoffman (1981) actually classifies Haley's position as a structural-strategic approach; Haley's concern with family hierarchy and coalitions and other family structure issues places him in the former group, while his interest in paradoxical directives and other unobtrusive ways of managing resistance identifies him with the latter. By 1974 Haley and his wife Cloë Madanes had formed the Family Therapy Institute in Washington,

D.C., a highly respected training program for family therapists. Haley, a prolific writer, described his strategies for changing the way a family is organized in *Problem-Solving Therapy* (1976); more recently, Haley published *Ordeal Therapy* (1984), an account of treatment based on the premise that if a client is maneuvered into a position where he or she finds it more distressful to maintain a symptom than to give it up, the client will abandon the symptom. Madanes has presented recent innovations in the field in *Behind the One-Way Mirror: Advances in the Practice of Strategic Therapy* (1984). Haley and Madanes have demonstrated their active, directive, highly focused therapeutic techniques around the world.

Strategic therapists concern themselves with family communication patterns as well as repetitive sequences of behavior between and among family members. Like the communication/interactionists, they believe that communication defines the nature of the relationship between partners. If a husband is willing to discuss only the weather when he and his wife are together in the evening, he may be defining the relationship as one where they talk only about conventional matters. If the wife refuses to comment on tomorrow's forecast but instead expresses the idea that they seem distant from each other this evening, she is attempting to redefine the relationship on more personal and intimate terms. Implicit in every relationship, according to an early Haley formulation (1963), is a maneuver for power, not a struggle to control another person but a struggle to control the definition of the relationship. In some marriages, a partner's symptoms (for example, anxiety attacks, phobias, depressions, heavy drinking) control what takes place between the partners—where they go, what they do together, whether one can leave the other's side for any length of time, and so on. Traditionally, such symptoms have been explained as expressions of intrapsychic conflict and therefore as involuntary aspects of one person's "illness." Haley, strongly opposed to intrapsychic explanations, defines symptoms as interpersonal events, as tactics used by one person to deal with another. The therapist's goal is to encourage the patient to develop other ways of defining relationships so that the symptomatic methods will be abandoned.

Strategic family therapists tailor their interventions to a particular set of presenting problems, deal with the present rather than the past and devise novel strategies for helping the family prevent the repetition of destructive behavior. Rather than offer interpretation or provide insight—the family may actually resolve a problem without ever knowing why or how—strategic therapists attempt to change only those aspects of the family system that are maintaining the problematic or symptomatic behavior.

Haley (1963) points out that therapists and patients continually maneuver each other in the process of treatment. Elements of a power struggle exist in psychoanalysis, hypnosis, behavior therapy, family therapy, and other forms of treatment. Family members may try to manipulate, deceive, exclude, or subdue a therapist in order to maintain the homeostatic balance they have achieved, even if it is at the expense of symptomatic behavior in one of their members. The therapist, therefore, must take an authoritative stance. Haley (1976) sees his task as taking responsibility for changing the family organization and resolving the problem that brought the family to see him. He is highly directive, giving the family members precise instructions and insisting that they be followed. Thus, he is highly manipulative in his procedures. For example, Haley cites the case (1976) of a grandmother siding with her grandchild (age 10) against the mother. He saw the mother and child together, instructing the child to irritate the grandmother and instructing the mother to defend her daughter against the grandmother. This task forced a collaboration between mother and daughter and helped detach the daughter from her grandmother.

As we can see from this example, Haley is an active, take-charge family therapist. Artfully gaining the position of family change-maker, he intervenes when he chooses (rather than when the family requests his participation), comments openly about the family's efforts to influence or control him, gives directions and assigns tasks, and assumes temporary leadership of the family group. He avoids getting enticed into coalitions within the family; adroitly, he takes sides[3] to overcome an impasse but quickly disengages before becoming allied with one or another family faction.

Another Haley tactic is to emphasize the positive, usually by relabeling seemingly dysfunctional behavior as reasonable and understandable. In one often quoted example, Haley boldly and somewhat outrageously told a wife whose husband had chased after her with an axe that the man was simply trying to get close to her! Haley is simply following a principle of communication theory described earlier; namely, that all communication occurs at two levels and that the message at the second level (metacommunication) qualifies what takes place on the surface level. A remark made by a sender in normal conversation can be taken as a joke or an attack, as praise or as blame, depending on the context in which the receiver places it. By relabeling or reframing, Haley changes the context, freeing the participants to behave differently in the new context.

Directives, or tasks, are given to individuals and families for several reasons: (1) to get people to behave differently in order for them to have different subjective experiences; (2) to intensify the therapeutic relationship by involving the therapist in the family's actions during the time between sessions; and (3) to gather information, by their reactions, as to how the family members will respond to the suggested changes. In most cases, Haley issues a directive to family members (for example, instructing a mother to stop intruding when the father and son try to talk to each other) because he wants or expects them to follow it in order for them to change their behavior toward one another.

---

[3]Another noteworthy side-taker is Gerald Zuk (1981). Although Madanes and Haley (1977) classify him as a strategic therapist, Zuk does not use the term himself. Nevertheless, as Stanton (1981) notes, Zuk often displays the kind of planning and forethought exercised by strategists. A systems-oriented psychologist long affiliated with The Eastern Pennsylvania Psychiatric Institute in Philadelphia, Zuk offers a **triadic-based therapy** in which the therapist acts as go-between in working with a couple, setting the rules for communicating, in order to shift the balance of "pathogenic relating" among family members. As go-between and as side-taker, Zuk may select an issue to be negotiated, with himself as mediator, deliberately siding with one and then the other family member. By taking control and setting limits, Zuk structures and directs the therapy process.

However, as this example illustrates, asking someone to stop engaging in certain behavior is a difficult directive to enforce; its success depends upon the status of the therapist giving the instruction, the severity or chronicity of the behavior, how often the directive is repeated, whether the father and son are willing to be cooperative so they might support the therapist in accomplishing the task, and so forth. In short, a key factor determining whether the therapist will succceed in this direct approach is the motivation of all the family members.

Another kind of task assignment, more indirect, is one in which the therapist wants the family to resist him or her so that it will change. These are called paradoxical tasks; it seems to the family members that through the assignment of the task the therapist is asking them not to change at the same time that the therapist has declared the intention of helping them change. **Paradoxical intervention,** as Haley uses it, represents a particularly ingenious way of forcing a person or family to abandon old dysfunctional behavior. Similar to "prescribing the symptom," this technique is particularly appropriate for Haley (1976), the strategist, because he assumes that families who come for help are also resistant to any help being offered. The result may be a standoff, a power struggle with the therapist trying to help family members change but unstabilizing their homeostatic balance in the process, and the family trying to get the therapist to fail but to go on trying because they realize something is wrong. Andolfi (1979), also considered a structural/strategic therapist, describes such an encounter as a game into which the therapist is drawn, and in which every effort on the part of the therapist to act as an agent of change is nullified by the family group. If not careful, Andolfi warns, the therapist can easily get entangled in the family's contradictory logic of "help me to change, but without changing anything."

Haley's paradoxical approach encompasses several stages. First, he attempts to set up a relationship with the family in which change is expected. Second, the problem to be corrected is clearly defined; third, the goals are clearly stated. In the fourth stage, the therapist must offer a plan; it is helpful if a rationale can be included that makes the paradoxical task seem reasonable. In the fifth stage, the current authority on the problem (such as a physician or a parent) is disqualified as not handling the situation the right way; in the sixth, the therapist issues the directive. In the seventh and last stage, the therapist observes the response and continues to encourage the usual problem behavior.

It is of utmost importance that the therapist using paradoxical intervention carefully encourage the member(s) with the behavior to be changed to continue that behavior unchanged[4]—a domineering wife to continue to run everything in the family; a daughter refusing to attend school to stay home; an

---

[4]There has been a great deal of interest recently in the use of paradoxical interventions (Weeks & L'Abate, 1982; Hare-Mustin, 1976; Papp, 1984). By now the reader is aware that this approach is employed by many family therapists, especially in dealing with defiant or resistant families. We particularly underline its use in our discussion of those therapies that emphasize clear communication because a paradoxical injunction (for example, "Be spontaneous") is a prototype of a double-bind situation. To command someone to be spontaneous is to demand behavior that by its very

adolescent boy masturbating in public to continue doing so but to keep a chart of how often, what days he enjoyed it most, and so on. Haley might tell a couple who always fight unproductively to go home and fight for three hours. The issue becomes one of control. The domineering wife no longer runs everything if the therapist is telling her what to do and if she resists his directive she will become less domineering. Similarly, Haley assumes in the other cases that the symptom presented, originally a way of gaining an advantage, will resolve if the symptom now places the person at a disadvantage. In the case of the couple, Haley expects them to stop fighting; people do not like to make themselves miserable because someone else tells them to do so. Haley is a master at bringing about change through the use of therapeutic paradox. By the use of this technique he forces the symptom bearer into a no-win situation: should the individual or family follow his instruction and continue the problematic or symptomatic behavior, Haley has been given the power and control to make the symptom occur at his direction. Should the individual or family resist the paradoxical intervention, the symptomatic behavior is, in the process, given up (and, again, the therapist retains power and control).

There are three major steps in designing a paradox, according to Papp (1984): *redefining, prescribing,* and *restraining.* Before a therapist can "prescribe the symptom," the behavior to be maintained must be redefined as a loving gesture in the service of preserving family stability. Thus, anger may be relabeled love, suffering as self-sacrifice, distancing as a way of reinforcing closeness. Next, the wording of the prescription ("practice being depressed," "continue being rebellious against your parents") must be brief, concise, and unacceptable (in order for the family to recoil at the instruction) but the therapist must appear to be sincere by offering a convincing rationale for the prescription. Later, when the family members show signs of changing, the therapist must restrain them.

Restraining strategies ("go slow") are efforts to emphasize that the system's homeostatic balance is in danger if improvement occurs too fast or, sometimes, if improvement occurs at all. Haley (1976) inquires, in a case of a young, middle-class couple concerned that their young child soils his pants, what the consequences would be if he began to go to the toilet normally. (This move suggested that Haley could help them with the problem but would rather not

---

nature cannot be spontaneous because it is commanded! Thus, with seeming innocence, the message sender is trapping the receiver into a situation where rule compliance entails rule violation (Watzlawick, Weakland, & Fisch, 1974). The receiver is faced with two conflicting levels of messages, is bewildered, and cannot make an effective response. As Haley, Milton Erickson, Watzlawick and others use the paradox therapeutically, the family is directed in effect to "disobey me." As in the case of commanding someone to be spontaneous, instructing that person to disobey what you are saying is to produce a paradox. Thus, the family told not to change in effect defies the therapist's injunction; the family begins to change to prove the therapist wrong in assuming it could not change. If the therapist allows himself or herself to be put down as wrong and even suggests that the change is very likely to be temporary and a relapse probable, the family will resist relapse and continue to change to prove the therapist wrong again. It is essential that the therapist never claim credit for helping the family—indeed, the therapist remains puzzled by the change—to preclude the family's need to be disobedient in the form of a relapse.

until he was sure of the consequences to the entire family.) When they returned the next week and indicated that they could think of no adverse consequences, the therapist suggested some possibilities; for example, could the mother tolerate being successful with her child? This effort to restrain the mother from changing her overinvolved but exasperated behavior contained messages at several levels: 1) Haley thought she could tolerate success; 2) he was benevolently concerned so he wanted to make sure she could tolerate it; and 3) the mother would find the suggestion of not tolerating success to be unacceptable. No mother is likely to think she cannot be successful with her own child, as Haley well knew. Thus provoked (the father was similarly confronted), both parents became highly motivated to solve their problem to prove they could tolerate being normal; the boy's encopretic behavior ceased.

Some critics have argued that Haley's methods are too manipulative and authoritarian, a charge he dismisses as baseless since he claims all therapies, whether they acknowledge it or not, rely to some extent on interpersonal influence, challenge, and therapist expertise to resolve family problems. Nevertheless, detractors charge that paradoxical intervention need not be so blatantly reliant on power and provocation. Madanes (1981, 1984) has developed a number of **pretend techniques** that are less confrontational, less apt to invite defiance and rebelliousness, but still help to overcome family resistance. Based on playfulness, humor, and fantasy, these gentler approaches would have a therapist suggest, for example, that a symptomatic child "pretend" to have a symptom and that the parents "pretend" to help. By manipulating the family through this kind of paradoxical intervention, Madanes manages to work out in make-believe what once produced an actual symptom. In many cases, if the family is pretending, then the actual symptom cannot be real and can be abandoned at will.

SYSTEMIC THERAPY AND THE MILAN ASSOCIATES (SELVINI-PALAZZOLI)

Three major related approaches to family therapy emerged from the work of the Bateson research project of 1952–1962: the MRI communication/interactional model; the strategic model developed by Haley and Madanes; and the model put forth by the Milan Associates led by Mara Selvini-Palazzoli. Of the three, the Milan group comes closest to constructing a model that is conceptually and methodologically consistent with Bateson's circular epistemology (MacKinnon, 1983). That is, they focus their approach on information, much like Bateson (1972)—and as exemplified in his famous definition of information as "a difference that makes a difference." Characterized by a systematic search for differences—in behavior, in relationships, in how different family members perceive and construe an event—and by efforts to uncover the connections that link family members and keep the system in balance, the approach has come to be known as **systemic family therapy.**

Although trained as a child psychoanalyst, Selvini-Palazzoli found greater success in treating anorexic children when she shifted her thinking from individuals to families and from the psychoanalytic to a more purely systems orientation. In the late 1960s in Milan, Italy, she set about organizing a team of therapists including three psychiatrists—Luigi Boscolo, Gianfranco Cecchin, Guiliana Prata—with whom she worked for the next decade on developing a radically new, systems-based approach for working with families with a wide variety of severe emotional problems. To date, the clearest and most comprehensive exposition of their work in book form can be found in *Paradox and Counterparadox: A New Model in the Therapy of the Family in Schizophrenic Transaction* (Selvini-Palazzoli, Boscolo, Cecchin, & Prata, 1978). However, the four colleagues have since separated into two autonomous groups (Boscolo and Cecchin; Selvini-Palazzoli and Prata) to continue their work, still systemically based but with somewhat different emphases. In the United States, the Milan group's outlook has found a particularly receptive audience among some members of the Ackerman Institute for Family Therapy in New York, especially Peggy Papp, Olga Silverstein and Lynn Hoffman (Hoffman has since founded her own family institute in Amherst, Massachusetts).

The Milan group's approach has been described as "long brief" therapy since relatively few sessions (generally about ten) are held approximately once a month and thus treatment may extend up to a year or so. Originally this unusual spacing of sessions was instituted because so many of the families seen at the Institute for Family Studies in Milan had to travel hundreds of miles by train for treatment. Later, however, the therapy team realized that their interventions—often in the form of paradoxical prescriptions aimed at changing the way an entire family system functioned—took time to incubate and finally take effect. Once the frequency is determined, the therapists will not grant an extra session or move up a session to shorten the agreed-upon interval. Such requests by families are seen as efforts to disqualify or undo the effects of a previous intervention (Selvini-Palazzoli, 1980). The Milan associates are adamant in their determination that the therapist not submit to the family's "game" or become subjugated to its rules for maintaining sameness and controlling the therapeutic relationship. Even in a dire emergency, these therapists remain unavailable in the belief that a request for an exceptional meeting actually means the family is experiencing rapid change and needs time to integrate any subsequent changes in family rules.

The Milan associates work in an unconventional but fairly set way. The entire family is seen together by one or sometimes two therapists (typically a man and a woman) while the remainder of the team watches behind a one-way mirror. From time to time during the session, the observers may summon one of the therapists out of the room in order to make suggestions, share opinions, provide their own observations or discuss the therapeutic progress. Following this strategy conference, the therapist rejoins the family group and before the family members leave they are assigned a task, usually a paradoxical prescription. Sometimes such a prescription is in the form of a letter, a copy of which is given to every member. In the rare event that a key member misses a session, a copy of the letter may be sent by mail, frequently with comments (again, often paradoxically stated) regarding his or her absence. Prescriptions may take the form of opinions ("We believe father and mother, by working hard to be good parents, are nevertheless . . ."), or requests that certain behavioral changes be attempted by means of rituals carried out between sessions ("the immediate family, without any other relatives or outsiders, should meet weekly for one hour, with each person allowed fifteen minutes to . . ."). By addressing the behavior of all the members, the connections in the family patterns are underscored. Prescriptions usually are stated in such a way that the family is directed not to change for the time being.

To the Milan group, family therapy begins with the initial telephone call from the family. The team member who takes the call talks to the caller at length, recording the information on a fact sheet. Who calls? Who referred the family? What is the problem? How disturbed was the caller's communication? What tone of voice was used? What was the caller's attitude regarding the forthcoming treatment? What special conditions, if any, did the caller attempt to impose (specific date or time)? These intake issues are then taken up with the entire team prior to the first interview, again in a lengthy and detailed way. In a similar fashion, such team conferences occur before each session, as the therapists meet to review the previous session, and, together, plan strategies for the upcoming one. All of these tactics affirm the Milan therapists' belief that the family and therapist(s) are part of one system.

The Milan model is more concerned with process than family structure. It views the family members as engaging in destructive, repetitive sequences of interaction in which no one can extricate himself or herself from the family's self-perpetuating "games." To attempt to change an individual player is to doom the intervention to failure. Even the identified problem is seen as serving the system in the best way possible at the moment. Why, then, can the family not find a better way to survive and function, one that does not involve sacrificing one of its (symptomatic) members? Perhaps the rules governing the system are too rigid, tolerating an extremely narrow range of behavior. Since the family members, through their communication patterns, maintain the system's rules and thus perpetuate the transactions in which the symptomatic behavior is embedded, the therapist must try to change the rules in order to change that behavior (Selvini-Palazzoli, Boscolo, Cecchin, & Prata, 1978).

Put more succinctly, systemic therapy tries to change the rules of the game before the players can change. In the following example (Selvini-Palazzoli, 1978), the therapist working with a family with an anorexic daughter must break the code inherent in the following family game, as each parent both insists upon and denies family leadership:

Mother: I don't let her wear miniskirts because I know her father doesn't like them.

Father: I have always backed my wife up. I feel it would be wrong to contradict her (p. 208).

Note the trap the therapist is drawn into if he or she tries to change such confusing and disqualifying statements. Direct interventions are likely to bring forth countermoves, as the family members fight off any challenge to their rules. Following Bateson's earlier work, Selvini-Palazzoli and her colleagues contend that a family double-bind message, a paradox, can only be undone by a therapeutic double-bind, which they call a **counterparadox.**

Several techniques have become trademarks of the Milan group. **Positive connotation** is a form of reframing in which symptomatic behavior is qualified as "positive" or "good" because it helps maintain the system's homeostatic balance. All members are considered to be motivated by the same desire for family cohesion and thus all are linked as participants in the family system. Because the positive connotation is presented as an approval rather than a reproach, the family does not resist such explicit confirmation and accepts the statement. However, the positive connotation has implicitly put the family in a paradox: why must such a good thing as family cohesion require the presence of symptomatic behavior in a member? Consistent with the Milan tactics, the therapists present paradoxes and issue directives and prescriptions to the entire family system, not just the symptomatic member. By uncovering connecting patterns, by revealing family "games," by introducing new information into the system through opinions or requests that certain family rituals be carried out between sessions, they are trying to bring about a transformation in family rules and relationships. Note that, unlike Haley, the Milan therapists do not issue prescriptions to arouse defiance and resistance. Rather, they offer "information" about family connectedness and the interrelatedness of its members' behavior. By deliberately trying not to provoke resistance to change, they help the family discover its own solutions (MacKinnon, 1983).

Several other Milan principles need to be reviewed briefly. **Hypothesizing** refers to the active efforts the team makes before the first session to formulate in advance what they believe might be responsible for maintaining the family's problems. This helps the team organize forthcoming information from the family and begin to comprehend why the symptomatic behavior manifested itself in this family at this time. If the hypothesis turns out to be incorrect, it may be amended in later conferences. **Neutrality** refers to the therapists' efforts to remain allied with all family members, avoiding getting caught up in family coalitions or alliances. Such a position, typically low-keyed and nonreactive, allows for maximum leverage in achieving change by not being drawn into family "games." **Circular questioning** is an effective diagnostic as well as therapeutic technique of framing every question so that it addresses differences in perception about events or relationships. Asking a child to compare his mother's and father's reactions to his sister's refusal to eat, or to rate each one's anger on a ten point scale, or to hypothesize what whould happen if they divorced—these are all subtle and relatively benign ways to compel people to focus on differences. By asking several people the same question about their attitude toward the same relationship, the therapist is able to probe more and more deeply without being directly confrontational or interrogating the participants in the relationship (Selvini-Palazzoli, Boscolo, Cecchin, & Prata, 1980). Here again we see the influence of Bateson's thinking, with its stress on information, differences, and circularity.

SUMMARY

Communication theories, emerging from the research at the Mental Research Institute in Palo Alto in the 1950s, have had a major impact on the family therapy field by recasting human problems as interactional and situational (tied to a set of circumstances that maintains them). The introduction of this epistemology by Bateson, Jackson, Haley and others laid the foundation for the therapeutic efforts of the MRI (interactional view), strategic family therapy as developed by Haley and Madanes, and the systemic approach of Selvini-Palazzoli and her Milan team. Particularly characteristic of these approaches is the use of therapeutic double-binds or paradoxical techniques for changing family rules and relationship patterns.

Paradoxes—contradictions that follow correct deductions from consistent premises—are used therapeutically to direct an individual or family not to change in a context that carries with it the expectation of change. The procedure promotes change no matter which action, compliance or resistance, is undertaken. "Prescribing the symptom," as used by Jackson, is a paradoxical technique for undermining resistance to change by rendering it unnecessary.

The strategic family therapy approach, currently receiving considerable attention from family therapists, is characterized by carefully planned tactics and the issuance of directives for solving a family's presenting problems. Haley, its most influential practitioner, uses task assignments, paradoxical interventions that force the willing abandonment of dysfunctional behavior by means of the family defying the directive not to change. Madanes, another strategic family therapist, uses "pretend" techniques, nonconfrontational interventions directed at achieving change without inviting resistance.

Selvini-Palazzoli and her Milan group practice systemic family therapy, a technique based on Bateson's circular epistemology. According to a "long brief therapy" procedure in which sessions are spaced at more or less monthly intervals, the family is seen by a team of therapists who plan strategy together; one or two therapists work directly with the family, the others observe from behind a one-way mirror. Families are assigned tasks between sessions, usually based on paradoxical prescriptions. The goal of the Milan model is to offer "information" in order to influence families to change the rules—the destructive repetitive sequences—of their self-perpetuating, self-defeating "games." The Milan approach contends that a family's paradoxical or double-bind messages can only be countered by a therapeutic double-bind or counterparadox.

Theoretical Perspectives: Behavioral Models

Behavioral models of family therapy are relatively recent additions to the field, since it is only within the last fifteen years or so that the application of **behavioral** concepts has been extended to the family unit. The use of behavioral methods with individuals goes back to the early 1960s when, as a reaction against psychodynamic theory and technique, a movement began to bring the scientific method to bear upon the psychotherapeutic process. Today, although many behavior therapists attend less exclusively to observable behavior and also try to modify a client's cognitive processes, they continue to "place great value on meticulous observation, careful testing of hypotheses, and continual self-correction on the basis of empirically derived data" (Lazarus, 1977, p. 550). The unique contribution of the behavioral approach lies not in conceptualizations of psychopathology or adherence to a particular theory or underlying set of principles but in its insistence on a rigorous, data-based set of procedures and a regularly monitored scientific methodology.

Despite the behaviorists' relatively recent entrance into the marital and family field, they have made a significant and lasting impact on current practices. Indirectly, we see their influence on therapists such as Haley and Minuchin who manipulate environments and attempt to change specific maladaptive patterns of interactive behavior. More directly, the behavioral approach is best illustrated by several types of treatment that we describe in this chapter: **behavioral marital therapy** (BMT), **behavioral parent training** (BPT) to acquire better child management skills, and **conjoint sex therapy** to ameliorate various forms of sexual dysfunction.

SOME BASIC BEHAVIORAL CONCEPTS

The behavioral methods in family therapy apply principles of human learning derived from the psychological laboratory to changing or modifying the maladaptive, problematic or dysfunctional behavior in which family members are engaged. For behavioral family therapists, theory precedes practice. That is, intervention procedures follow logically from behavioral theory; in most other approaches to family therapy, successful therapeutic techniques are developed first and only afterwards is a theory constructed to explain their success.

Before we consider some of the current forms of behavioral family therapy, we present some underlying theoretical assumptions (see Table 10-1) and define important terms. Behaviorists strive for precision in identifying a problem, employ quantification to measure change and conduct further research to validate their results. They design programs that emphasize assessment (the **behavioral analysis** of the family's difficulties) along with a number of direct and pragmatic treatment techniques to alleviate symptoms and teach the family to improve its skills in communication and self-management. The behavior therapist is interested in increasing positive interaction between family members, altering the environmental conditions that oppose or impede such interaction, and training people to maintain the improved behavior. No effort is made to infer motives, uncover unconscious conflicts, hypothesize needs or drives, diagnose inner pathological conditions producing the undesired behavior; the individual or family is not necessarily helped to gain insight into the origin of current problems. Instead, emphasis is placed on the environmental, situational, and social determinants that influence behavior (Kazdin, 1984).

TABLE 10-1. Ten Underlying Assumptions of Behavior Therapy

1. All behavior, normal and abnormal, is acquired and maintained in identical ways (that is, according to the same principles of learning).
2. Behavior disorders represent learned maladaptive patterns that need not presume some inferred underlying cause or unseen motive.
3. Maladaptive behavior such as symptoms is itself the disorder, rather than a manifestation of a more basic underlying disorder or disease process.
4. It is not essential to discover the exact situation or set of circumstances in which the disorder was learned; these circumstances are usually irretrievable anyway. Rather, the focus should be on assessing the current determinants that support and maintain the undesired behavior.
5. Maladaptive behavior, having been learned, can be extinguished (that is, unlearned) and replaced by new learned behavior patterns.
6. Treatment involves the application of the experimental findings of scientific psychology, with an emphasis on developing a methodology that is precisely specified, objectively evaluated, and easily replicated.
7. Assessment is an ongoing part of treatment, as the effectiveness of treatment is continuously evaluated and specific intervention techniques are individually tailored to specific problems.
8. Behavior therapy concentrates on "here and now" problems, rather than uncovering or attempting to reconstruct the past. The therapist is interested in helping the client identify and change current environmental stimuli that reinforce the undesired behavior, in order to alter the client's behavior.
9. Treatment outcomes are evaluated in terms of measurable behavioral changes.
10. Research and scientific validation for specific therapeutic techniques have continuously been carried out by behavior therapists.

(From Goldenberg, 1983, p. 221)

Since almost all behavior is learned rather than innate, behavior can be altered by new learning. Thus, behavior therapists attempt to train a person's behavior rather than probe those dimensions of personality that, according to other models, underlie behavior.

Classical conditioning is a form of learning first investigated by Ivan Pavlov in studying the physiology of digestion in dogs. In effect, the concept refers to the fact that a neutral stimulus, paired repeatedly with a stimulus that ordinarily elicits a response, eventually elicits the response by itself. As applied to human beings by John Watson (Watson & Rayner, 1920), an American psychologist, and later elaborated by Joseph Wolpe (1958), then a South African psychiatrist, the concept was particularly relevant to clinical work because it suggested that certain responses, such as phobias, might simply (and perhaps accidentally) be learned responses. Even more important, they could be unlearned or overcome through experimental **extinction** or various counterconditioning techniques. This last idea is especially germane to the removal or reduction of symptoms of sexual dysfunction, as we shall see later in this chapter.

An even more cogent concept for behavior therapists is Skinner's (1953) notion of **operant conditioning:** the process of strengthening a particular kind of responsive behavior in a particular situation by selectively rewarding, or reinforcing, that behavior so that it will occur more frequently than other responses that are not being rewarded. For example, what some voluntary, everyday actions (such as answering a doorbell, opening a refrigerator door, choosing a particular flavor of ice cream cone, or buying a ticket to a movie or concert) have in common is that they have usually led to pleasurable consequences in the past and are therefore more likely to occur again than is behavior that has not been so rewarded (such as making an appointment with the dentist). The point is that much of our behavior, especially that which is voluntarily emitted, is controlled and maintained primarily by its consequences. Behavior therapists believe that by altering the consequences that follow from undesired behavior, this behavior may become amenable to modification and control.

Behaviorists use the concept of **reinforcement** to refer to an increase in the frequency of a response when it is immediately followed by certain consequences that are contingent upon the behavior. Another way of looking at it is to say that a contingent event that increases the frequency of any behavior can be considered a reinforcer. **Positive reinforcement** denotes an increase in the frequency of a response that is followed by a favorable event (a reward or positive reinforcer). Thus, a student studying for an examination who receives an "A" is likely to increase study activity because of having achieved the desired payoff. By the same token, an infant who cries before going to sleep and is picked up by his or her parents is likely to increase the frequency of crying before sleeping, since the attention and physical contact provided by the parents are probably positive reinforcers (Kazdin, 1984). In interpersonal terms—as we shall illustrate in discussing how marital couples can be helped to change their interactive patterns—a smile, a kiss, a gift, a show of attention and affection are all positive reinforcements that lead to increases in the occurrence of behavior that gives rise to these consequences.

Negative reinforcement refers to an increase in the frequency of a response due to the fact that an ongoing painful, unpleasant or aversive stimulus or event is removed or terminated immediately after the desired response is made (mother to teenager: "When your room is straightened up to my satisfaction, you will no longer be grounded."). Having experienced the removal of the negative reinforcer, the teenager is more likely to repeat the (room-cleaning) response.

Note that in operant conditioning, reinforcement is always contingent on the emission of a response; the response, whether positive or negative, leads to an increase in the targeted behavior. Unlike classical conditioning, operant conditioning usually concerns behavior we consider voluntary. It derives its name from the fact that some voluntary action, or "operation," must be carried out by the individual in relation to the environment. The concept has applicability to managing young children (especially when parents are able to exercise control over the reinforcers, both positive and negative) as well as to promoting changes, through the exchange of reinforcers, in marital relationships.

Another operant technique useful in achieving behavioral changes is called **shaping.** Developed by Skinner, shaping involves the reinforcement of successive approximations of a targeted behavior until the desired behavior is achieved. In many cases, the behavior therapist hopes to produce an outcome that is so complex, or involves elements so unlike those in the individual's or family's current repertoire, that it cannot be reached simply by reinforcing existing responses. Under such circumstances, the therapist may employ shaping—achieving the desired behavior by gradually reinforcing small steps along the way instead of reserving reinforcement for the final response itself.

Contingency contracting refers to a written agreement or signed contract between parties (for example, parents and children; teachers and students) specifying the circumstances under which who is to do what for whom; in effect, the contracting parties exchange positively rewarding behavior with each other. In behavioral terms, the contract specifies the relationship between certain kinds of behavior and their consequences. As an instrument that is easy to understand, straightforward, simple to devise, and noncoercive, the contract has proven to be useful in negotiating parent-child differences. By specifying contingencies, the family members together can agree on the explicit rules for their interaction and determine the consequences of compliance with those rules.

Social-learning theory represents an effort to integrate the basic principles of learning with an appreciation of the social conditions under which that learning takes place. In the social-learning view, individuals are neither exclusively driven by inner forces nor helplessly buffeted by forces in their environment. Instead, their psychological functioning might best be understood as the result of a continuous reciprocal interaction between behavior and its controlling social conditions. Cognitive functioning—the ability to think and to make choices—must also be taken into account. People are capable of learning vicariously, by observing the behavior of others as well as its consequences and by imitating that behavior; children in particular learn a great many behavioral patterns in this way (Bandura, 1977).

Social-learning theory, then, offers a broader perspective than the classical or operant conditioning theories of learning, since it views behavior as more than the product of directly experienced response consequences. Moreover, it enables many behavior therapists to recognize the role of cognition and feelings in influencing behavior. They focus their attention on the contribution of faulty thought patterns (self-defeating, anxiety-engendering statements a person consciously makes to himself or herself) to producing dysfunctional or maladaptive behavior and on the acquisition of new behavior through observing a model of that behavior. Social-learning theory is highly applicable to problematic family behavior. A therapist or family member, through **modeling** the desired behavior, provides an example for an observer to imitate; the imitation eventually becomes part of the observer's own behavioral repertoire. For example, parents may watch and then reproduce a therapist's child management strategies in their own home; a child learns to attend to cues, emulate the behavior of a parent, and finally make that behavior his or her own response to a given situation.

VARIETIES OF BEHAVIORAL FAMILY THERAPY

The following broad definition of behavior therapy has been endorsed by the Association for the Advancement of Behavior Therapy: "Behavior therapy involves primarily the application of principles derived from research in experimental and social psychology for the alleviation of human suffering and the enhancement of human functioning" (Franks & Wilson, 1975, p. 2).

The application of research principles suggests that assessment and evaluation play a key role, not merely in treatment planning but throughout therapy as the behavior therapist continues to appraise, modify and even change interventions as behavioral data direct. The treatment approach is tailored to fit the family's specific needs. To begin, the behavior therapist makes a careful, systematic analysis of the family's maladaptive behavior patterns, pinpointing exactly which behavior needs to be altered and what events precede and follow manifestation of the behavior. Working with a distraught family in which the presenting problem is a 4-year-old boy's "temper tantrums," the behavior therapist might want to know exactly what the family means by "tantrums," the frequency and duration of such behavior, the specific responses to the behavior by various family members, and especially the antecedent and consequent events associated with these outbursts. By means of this inquiry, the behavior therapist is attempting to gauge the extent of the problem and the environmental factors (such as the presence of a particular family member, a particular cue such as parents announcing bedtime, a particular time and place such as dinnertime at home) that maintain the problematic behavior. The assessment of environmental circumstances is especially crucial, since the behavior therapist believes that all behavior (desirable and undesirable) is maintained by its consequences.

Generally speaking, the work of behavior family therapists has a number of characteristics that distinguishes it from the approaches taken by other family therapists we have considered: (1) a direct focus on observable behavior, such as symptoms, rather than an effort to establish causality intrapsychically or interpersonally; (2) a careful, ongoing assessment of the specific, usually overt, behavior to be altered; (3) a concern with either increasing (accelerating) or decreasing (decelerating) targeted behavior by directly manipulating external contingencies of reinforcement; (4) an effort to train families to self-monitor and self-modify their own reinforcement contingencies; and (5) an interest in empirically evaluating the effects of therapeutic interventions.

Moreover, behaviorally oriented therapists, with few exceptions, adopt a linear rather than a circular outlook on causality. For instance, a parent's inappropriate, inconsistent, or otherwise flawed response to a temper tantrum is believed to cause as well as maintain a child's behavioral problem (contrary to the more commonly held view among family therapists that the tantrum constitutes an interaction, including an exchange of feedback information, occurring within the family system). Predictably, the behavioral family therapist is likely to aim his or her therapeutic efforts at changing dyadic interactions (for example, a mother's way of dealing with her child having a tantrum) rather than adopting the triadic view more characteristic of systems-oriented family therapists, in which the participants in any exchange are simultaneously reacting to other family transactions (for example, a mother who feels neglected by her husband and who attends too closely to the slightest whims of her child; a father who resents his wife taking so much attention away from him in order to interact with their son).

While some of the leading behavioral family therapists such as Gerald Patterson, Robert Liberman, and Richard Stuart do view the family as a social system (whose members exercise mutual control over one another's social reinforcement schedules), others remain far from convinced. Gordon and Davidson (1981), for example, acknowledge that in some cases a strained marital relationship may contribute to the development and/or maintenance of deviant child behavior (or vice versa), but they argue that systems theorists have exaggerated the prevalence of the phenomenon. Their experiences lead them to conclude that deviant child behavior may occur in families with and without marital discord; they state that "the simple presence of marital discord in these families may or may not be causally related to the child's problems" (p. 522).

Behavioral Marital Therapy (BMT)

Not long after the behavioral approach in psychology began to be applied to clinical problems in individuals, interest grew in adapting this perspective to problems of marital discord. By the end of the 1960s, Liberman and Stuart had

Robert Liberman, M.D.

published their early efforts in this regard, each offering a straightforward, step-by-step set of intervention procedures in which some basic learning principles were applied to distressed marital relationships.

Liberman (1970), for example, saw marital therapy as an opportunity to induce significant behavioral changes in both partners by restructuring their interpersonal environments. After creating a positive therapeutic alliance with the couple, he began his assessment (or behavioral analysis) of their problems. What behavior is maladaptive (that is, should be increased or decreased) in each partner? What specific changes would each like to see in the other? Answers to questions such as these force the therapist to specify the behavioral goals of the treatment, a step that behaviorists argue is conspicuously lacking in other therapeutic approaches. In addition, as we noted earlier, the behavior therapist wants to know what interpersonal contingencies currently support the problematic behavior. In the following early example of behavioral marital therapy (BMT), note how Liberman (1970) had couples collect data on their problems in order to discover what triggered the undesirable behavior and what consequences maintained it; note also how the therapist applied such basic principles of learning as positive reinforcement and shaping to change behavior patterns.

Mr. and Mrs. F. have a long history of marital strife. There was a year-long separation early in their marriage and several attempts at marriage counseling lasting three years. Mr. F. has paranoid trends which are reflected in his extreme sensitivity to any lack of affection or commitment toward him by his wife. He is very jealous of her close-knit relationship with her parents. Mrs. F. is a disheveled and unorganized woman who has been unable to meet her husband's expectations for an orderly and accomplished homemaker or competent manager of their five children. Their marriage has been marked by frequent mutual accusations and depreciation, angry withdrawal and sullenness.

My strategy with this couple, whom I saw for 15 sessions, was to teach them to stop reinforcing each other with attention and emotionality for undesired behavior and to begin eliciting desired behavior in each other using the principle of *shaping.* Tactically, I structured the therapy sessions with an important "ground-rule": No criticism or harping were allowed and they were to spend the time telling each other what the other had done during the past week that approached the desired behaviors. As they gave positive feedback to each other for approximations to the behavior each valued in the other, I served as an auxiliary source of positive acknowledgment, reinforcing the reinforcer.

We began by clearly delineating what specific behaviors were desired by each of them in the other and by my giving them homework assignments in making gradual efforts to approximate the behavioral goals. For instance, Mr. F. incessantly complained about his wife's lack of care in handling the evening meal—the disarray of the table setting, lack of tablecloth, disorderly clearing of the dishes. Mrs. F. grudgingly agreed that there was room for improvement and I instructed her to make a start by using a tablecloth nightly. Mr. F. in turn was told the importance of his giving her positive and consistent attention for her effort, since this was important to him. After one week they reported that they had been able to fulfill the assignment and that the evening meal was more enjoyable. Mrs. F. had increased her performance to the complete satisfaction of her husband, who meanwhile had continued to give her positive support for her progress.

A similar process occurred in another problem area. Mr. F. felt that his wife should do more sewing (mending clothes, putting on missing buttons) and should iron his shirts (which he had always done himself). Mrs. F. was fed up with the home they lived in, which was much too small for their expanded family. Mr. F. resolutely refused to consider moving to larger quarters because he felt it would not affect the quality of his wife's homemaking performance. I instructed Mrs. F. to begin to do more sewing and ironing and Mr. F. to reinforce this by starting to consider moving to a new home. He was to concretize this by spending part of each Sunday reviewing the real estate section of the newspaper with his wife and to make visits to homes that were advertised for sale. He was to make clear to her that his interest in a new home was *contingent* upon her improvements as a homemaker.

Between the third and sixth sessions, Mrs. F.'s father—who was ill with terminal lung cancer—was admitted to the hospital and died. During this period, we emphasized the importance of Mr. F. giving his wife solace and support. I positively reinforced Mr. F.'s efforts in this direction. He was able to help his wife over her period of sadness and mourning despite his long-standing antagonism toward her father. Mrs. F., in turn, with my encouragement, responded to her husband's sympathetic behavior with affection and appreciation. Although far from having an idyllic marriage, Mr. and Mrs. F. have made tangible gains in moving closer toward each other [pp. 114–115].

A decade later, Liberman and his colleagues (Liberman, Wheeler, deVisser, Kuehnel & Kuehnel, 1980) prepared a *Handbook of Marital Therapy* in which they described a variety of more sophisticated behavioral techniques, including the contributions of social-learning theory as well as the communication approach to marital therapy. In general, the techniques are directed at: (1) increasing the couple's recognition, initiation and acknowledgment of pleasing interactions; (2) decreasing the couple's aversive interactions; (3) training the partners in the use of effective problem solving/communcations skills; and (4) teaching them to use contingency contracting in order to negotiate the resolution of persistent problems.

Stuart (1969) utilized operant conditioning theory and what he called **operant-interpersonal therapy** to treat marital discord. He assumed, from the beginning, that the pattern of interaction taking place between spouses at any point in time is the most rewarding of all available alternatives—that is precisely why they choose it. (For example, a wife who complains that her husband spends too much time with his friends and not enough with her should not simply be angry at him but should face up to the fact that his friends offer greater relative rewards for him than she does.) Stuart assumed further that successful marriages involve a quid pro quo ("something for something") arrangement; here he is in agreement with communication theorist Don Jackson. In behavioral terms, successful marriages can be differentiated from unsuccessful ones by the frequency and range of reciprocal positive reinforcements the partners exchange ("I'll be glad to entertain your parents this weekend if you accompany me to that baseball game [or ballet performance] next month."). In unsuccessful marriages, coercion, withdrawal, and retaliatory behavior are more common. Presumably, the rejected wife in the example above must take the "positive risk" of changing her behavior (that is, making a positive move toward her mate before expecting one from him). In behavioral terms, she must be willing to give reinforcement before receiving it. The consequences of her behavioral change increase the likelihood of a "positive risk" from her spouse. The new social exchange reshapes and redefines their relationship.

In a troubled relationship, according to Stuart, the couple is "locked into" a problematic pattern of interaction, each requiring a change in the other before changing his or her own behavior. Stuart proposed that the couple make explicit reinforcement contracts with each other, negotiating exchanges of desired behavior. Negative statements and complaints are restated in terms of specifically desired positive behavior (wife: "I would like you to spend at least 30 minutes with the children before their bedtime"; husband: "I would like you to have dinner on the table within 15 minutes after I arrive home"). Next, each person records the frequency with which the other completes the desired behavior. Stuart even suggested a token system, somewhat in the style of hospital **token economy** programs, to facilitate behavioral change. The husband may earn tokens for conversing with his wife, let us say, for at least 30 minutes of each hour (these criteria can be negotiated depending on circumstances). Conversation tokens accumulated by the husband could later be redeemable for increased physical affection and sexual activity.

Although probably considered naive, too mechanical, or too simplistic by most family therapists, Stuart was beginning to blend Skinner's operant learning principles with social exchange theory (Thibaut & Kelley, 1959). The contribution of the operant model—the key determinants of behavior are to be found in the external environment—and the contribution of the social exchange model—ongoing behavioral exchanges influence long-range outcomes in relationships—are quite compatible. As contemporary behavioral marital therapist Jacobson (1981) points out, relationship satisfaction in marriage can be appraised according to long-term reward/cost ratios. If missing but potentially rewarding events can be identified and maximized and displeasing events occurring in excess can be identified and minimized, then the reward/cost ratio should increase greatly and each partner should not only feel more satisfied but also more willing to provide more rewards for the partner. This is in contrast to unsuccessful marriages, where each partner, out of self-protection, acts to minimize costs from the relationship but makes no effort to exchange rewards. In addition to Stuart, a number of other behavioral marital therapists use behavior exchange procedures in their work (O'Leary & Turkewitz, 1978; Jacobson & Margolin, 1979; Liberman and Associates, 1980).

In recent years, Stuart (1976, 1980) has refined his techniques for working with maritally troubled couples. He begins by noting that every dimension of a marriage is subject to continued fluctuation, ranging from issues such as who is to provide what kind of new and stimulating activities to how old and new responsibilities should be allocated and reallocated over time. In the same way, Stuart recognizes that each spouse's commitment to the marriage varies over time, depending on his or her experience within the marriage or outside of that relationship. Stuart makes the further assumption that at least one of the spouses has doubts about remaining married, and that is why the couple has sought treatment or counseling. Therefore, he views the therapist's task as helping both spouses create the best relationship possible at this point in time. Then, he reasons, if even at its current best it is not good enough (that is, in behavioral terms, the marriage offers insufficient reinforcements relative to the rewards each partner expects to earn living alone or with someone else), they can decide to end their marriage. On the other hand, if the husband and wife—having changed their behavior toward each other—evaluate the changes positively, they can recommit themselves to maintaining the marriage.

Orderly and precise in his approach, Stuart (1976) presents an eight-stage model (see Figure 10–1) with the central theme of accelerating positive behavioral change. After each spouse independently completes a Marital Pre-Counseling Inventory (detailing daily activities, general goals, current satisfactions and targets for change, and level of commitment to the marriage), the therapist can plan an intervention program in an organized and efficient manner. The couple is asked to agree by telephone to a treatment contract stipulating joint sessions, permission granted to the therapist to reveal to both partners

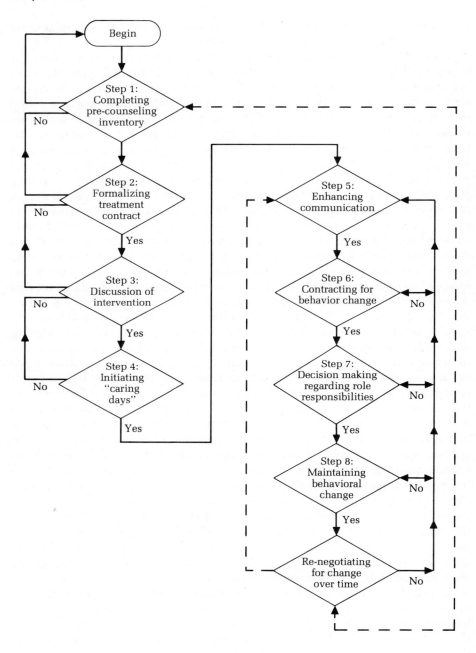

Figure 10–1. Flow chart of a behavioral treatment process for marital discord. (From Stuart, 1976)

the information each has already provided, and a commitment to participate in six sessions, after which a decision about further treatment can be made. In the process of contracting, Stuart has made it clear that he will not enter into collusion with one spouse (for example, keeping a secret) against the other, that he expects both of them to become involved in the process, and that he expects them to initiate change within a finite period.

During the first conjoint session (Step 3), in which Stuart discusses the rationale of this therapeutic approach, he attempts to indoctrinate the partners with the idea that the most effective way to initiate change in a troubled marriage is to increase the rate at which they exchange positive behavior. Step 4, creating "caring days,"[1] is consistent wih the notion of motivating both partners to achieve their treatment objectives. As seen in Figure 10–2, each person defines the specifics of the behavior he or she desires on the part of the other and is asked to carry out from eight to twenty of the requests made by the partner, on a daily basis. Each partner is to exhibit caring behavior independently of the other's actions, as a demonstration of commitment that is consistent with Stuart's idea of "positive risks" described earlier. Each partner records the number of instances and the type of caring behavior he or she offers each day (a "commitment index") and experiences each day (a "pleasure index").

The remaining four steps in Stuart's approach are tailored to the unique needs of each couple. Step 5 is devoted to training the partners to accurately communicate honest, timely, and constructive messages without subterfuge, misinterpretation or superfluous innuendo. A behavioral contract can then be negotiated (Step 6). At this point, for example, efforts might be made to modify ritualized role expectations, a wife asking her husband to babysit so that she might attend an evening class or a husband asking her to take over responsibility for balancing a checkbook. They might work on developing specific strategies for dealing with arguments, perhaps even arranging signals to alert one person to the other's willingness to end the argument. Changes oriented toward producing greater trust between the partners are also negotiated. A behavioral contract, implicit and explicit, is established based on the quid pro quo ("something for something") exchange of desirable behaviors.

In Step 7, the couple learns more effective decision-making strategies (that is, formulating a goal and problem-solving set, assembling facts, and so on), particularly regarding who will take major responsibilities for what areas of life. In Step 8, the partners are helped to maintain the changes they have made by learning specific "relationship rules"; the rules summarize what they have agreed on as the best methods for continuing to make communicational, behav-

---

[1]In *Helping Couples Change* (1980), Stuart spells out in greater detail his "caring days" technique for building commitment in a faltering marriage. All requests must meet the following criteria: (1) they must be positive ("Please ask how I spent my day" rather than "Don't ignore me so much"); (2) they must be specific ("Come home at 6 P.M. for dinner" rather than "Show more consideration for your family"); (3) they must be "small" instances of behavior that can be demonstrated at least once daily ("Please line up the children's bikes along the back wall of the garage when you come home" rather than "Please train the children to keep their bikes in the proper place"); and (4) they must not have been the subject of recent sharp conflict (since neither spouse is likely to concede major points at this stage of teatment).

Wife's Requests	Husband's Requests
1. Greet me with a kiss and a hug in the morning before we get out of bed.	1. Wash my back.
2. Bring me pussywillows (or some such).	2. Smile and say you're glad to see me when you wake up.
3. Ask me what record I would like to hear and put it on.	3. Fix the orange juice.
4. Reach over and touch me when we're riding in the car.	4. Call me at work.
5. Make breakfast and serve it to me.	5. Acknowledge my affectionate advances.
6. Tell me you love me.	6. Invite me to expose the details of my work.
7. Put your things away when you come in.	7. Massage my shoulders and back.
8. If you're going to stop at the store for something, ask me if there is anything that I want or need.	8. Touch me while I drive.
9. Rub my body or some part of me before going to sleep, with full concentration.	9. Hold me when you see that I'm down.
10. Look at me intently sometimes when I'm telling you something.	10. Tell me about your experiences at work every day.
11. Engage actively in fantasy trips with me—e.g., to Costa Rica, Sunshine Coast, Alaska.	11. Tell me that you care.
12. Ask my opinion about things which you write and let me know which suggestions you follow.	12. Tell me that I'm nice to be around.
13. Tell me when I look attractive.	
14. Ask me what I'd like to do for a weekend or a day with the desire to do what I suggest.	

Figure 10–2. A sample request list for caring days, a crucial aspect of Stuart's "operant-interpersonal" approach for couples. (From Stuart, 1976)

ioral, and decision-making changes. Stuart insists that the couple evaluate the relationship at four-month intervals using the Marital Pre-Counseling Inventory, in order to gauge progress and choose new objectives for further change.

As we observed with Liberman and Associates (1980), Stuart (1980) also has moved in the direction of helping couples improve their communication skills. Specifically, Stuart proposes these exercises as part of a five-skill training sequence: listening to one's partner more effectively (and, as far as possible, without preconceived notions of the other's motives); learning self-expression (making self-statements for which the person takes responsibility); learning to make requests (framed and timed properly); exchanging appropriate feedback information with each other; and using clarification (to check out the meaning of one person's message until mutual meaning is achieved).

Marital skills training—teaching couples strategies for improving their communication patterns—is an important feature of the BMT approach. As developed by Gerald Patterson and his colleagues at the Oregon Marital Studies Program (Patterson, Weiss, & Hops, 1976), a ten-session assessment/intervention package is now available for helping couples track, self-monitor and then self-report their home behavior, rating pleasing and displeasing interactions on a checklist containing categories such as companionship, spouse independence, and so on. These ratings (based on a family interaction coding system that records, for example, number of positive or negative responses; extent of communication-facilitating and communication-impeding behavior) are then used for assessment purposes. Intervention, based on such an assessment, provides training in such areas as conflict resolution, communication skills, negotiation and contracting.

Contracts, used by Stuart, Jacobson and other practitioners of BMT, are written agreements between spouses stipulating specific behavioral changes. Each spouse explicitly states what behavior he or she wants increased, thus avoiding the all-too-familiar marital plea for clairvoyance "If you really loved me, you'd know what I want." Note how the agreement developed by Stuart (1980) in Figure 10-3 offers each partner a range of constructive choices, any one of which can satisfy their reciprocal obligations. By not creating the expectation that reciprocation should be forthcoming immediately ("I'll do this if you do that"), behavior marital therapists believe that the likelihood of spontaneous reciprocation will increase.

Clearly, BMT is a treatment model in transition (Gurman, 1980). Some of its earlier assumptions were too simplistic: that both partners, as rational adults, will not resist change but will follow the therapist's suggestions; that a focus on

It is understood that Jane would like Sam to:	It is also understood that Sam would like Jane to:
wash the dishes;	have dinner ready by 6:30 nightly;
mow the lawn;	weed the rose garden;
initiate lovemaking;	bathe every night and come to bed by 10:30;
take responsibility for balancing their checkbooks;	call him at the office daily;
invite his business partners for dinner once every six or eight weeks;	plan an evening out alone for both of them at least once every two weeks;
meet her at his store for lunch at least once a week.	offer to drive the children to their soccer practice and swim meets;
	accompany him on occasional fishing trips.

It is expected that Sam and Jane will each do as many of the things requested by the other as is comfortably manageable, ideally at least three or four times weekly.

Figure 10-3. A holistic therapeutic marital contract (Stuart, 1980, p. 248).

overt behavior change is sufficient, without attending to underlying perceptual processes; that marital disharmony derives from the same sources, such as insufficient reciprocity, throughout the marital life cycle; that displeasing behavior, such as anger, should be extinguished without exploring the covert reasons for conflict; that the couple–therapist relationship can be ignored (Gurman & Knudson, 1978). Nevertheless, these therapists made a valuable contribution to the field with their insistence on careful assessment procedures, their emphasis on pinpointing the contingencies that help maintain current dysfunctional patterns, their concern with teaching specific interpersonal marital skills, and their efforts to evaluate outcomes through integrated clinical/research endeavors.

Although BMT today is still largely based on social-learning and behavior-exchange principles (Jacobson & Margolin, 1979), the approach is becoming less technological and more flexible as it attempts to incorporate other theoretical perspectives. Increasingly, attention is being paid to such "internal" processes as thoughts, feelings and attitudes, and the role of cognitions in marital dysfunction (for example, unrealistic expectations of marriage, faulty attributions for relationship problems) (Margolin, 1983). Patterson, once a staunch operant behavior advocate, has begun to acknowledge value in the systems view. Margolin (1983), primarily identified with the BMT approach, now believes that systems theory provides a greater appreciation of the interdependence of behavior of marital partners and the cohesiveness of the marital system and offers such useful intervention techniques as reframing and "prescribing the symptom." The future promises even greater rapprochement between BMT and other models of marital/family therapy.

Behavioral Parent Training (BPT)

Much behavioral work, generally following a social-learning model, has been directed at problems of child management within the family. While nonbehavioral family therapists might question whether such efforts should be considered methods of family therapy, in actual practice clinicians representing a variety of theoretical approaches are frequently called upon to help parents cope with various behavior problems in their children. In the last decade or so, increased attention has been paid to training parents themselves in behavioral principles and techniques, so that they might apply these at home—utilizing their daily contact with the child to act as change agents in bringing about a modification of the child's undesirable behavior (Berkowitz & Graziano, 1972). Although most behavioral parent training (BPT) advocates have as their goal the alteration of the undesirable behavior in the child, accepting the parents' view that the child is the problem, Falloon and Liberman (1982) adopt a broader view, arguing that BPT ultimately modifies the entire family interactive system.

Parent training has many practical features to recommend it. It minimizes the family's reliance on qualified professional therapists, who may be in short supply. The training process, if successful, builds competence in parents. Intervention generally begins early, thus reducing costs and the difficulties inherent in correcting an established problem; parent training thus has a preventive aspect. Perhaps most important, parents possess the greatest potential for generating behavior change because they have the greatest control over the significant aspects of the child's natural environment (Gordon & Davidson, 1981). The use of parents as trainers makes it easier for children to actually use the new behavior they learn, since they do not have to go through the process of transferring what they have acquired from a therapist to their home situation.

The initial request for treatment rarely comes from the child. It is likely to be the parents who are concerned about their child's disturbed behavior (see Figure 10–4) or failure to behave in ways appropriate to his or her age or sex. According to the group at the influential Oregon Social Learning Center led by Gerald Patterson and John Reid (Patterson & Reid, 1970), a faulty parent (usually mother)–child interaction pattern has probably developed and been maintained through reciprocity (a child responding negatively to negative parental input) and coercion (parents influencing behavior through the use of punishment). BPT intervention aims to change this mutually destructive pattern of interaction, usually by training parents to observe and measure the child's problematic behavior and then to apply behavioral techniques for accelerating desirable behavior, decelerating undesirable behaviors, and maintaining the consequent behavioral changes.

Behavioral Problem	Percentage Rating as "Severe"
Disobedience; difficulty in disciplinary control	52
Disruptiveness; tendency to annoy and bother others	49
Fighting	45
Talking back	43
Short attention span	42
Restlessness; inability to sit still	40
Irritability; easily aroused to intense anger	37
Temper tantrums	35
Attention seeking; "show-off" behavior	35
Crying over minor annoyances	33
Lack of self-confidence	33
Hyperactivity; "always on the go"	33
Distractibility	33
Specific fears; phobias	17
Bed wetting	16

Figure 10–4. Behavior problems self-described as "severe" by over 4000 parents during 10 years of offering workshops to help them improve their child-management skills (From Falloon and Liberman, 1982, p. 123).

With few exceptions, therapeutic efforts are designed to change the child's deviant behavior, rather than viewing that behavior as part of a system in disarray or disequilibrium. Patterson (1976), the leading advocate of this approach, questions whether the resolution of the underlying family tensions or marital discord will necessarily change the problem behavior. Instead, Patterson relies on behavioral interviews, checklists, and naturalistic observations of parent–child interactions in order to identify the specific problem behavior along with its antecedent and consequent events. Through such a behavioral assessment, the therapist is able to identify the problem more exactly; evaluate the form, frequency and extent of its impact on the family; and systematically train parents to utilize social learning principles to replace the targeted behavior with more positive, mutually reinforcing interaction.

The actual training of parents in behavioral techniques may be as simple as instructing them in how to enforce rules or act consistent, or as sophisticated as the use of behavioral deceleration procedures such as the **time-out** from positive reinforcement or acceleration procedures such as token economy techniques (Gordon & Davidson, 1981). Most training programs include verbal or written instructions, often in the form of lectures, books, or instructional guides that illustrate social learning theory. Applied to family life, the theory emphasizes that parents control many of the contingencies that influence the child to acquire and maintain certain behavior patterns; parents are therefore in a logical position to change that behavior, if properly taught to do so. In *Families*, Patterson (1971) outlined procedures for parents to acquire "behavior management skills" toward more effective child management. Presumably, many adults come by these skills "naturally," that is, without deliberately following a prescribed program. For less well-equipped parents, Patterson spelled out a plan for observing a child's behavior to establish a baseline, pinpointing the specific behavior the parents wish to change, observing and graphing their own behavior, negotiating a contract with the child, and so on. Figure 10–5 represents a checklist constructed for a boy who displayed a wide range of out-of-control behavior. The parent/child contract, jointly negotiated, stipulated that the parent would check with the teacher daily to get the necessary information and would regulate the consequences for the child's behavior. These consequences included mild but fair punishment for continued problem behavior in addition to "payoffs" (such as no dishwashing chores, permission to watch TV) for adaptive behavior.

In establishing the contract, the child helps set the "price" in points for each item, sees the results daily (the program is posted in a conspicuous place at home, such as the refrigerator door), and negotiates the backup reinforcers (for example, TV programs) for the accumulated points. The parents are rehearsed and then supervised in the use of these procedures; additional performance training, such as demonstrations by the therapists, may be provided for those having difficulties in carrying out the program. Gordon and Davidson (1981), surveying the literature on the usefulness of the procedures, conclude that "it is an effective intervention for discrete, well-specified behavior problems. In cases of more complex deviant behavior syndromes, the research is encouraging but not conclusive" (p. 547). A major concern, of course, is how long therapeutic changes are maintained after treatment ceases; longer range follow-up studies are indicated.

Dave's Program						
	M	T	W	T	F	S
Gets to school on time (2)	2					
Does not roam around room (1)	0					
Does what the teacher tells him (5)	3					
Gets along well with other kids (5)	1					
Completes his homework (5)	2					
Work is accurate (5)	3					
Behavior on the schoolbus is OK (2)	2					
Gets along well with brother and sisters in evening (3)	0					
TOTAL	13					

1. If Dave gets 25 points, he doesn't have to do any chores that night and he gets to pick all the TV shows for the family to watch.
2. If Dave gets only 15 points, he does not get to watch TV that night.
3. If Dave gets only 10 points, he gets no TV and he also has to do the dishes.
4. If Dave gets only 5 points or less, then he gets no TV, washes the dishes, and is grounded for the next two days (home from school at 4:00 and stays in yard).

Figure 10-5. A parent/child negotiated contract checklist indicating specific duties to be performed and a point system based on the degree of goal achievement. (From Patterson, 1971)

The behavior therapist may also work through the parents when the target for intervention is an adolescent's behavior. By observing the natural interaction between family members (sometimes in a home visit), the behavior therapist performs a **functional analysis** of the problem behavior, determining what elicits it, what reinforces and maintains it, and how the family members' interaction reflects their efforts to deal with it (passive acceptance, resignation, anger, bribes, encouragement, and so forth). Behavioral intervention strategies chosen by the therapist are apt to be specific and directed at helping to resolve or eliminate the problem.

Contingency contracting is a particularly useful technique with teenagers. As we defined the process earlier in this chapter, the technique is simple and straightforward, usually involving a formally written agreement for the exchange of positively rewarding behaviors between the teenager and his or her parents. A number of prominent BPT advocates such as Stuart (1969), Liberman (1970), and Patterson and Reid (1970) have applied such a reciprocity concept to family conflict where the previous excessive use of aversive controls by parents (nagging, demanding, threatening) has been met by equally unpleasant responses from the adolescent. The goal is to reverse this persistent negative exchange by means of a mutual exchange of pleasurable behavior.

A contract is negotiated wherein each participant specifies who is to do what for whom, under which circumstances, times, and places. Negotiations are open and free from coercion; the terms of the contract are expressed in clear and explicit statements. For example, a contract negotiated between parents and an adolescent with poor grades refers to "a grade of 'C' or better on the weekly quiz" rather than "do better in school." The latter is too vague and open to different interpretations by the participants; by that kind of definition the adolescent may believe he or she has done better and fulfilled his or her part of the agreement, while the parents believe the gain is insignificant, and the conflict between them over school performance remains unresolved. By the same token, the rewards must be specific ("We will give you $5 toward the purchase of new clothes for each week your quiz grade is 'C' or better") and not general or ambiguous ("We'll be more generous about buying you clothing if you get good grades"). The point here is that each participant must know exactly what is expected of him or her and what may be gained in return.

A contract (Figure 10–6) is an opportunity for success, accomplishment, and reward. However, the desired behavior, such as a "C" grade, must be realistic and within the grasp of the contractor. In addition, each member must accept the idea that privileges are rewards made contingent on the performance of responsibilities. Behavior therapists believe that a family member will exchange maladaptive behavior for adaptive behavior in anticipation of a positive consequence, a desired change in the behavior of the other. The teenager's responsibilities (that is, better grades) are the parents' reinforcers and the parents' responsibilities (money) are the teenager's reinforcers. BPT helps a family set up a monitoring or record-keeping system that enables the contractors and the therapist to assess the reciprocal fulfillment of the terms of the contract. Bonuses are given for consistent fulfillment of the terms and penalties imposed for failure to adhere to them. Note that, as in all behavioral procedures, the success of treatment can be measured by the extent to which the contract works for all parties.

Contingency contracting is not an end in itself but merely one motivating and structuring device among a variety of family intervention techniques (for example, modeling, shaping, time-out, use of tokens and other operant reinforcement strategies) used in the BPT approach. Contracting may open up communication within a family and help members express for the first time what each would like from the others. In some cases, the contracting process even makes family members aware of wishes or desires they had not previously recognized within themselves. Finally, an important aspect of this approach is its focus on goals and accomplishments. Liberman (1970) contends that contingency contracting formalizes the family's natural expectations into concrete actions. By giving recognition for achievement, the family becomes more positive in its future interactions.

Conjoint Sex Therapy

Sexual dysfunction in a marriage has so many repercussions in family life that we believe sex therapy should be included in our consideration of approaches to family therapy. Probably the most promising therapeutic work in this field has been done at the Masters and Johnson Institute in St. Louis under the direction of physician William Masters and psychologist Virginia Johnson; the procedures pioneered there have been incorporated into the programs of nu-

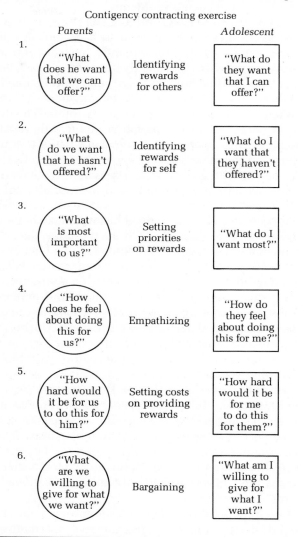

Figure 10–6. Steps in a contingency contract negotiated between parents and an adolescent. The Family Contracting Exercise is a structured learning experience conducted by the behaviorally oriented family therapist to help family members, stepwise, to identify their needs and desires (rewards) for themselves and each other, to set priorities for rewards for self, to empathize with the other, to set costs on providing rewards to others, and finally to bargain and compromise. This sequence is outlined for the parents in circles and for the adolescent in squares. (From Weathers and Liberman, 1975)

merous sex-therapy clinics throughout the United States. The Institute offers a treatment program that relies heavily on behavior-therapy techniques. It is distinguished by its brevity (generally two weeks) and its proven high rate of success for certain types of sexual problems.

A basic assumption in the Masters and Johnson (1970) approach is that there is no such thing as an uninvolved partner in a relationship in which some form of sexual inadequacy exists. Consequently, husband and wife are always treated conjointly to emphasize that any dysfunction is a problem for the marital couple rather than one that belongs to only one partner. Each couple is seen by a male–female co-therapy team; ideally, one member is trained in the biological sciences and the other in a behavioral discipline. The dual-sex team is designed to avoid potential misinterpretation due to a therapist's male or female bias, consistent with Masters' and Johnson's belief that neither sex can ever fully understand the other's sexual experiences. The two-week program of daily sessions begins with an extensive assessment; a detailed sexual history is taken from each partner, not only in regard to chronological sexual experiences but, more importantly, in respect to sexually oriented values, attitudes, feelings, and expectations. Next, a medical history is taken and each partner is given a thorough physical examination. On the third day, the co-therapists and the marital partners meet to review the accrued clinical material and to begin to relate individual and marital histories to current sexual difficulties. During the next several days, the therapists concentrate on giving the couple instruction in "sensate focus"—that is, learning to touch and explore each other's bodies and to discover more about each other's sensate areas—but without feeling any pressure for sexual performance or orgasm. During this period, regular roundtable meetings that include both therapists and both marital partners are held to deal with either partner's discomfort, guilt feelings, or apprehensions. In the time remaining, the therapists utilize procedures aimed at teaching both partners to work together on their specific sexual dysfunction.

According to Masters and Johnson, a primary reason for sexual dysfunction is that the participant is critically watching (they refer to it as "spectatoring") his or her own sexual performance instead of abandoning himself or herself to the giving and receiving of erotic pleasure with a partner. In order to enjoy fully what is occurring, Masters and Johnson point out that it is necessary to suspend all such distracting thoughts or anxieties about being evaluated (or evaluating oneself) for sexual performance.

Psychiatrist Helen Singer Kaplan (1974) distinguishes a variety of immediate causes of sexual dysfunction in a couple attempting intercourse (sexual ignorance, fear of failure, demand for performance, excessive need to please one's partner, failure to communicate openly about sexual feelings and experiences). In addition, she points out that there may be various intrapsychic conflicts (such as early sexual trauma, guilt and shame, repressed sexual thoughts and feelings) within one or both partners that impede satisfying sexual activity. Finally, Kaplan cites a third set of psychological determinants of sexual dysfunction—namely, factors arising from the relationship such as various forms of marital discord, lack of trust, power struggles between partners, and efforts to sabotage any pleasure being derived from the sexual experience. In combination or singly, any of these problems or conflicts can lead to distressing sexual symptoms (for example, impotence or premature ejaculation in a male, nonorgasmic responses in a female) that threaten a marriage by heightening tensions and even lead to its dissolution.

Unlike Masters and Johnson, who require participating couples to spend two weeks in residential treatment, Kaplan treats couples on an outpatient basis once or twice per week. No time limit is placed on treatment; the program terminates when the couple achieves good sexual functioning (that is, when the presenting symptom is eliminated) and there are indications that the changes are more or less permanent. Rather than the dual-sex team used in Masters' and Johnson's approach, one therapist treats the couple. Kaplan uses a combination of psychoanalytic and behavioral theories and techniques and assigns couples various sexual tasks (for example, taking turns stimulating or "pleasuring" each other's erotic areas, free of the demand for orgasm or coitus) to practice at home. Six to fifteen visits are generally required for successful treatment.

Unlike psychotherapeutic undertakings that have loose or vague criteria for defining their effectiveness (for example, "patient is happier," "more productive," "feels more fulfilled"), sex therapy is considered successful only if the presenting symptom in the marital unit is eliminated. Masters and Johnson have reported a remarkably high overall success rate despite their stringent criterion of success—no recurrence of the symptom within five years. Their greatest success (97.8%) has come with treating premature ejaculation in men; for secondary impotence (losing the capacity to achieve or maintain an erection long enough to engage in intercourse) the success rate, while lower (73.7%), is nevertheless extraordinarily high compared to that of other therapeutic interventions having to do with secondary impotence. Similarly, a success rate of 83.4% for treating primary orgasmic dysfunction in women (never having reached a climax) is very impressive. Kaplan reports similar results for rapidly relieving a wide variety of sexual dysfunctions. As she points out, however, sex therapy may represent a major advance in our understanding and treatment of a couple's sexual difficulties but it is no panacea for a marriage that has already failed.

The use of explicitly behavioral sex therapy techniques has proliferated in recent years (LoPiccolo & LoPiccolo, 1978) with about the same levels of success as those reported by the Masters and Johnson program, especially for procedures treating premature ejaculation and primary orgasmic dysfunction (Kinder & Blakeney, 1977). In a review of treatment programs for sexual dysfunction in heterosexual couples, Heiman, LoPiccolo and LoPiccolo (1981) concluded that the various behavioral approaches have the following elements in common: the reduction of performance anxiety, sex education, skill training in communication as well as in sexual technique, and attitude change procedures. As currently practiced, sex therapy appears to be a type of **cognitive behavior therapy** applied to couples with sexual problems.

SUMMARY

Behavioral family therapy, the latest entrant in the field, attempts to bring the scientific method to bear upon the therapeutic process by developing regularly monitored, data-based intervention procedures. Drawing on established principles of human learning—such as classical and operant conditioning, positive and negative reinforcement, shaping, extinction, and social learning—the behavioral approach emphasizes the environmental, situational, and social determinants of behavior. The behaviorally oriented therapist attempts to increase positive interaction between family members, alter the environmental conditions that oppose such interactions, and train people to maintain their newly acquired positive behavioral changes.

Currently, the approach is making a significant impact in three distinct areas: behavioral marital therapy (BMT), behavioral parent training (BPT), and the treatment of sexual dysfunction. Primary theoreticians and practitioners of BMT are Liberman, Stuart, and Jacobson, as well as Patterson and colleagues at the Oregon Marital Studies Program. Blending principles of social-learning theory and social-exchange theory, BMT advocates teach couples how to improve certain marital skills so that their relationship will have more pleasing consequences for both partners. Contracts are frequently used to reinforce the partners' commitment to the reciprocal exchange of satisfying behavior.

Behavioral parent training (BPT), also largely based on social-learning theory, represents an effort to train parents in behavioral principles and procedures so that they might ameliorate certain specific undesirable or problematic behavior in their child, who is considered the problem. Patterson has been particularly influential in focusing attention on the parent (usually mother)–child dyad by stressing that the child's behavior has probably developed and been maintained by means of the reciprocity and coercion inherent in their interaction. Intervention typically attempts to change the child's deviant behavior, rather than seeing that behavior as part of a family system in disarray.

Conjoint sex therapy is a rapid-treatment program involving both marital partners in an effort to alleviate problems of sexual dysfunction; the treatment may strengthen a marriage by correcting a disharmonious (thus potentially destructive) aspect of the relationship. First developed by Masters and Johnson and elaborated by Kaplan, the treatment of sexual dysfunction now utilizes a variety of explicitly behavioral techniques; conjoint sex therapy in its present form may be conceptualized as a type of cognitive behavior therapy applied to couples with marital problems.

PART THREE

The Practice of Family Therapy

CHAPTER ELEVEN

The Process of Family Therapy

In Part One of this book, we considered a variety of family transactional patterns, some less functional than others. We described a family as a natural social system with its own rules of behavior, its own degree of closeness among members, its own power structure. Each family develops and perpetuates its own myths, has its own way of coping with crises, and its unique communication patterns. In Part Two, we looked at how the family therapy movement evolved and what theoretical models exist today for the practice of family therapy.

We are now ready to look at various controversial issues and forms of clinical practice in the family therapy field. In this chapter, some definitions and basic features of family assessment and family therapy will be considered. The following chapter will be devoted to a discussion of some contemporary therapeutic techniques, frequently extensions of the theories considered in Part Two.

BASIC CHARACTERISTICS OF FAMILY THERAPY

Family Therapy versus Individual Therapy

Family therapy is a psychotherapeutic technique for exploring and attempting to alleviate the current interlocking emotional problems within a family system by helping its members change the family's dysfunctional transactional patterns together. Unlike individual psychotherapy, which focuses on the person's intrapsychic difficulties while sometimes recognizing that the patient's disturbed interpersonal relationships may have contributed to those difficulties, family therapy zeros in on the relationships (for example, alliances, rules, covert loyalty pressures) as they transpire during therapeutic sessions. The family therapist is interested in the family *of* the psychiatric patient and in the family *as* the psychiatric patient (Bloch, 1974).

Family therapy may be further differentiated from individual therapy along three dimensions: (1) views of the nature and location of forces active in personality development; (2) views of symptom formation; and (3) the approach to therapeutic change (Robinson, 1975). In family therapy, it is assumed that external forces dominate personality formation through the organized behavioral characteristics of the family that manage and regulate the interpersonal lives of its members. In individual therapy, internal events (thoughts, fears, conflicts) are believed to be dominant. From the former perspective, it is the family, as a rule-governed, change-resistant transactional system evolved over several generations, that sustains itself by evoking conformity among its members. Robinson cites the example of a mother–infant relationship being influenced as much by the quality of the mother's relationship with her husband and the satisfactions derived from her marriage as by the specific characteristics of the infant. If the infant ultimately fails to develop into a mature adult, independent of the mother, it is less a reflection of his or her unresolved internal conflicts than of a family conspiracy of needs. Parental marital tensions may have exaggerated the mutually dependent mother–child relationship in order to satisfy the void in the marital relationship.

Similarly, whereas individual therapies emphasize symptom formation as a result of conflict between component parts of the self (for example, id/ego/superego conflict in psychoanalysis), family therapy locates conflict in the transactional interface between the individual and the dysfunctional family system. A disturbed person becomes trapped in a role designated for him or her by the family system, which results in impaired or arrested development. Efforts to become independent may lead to high levels of anxiety and guilt. Thus, the family context must be attended to in understanding the appearance of symptoms in a family member.

In regard to treatment, the individual therapist structures the sessions to assist the patient in achieving **insight** or having new experiences in order to understand or overcome previous failures and gain relief from disabling symptoms. The family therapist, on the other hand, sees the family as committed to the status quo, behaving in a repetitive manner, protecting itself and maintaining homeostasis by opposing change in one of its members. Robinson (1975) describes the therapist as helping the family as a unit to isolate and change family behavior patterns that support the appearance of symptoms in family members, thus allowing individuals in each generation to separate from the family and become independent as they mature and establish emotional bonds with their peers. Zuk (1971) puts the goal of family treatment somewhat differently, but also feels that it involves a change in the family's homeostatic balance. He attempts to "shift the balance of pathogenic relating among family members so that new forms of relating become possible" (p. 213).

Indications and Contraindications for Family Therapy

The systems orientation—the theoretical viewpoint of most family practitioners—dictates that the therapist never lose sight of the family system as he or she works; it does not necessarily demand that all family members be present at all sessions. In practice, the family therapist may choose to work with the entire family, subsystems within the family (for example, husband and wife, both parents plus all children over the age of nine, father and adolescent son, mother and school-phobic daughter), or individual family members in order to bring about change in the functioning of the overall family social system. In some cases, the therapist may combine all three or parts thereof during different stages of treatment.[1] A common sequence is for the entire family to begin treatment together, with various dyads or triads then selected for special attention. Most often it is the marital pair that receives further therapeutic help, particularly in outpatient treatment; in current practice, a family therapy case often becomes a case for marital therapy (Framo, 1975).

Generally speaking, family therapy is indicated when the family's ability to perform its basic functions becomes inadequate to the task. Consider, for example, the case of a teenage family member who is being seen in individual outpatient treatment. The therapist and adolescent may reach an impasse as the enmeshed, pathology-producing family resists therapeutic efforts to bring about changes in the patient and upset the longstanding homeostatic balance in the family. In this event, the entire family may then be seen for a period of time, or the adolescent and his or her parents, minus siblings, may come together for family therapy aimed at reducing the overinvolvement, creating clearer boundaries, and breaking the impasse. In the case of another youngster, improvement as a result of individual psychotherapy may lead to considerable distress and the appearance of symptoms in one or more of the other family members, again suggesting family sessions. In both these situations, a clinician with a family therapy orientation is likely to assume that the identified patient is the symptom bearer for a disturbed or dysfunctional family system.

When children are placed in an inpatient psychiatric unit, the presenting symptoms are usually serious enough that a number of therapeutic approaches, individual as well as family-focused, are attempted simultaneously. Because the symptom bearer may be reflecting a family problem and because the child will be returning home after hospitalization, family intervention is essential. Zimmerman and Sims (1983) suggest that this can be accomplished indirectly by working with the child on family-related issues or more directly by bringing the family to the hospital for regular, ongoing family therapy sessions.

There are situations in which family therapy is clearly indicated, when the presenting problem appears in a family relationship context. Marital conflict, severe sibling rivalry, and intergenerational conflicts are the clearest examples of such situations (Bloch & LaPerriere, 1973). The individual-oriented therapist who simply chooses to treat the most obviously disruptive or most obviously suffering family member may miss the point of the disturbed transaction. Such

---

[1]In recent years, as a variety of techniques have been developed, some therapists divide a single session into parts, doing family intervention, marital therapy, behavioral management or individual therapy as needed (Zimmerman & Sims, 1983). However, it should be emphasized that getting the entire family involved at the beginning usually makes it easier to carry out such procedures later in the treatment.

a therapist may waste a lot of time listening to the patient declare how the other, absent person(s) is to blame and must change if the patient is to gain relief. In marital therapy, for example, if the difficulties presented by a couple pertain largely to the relationship, if there is at least minimal communication between the partners, and if they are reasonably motivated to work on their marital problems, a conjoint approach is most likely to prove successful (Baruth & Huber, 1984). On the other hand, if one partner comes to marital/family therapy in response to an ultimatum ("I'm leaving unless we get professional help together"), is looking for permission to get out of the relationship, attempting to avoid any personal responsibility for the marital problems, or simply seeking validation from a therapist that the other partner is the cause of their difficulties, conjoint treatment is unlikely to be effective.

In the case of intergenerational conflicts, as many as three generations may be involved simultaneously, as the following example illustrates:

> The index patient was an eighteen-year-old girl with an out-of-wedlock pregnancy. There was open and continued conflict between the parents and the girl over her behavior in general and in regard to plans for this pregnancy specifically. The parents wanted her to terminate the pregnancy with an abortion; her stated wish was to carry the child to term and place the baby for adoption. Much of the parental concern was centered around the issues of the reaction of the community to the pregnancy. While the generational conflict was the initial basis for the consultation, the first family interview revealed severe concealed disagreements between the parents, which were long-standing and antedate the present complaint, and seemed to be related to it, at least in the sense that the pregnancy restored and healed over a split between the girl's parents. Further study also demonstrated that the grandparental generation had opposed the parents' marriage and had been consistently involved in intense maneuvering designed to split the parental pair. The extended families of the girl's parents had never reconciled themselves to the marriage, nor had they been willing to free *their* children from bonds of dependency.
>
> In the foregoing instance, it was necessary ultimately to involve elements of all three generations and of both extended families in order to explore and resolve the conflicts most efficiently. As the parents were able to clarify the nature of their own involvement with their own extended families and with *their* parents in particular, it was possible to reduce the intensity of their competitive struggle for their daughter's allegiance. This in turn permitted the girl to make an adequate decision about her pregnancy [Bloch & LaPerriere, 1973, p. 7].

Family therapy is not a panacea for all psychological disturbances but a valuable option in a therapist's repertoire of interventions. As we have just pointed out, it is especially useful—the treatment of choice—for certain systems problems within the family. Even if the therapist sees one family member at a time (the others may simply refuse to come in!), a family orientation in which an individual's problems are seen in a family context is still possible (Wynne, 1971).

Most clinicians who accept the premises of family therapy would agree with Wynne's (1965) observation that this approach is particularly applicable to clarifying and resolving relationship difficulties within a family. Here Wynne is referring to those reciprocal interactional patterns to which all family members contribute, collusively or openly, consciously or unconsciously. Some members will continue to insist, months later, that the problem (for example, drug abuse in an adolescent or sexual dysfunction in a spouse) resides in some other family member (the identified patient); despite their claims that they are attending family sessions only to help that troubled member, they may ultimately become active participants themselves and benefit from the sessions, individually as well as in a family sense. Wynne is suggesting that it is not necessary for all members to verbally acknowledge their motivation for treatment in order for family therapy to be effective.

Wynne (1965, 1971) cites a number of cases from his work at NIMH for which family therapy was especially well suited. He includes a variety of adolescent separation problems (for example, rebellious, often delinquent teenagers trying to break away from a family or, in some cases, simply seeking the degree of separation necessary to go away to college), especially when the parents share in the adolescent's ambivalence and confusion about the pending separation. As indicated by his previously cited work on pseudomutuality (see Chapter 3), Wynne is also interested in families whose members make a shared effort to avoid separation or the development of mutuality. In such families, boundaries to the outside world are rather impermeable, so extrafamilial experiences are limited. Should the developing adolescent or young adult become exposed to totally unfamiliar feelings in the outside world (for example, hostile, angry feelings or even loving, tender feelings), he or she may suffer an abrupt breakdown and perhaps become schizophrenic. On the family level, according to Wynne, the breakdown is both dreaded and collusively supported. It is during the period of trying to cope with an acute schizophrenic episode in one of its members that Wynne has found family therapy exceedingly helpful in getting the family in touch with previously excluded and denied feelings that erupt in the course of this experience.

Under what circumstances is family therapy contraindicated? Some family therapists take the extreme position that family therapy is the treatment of choice in all conditions where psychotherapy is indicated. The only practical exceptions to this rule might be the limited ability of the therapist to work with entire families or the unwillingness of the family system to cope with the changes necessary in all its members. That is, some families simply refuse to give up scapegoating the identified patient because the alternative behavior patterns cause intolerable discomfort; these families are likely to discontinue treatment (Bloch & LaPerriere, 1973).

A more moderate view of contraindications holds that not all disturbed families necessarily benefit from family therapy. For some families, it may be too late to reverse the forces of fragmentation. In other families, it may be too difficult to establish or maintain a therapeutic working relationship with the family because key members are unavailable (for example, children away at school, parents hospitalized or dead, certain members refuse to attend family sessions). Sometimes one grossly disturbed member may so dominate the family with malignant, destructive motives and behavior (openly violent and/or filled with paranoid ideation) that the family therapy approach is unworkable (Ackerman, 1970b). While family therapy may often be useful in treating schizophrenia in a family member, sometimes acute schizophrenics are so panicked that they cannot tolerate the complexity and stress of family interviews without having already established a relationship with the therapist (Wynne, 1965). In another type of case, two emotionally fragile, socially isolated individuals, married to each other, may have learned to stabilize their lives so long as few demands are made on them. Family therapy, in such a situation, may have a catastrophic effect on their equilibrium. Sometimes, as in the following example, this approach may even precipitate paranoid schizophrenic episodes.

> The wife was the index patient in this instance. She had adapted to a childless, lonely, restricted married life, spending most of her time cleaning and caring for a tiny, immaculate apartment, while her highly successful executive husband occupied himself with 16-hour work days at his factory. This functioning adaptation was twice upset by efforts of the childless couple to become more intimate with each other, under the guidance of a family therapist. Each effort seemed brilliantly successful, with heightened sexual contact and enjoyment and an increase in shared activities, but each instance led to a psychotic decompensation for the wife, under the unmanageable pressures of their increased intimacy [Bloch & LaPerriere, 1973, p. 11].

Family therapy demands open communication and the courage to risk exposing the truth. Parents, unaccustomed to sharing personal or marital secrets with their children (or family secrets with their therapist), may balk at family sessions.[2] Ackerman (1970a) has noted that some family members have such extremely rigid defenses that breaking through them may induce an acute depression, psychosis, or psychosomatic crisis. On the other hand, if the rigid defenses remain impenetrable, the individual remains walled off from his or her own feelings and inaccessible to the rest of the family, rendering intervention by family therapy ineffective.

None of these arguments necessarily rules out using family therapy. Instead, they indicate that certain family circumstances or characteristics may excessively limit the potential benefits of therapeutic intervention on a family level.

FAMILY ASSESSMENT

Is Diagnosis Necessary?

Is **diagnosis** an integral part of treatment planning and choosing of therapeutic goals in family therapy or merely an irrelevant counterproductive exercise in labeling left over from the **medical model**? Both views have their supporters

---

[2]Handling secrets or other confidential items presents a special ethical problem in family therapy. In individual psychotherapy, the patient's privacy is protected; his trust in the therapist maximizes his openness. In family therapy, the situation is more complicated, with different family

and detractors among family therapists. As an advocate of diagnosis, Ackerman (Ackerman & Behrens, 1974) stresses the interdependence of diagnostic and treatment procedures in family therapy. According to Ackerman, there can be no scientific approach to treatment without a prior evaluative or diagnostic effort to conceptualize and categorize various family types.

Those who take the more commonly held position that disregards diagnosis are equally adamant in their views. Kempler (1974) considers history taking useless, psychological analysis of people distracting. Haley (1971a) believes experienced family therapists need to intervene as soon as they have some grasp of what is going on during a family session; they should not delay therapy for diagnosis. He contends that careful diagnosis—most likely to be carried out by the novice family therapist—is done more to allay the anxiety of the therapist than to benefit the family. Bell (1975) assigns little value to diagnosing individual family members in advance of family meetings, preferring to observe directly how they relate to each other once they are together. According to Bell, diagnosis and treatment should proceed simultaneously throughout the family sessions, up to termination.

Most family therapists probably agree with Haley's (1976) notion that to begin therapy by interviewing one family member is to begin with a handicap. Such an approach, a carry-over from individual psychotherapy, assumes the therapist is dealing with a disturbed person whose symptoms indicate maladaptive or inappropriate behavior. Thus, a wife experiencing anxiety attacks is traditionally thought to be acting in a way that is not adaptive to her surroundings and therefore she is in need of treatment. From a family perspective, however, her "symptom" needs to be seen in the context of her family life, where it may be quite adaptive to the husband–wife relationship that she and her spouse maintain. Family therapy attempts to deal with the interactional life of the family group, not merely the symptoms in its separate members.

Howells (1975), a British psychiatrist, is perhaps the staunchest advocate of formal family diagnosis in planning therapeutic strategy. Working with as many family members as can be induced to attend, Howells undertakes a broad investigation aimed at obtaining as complete a picture as possible of the family's strengths and weaknesses, the areas where they function effectively and the areas where dysfunction occurs. Essentially medical in his orientation, Howells tries first to establish the nature of the "disorder" and then to seek its cause. Beginning with the presenting complaint ("Our family is breaking up."; "We seem to quarrel all the time we're together."), he inquires further into the family symptomatology ("My husband and I have not had sexual relations for several years."; "Both our children have a tendency toward depression.") and traces the history of these problems with the family members. At the same time,

---

members feeling varying degrees of trust or openness in front of the rest of the family and the therapist. Many family therapists consider secrets to be part of the family's problems in communication. Consequently, they may announce at the start that, in an effort to facilitate more open communication, they will not keep secrets of one family member from the whole family.

he observes family interaction patterns for signs of psychopathology. Finally, he gives the family a diagnosis—not simply a label (for example, "anxious family" or "delinquent family"), but an indication of the degree of disturbance in each member and a brief description of family interaction patterns, as in the following:

(i) The individuals (symptomatology can be added in each case):
Marked degree of **psychonosis** in father
Moderate degree of psychonosis in mother
Moderate degree of psychonosis in son
Severe degree of psychonosis in daughter

(ii) Internal interaction:
Father-Mother relationship—negative, hostile relationship
Father-Children relationship—marked mutual antipathy to daughter and somewhat less to son
Mother-Children relationship—grossly overprotective to both with rejection of daughter, and hostility of children toward mother

(iii) General: Father isolated by rest of family members; fragmentation of family imminent

(iv) External interaction: Failure at employment with impending bankruptcy; school failure of daughter; delinquency of son; isolation of family

(v) Physical: Feeding difficulties in daughter; enuresis in son; gastric ulceration in father; frigidity in mother

The family diagnosis at this point may be:
(i) Unclear. Thus further investigations are required
(ii) Provisional
(iii) Final

[Howells, 1975, pp. 207–208]

Under Howells's system, therapeutic work may proceed with an individual, a pair, or the entire family, although most likely the entire family will be involved. Howells clearly distinguishes family diagnosis from family therapy. The former involves describing and understanding family events; family therapy, a separate procedure, focuses on changing dysfunctional family patterns.

Family diagnosis and family therapy must be parallel, interdependent activities, according to Ackerman (Ackerman & Behrens, 1974). Just as family functioning is an ever-changing phenomenon, the diagnosis changes as the family changes. Thus family diagnosis is a guide to action for the therapist, providing strategy and objectives for therapeutic intervention. Although Ackerman would agree with Howells on the need for family diagnosis, the two differ in their views of diagnostic procedures. While Howells is more structured and formal in his approach and is careful to keep the diagnostic and therapeutic phases of family interviews quite separate, Ackerman does not seem bound by such restrictions. He views family sessions as opportunities to confront the members of a troubled family face to face, continuously testing out clinical hunches derived from his observations of the family and his knowledge of psychodynamic and psychosocial processes.

Ackerman believes that therapists inevitably formulate judgments about the families they treat, even if some prefer to call this process evaluation rather than diagnosis. He understands that the concept of diagnosis is repugnant to many family therapists who are disenchanted with the medical model and critical of psychiatric labeling. Nevertheless, he believes a clinically oriented classification of families is necessary if we are truly to understand what distinguishes "well" from "sick" families. While acknowledging that diagnosis is often abused—pigeonholing people with scant information—he argues that the solution is better diagnosis, not ridding ourselves of the diagnostic responsibility altogether.

Diagnostically, Ackerman maintained an interest for over 25 years in developing a classification system for family disturbance. Unfortunately, he failed to develop a comprehensive system, offering instead a set of partial hypotheses and observations regarding family functioning. Other attempts at classifying family functioning (described in Chapter 2) have been less ambitious than Ackerman's, limited to such family dimensions as transactional style or structural development.

METHODS OF FAMILY EVALUATION

In practice, as we have just pointed out, most family therapists find little if any use for the formal psychiatric labels (neurotic, schizophrenic, psychopathic) originally intended for individual diagnosis. The reasons should be obvious: families are too complex, relationships too much in flux over time, and the existing labels inadequate to capture the full flavor of ongoing family life. According to Kempler (1974), even a term like "double-bind" or "scapegoating" is useless in characterizing families, since such behavior occurs at times in any family and refers to only one aspect of the family's overall functioning; moreover, the use of the term offers the therapist no guidance in planning treatment (in contrast to a medical diagnosis that indicates a specific course of treatment). Instead, family therapists are apt to evaluate each new family by viewing the members' behavior in the context of the family, assuming that problematic or symptomatic conduct in any individual family member is a response to that person's current situation. Consequently, observing the family as a whole affords an excellent diagnostic opportunity (not available in individual therapy) to see how the members interact, how they communicate thoughts and feelings, and what alliances and coalitions are formed (parents versus children, males versus females, father and daughters versus mother and sons, and so on) that may be related to the symptomatic behavior in the identified patient. Haley (1971b) views the symptom as always having an adaptive function and therefore as appropriate behavior, rather than being irrational and maladaptive. Thus, rather than assume that a depressed family member has a predisposition to that behavior under stress, the family therapist tries to help the family become aware of how depression in one of its members is an appropriate response to what is happening to them here and now. A family rarely enters therapy with a clearcut idea of where its problems lie. As Guerin and Pendagast (1976) see it:

> The therapist's major job in the first interview is to elucidate and organize the facts and characteristics of the family, and dissect the emotional process in a way that pinpoints the trouble spots in the relationship system. It is to the advantage of both the therapist and the family that this process be simple, and accomplished in a relatively short period of time [p. 450].

The family therapist, during this brief evaluative process at the start of the treatment, is likely to pose the following questions to himself or herself: Who is attending and why are the absentees not present? What is the family structure (intact or single-parent family; nuclear or extended-family household)? Is the family in crisis? What is the apparent attitude of each of the family members regarding treatment (in other words, to what extent does each member want to be here)? How do they define their problem (marital conflict, parent–adolescent difficulties, or other kinds of distress)? Should the children be included in future sessions? How does the family enter the consultation room and in what arrangement do they seat themselves? Who joins with whom, and against whom? Who speaks for the family? Who is silent? Who reaches out to the therapist or to other family members, who withdraws because of fear, distrust or hostility? Answers to these and other questions help the therapist appraise the family's patterns of conflict and coping, its rules and possible secrets, its sources of anxiety, its alliances and collusions, its image of itself, and finally, its capacity for change and growth. Frequently, the therapist attempts to gauge the current phase of the family's life cycle, and identify any ethnic or socioeconomic factors, intergenerational influences, current external pressures, and any other issues that bear on the presenting problem and help define the goals of treatment.

Although many family therapists carry out such evaluations informally, as part and parcel of the overall therapeutic process, others prefer a more structured format for gathering information about the family. Typically, they believe that a formal evaluation process helps involve the entire family more directly in the treatment to follow.

In the following sections we will consider five evaluation procedures: the Structured Family Interview, the Family Life Chronology, the Genogram, the Family Environment Scale, and Behavioral Coding Systems. The choice of any particular method depends largely upon the theoretical views of the user.

The Structured Family Interview

Paul Watzlawick (1966) of the Mental Research Institute, a family therapist with a communication viewpoint, developed what he calls a "structured family interview" as a standardized evaluative technique designed to reveal family interactive patterns. The instrument, usually requiring about one hour to administer, is intended to stimulate participants to explore their relationships through directed conversation, and thus to involve them in the tasks of marital/family therapy from the outset. Through a series of predetermined questions to each member and the assignment of tasks to the family group, the interviewer gathers data useful in evaluating the family's functioning. According to Watzlawick, it is even possible for the therapist to observe another interviewer and the family through a one-way mirror and then to take over at the end of the interview to begin therapy with an understanding of the family's dynamics and patterns of interaction. More likely, the therapist will conduct the family interview as a prelude to initiating family therapy.

A structured interview might begin with the therapist asking each family member individually what he or she thinks are the family's main problems. After each person is questioned separately, the family is brought together. The interviewer indicates there are discrepancies in their viewpoints, although these are not disclosed because confidentiality is protected. These discrepancies suggest the family may wish to discuss their problems together now, and the interviewer leaves to go behind the one-way mirror to observe and record their discussion. Their assignment is to reach a consensus regarding the family's main problems. In this way, the therapist is showing the family that each member has his or her own views, that all views are considered important, that the problems belong to the family and not just the identified patient, and that the interviewer assumes the existence of not just one but a variety of problems.

Later, the interviewer may ask the family to plan something *together* that they can do as a group, as he or she observes them through the mirror. Here, of course, it is not so much the content of what they plan (for example, a family picnic or trip by car) that interests the interviewer but the process (including possible conflicts and impasses) that is important. An interviewer may also question the parents alone, inquiring how they met.[3] Frequently such questioning elicits highly significant patterns of marital interaction. The parents may also be asked to arrive at a mutually satisfactory interpretation of a proverb (such as "A rolling stone gathers no moss") and then to teach its meaning to their children. Whether or not they agree on the meaning—the proverb may actually be interpreted in two ways[4]—how they tolerate or otherwise deal with disagreement and the way they involve the children in the explanation provides valuable information for appraising family functioning.

The structured family interview has been used extensively at the MRI, with various features added or deleted as necessary in a particular family situation. Bodin (1981) discusses the use of this technique within the framework of the interactional approach to family therapy currently practiced at the MRI.

---

[3]The transcript of such an interview is reproduced in Chapter 3.

[4]Either that moss is desirable (representing roots, stability, friendships) or that rolling is desirable (because it keeps a person from stagnating).

The Family Life Chronology

Another early effort from the MRI, this technique developed by Satir (1967) emphasizes the importance of family-history taking in order to shed light on current relationships. As Satir puts it, just to take a detailed history is "like diagnosing an illness without doing all the appropriate tests. The therapist can always be wrong in his perceptions" (p. 144). To carry the medical analogy a bit further, Satir likens the family therapist to a dentist who asks the patient "Where is the pain?" and then proceeds first to where the patient points before exploring further. Similarly, the family therapist relies on the family to help him or her get started, so that the therapist can decide what to work on first, and what can wait.

As outlined in Table 11–1, and as described in great detail by Satir (1967), the family life chronology goes beyond the gathering of historical facts. Rather, Satir attempts to force family members to think about the relevant concepts that formed the basis for their developing relationships, how the family's ideology, values, and commitments emerged and changed over time, and, in general, what the impact of the past has been on the family as a whole as it functions currently. In the process, she carefully comments on possible trends and introduces ideas to which she will return in later sessions.

Satir attempts to be flexible and creative in using the family life chronology, sometimes taking up to five sessions to gather what she considers the necessary information from the past to understand current patterns. Table 11–1 presents an overview of the general areas Satir covers by this approach, as she pieces together what has happened in the past that remains and impacts on the present. Many of the issues and bits of unfinished family business she discovers through these efforts are dealt with later in the course of family treatment.

Genograms

One of the best known objective family-assessment devices, developed largely by Bowen and used by many therapists he has trained (Philip Guerin, Elizabeth Carter), is the **genogram.** A genogram is a structural diagram of a family's multigenerational relationship system (Guerin & Pendagast, 1976), schematically depicting the various family members in family-tree fashion and noting pertinent data such as sex, age, year of marriage, offspring, current marital status, year of death. Males are represented by squares, females by circles, their present ages are written inside the figures. Horizontal lines indicate marriages and vertical lines show family lineage.

The genogram illustration in Figure 11–1 depicts a three-generational family. It should be read as follows: Carl and Linda were married in 1940 and had one daughter, Vickie, before Linda was killed in an auto accident in 1943. Two years later, Carl remarried and together, he and Carol (now the paternal grandparents) had two sons, Tom and Sam. Carl is now 65, Carol 63, Vickie 43, Tom 37, and Sam 32.

On the maternal side, the grandparents Paul (now 62) and Martha (58) married in 1947 and had four children—three daughters and a son. All are alive and range in age from Sue, the oldest (35), to Paul (28), the youngest.

TABLE 11–1. Main Flow of Family Life Chronology to Family as a Whole

Therapist asks about the problem

TO MATES:

Asks about how they met, when they decided to marry, and so on.

TO WIFE:	TO HUSBAND:
Asks how she saw her parents, her sibs, her family life.	↔ Asks how he saw his parents, his sibs, his family life.
Brings chronology back to when she met her husband.	↔ Brings chronology back to when he met his wife.
Asks about her expectations of marriage.	↔ Asks about his expectations of marriage.

TO MATES:

Asks about early married life. Comments on influence of past.

TO MATES AS PARENTS:

Asks about their expectations of parenting. Comments on the influence of the past.

TO CHILD:

Asks about his views of his parents, how he sees them having fun, disagreeing, and so on.

TO FAMILY AS A WHOLE:

Reassures family that it is safe to comment.

Stresses need for clear communication.

Gives closure, points to next meeting, gives hope.

(From Satir, 1967, p. 135)

In 1974, Tom and Sue married but were divorced two years later, in 1976. Sue married Jack, to whom she is currently wed. The genogram indicates that Tom and Sue had one child, Linda, during their brief marriage, and she is now 9 years old. Sue and her second husband, Jack, have had three children to-gether—two boys, Bob (6) and Joe (5), and one daughter, Jean (2), the youngest in the family.

Consistent with Bowen's overall approach, as we described it in Chapter 7, the use of the genogram represents objectivity, accuracy and orderliness. A family presenting itself for help generally displays a high level of emotional reactivity that limits the ability of the family members to define themselves in relationship to each other and to the issues that exist. According to Kerr (1981), the situation calls for a therapist to stay clear of the family's emotional turbulence, in order to objectively evaluate the situation and carefully work out a treatment plan. The genogram is a means toward those ends.

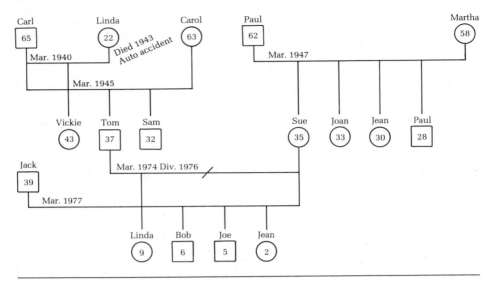

Figure 11-1. Genogram of a three-generational family. (Courtesy of Kathleen Austin)

The content and the mechanisms of the evaluation process are determined by Bowen's family systems theory. The evaluation has five parts: (1) the history of the presenting problem (who has the symptom, when it originated, how it developed, how the family reacted); (2) the history of the nuclear family (ages, nature of parents' courtship and marriage, impact of having children, and similar issues); (3) the history of husband's extended family (sibling position, degree of differentiation from family of origin, and so on); (4) the history of wife's extended family (same as for husband, above); and (5) conclusion (in which the family focus is turned away from the presenting symptom in order to look at the emotional processes and tensions within the family to which every member is presently reacting and, in some way, contributing).

Exact dates of birth, death, separation or divorce, geographic moves, periods of ill health, and so forth, may all be schematicized so that the Bowenian therapist obtains a picture of the family's structure and key life events extending back over several generations. According to Papero (1983), the genogram is, in effect, the therapist's roadmap of the family emotional process. As family therapy proceeds, questions can be directed at relationship patterns within and between generations and any emotional cutoffs can be addressed; in general, the genogram facilitates a clearer understanding of why and how certain family members got caught up in the emotional currents and others were less involved (Papero, 1983).

Family Environment Scale

A psychometric evaluative approach introduced by Moos (1974) attempts to assess the impact of the family environment on individual and family functioning. Moos assumes that all social climates have characteristics that can be portrayed accurately. For example, some are more supportive than others, some more rigid, controlling, and autocratic; in others, order, clarity, and structure are given high priority. Moos argues that, to a large extent, the family environment regulates and directs the behavior of the people within it. The Family Environment Scale contains 90 statements to be labeled "true" or "false" by the respondent ("Family members really help and support one another."; "Family members often keep their feelings to themselves."; "We fight a lot in our family."). The set of responses characterize the family climate and its influence on behavior. It provides a framework for understanding the relationships among family members, the kinds of personal growth (for example, intellectual, religious) emphasized in the family, and the family's basic organizational structure.

Ten subscales make up the Family Environment Scale. As indicated in Table 11-2, three subscales (cohesiveness, expressiveness, and conflict) are conceptualized as relationship dimensions. They characterize the interpersonal transactions that are taking place within the family. Five subscales (independence; achievement, intellectual-cultural and active recreational orientations; moral-religious emphasis) refer to personal development or growth dimensions. Two subscales (organization, control) refer to system maintenance dimensions. They provide information about the family structure and its roles. A score is obtained for each subscale and average scores for the family are placed on a family profile. (If desired, the differing perceptions of various family members—for example, parents and children or husband and wife—can be compared for possibly divergent views of the same family environment.)

The family in Figure 11-2, made up of parents and two children in their early twenties, is strongly upwardly mobile, emphasizing personal development (especially achievement and moral-religious emphasis) above other aspects of family life. These same two factors are deemphasized by the young couple (no children) depicted in Figure 11-3. They agree that, for them, relationships are far more important than achievement, conflict is minimal, and control is low. This couple feel very positive about the social environment they have created.

Functional Analysis: A Behavioral Coding System

As we emphasized in our earlier discussion of behavioral family therapy, assessment and evaluation are ongoing processes in behavioral forms of treatment. Some therapists, such as Patterson and Reid (1970), have developed standardized coding schemes whereby trained observers making home visits can identify the frequency of particularly significant sequences of behavior between and among family members, as in the case of aggressive children and their parents. Other therapists, as reported by Alexander and Parsons (1982), have developed individualized coding schemes to evaluate a wide

243

TABLE 11-2. Description of Subscales of Moos's Family Environment Scale

Relationship Dimensions

1. Cohesion	The extent to which family members are concerned and committed to the family and the degree to which family members are helpful and supportive of each other.
2. Expressiveness	The extent to which family members are allowed and encouraged to act openly and to express their feelings directly.
3. Conflict	The extent to which the open expression of anger and aggression and generally conflictual interactions are characteristic of the family.

Personal Growth Dimensions

4. Independence	The extent to which family members are encouraged to be assertive, self-sufficient, to make their own decisions and to think things out for themselves.
5. Achievement orientation	The extent to which different types of activities (for example, school and work) are cast into an achievement oriented or competitive framework.
6. Intellectual-cultural orientation	The extent to which the family is concerned about political, social, intellectual and cultural activities.
7. Active recreational orientation	The extent to which the family participates actively in various kinds of recreational and sporting activities.
8. Moral-religious emphasis	The extent to which the family actively discusses and emphasizes ethical and religious issues and values.

System Maintenance Dimensions

9. Organization	Measures how important order and organization are in the family in terms of structuring the family activities, financial planning, and explicitness and clarity in regard to family rules and responsibilities.
10. Control	Assesses the extent to which the family is organized in hierarchical manner, the rigidity of family rules and procedures and the extent to which family members order each other around.

(From Moos, 1974)

range of problem situations, from marital arguments and dysfunctional problem solving to bedtime conflicts and the granting of privileges to adolescents. Such schemes, based on independent observation, may prove especially helpful when family members admit confusion or outright disagreement about how problem behavior sequences started or developed—a more than likely scenario.

The observation of a couple's or a family's attempt to solve a problem together illustrates the way a behavior therapist carries out a behavioral assessment. Particular attention is paid to small but possibly significant bits of behavior that lead to communication problems—poor eye contact, verbal interruptions, speaking for the other person, digressing from the subject, making inappropriate nonverbal expressions such as frowning or eye-rolling in feigned disbelief, leaving the room in the midst of a conversation and so forth. The behavior therapist may also note problem-solving defects (for instance, the quarreling couple may never define what they are fighting about or what alternative solutions are available) or specific detrimental patterns of interaction (such as excessive use of criticism, baiting the other person, aggressive threats). By coding and recoding these patterns, the therapist is able to feed back to the participants what was observed, and help them to change the nature of their transactions.

Behavior therapists postulate that certain family interactive patterns are acquired through repeat performances and numerous trial-and-error experiences. In carrying out a functional analysis, an appraisal is made of how an individual, his or her family members, and his or her social network respond to the problem behavior, either reducing its threat or learning to live with it by incorporating it into their usual pattern of interaction. Falloon and Liberman

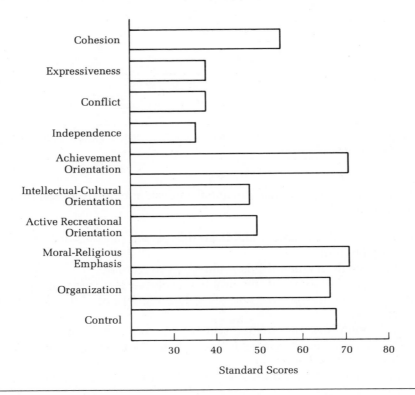

Figure 11–2. Family Environment Scale scores for an achievement-oriented family. (From Moos, 1974)

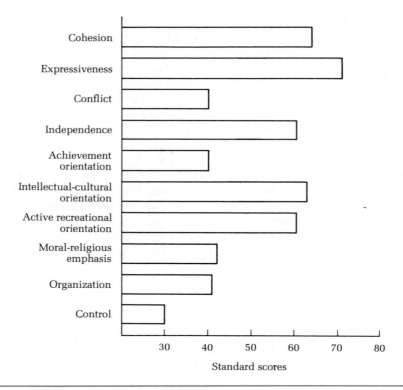

Figure 11–3. Family Environment Scale for a higher relationship, low control family. (From Moos, 1974)

(1982, p. 129) propose that the functional analysis attempt to answer the following questions:

1. How does this problem handicap this person (and his or her family) in everyday life?
2. What would happen if this problem were ignored?
3. What would happen if this problem occurred less frequently?
4. What would this person (and his or her family) gain if the problem were removed?
5. Who reinforces the problem with attention, sympathy, or support?
6. Under what circumstances is the problem reduced in intensity? Where? When? With whom?
7. Under what circumstances is the problem increased in intensity?

Answers to these questions provide the basis for the behavior therapist to devise a treatment plan tailored to the specific problems from which the clients seek relief.

DIMENSIONS OF FAMILY ASSESSMENT

Apart from using one or more of these specific methods of family evaluation, are there general areas of family functioning to which therapists characteristically pay attention? Certainly all family therapists attend to family interaction patterns (how a family communicates, what relationships it forms, how it negotiates differences), although those with different theoretical orientations may look for different patterns or attribute different meaning and significance to the same pattern.

One well-known family assessment effort (Lewis, Beavers, Gossett, & Phillips, 1976; Beavers, 1977, 1982), described in Chapter 2, studied volunteer families by filming their members as they carried out a series of assigned tasks with varying degrees of competence; each family's activity was later scored according to a group of process-oriented, interactional rating scales and categorized as "healthy," "midrange," or "severely dysfunctional." A number of systems-oriented, family-level variables were studied: the clarity of boundaries (for example, between the generations), the hierarchy of power, the process of expressing intimacy, the expression of affect, the degree of skill at organizing family members and mediating their differences, the extent of members' comfort and joy at being together, the degree of encouragement of members' autonomy, and so on. Each family received a global rating of competence based on a composite of these subscale scores.

A similar family assessment technique, the McMaster Model of Family Functioning, was initially developed at McMaster University, Hamilton, Ontario, Canada, and later refined at Brown University in Providence, Rhode Island (Epstein, Bishop, & Baldwin, 1982). The McMaster model focuses on those dimensions of family functioning selected by the research team as having the most impact on the emotional and physical well-being of family members. The model, having evolved through a series of refinements over a period of 25 years, is a systems-based approach to family evaluation. Families are assessed with respect to their functioning in three areas: (1) the Basic Task Area (how family members deal with problems of providing food, money, transportation, and shelter); (2) the Developmental Task Area (how they deal with problems arising as a result of changes over time, such as first pregnancy, or last child leaving home); and (3) the Hazardous Task Area (how they handle crises that arise as the result of illness, accident, loss of income, job change, and so forth). Families unable to deal effectively with these three task areas have been found to be those most likely to develop clinically significant problems.

To appraise the structure, organization, and transactional patterns of a family, the McMaster group attends particularly to six dimensions of family functioning: (1) family problem solving (the ability to resolve problems to a level that maintains effective functioning); (2) communication (how, and how well, a family exchanges information and affect); (3) roles (how clearly and appropriately roles are defined, how responsibilities are allocated and accountability is monitored in order to sustain the family and support the personal development of its members); (4) affective responsiveness (the family's ability to respond to a given situation with the appropriate quality and quantity of feelings); (5) affective involvement (the extent to which the family shows interest in and values the particular activities and interests of family members); and (6) behavior control (the patterns the family adopts for handling dangerous situations; for handling social interaction within and outside the family; for meeting and expressing members' psychobiological needs [eating, sleeping, eliminating, sex] and drives [such as aggression]).

From the various conceptual schemas for family assessment available in the literature at the time of his survey, Fisher (1976) derived five broad categories (see Table 11-3). Generally speaking, structural descriptors (roles, splits, alliances, boundaries, patterns of interaction and communication, rules, conflict and its resolution, and family views of life) are the primary dimensions for family assessment. Control, power, leadership, and the degree of fusion within the family also interest family therapists, as does the family's ability to deal with emotional expression and need satisfaction. Note, however, that cultural aspects (social class, race, urban versus rural or suburban setting) and developmental aspects (the phase of the family's life cycle) help provide a context in which the family can be viewed and evaluated.

TABLE 11-3. **An Overview of Dimensions Used by Practitioners in Making Family Assessments**

I) Structural Descriptors
    1) role: complementarity, acceptance, confusion, adequacy
    2) splits, alliances, scapegoating
    3) boundaries: internal and external
    4) patterns of interaction and communication: rules and norms of relating
    5) conflicts and patterns of resolution
    6) family views of life, people, and the external world
II) Controls and Sanctions
    1) power and leadership
    2) flexibility
    3) exercise of control
    4) dependency—independency
    5) differentiation—fusion
III) Emotions and Needs
    1) methods and rules for affective expression
    2) need satisfaction: giving and taking
    3) relative importance of needs vs. instrumental tasks
    4) dominant affective themes
IV) Cultural Aspects
    1) social position
    2) environmental stresses
    3) cultural heritage
    4) social and cultural views
V) Developmental Aspects: appropriateness of structural, affective, and cultural
    aspects to developmental stage.

(From Fisher, 1976)

VALUES AND GOALS IN FAMILY THERAPY

Inherent in the family therapy approach are a set of moral values and sentiments that are largely middle class—respect of the institution of marriage and a stable and harmonious family life, the importance of exercising good childrearing techniques adapted to the needs of each child, the desirability of passing along the family's cultural values to the next generation, and so on. According to Bloch and LaPerriere (1973), family therapy—by its very orientation—speaks to a value and belief system in which a family (of whatever type or composition) is necessary for maintaining good mental health and an individual who functions in isolation is underfunctioning or malfunctioning. On the other hand, social critics such as British psychiatrist David Cooper (1970), a colleague of R. D. Laing, see the family structure in capitalist society as the ultimate form of imperialism, destroying individual initiative and spontaneity. Nevertheless, most family therapists—deliberately or unwittingly, consciously or unconsciously—proselytize for maintaining a family way of life.

The reader can easily glean from the theories discussed so far the dominant value-orientations of some of the leading family therapists: the avoidance of interlocking pathology within the family (Ackerman); freedom from hidden transgenerational introjects from the past (Framo); resolution of family legacies and obligations owed over time (Boszormenyi-Nagy); the differentiation of the self from the family of origin (Bowen); the development of mutuality within a family, rather than simply maintaining the appearance of a relationship, as in pseudomutuality (Wynne); the acknowledgment of self-deceptive family myths and scapegoating (Ferreira); differentiation and clarification of boundaries between family members (Minuchin); simple, straightforward communication of needs, feelings, and thoughts and the development of self-esteem (Satir); and the modification of reinforcement contingencies so that family members learn to positively reinforce only desirable behavior in each other (Liberman).

Beyond these specific values (most of which are shared but given different emphasis by different therapists), there appears to be a common core of operational assumptions made by therapists working with families. Warkentin and Whitaker (1967) indicate the following as their "secret agenda" in working with couples and families: that marital partners have chosen each other with great wisdom (including the wisdom of their unconscious motives); that people are good for each other to the degree that they are intimate together; that the force or power of marriage is greater than the positive and negative sums of the two people; that a satisfying sexual relationship is the primary axis in the dynamics of a marriage; that the type and intensity of exchange of feeling in a marriage must be continuously balanced by the partners; that the usual rules of human social behavior (for example, fairness) do not apply to marriage or any other intimate relationship; that a normal marriage proceeds through a series of developmental crises or impasses as the years go by; that both partners bring their unconscious secret goals into marriage, and that these secret purposes determine the dynamic line of forces between them; that the course of marriage hinges on the conscious determination of two people to remain intimately related. Finally, Warkentin and Whitaker contend that human character structure changes little once it is formed, so that someone who divorces and remarries may very likely choose as a second spouse someone who is a reasonable facsimile of the first and eventually get involved in similar marital struggles; accordingly, the current marriage is probably the best that person can achieve in his or her lifetime.

How do family therapists decide on treatment goals, on what they wish to change in a family? Ferber and Ranz (1972) caution that the therapist may, knowingly or unknowingly, impose on families his or her own version of what makes for a good family life (for example, less rigidity in family roles, better sex relations, more fun together).[5] In such a case, the therapist's values, rather than the problems presented by the family, influence the direction of the treatment. Therapists and families from similar cultural and social-class backgrounds may share similar assumptions about the definition of problems and how they should be solved. However, therapists and families from widely divergent backgrounds may have different expectations about what the family problems are and how they can be resolved. Ferber and Ranz suggest as a general rule that the therapist try to deal with the problems the family labels as problems or, at the very least, explain to the family the basis on which he or she redefined their problems.

Generally speaking, the main purpose in therapeutic work with a family is to improve the members' functioning as a working, interdependent group. In addition, each member should derive personal benefit from the therapeutic experience. Haley (1976) attempts to obtain from the family in the first session some statement of what changes everyone wants; this helps the family focus on why they are in family therapy and helps set the goals of treatment. Satir (1967) suggests asking the family members to state their goals, in terms of what they hope to gain for the identified patient as well as for themselves, as a way of consolidating their commitment to the treatment. Behaviorists are apt to negotiate a contract with clearly stated objectives (for example, fewer quarrels, more frequent sexual relations, more help around the house from the children with more recognition of their contribution). Glick and Kessler (1980) suggest that, in general, family therapists have three broad therapeutic goals: to facilitate communication of thoughts and feelings between family members; to shift disturbed, inflexible roles and coalitions; to serve as role models, educators, and demythologizers, showing by example how best to deal with family quarreling and conflict.

---

[5]Some clinicians such as Rachel Hare-Mustin (1978) advocate a feminist approach to family therapy, encouraging practitioners to examine the consequences of traditional socialization practices that may be disadvantageous to women. Specifically, Hare-Mustin urges family therapists to be aware of their own biases regarding stereotyped sex roles and sexist attitudes. She is concerned that in attempting to restore family equilibrium, some therapists may simply be perpetuating traditional norms and expectations rather than seeking ways of freeing women (and themselves) from these notions.

ETHICAL ISSUES IN FAMILY THERAPY

A number of important considerations of an ethical and professional nature arise as therapy shifts from an individual focus to one that involves a marital/family system. For example, to whom and for whom does the therapist have primary loyalty and responsibility? The identified patient? The separate family members as individuals? The entire family? Only those members who choose to attend sessions? More than academic hairsplitting is involved here. Hare-Mustin (1980) has warned that "family therapy may be dangerous to your health"; the changes that most benefit the entire family may not in every case be beneficial to each of its members.

Whether the therapist's values are such that he or she chooses to be responsible to the individual or, say, to a marriage, the choice has significant consequences. To use an example offered by Bodin (1983), suppose a husband is contemplating divorcing his wife, an action his wife opposes. The husband may feel his individual happiness is so compromised by remaining in the marriage that he hopes the therapist attaches greater importance to individual well-being than to maintaining some abstraction called "the family system." The wife, on the other hand, hopes the therapist gives higher priority to collective well-being, helping individuals adjust their expectations for the sake of remaining together. Many therapists caught in such a situation take the position that a strife-torn marriage all but guarantees unhappiness for everyone, including the children. Others argue that the stress and uncertainty of separation and divorce may do irreparable damage to the children and thus the maintenance of family life, imperfect as it is, is preferable to the breakup of the family. As Bodin (1983) notes, the therapist's position may have a profound impact not only in terms of the rapport established with the various family members but also on the therapist's formulation of the problems, the goals, the plans for treatment.

Morrison, Layton, and Newman (1982) identify four sets of ethical conflicts in the therapist's decision-making process. We have touched on the first—whose interest should the therapist serve? When working with an individual, the therapist must decide whether, and to what extent, to involve family members in the treatment. On the other hand, when working with a family group, should certain individuals or combinations of family members be seen separately? How should confidentiality be handled under those circumstances? The second set of ethical issues involves the handling of secrets. Should parental secrets (for instance, sexual problems) be aired before the family or brought up in a separate couple's session? How should an extramarital affair—hidden from one's spouse but revealed to the therapist in an individual session—be handled? What about family secrets—incest between the father and teenage daughter, or physical abuse of the wife or young children? Here the therapist in many states has legal responsibilities to report such behavior to the police or child welfare authorities. Even when reporting is not mandatory, the therapist must exercise clinical judgment to insure the safety and well-being of family members.

The third set of ethical considerations offered by Morrison, Layton and Newman (1982) concern the careful use of diagnostic labeling of individuals, since such labels may ultimately be used by others in litigation (for example, child custody disputes) or other forms of intrafamilial power struggle. The fourth set of issues involves awareness by the family therapist of his or her power to increase or decrease conflict. As we indicated earlier, the family therapist may impose certain traditional male–female role expectations that are disadvantageous to a particular family. Such gender-related issues must be dealt with in an especially sensitive manner in view of changing social attitudes and to insure that both male and female clients believe that the therapist represents their best interests.

Because ethical issues are not necessarily discussed in family therapy training programs, Hines and Hare-Mustin (1978) have urged that the subject of ethics become a regular feature of such programs as well as of **continuing education** offerings. In addition, various professional organizations have established ethical guidelines for practitioners, although these guidelines typically specify only minimal standards and cannot, of course, encompass all the issues that the clinician must deal with in actual practice. Table 11–4 reprints the basic code of ethics of the American Association for Marriage and Family Therapy (AAMFT), which appears in its entirety in the appendix of this book.

TABLE 11–4. Code of Professional Ethics, American Association for Marriage and Family Therapy

Section I: Code of personal conduct

1. A therapist provides professional service to anyone regardless of race, religion, sex, political affiliation, social or economic status, or choice of lifestyle. When a therapist cannot offer service for any reason, he or she will make proper referral. Therapists are encouraged to devote a portion of their time to work for which there is little or no financial return.
2. A therapist will not use his or her counseling relationship to further personal, religious, political, or business interests.
3. A therapist will neither offer nor accept payment for referrals, and will actively seek all significant information from the source of referral.
4. A therapist will not knowingly offer service to a client who is in treatment with another clinical professional without consultation among the parties involved.
5. A therapist will not disparage the qualifications of any colleague.

Section II: Relations with clients

1. A therapist, while offering dignified and reasonable support, is cautious in prognosis and will not exaggerate the efficacy of his or her services.
2. The therapist recognizes the importance of clear understandings on financial matters with clients. Arrangements for payments are settled at the beginning of a therapeutic relationship.
3. A therapist keeps records of each case and stores them in such a way as to insure safety and confidentiality, in accordance with the highest professional and legal standards.
   a. Information shall be revealed only to professional persons concerned with the case. Written and oral reports should present only data germane to the purposes of the inquiry; every effort should be made to avoid undue invasion of privacy.
   b. The therapist is responsible for informing clients of the limits of

6. Every member of the AAMFT has an obligation to continuing education and professional growth in all possible ways, including active participation in the meetings and affairs of the Association.
7. A therapist will not attempt to diagnose, prescribe for, treat, or advise on problems outside the recognized boundaries of the therapist's competence.
8. A therapist will attempt to avoid relationships with clients which might impair professional judgment or increase the risks of exploiting clients. Examples of such relationships include: treatment of family members, close friends, employees, or supervisees. Sexual intimacy with clients is unethical.
9. The AAMFT encourages its members to affiliate with professional groups, clinics, or agencies operating in the field of marriage and family life. Similarly, interdisciplinary contact and cooperation are encouraged.

    confidentiality.
c. Written permission shall be granted by the clients involved before data may be divulged.
d. Information is not communicated to others without consent of the client unless there is clear and immediate danger to an individual or to society, and then only to the appropriate family members, professional workers, or public authorities.
4. A therapist deals with relationships at varying stages of their history. While respecting at all times the rights of clients to make their own decisions, the therapist has a duty to assess the situation acording to the highest professional standards. In all circumstances, the therapist will clearly advise a client that the decision to separate or divorce is the responsibility solely of the client. In such an event, the therapist has the continuing responsibility to offer support and counsel during the period of readjustment.

(*Code of Professional Ethics*, by the American Association for Marriage and Family Therapy. Copyright by the American Association for Marriage and Family Therapy. Reprinted by permission.)

Family therapy, as we have seen, poses a variety of complications in respect to a therapist's social responsibilities. The help offered to one family member may be harmful or depriving to another. A preference for one or the other spouse implies favoritism and, potentially, the loss of necessary impartiality. The balancing of the needs of each individual with the needs of the marital relationship can become a monumental task (Margolin, 1982). The importance of maintaining confidentiality is well established, but when there is a clear and imminent danger to a client or to others, or when a specific requirement of the law takes precedence, the therapist may have to reveal information gained during a therapy session (Baruth & Huber, 1984). (Whatever the therapist's decision in such circumstances, he or she must inform the clients before such information is forthcoming.)

Corey (1982) has offered the following guidelines for developing a therapist's personalized code of professional ethics:

1. Therapists must be aware of their own needs, what they are getting from their work, and how their needs and action influence their clients.
2. Therapists should have the necessary training and supervised experience in the use of assessment techniques and intervention strategies they employ.
3. Therapists should be aware of the ethical standards of their professional

organizations and realize that many situations have no clear-cut answers; therapists have to exercise their own professional judgment.

4. Therapists should have some theoretical framework of behavior change to guide them in their practice.
5. Therapists must remember that their needs should not be met at the clients' expense.
6. Therapists need to be aware of the importance of continuing education as a way of updating their knowledge and skills.
7. Therapists should avoid any behavior that could jeopardize the therapeutic/ professional relationship with clients.
8. Therapists are responsible for informing clients about confidentiality and other matters that may affect the therapist-client relationship.
9. Therapists must recognize their own values and beliefs and avoid imposing them on their clients.
10. Therapists must provide the information necessary for clients to give informed consent.
11. Therapists must be aware of the boundaries of their competence and, when they have reached their limits with a particular client, should seek supervision or refer clients to other professionals.
12. Therapists should strive to practice in their own lives the behaviors that they encourage in their clients.

STAGES OF FAMILY THERAPY

The Initial Interview

Family therapy gets underway with the first contact made by a family member concerning the presenting problem or symptom. Most often this contact is made by telephone by the identified patient or someone calling on his or her behalf (especially when the identified patient is a child). Family therapists assume that a symptomatic person is calling out for help for the entire family, regardless of whether the symptom is physical ("I have frequent headaches."; "My child is hyperactive."), psychological ("I'm always frightened and apprehensive."; "My husband has been depressed for two months now."), or interpersonal ("My teenage son and I have been at each other's throats all summer."; "My wife and I stopped having a sexual relationship six months ago."). As Kempler (1974) puts it, the individual with the symptom is simply saying "Ouch! I have a pain in my family." Consequently, most family therapists prefer to ask everyone living in the household to come in together for the initial interview. Even if the therapist later chooses to work with only some members, excluding others (for example, young children), this opportunity to gather information firsthand about the family's style of operation and strategies for coping with the stress of the interview situation may later prove invaluable.

As we noted earlier, a family may refuse to involve one or more of its members (for example, the parent who states that it is not possible to leave work to attend, but who may also be avoiding the sessions out of fear of being blamed or exposed by the therapist or family). Most families, however, will include all members if the therapist indicates it is his or her way of working—to see the entire family together. Therapists such as Bell (1975) point out over the telephone that in their experience such problems always involve the total family, so it is therapeutically best for all members to attend. Franklin and Prosky (1973) go so far as to regard the willingness of the entire family to participate as a favorable prognostic sign. They point out the risk of seeing one member (for example, an anguished wife) alone, since the other members who later join her may see her as the person with the problem, or she may mistakenly look to "her" therapist for protection against the others. Family therapists report that, despite the protests of a telephone caller that his or her spouse would never agree to family sessions, most people are willing to come in if troubled enough about the state of their marriage or other family relationships.[6]

What about children? Is there an age below which the child's short attention span is countertherapeutic? If a child is the identified patient (for example, a 12-year-old bedwetter) should he or she and the parents come together for family sessions, or should all the other children in the family also attend? When should children be included, for how long, and when excluded? Satir (1964) usually insists on seeing the husband and wife first for at least two sessions without the children, in order to emphasize to them that they are individuals and mates, not strictly parents. However, in the event that the family is so dysfunctional that the spouses cannot bear to look at their own relationship but must have the child present to focus on, Satir may make an exception and include the child from the start. Children under four years of age may attend some early sessions, according to Satir, but she prefers working with the marital pair and possibly including the young children later in the therapy. All the children in the family above four, and not merely the symptomatic child, are included for most if not all the family therapy sessions.

Bell (1975) also insists on seeing the parents first, then the entire family. He will not see one parent from an intact family (mother and father living together in one household) without the other—a practice followed by most family therapists. Bell's rule of thumb is to exclude children younger than nine because of their limited ability to verbalize or to think in abstract terms about the family's problems beyond their own self-centered feelings. Otherwise, all family members living together are included in the family sessions once the parents are oriented to the family therapy approach.

Some therapists compile a family life history (for example, Satir, 1967; Franklin & Prosky, 1973) during the initial interview, perhaps comparing each member's perspective on the events that person deems significant. Other therapists (for example, Zuk, 1976) are interested in family history but focus primarily on current family functioning and activities. Still others, such as

[6]There are situations where only one person is available, of course, so that the initial session is by necessity a one-to-one encounter. A college student away from home, a member of the armed forces stationed far from his family, a person in jail or in a mental hospital may all need to be seen individually, although the therapist may retain a family-oriented outlook regarding the causes of the presenting difficulties and their alleviation.

Wynne (1971), determine the feasibility of family therapy through a series of exploratory conjoint family sessions, search for difficulties in ongoing family interactions, and believe discussion of the past is merely an intellectual exercise unless an understanding of current experiences is achieved.

A number of family therapists, such as Haley (1976), proceed systematically, with the initial interview comprising a series of stages. The therapist negotiates with the family to decide what problem(s) need attention, then formulates a plan of intervention to change the dysfunctional behavior patterns in order to eliminate the problem(s). In the opening *social stage*, Haley observes family interaction and tries to get all family members to participate; he then shifts to a *problem stage*, getting down to the business of why the family is there. Here he tries to get all family members to specify what changes in the family they want. Why is the family here and why now? In some cases it is best to start with the least involved child, the one seemingly most distant and detached, thus making it clear that all members are expected to participate, not merely the adults. In what Haley calls "problem-solving therapy," the focus is on establishing the problem to be solved and suggesting the new kind of behavior needed, not only to solve the problem but as a lever for changing family relationships, as in the following example:

> A mother may say that her nine-year-old son is afraid to go outside the house and clings to her all the time. In the room the therapist may see that he sits beside her and holds on to her. She also may say he lies and will not do anything around the house, but that the problem is mostly that he is afraid and never leaves her side. He even sleeps with her so that the father has to sleep on the livingroom couch. The other children do not behave this way, but seem normal.
>
> This information from the mother does not tell the therapist what the problem is or what to do about it. He has only her version that the problem is inside the child and no one else has anything to do with it. To get more information and begin to make a change is the purpose of skillful family interviewing. After the mother has stated that problem the therapist needs to listen to the father and his views. Then he needs to listen to the brothers and sisters and what they say about it. After having spoken to each one, he will see disagreements appearing. For example, he will notice that the father does not quite agree with the mother and thinks she is taking care of the child too much and not letting him be on his own enough. He also does not like to be moved out of his own bed, he may say, although he is willing if it will keep the child from being afraid. Perhaps mother argues that father neglects the child. When mother and father talk about their disagreements, information may appear about how much the child is an issue between them.
>
> During this stage of the interview, it will probably become clearer how to think about this problem in terms of more than the child. The therapist may think of it as a peculiar relationship between mother and son; she has as much difficulty leaving him as he has leaving her. He may also be able to think in terms of three people and consider the possibility that the child is helping mother and father. If they cannot get together without fighting, particularly in bed, then the child is helping them by acting so fearful that they are kept more separate. They can then say it is the child who is the problem, and not bad feelings between them [Haley, 1976, p. 35].

In this family therapy scene, cotherapists work together with a husband and wife who sought help because of their frequent quarrels over disciplining their 6-year-old hyperactive daughter.

Notice in this example how Haley tries to define the family problem as carefully and fully as possible before treatment gets underway. He believes the responsibility for change rests entirely with the therapist. The therapist must use this family-focused information gathered during the initial interview to formulate ideas about how to bring about behavior change and, ultimately, problem resolution. Beyond the problem stage, there is an *interaction stage* in which the family members are encouraged to talk to each other, rather than to the therapist. The *goal-setting stage* is reached next and the family members are asked just what changes they seek. This technique is similar to a therapeutic contract used by behavior therapists (see Chapter 10) and is based on a similar premise: the clearer the goal (the elimination of a problem or the alleviation of a symptom), the easier the evaluation of progress and the greater the likelihood of therapeutic success. In the *closing stage*, the therapist offers the family some observations about its problems as well as recommendations for a specific plan of action.

By way of contrast to Haley's rather set, by-the-book procedure, therapists with an experiential viewpoint take a more spontaneous and personally involved approach to the encounter with the family. Whitaker (1977) emphasizes that a therapist's usefulness is more related to his or her presence and the characteristics of his of her personality than to any formal procedure or effort to create an image of a take-charge figure. He is likely to begin broadly— "What's with your family?"—perhaps addressing the father first before moving around the family. Whitaker's therapeutic tactic here is to acknowledge the father's importance and to involve him early in the treatment, particularly since he is the most likely of the family members to resist seeking help and usually has the power to pull the family out of treatment if some rapport is not established with the therapist from the beginning.

Minuchin's (1974a) opening gambit is to join the family, accommodating to its ways and its style of communicating. He listens carefully to what family members tell him about their experiences, perhaps sharing his own related experiences and views of the world. He uses their language as he solicits personal information about their daily activities and concerns. To use Minuchin's metaphor, all effective interventions involve both "a kick and a stroke" (Minuchin & Fishman, 1981, p. 6), a supportive statement alongside a push to change. For Minuchin, all of therapy is a process of kicking and stroking, with stroking perhaps more prominent during the initial structural interviewing.

Generally speaking, the first interview with a family calls for the therapist to try to accomplish the following tasks: "joining the family, as individuals and as a group; accurately assessing the problem; formulating a treatment plan; getting the family to agree to treatment; and making sure they come back for the next session." (Schultz, 1984, p. 325.)

The Middle Phase

The middle phase of family therapy comprises the heart of the therapeutic process (Framo, 1965). Let us assume that, on the basis of the initial interview or brief series of interviews, the therapist and the family agree to meet regularly, usually once a week for an hour to an hour and a half. It would be rare indeed for the members to unanimously express the need for help as a family; much more likely, some family members will be far more strongly motivated than others, some will express a willingness to participate if it will help the "sick" family member, all will be to a greater or lesser extent resistant to self-exposure or revealing family "secrets." Both conscious resistance (expressed as fear of rejection, shame, distrust of the therapist) and unconscious resistance (expressed through silences or too much chatter, lack of affect or too much intensity of affect, intellectualizations and clichés about family problems and their solutions, acting-out behavior, regression in various family members) are operating here. Haley (1976) has found it helpful to set a fixed number of family interviews (for instance, six sessions) if he finds the family particularly resistant or doubtful about continuing after the initial interview, with the proviso that they can all decide at the end of that time if more sessions are necessary.

Emotionally disturbed children, often the identified patients, usually reflect disturbed marriages and often cover up deeper family splits. When such families are told the entire family will be seen together, according to this account by Framo,

> they initially accept the idea with equanimity, saying, "Yes, doctor, we understand. We want you to know that we will do everything in our power to cooperate to get our daughter well. No sacrifice is too great." In our early years of operation we

used to allow discussion about the designated patient to go on for a number of sessions; our rationale was that the sessions should begin with what most concerned the family, which obviously would be the illness of a member of the family. A typical exchange at that time was as follows: The parents would turn to the patient with the words: "Tell us what is wrong, dear. Why don't you talk to the doctor? Don't be afraid to say anything; we can take it. Would you like to tell us off or hit us? Will that make you feel better?" The majority of the time the patient, sensing the concealed injunction that she'd better say the right thing or at least avoid self-incrimination, would respond, "Nothing's bothering me," or she would behave in some irrational way to confirm the view of her as a demented or inept person. If the patient, particularly if she has undergone individual psychotherapy and feels the support of her therapist, actually reveals what's on her mind, for example, in the form of "disloyally" commenting on the parents' unhappy marriage or angrily passing a judgment on mother (thus violating family dictum number one), a series of events follows very quickly. Father quickly changes the subject, a sibling begins to laugh, and mother, after a dumbfounded look, hits her hand on her thigh, turns to the doctor, and says, "See, doctor, this is what I mean. She's getting sick again." We have repeatedly noticed in most families that the mother can never consider her daughter well until the patient no longer manifests anger of deep resentment toward her [Framo, 1965, p. 162].

The task of the therapist, then, is to keep the family redefining the presenting problem or symptom of the identified patient as a relationship problem to be viewed within a family context.

As the entire family becomes oriented to therapy, the members begin to understand the role of the therapist. For example, the therapist will offer guidance and direction but will not take over the parental functions; will not take sides with certain family coalitions against others within the family; will not meet privately with one member; will try to facilitate open and honest communication among family members; will insist all members, children included, participate. At the same time, the family learns its obligations: all members must attend unless otherwise agreed beforehand; they must all be available at the agreed upon time; they should be prepared for the possibility of increased strain and expression of open hostility within the family as underlying sources of conflict are revealed, and so on.

During the middle phase of therapy, families begin to consider that relationships can change and that destructive alliances within the family (for example, between one parent and a child against the other parent) can be broken. The following case illustrates just such a situation in which a variety of therapeutic techniques were undertaken simultaneously.

Lisa Ash, a 5-foot-tall, 260-pound, 13-year-old girl, was brought to a mental hospital by a distraught mother who complained that she couldn't control her daughter's eating habits and was alarmed about the danger to her health. Lisa, a junior high school student, was the oldest of three daughters in a middle-class Jewish family. Both the father, a moderately successful shoe-store owner and his wife, a housewife, were overweight, as were various other uncles, aunts, and to a lesser extent, Lisa's two younger sisters.

The mother/daughter conflict was evident from the intake interview. In particular, both agreed that they battled frequently over discipline or any restrictions imposed by Mrs. Ash on Lisa's eating behavior. Whenever this occurred, the mother complained, Lisa would lock herself in her room, wait for her father to come home, and then tell him how "cruel" the mother had been to her. Usually, without inquiring further or getting the mother's story, he would side with Lisa and countermand the mother's orders. Occasionally he would even invite Lisa out for a pizza or other "snack."

Needless to say, the mother/father relationship was poor. They had not had sexual intercourse for several years, and Mrs. Ash assumed that her husband was impotent, although she was too embarrassed to ask him. She had become increasingly unhappy and had seen a psychiatric social worker a year earlier for several sessions, although then, as now, her husband refused to participate in therapy. He also opposed Lisa's hospitalization and for several months would not speak to any member of the hospital staff about his daughter's progress.

Lisa was placed on the adolescent open ward of the hospital and attended the special school within the hospital complex, remaining there for 12 months. During that period, four coordinated therapeutic programs were introduced: nutritional control (including a careful watch on calorie intake), individual psychotherapy twice weekly, family therapy (after much resistance, Mr. Ash agreed to attend), and ward milieu therapy. The picture that emerged was of an emotionally intense and chaotic family existence in which Lisa often screamed, hit, swore, and threatened to break household objects if she didn't get her "sweets." There was no regular mealtime at the Ash house; each member ate when and what he or she wanted. Lisa would regularly visit her father's store after school, and they would go out together for an ice cream soda or sundae. Finally acknowledging, during one family-therapy session, that the situation had gotten out of hand, Mr. Ash defended his actions by saying that he could never get himself to say "no" to Lisa for fear of losing her love. Mrs. Ash quickly conceded her resentment about her husband's relationship with Lisa, her own feeling of isolation, and her sense of helplessness; she was finally able to separate the two only by hospitalizing the daughter.

The program of calorie restriction was immediately successful. After 2 months, Lisa had lost 35 pounds; after 7 months, 80 pounds; and by 10 months, a full 100 pounds. Family therapy was less immediately successful. Mr. Ash and Lisa continued to play seductive games with each other: he called her on the telephone frequently, sent her flowers, and even visited her with a box of candy on her birthday, and she deliberately delayed coming to the telephone or lobby, to make her ultimate appearance more appealing. Finally, Lisa put an end to this kind of transaction, to Mrs. Ash's relief; Lisa learned limits on her own behavior largely from milieu therapy on her ward. Eventually, Mr. Ash was able to give up his seductive and overprotective behavior, realizing that if he really wanted to help his daughter, he should limit her self-indulgent, self-destructive behavior rather than encourage it.

Upon her discharge from the hospital, Lisa weighed 140 pounds, had some insight into her eating behavior, and had dealt with a number of other preadolescent problems. She agreed to undergo weekly individual psychotherapy for a while so that she would not regress to her former ways once she was home. A two-year follow-up found her able to control her eating and generally proud that she could take care of herself successfully [Goldenberg, 1977, pp. 350–351].

Not all interventions are as successful as the case just described, nor does family therapy necessarily proceed smoothly. Like any other form of psychotherapy, family therapy moves in fits and starts as therapist-initiated interventions reverberate throughout the family system. As one family member begins to change his or her behavior, or the family rules are challenged or made more explicit, family members display a variety of reactions. Some are positive moves, others are more regressive efforts to revert to the family's earlier, more dysfunctional mode of operation. Resistances to change—familiar to all therapists—occur at various times throughout treatment, and signal the therapist that the family is struggling—consciously or unconsciously, purposefully or inadvertently—against changes in the way they function as a family unit. Anderson and Stewart (1983) offer a number of examples of common forms of resistance in family therapy (denial of the problem, intellectualization, nonstop talking, insistence that the problem resides within the identified patient, increased hostility and sullen behavior in an adolescent) along with suggestions for overcoming them.

As families become involved in treatment, and resistances are dealt with successfully, reorganization of the family structure starts to take place. Family members open themselves to these possibilities: increased autonomy, less rigid roles, the sharing and acceptance of previously concealed feelings and experiences, the giving and receiving of feedback in response to new behavior. Weekly therapy sessions do not, of course, produce steady progress. Some old patterns of interaction may be highly resistant to change and family members may even demonstrate regression in some of their relationships. But the overall result of the middle phase of family therapy is a family that is better prepared to accept the idea of change and more willing to work to achieve its potentially positive consequences.

Termination

Generally speaking, family therapy is of shorter duration than individual therapy. Because it focuses so precisely on eliminating a specific problem or alleviating a presenting symptom, it is clear to all participants when the goal has been achieved. Although the process may last anywhere from several weekly sessions to several months (or, in rare cases, even years), Bell (1975), an experienced family therapist, estimates that eight to twenty sessions are a reasonable expectation.

No family leaves treatment problem-free, nor have all members progressed to the same point by termination time. Several members may be ready to move into new kinds of relationships, but one member may continue to obstruct the process, or two members in combination may retard a third (Framo, 1965). Nevertheless, the family members and therapist are apt to sense at about the same time that the family is ready to go off on its own, not without trepidation about the forthcoming loss of support from the therapist, but eager to function independently.

Most therapists agree that termination is easier in family therapy than in individual treatment. The family, now accustomed to working as a unit to solve

261

its own problems, has developed an internal support system and is not usually overdependent on an outsider, the therapist. In family sessions, family members have had considerable practice in working together on relationship issues, developing clearer and more explicit ways of communicating, assigning roles more flexibly, redistributing power more equitably or appropriately.

Families may or may not announce that they are ready to conclude the therapy, but the signs are apparent in either case. For example, the family now resolves interpersonal conflicts at home rather than bring them to the therapist. The presenting complaint or symptom has usually disappeared, the family engages in more mutually satisfying activities, independent activities outside the family bring new satisfactions, the family has developed through its own efforts effective ways of solving problems. It is time for disengagement from family therapy.

SUMMARY

Family therapy aims at alleviating the interlocking emotional problems that develop within any type of family organization. A family-oriented therapist may choose to work with entire families, subsystems within the family, or individual family members in order to help change the family social system. Family therapy is indicated especially for cases of marital conflict, severe sibling rivalry, or intergenerational conflict, or for clarifying and resolving relationship difficulties within a family, but contraindicated when one or more grossly disturbed family member(s) may be too destructive, violent, or too psychologically fragile.

Family therapists differ in their views regarding family diagnosis. Detractors find the process unproductive and distracting, while proponents argue that it is a necessary and useful guide to treatment planning. The latter group may rely on systematic observation of the family functioning together, on interviews, on psychological assessment techniques (such as a family life chronology, a genogram, or the Family Environment Scales), or on behavioral assessment procedures.

Therapists' values, such as belief in marriage and family life, tend to be middle-class in origin and affect the therapy process and choice of therapeutic goals. Despite differences in value-orientation, the main goal of therapists appears to be improvement in family members' ability to function as a working, interdependent group. Ethical issues involving the therapist's loyalty and responsibility, handling of family secrets, diagnostic labeling, and awareness of power to increase or decrease conflict must be taken into consideration by the family therapist.

Family therapy proceeds in stages beginning with the first contact with the family, which is usually by telephone. Most therapists will insist on seeing the entire family or as many members as possible, although children (especially young children) may be excluded in certain cases. There is no single way of conducting initial interviews; they range from a carefully planned strategy

(Haley), to a spontaneous encounter between therapist and family (Whitaker), to an effort to join the family, accommodate to its style, and attempt to change it from within (Minuchin). During the middle phase of family therapy, families are encouraged to look at their relationships, work on specific problems that brought them into treatment, and attempt to reorganize the family structure. If successful in overcoming resistances and involving themselves in the treatment, families are usually ready to terminate treatment after several months, now better able to work as a group to solve their problems and change destructive behavior patterns.

CHAPTER
TWELVE

Innovative Techniques in Family Therapy

A number of noteworthy forms of family therapy—in a sense, variations on the themes presented in Part Two—will be discussed now. Some forms, such as multiple family therapy or multiple impact therapy, represent well-established approaches to family treatment while others, such as **family sculpture** or **family choreography,** are useful supplemental techniques rather than full-fledged therapeutic approaches. Some are based on technological break-throughs (for example, **videoplayback** techniques). Others represent the appli-cation of previously developed intervention techniques to changing family needs (**divorce therapy**), or the extrapolation to families of individual clinical procedures (for example, family **crisis intervention**). Family therapy in the home is also represented here in the form of **social network intervention,** as is the MRI's Brief Therapy Center approach.

We will present these special forms and innovations in terms of their clinical application to situations calling for non-verbal treatment procedures, to crisis situations, to time-limited treatment and to situations where large-group treat-ment is indicated.

NONVERBAL TREATMENT PROCEDURES

Family Sculpture and Choreography

Family sculpture is a metaphor for understanding a family's relationships through the eyes of one of the family's members. Developed by Duhl, Kantor, and Duhl (1973) at the Boston Family Institute, the technique attempts to trans-late systems theory into physical form by creating an arrangement of people placed in various physical positions in space that represent their relationships to each other at a particular moment in time. While it may be very difficult for an individual to verbalize his or her perceptions of how family members relate—how intimate or distant they are, how loving or indifferent—sculpting allows the person to reveal his or her private view of invisible but meaningful boundaries, alliances, subsystems, roles, and so on. When each member has created a sculpture, conflicts are removed from the verbal arena and given a graphic, more active mode of expression. The entire family and the therapist are able to grasp each member's experiences and perceptions more easily and immediately. In this manner, the family is prepared for choosing new options—taking new actions—to change relationships.

The technique has been popularized by Satir (1972) as a way of permitting each family member to put his or her feelings into action. In recent years Satir (1982) has used sculpting to place people in certain postures herself, saying that she "activated the right brain experience so people could feel their experience with minimal threat. They were *experiencing* themselves, instead of only hearing about themselves" (p. 18). Constantine (1978) observes that the act of externalizing one's perception of relationships between family members often provides insights about those relationships for all family members and the therapist alike. Bandler and Grinder (1975) contend that these visual, spatial, metaphorical representations reveal in compact form each person's map of the world—the way each person perceives his or her complex interpersonal landscape.

The family therapist may use sculpting at any point in the assessment or therapeutic process. Preferably at least three or four persons should be present, although at times a movable piece of furniture can pinch-hit for an absent member. The request for a member to make a sculpture is often timed to cut through excessive verbalizations or, on the other hand, when a member (often an adolescent) sits silently through a session or cannot easily express his or her thoughts verbally. According to Simon (1972), adolescents usually make excellent sculptors because of their awareness of family truths and their relish in manipulating their parents. Younger children, by contrast, typically lack comprehension of what is really taking place in the family; parents are often too anxious about losing their dignity to participate fully themselves. Once the ice is broken by the first presentation, however, all family members are likely to want a turn at sculpting in order to present their points of view. Family sculpting can be repeated at various points during the course of family therapy, revealing to all participants how their individual perceptions of their relationships are undergoing change.

The procedure calls for each member to arrange the bodies of all the other family members in a defined space, according to his or her perception of their relationships either at present or at a specific point in the past. Who the sculptor designates as domineering, meek and submissive, loving and touching, belligerent, benevolent, clinging, and so on, and how those people relate to each other becomes apparent to all who witness the tableau. The sculptor is invited to explain the creation, and a lively debate between members may follow. The adolescent boy who places his parents at opposite ends of the family group while he and his brothers and sisters are huddled together in the center conveys a great deal more about his views of the workings of the family system than he would probably be able to state in words. By the same token, his father's sculpture—placing himself apart from all others, including his wife—may reveal his sense of loneliness, isolation, and rejection by his family. The mother may present herself as a confidante of her daughter but ignored by the males in the family, and so forth. Nonverbally—without emotional outburst or intellectualization—the members have openly portrayed their various views of the family's difficulties. Their actions have indeed spoken louder than words, often revealing to others for the first time what each had felt but never expressed before.

Constantine (1978) offers a useful typology of sculpting and related mapping techniques. These range from simple, individualized spatializations to boundary sculptures (sometimes involving two or more family members simultaneously portraying their sense of space) to system sculptures (including not only the current family members playing themselves, but also the families of origin of adult family members).

Family choreography (Papp, 1976) is an outgrowth of family sculpture, so named because the sculpture moves to show the dynamic, shifting transactional patterns within the family (see Figure 12-1). Choreography is a method for actively intervening in the family, realigning relationships, creating new patterns, and changing the system. While family members seldom surprise each other by what they say—in most families the pattern of verbal exchange is all too predictable—they may be surprised by what they choreograph. Alliances, triangles, and shifting emotional currents are all represented by the family movement. Choreography may help a family to physically retrace old interactive patterns and create new ones. An entrenched vicious cycle of behavior within a family, dramatized in the therapist's office, may be replayed using alternative ways of reacting and relating. With the old pattern experienced differently by the entire family, under the direction of the therapist, the newly enacted changes may be easier to recreate at home.

Videoplayback

The use of videoplayback during a family session provides unique opportunities both to capture objective behavioral data and to examine (and reexamine) it on the spot (Alger, 1976a). The advent of videotape equipment has also opened new avenues in clinical training, such as studying the demonstrations of master therapists as well as recording sessions conducted by beginning family therapists for supervisory purposes. In the latter case, the "instant replay" of an interview can provide the trainee with immediate feedback information. Away from the emotional intensity of the family session, the therapist can see how he or she presents himself or herself to the family, what was missed or overlooked, what characteristic patterns of communication appear and reappear, what facial expressions belied what member's verbal comments, and so on (Berger, 1978). Other students, viewing the tape, can learn a

Figure 12-1. In this simulation of a family choreography session, therapist Papp (rear) observes as a mother creates a tableau to illustrate her perception of her family's relationship to her. (Bernard Gotfryd–Newsweek)

variety of styles and profit from each other's mistakes. For the purposes of this chapter, however, we will concentrate on the use of videoplayback as an intervention that supplements various approaches (for example, couples groups, family crisis therapy) in family therapy.

Videotape playback is ideally suited for the practice of family therapy. Becoming technically feasible at the time that communication theory and general systems theory were directing clinical attention to transactional patterns between people, videoplayback permitted a look at the behavioral sequences and signaling of responses that go on within a family system. By allowing family members to view their behavior immediately after it takes place, a corrective maneuver is introduced. Put another way, videoplayback adds negative feedback into the system, calling for a change in the ongoing system's direction and promoting the development of equilibrium and stability (Alger, 1973).

Technically, videotape's great advance over filming a family session is in providing playback without any time lost for film processing. In a teaching hospital, clinic, or university, audiovisual personnel are usually available for taping a session from behind a one-way mirror. Later, the tape can be studied by a class and/or supervisor or shown to the family involved. An even more immediate therapeutic effect is achieved when the therapist (or the co-therapist) operates a camera equipped with a zoom lens, focusing on one person and then another during the session, or perhaps sets the camera up with a wide-angle lens covering the entire group, therapist(s) included. The tape can then be stopped, reversed, or shown in slow motion for everyone to see. Facial expressions, gestures, changes in body positions, covering of the face, raised eyebrows, a flushed face—these are all nonverbal signals, forms of communication whose meaning is clarified when captured by the camera. At certain times, it may be advantageous to have different family members operate the camera, in order to give each a fresh perspective on how the family operates. What the member chooses to focus on (for example, angry expressions) or avoid (for example, consistently excluding one member) may be clinically meaningful.

Alger (1976a) invites each family member to ask for an instant replay during a session whenever he or she wants to review or clarify what just took place. Typically, he reports, family members may ask for two or three playback interventions in the course of an hour. In some cases the family may request that the same sequence be replayed several times during a session, as different members react to their own perceptions and memories of what just took place. With more sophisticated equipment, involving a second camera, it is even possible to use a split-screen replay technique. While the entire family is interacting on the television screen, a closeup of one member may be inserted in one corner of the screen, showing the details of that person's responses. In working with couples,[1] each partner may be seen, side by side on the screen, during a replay. A camera may even be brought into the home to record what transpires there for later playback.

Seeing oneself on the screen is, inescapably, an experience in self-confrontation. A person may deny having an angry feeling, insisting that all he or she did was sit and listen, but the camera has caught the sneer. Another member's hurt feelings, verbally unacknowledged, are exposed. It is not possible to pretend a transaction never took place when confronted with evidence to the contrary. As a result, the effects of gaining self-awareness visually ("I'll never forget seeing that look on my face when . . . ") may outlast the effects of verbal insights and interpretations. Through videoplayback, family members are likely to gain a new perspective on family functioning, seeing individual behavior as arising within a particular family context. As videotape recorders have become more economical and reliable, they have become an invaluable tool for many family therapists.

Other Projective and Expressive Techniques

A number of procedures ancillary to family therapy have appeared in recent years, some intended to help family members reveal current interpersonal stresses, others to evoke memories, and still others to improve problem-solving skills.

---

[1]Most marital therapists are accustomed to hearing one or both spouses say "I wish I'd had a tape recorder when we had that argument last night. Then you would see how you started it by looking for a fight." A videoplayback recaptures the action and its context for greater clarification of exactly what took place.

The techniques designed to uncover current problem areas include: **family drawings** (Bing, 1970) in which each of the members is asked to draw a picture of how he or she sees the family as a unit; the **family floor plan** (Coppersmith, 1980) in which children draw a floor plan of their current dwelling, providing the stimulus for verbal descriptions of their surroundings, as parents observe and later respond; **family puppet interviews** (Irwin & Malloy, 1975) in which family members act out family scenes, in some cases accompanying the puppet play with a narrative of what is transpiring (the technique is especially useful with young children).

Memory aids include the use of family photos and home movies (Kaslow & Friedman, 1977) in a procedure called **family photo reconnaissance.** The family brings in such historical evidence of family life as snapshots, slides, or films in an effort to retrieve emotionally significant events in the past, as a means to better understanding each other's current experiences and perceptions. In the adult version of the family floor plan, Coppersmith (1980) asks family members to draw plans for homes in which they lived as children, as aids to helping them recall the sights, smells, moods, significant friends and relatives, and key events of those earlier times.

The behaviorist Blechman (1974) has developed a "contracting game" to teach families negotiation and problem-solving skills. Although reluctant to confront problems directly, the members of families in conflict can be helped to strengthen their abilities at, and decrease their aversion to, solving problems. Blechman utilizes a game board with 14 squares. Each square makes a statement (for example, "Red, tell Blue what to do more of and when") or asks a question (for example, "Blue, ask Red if he agrees to the reward you choose"). The game involves participants (family members) going around the board through each square, selecting a target for change ("Red, draw a problem card"), agreeing on more pleasing behavior to replace problem behavior, deciding on rewards—such as play money or humorous bonus cards—and, finally, writing out and signing a contract together (for example, "how to deal with clothes left on the floor"). The **family contract game** is designed to provide powerful antecedents to and consequences for effective problem-solving behavior; learned problem-solving skills will presumably transfer from the game to actual use at home, becoming useful family tools for negotiating problems.

CRISIS-ORIENTED TREATMENT PROCEDURES

Multiple Impact Therapy

With the goal of providing brief but intensive intervention for a family with a disturbed adolescent in crisis, MacGregor, Ritchie, Serrano, and Schuster (1964), of the University of Texas Medical Branch in Galveston, developed a unique, crisis-focused approach to family therapy. Psychologist MacGregor and his associates operated as a clinic team, devoting a full two days or so to the study and brief treatment of a single family in crisis. Called multiple impact therapy (MIT), this highly focused procedure is based on two assumptions: (1) that individuals and families facing a crisis are motivated to mobilize family resources to meet it, and thus are more likely to be receptive to professional help than at other times, and (2) that psychotherapy is likely to produce faster results in the early stages of treatment, so rapid intervention is highly desirable (Ritchie, 1971).

Essentially an expanded intake procedure focused on adolescents with behavior problems, MIT involves an entire family in a series of continuing interactions with a multidisciplinary team of mental health professionals over the two-day period. Beginning with a diagnostic team/family conference, the team starts to gather information about the family's role in the social development of the adolescent in crisis. Following this first collective conference, private individual interviews are arranged, each family member meeting with a different therapist. The venting of grievances, the presentation of each person's viewpoint, and attempts at self-justification are common at this point. Later, various combinations of team members and family members may hold joint sessions, such as when the teenager and his or her interviewer join with one or both parents and their interviewer(s). Therapists may overlap in working with different individuals or combinations; multiple therapists may work with the same individual or same pair of family members; occasionally two family members (for example, father and son) may be left alone to work on their problems themselves. After the team has had an opportunity to discuss their findings at lunch—the family is also encouraged to talk together at this time—individual interviews resume but with a switch in interviewers (that is, the husband's interviewer in the morning may become the wife's interviewer in the afternoon, and vice versa). While the adolescent is being given psychological tests, joint sessions between the parents and their interviewers are held, as the team begins to close in on the dysfunctional aspects of the family's functioning that are being revealed. At the end of the first day, the team and family reassemble for a group discussion of what they have learned.

The second day accelerates many of the first day's interviewing procedures, with family members likely to produce more emotionally charged responses to what is taking place. The overlapping material from interviews is used more freely; insights gained from one interview are shared in the next one. Factors interfering with family communication in general and intimate communication between the parents in particular are likely to become the focus of interest. A final team/family conference is held, findings are reviewed, and specific recommendations are made for dealing with "back-home problems." In some cases, an additional half-day is needed. Before the family leaves, arrangements are made for follow-up sessions to be held several months later in order to evaluate the extent to which any gains made during the intensive treatment period are sustained (MacGregor, 1971).

During the course of two days, the team has examined the marital relationship closely and taken initial steps toward strengthening it. Parent–adolescent transactions are investigated, with the objective of clarifying lines of authority.

All members have undergone a powerful emotional experience and, as a result of the team's efforts, are oriented to the future rather than the past. The treatment team's solidarity, its prior experience with families, and the sheer number of mental health professionals involved has a positive impact on the family and its value system. More than simply providing insights, MIT aims to change the family from a relatively closed system to an open system conducive to growth. MIT encourages more open communication between members, greater mutual acceptance, clearer role differentiation, and increased flexibility in attempting new ways of relating—especially to and by the disturbed adolescent—so that family members can give up old and unsatisfying roles and begin to explore new ways of growth.

Although many professional working hours were consumed in this experimental approach, thus raising questions about cost efficiency, overall results with 62 families indicated somewhat more success than that obtained by traditional therapeutic approaches (MacGregor and associates, 1964). Moreover, it should be noted that the team dealt with families not likely to remain involved in weekly child guidance clinic sessions; brief, direct, action-oriented, problem-solving procedures were a matter of necessity, not choice. If the team was able to make an impact in a brief period, then the possible prevention of behavioral problems in the future would be justification indeed for the time and intensive effort involved.

Family Crisis Therapy

Crises of varying magnitude, duration, and frequency occur in all families throughout their life cycles. As we discussed in Chapter 3, the family's usual functioning may become temporarily disrupted, as the members try, unsuccessfully, to impose their customary problem-solving strategies in a situation where such strategies are inappropriate or inadequate. Since the crisis period is a time of increased vulnerability as well as an opportunity for growth and change, prompt, action-oriented intervention focused on resolving the urgent problem may have great benefits for all concerned. Designed for such emergency situations, family crisis therapy seeks to help the family resolve the crisis through a process of systems change and to restore its functioning to its previous adaptational level. In some cases, immediate aid to the family on an outpatient basis may prevent the hospitalization of one or more of its members.

Family crisis therapy aims to help a distressed individual and his or her family to actively define the crisis in terms of the family system and then utilize the family's combined coping skills to deal with the existing, as yet unresolved, situation. It is time-limited (typically no more than six sessions) and highly focused on the management of the current crisis and the prevention of future crises.

The first extensive and systematic treatment of families in crisis came with the establishment of the Family Treatment Unit at the Colorado Psychiatric Hospital in 1964 (Langsley & Kaplan, 1968). This unit was set up to offer brief, crisis-focused outpatient therapy to families in which one member, usually diagnosed as acutely schizophrenic, would ordinarily be hospitalized. Part of the rationale for the unit was the belief that removing a disturbed young person from the home and placing him or her in a hospital has two drawbacks: it scapegoats that person as the cause of all family problems, and it thereby helps the family to avoid those very problems that may have precipitated the crisis that led to the person's disturbed behavior. In this alternative approach, the family in an acute crisis situation remains together, receiving intensive family therapy on an outpatient basis. Family crisis therapy typically lasts about three weeks and includes five office visits and one home visit. The home visit is especially valuable for observing family interaction and functioning in a natural environment, in addition to strengthening the family's commitment, involvement, and belief that the hospital team cares (Langsley, Pittman, Machotka, & Flomenhaft, 1968).

As practiced by the Colorado group, there are seven overlapping steps in the process: (1) immediate aid is offered at any hour of the day or night; (2) the crisis is defined as a family problem and all relevant family members are involved in the treatment from the outset; (3) the focus remains on the current crisis, placing immediate responsibility for change on all the family members; (4) a nonspecific treatment program (discouraging regression, offering reassurance and hope, lowering the family's tension level, prescribing medication for the identified patient for symptom relief) is begun; (5) specific tasks are assigned to each family member in an effort to resolve the crisis; (6) resistances to change are negotiated, as are role conflicts that have hindered the members' ability to deal with the crisis; and (7) therapy is terminated, with the understanding that further treatment is available in the event of a future crisis. If necessary, referral for long-term family therapy may be made during this step.

In a carefully designed experiment on the effectiveness of family crisis therapy (FCT) in avoiding mental hospital admission, Langsley and associates (1968) responded to requests for immediate hospitalization of a family member by assigning alternate applicants to the outpatient Family Treatment Unit or to the university psychiatric hospital. In the former group, the patient and his or her family were seen together for crisis therapy for six visits over a three-week period. The latter group of matched patients received the customary hospital treatment—individual and group psychotherapy, medication, participation in the hospital's therapeutic community—for an average stay of slightly less than a month. In addition, their families were seen separately from them by the hospital's psychiatric social worker. A follow-up study showed that the FCT patients were less likely to be hospitalized within six months following treatment than the hospitalized patients were to be rehospitalized. A later study (Langsley, Machotka, & Flomenhaft, 1971), comparing 150 FCT patients and 150 hospitalized patients 18 months after treatment, showed similar benefits for FCT patients, although the differences in hospitalization rates between the groups tended to decrease with time. If hospitalization became necessary by the 6-month or 18-month checkpoint, the FCT patients were likely to spend considerably less time in the hospital than did their previously hospitalized counterparts. Hospital treatment apparently encourages further hospitalization. Family crisis therapy can be a cost-effective, preventive measure in avoiding hospitalization, returning patients and families to a functional level, and helping them manage hazardous events in the future.

If a crisis period is an optimum opportunity for positive behavioral changes and rearrangements in the relationships between family members, as we have indicated, then why not therapeutically induce a crisis as a way of helping families to break old dysfunctional patterns and learn new ones? Minuchin and Barcai (1972) suggest doing just that—deliberately causing temporary upheaval in a family—by intervening in a manner that will produce an unstable situation requiring change and the restructuring of the family organization. We saw an example of the technique in Chapter 8, when Minuchin urged the parents to insist that their anorexic daughter eat, forcing them to change their ways of dealing with each other in order to cope with the situation. In very rigid families with seriously ill anorexic girls, Minuchin (Minuchin, Rosman, & Baker, 1978) pits the patient against the parents, reframing the issue as one of control versus disobedience rather than one in which the adolescent is treated as an incompetent and ineffective person, too sick to help herself. The daughter's refusal to eat is voluntary, Minuchin points out to the parents, aimed at frustrating and defeating them, rather than being an involuntary symptom over which she has no control. She has won over them, unless they mobilize together to deal with her rebelliousness. At the same time, Minuchin shows the adolescent that she is not helpless as she feared, but actually—through her symptoms—demonstrating considerable power. By precipitating the crisis, Minuchin has maneuvered the family members into a position where they must respond in new ways. There is considerable clinical evidence (Doyle & Dorlac, 1978) to indicate that the entire family unit is most receptive to change, to restructuring previously maladaptive coping patterns, while the crisis is in progress.

TIME-LIMITED TREATMENT PROCEDURES

Brief Family Therapy

The Brief Therapy Project at the Mental Research Institute at Palo Alto, in operation since 1967, has developed a number of ingenious systems-based tactics for treating a wide assortment of clinical problems, including anxiety, depression, marital discord, sexual dysfunction, family conflict, psychosomatic illness, and drug and alcohol dependence (Watzlawick, Weakland, & Fisch, 1974; Fisch, Weakland, & Segal, 1982). These interventions represent the clinical application of some of the communication/interaction theories and techniques of Bateson, Jackson, Haley and especially Erickson to families seeking immediate resolution of problems and relief from symptoms.

Brief family therapy is a time-limited (no more than ten sessions), pragmatic, nonhistorical, step-by-step strategic family therapy approach based on the notion that most human problems develop through the mishandling of normal difficulties in life. In such cases, the attempted "solutions" themselves become the problem, as people persist in self-perpetuating and self-defeating "more of the same" attempts at problem resolution. The patient (or, correspondingly, the family) is like a person caught in quicksand: the more struggling, the more sinking; the more sinking, the more struggling (Segal, 1982). In other words, wrong attempts persist, and now the "solution" itself only makes matters worse. According to advocates of this approach, it is only by giving up solutions that perpetuate the problem and attempting new solutions that are different in kind that changes can occur in behavior and/or the view of the problem.

According to Watzlawick, Weakland, and Fisch (1974), the kinds of problems presented in psychotherapy persist because people maintain them through their own behavior and that of others with whom they interact. (Note the influence of behavior therapy as well as the concepts of feedback and circular causality from cybernetics and systems theory.) If, however, the current system of interaction is changed, then the problem will be resolved regardless of its history and etiology. Accordingly, the strategically oriented brief therapist tries to obtain a clear picture of the specific problem as well as the current behavior that maintains it, then devise a plan for changing those aspects of the system that perpetuate the problem. By restraining people from repeating old unworkable solutions (and by altering the system to promote change) the therapist can help them break out of their destructive or dysfunctional cycle of behavior.

Brief therapy advocates argue that most therapists, in attempting to help a distressed person, encourage that person to do the opposite of what he or she has been doing—an insomniac to fall asleep, a depressed person to cheer up, a withdrawn person to make friends. These approaches, by emphasizing opposites or negative feedback, only lead to internal reshuffling; they do not change the system. Watzlawick and associates (1974) call such moves superficial **first-order changes** (effecting change within the existing system without changing the structure of the system itself). In the example of feedback loops we used in Chapter 2, such a therapeutic effort is equivalent to the thermostat that regulates room temperature, activating the heating system to cool down when the room gets too hot. Real change, however, necessitates an alteration of the system itself; it calls for a **second-order change** to make the system operate in a different manner. To continue the analogy, the thermostat on the wall must be reset. First-order changes, according to Watzlawick, Beavin, and Jackson (1967), are "games without end"; they are wrong attempts at changing ordinary difficulties that eventually come to a stalemate by continuing to force a solution despite available evidence that it is precisely what is *not* working (Bodin, 1981).

Clinicians report three ways that a family mishandles solutions so that they lead to bigger problems: (1) some action is necessary but not taken (for example, the family attempts a solution by denying there is a problem—the roof is not leaking, sister is not pregnant, money is no problem even though father has lost his job); (2) an action is taken when it is unnecessary (for example, newlyweds separate because their marriage is not as ideal as each partner fantasized it would be); (3) action is taken at the wrong level (for example, marital conflicts or parent–child conflicts are dealt with by "common sense" or first-order changes, such as each party agreeing to try harder next time, when revisions in the family system—second-order changes—are necessary). The third type is probably most common, since people with problems attempt to deal with them in a manner consistent with their existing frame of reference. Repeated failures only lead to bewilderment and "more of the same" responses.

The MRI version of brief therapy focuses on resolving problems that result from prior attempts to solve an ordinary difficulty. Paradoxical interventions, especially reframing, are emphasized in order to redefine the family's frame of reference so that members conceptualize the problem differently and change their efforts to resolve it. As we saw in our earlier discussions of the structural (Chapter 8) and strategic (Chapter 9) approaches to therapy, reframing involves a relabeling process in which a situation remains unchanged but the meaning attributed to it is revised. Reframing allows the situation to be viewed differently and thus facilitates new responses to it.

As practiced at the MRI, brief therapy's short-term duration sets up a powerful expectation of change. At the same time, the therapists tend to "think small," to be satisifed with minor but progressive changes. They also urge their clients to "go slow" and to be skeptical of dramatic, sudden progress; this paradoxical technique is actually designed to promote rapid change as the family is provoked to prove the therapist wrong in his or her caution and pessimism. In general, the therapists "go with the resistance," neither confronting the family nor offering interpretations to which the members might react negatively or defensively. Brief therapy aims to avoid power struggles with the family while it reshapes the members' perspectives on current problems and on their previous attempts to overcome difficulties.

The brief therapy program is a team effort. Although each family is assigned a primary therapist who conducts the interviews, other team members watch from behind the one-way mirror and may telephone the therapist with suggestions while treatment is in progress; in special cases (for example, a therapist–family impasse) one of the team members may enter the room and address the primary therapist or the clients, perhaps siding with the client to increase the likelihood that forthcoming directives from the observer will be implemented. Families are not screened prior to treatment and are taken into the program on a first-come, first-served basis. Team discussions precede and follow each session. A follow-up evaluation of each family receiving treatment at the center takes place 3 months and 12 months after the last interview. Although the treatment is not conducted under ideal research conditions, overall results indicate that this technique is cost-effective and has a positive impact on family systems—sometimes a significant one—in a relatively short period of time (Segal, 1982).

The reader will recognize the similarity of the Brief Therapy Project model to the work of Haley and an even greater resemblance to the work of the Milan group discussed in Chapter 9. All three approaches have their focus, at least initially, on a presenting problem that is thought to occur within, and be maintained by, a repetitive sequence of behavior. All three pay attention to the family's developmental stage and deliberately design interventions (most likely, paradoxical strategies) to fit the particular problems of that stage (MacKinnon, 1983). However, the brief therapy approach differs from Haley's efforts in being less concerned with power issues or family structures (such as hierarchies or coalitions). Also, they are more likely to be active, practical, and problem-focused, and to offer suggestions that activate the family system than do the Milan Associates, who emphasize neutrality and view the therapist and family as one large system.

The following example illustrates the effectiveness of the brief therapy approach. The therapy team helps a concerned wife to revise her earlier self-defeating solutions to a problem and thus to institute second-order changes in her interactions with a resistant husband:

the author and Dr. Fritz Hoebel studied and treated 10 families in which the husbands had suffered a major heart attack but were still continuing to engage in high risk behaviors: poor diet, smoking, lack of exercise, and excessive consumption of alcohol. All of these families were referred by cardiologists, or by the staff of a cardiac rehabilitation program, who had given up on these individuals, fearing they were on a suicide course. In all 10 cases the identified heart patient would have nothing to do with any further treatment or rehabilitation efforts.

Rather than wasting a lot of time and energy trying to convince the patient to come for treatment, we worked with their spouses. Using a five-session limit, we focused our attention on the way the wives had attempted to reduce their husband's high-risk behavior—our aim was to change the system, that is, the husband's behavior, by getting the wives to change their attempted solutions. In most cases the wives struggled, argued, and nagged their men to change, so our primary effort was getting the women to back off from this position. In one case that worked particularly well; on our instructions the wife returned home and told her husband that she had been doing a lot of thinking about him. She said she had decided that he had a right to live out the rest of his life in his own style, no matter how short that might be. Her primary concern now was herself and the children and how they would be provided for when he died. She than insisted that her husband go over all the life insurance and estate planning, instructing her how to handle things after his death. She also called life insurance agencies and asked whether there was any way her husband's life insurance could be increased. As instructed, she told them to call her back at times she knew she would not be home but her husband would be there to take the calls. Within 2 weeks after she had begun to deal with him this way, the husband had resumed his participation in the cardiac rehabilitation exercise program and was watching his diet [Segal, 1982, pp. 286-287].

Divorce Therapy

Although most of the intervention strategies related to marriage presuppose that the couple wishes to continue in the relationship, it would be naive and unrealistic to assume that all marriages remain intact as a result of marital therapy. As we attempted to show in Chapter 1, divorce is an increasingly common and acceptable fact of modern life; as Stuart (1980) points out, couples seeking marital therapy more and more often do so with the possibility of divorce their prime concern.

Spouses enter marital therapy with a variety of expectations and desires, as well as different degrees of commitment to remaining together. Some may have concluded before treatment that their marriage is no longer satisfying, although they are prepared to engage briefly in marital therapy as a last resort or perhaps to give the appearance of making a final effort before separating and filing for divorce. Others may deny their internal sense of hopelessness about the marriage, although they remain fearful even about saying the word "divorce" publicly. Still others think of divorce as personal failure, or perhaps as something that occurs to other people but not themselves or their families. Finally, some couples enter marital therapy sincerely hoping to improve their relationship only to find their goals increasingly unrealistic when no progress or change transpires, or because one or both partners is insufficiently satisfied even though obviously positive changes have occurred (Baruth & Huber, 1984). In all of these instances, divorce is seen as a feasible alternative for resolving relationship problems.

Considering the prevalence of divorce and the fact that therapists must deal with the issue repeatedly in their clinical practice, it is curious that no intervention strategies have been developed to deal specifically with the emotional, behavioral and interpersonal difficulties caused by separation and divorce (Gurman & Kniskern, 1981b). However, some beginning efforts have been made to study the divorce process from a clinical "stages" or developmental view. Most noteworthy in this regard is the work of Kaslow (1981) who conceptualizes the process as involving three distinct phases. As indicated in Table 12–1, each period has an accompanying set of feelings likely to be experienced by the couple, as well as tasks to be undertaken and possible actions to be contemplated.

Kaslow (1981) believes individuals cope with the experiences of separation and divorce in much the same way that they have coped with other stresses and crises during their life cycle. That is, reasonably levelheaded people, although they may experience some "craziness" for a brief period, will nevertheless remain functional, will not seriously consider suicide, and will be determined not to be destroyed by the experience. On the other hand, "those whose general pattern is to somaticize, play helpless, feel hopeless and become desperate are likely to react in these ways in this stage as well" (Kaslow, 1981, p. 675).

During the predivorce period, therapists would do well to heed the caution of Whitaker and Miller (1969) against seeing one spouse alone (and thus aligning with, or at least appearing to align with, that partner), since the other partner is likely to feel outnumbered and threatened by the coalition. Conjoint therapy is the treatment of choice, perhaps couples-group therapy as conducted by Framo and others. During the divorce period, Kaslow (1981) recommends that the therapist help the partners deal with their sense of failure, anger, and similarly explosive and debilitating feelings. During the postdivorce

TABLE 12-1. Typical Sequences in the Divorce Process

Divorce period	Feelings	Requisite actions and tasks
Predivorce: Deliberation Period	Disillusionment Dissatisfaction Alienation	Confronting partner Quarreling Seeking therapy Denial
	Dread Anguish Ambivalence Shock Emptiness Chaos Inadequacy Low self-esteem	Withdrawal (physical and emotional) Pretending all is okay Attempting to win back affection
During Divorce: Litigation Period	Depression Detachment Anger Hopelessness Self-pity	Bargaining Screaming Threatening Attempting suicide Mourning
	Confusion Fury Sadness Loneliness Relief	Separating physically Filing for legal divorce Considering economic arrangements Considering custody arrangements Grieving and mourning Telling relatives and friends
Postdivorce: Reequilibration	Optimism Resignation Excitement Curiosity Regret	Finalizing divorce Begin reaching out to new friends Undertaking new activities Stabilizing new life-style and daily routine for children
	Acceptance Self-confidence Energy Self-worth Wholeness Exhilaration Independence Autonomy	Resynthesis of identity Completing psychic divorce Seeking new love object and making a commitment to some permanency Becoming comfortable with new life-style and friends Helping children accept finality of parents' divorce and their continuing relationship with both parents

(Source: Kaslow, 1981, p. 676)

period, it may be necessary at times to facilitate adaptation to the changes in the couple's and their children's lives by holding family therapy sessions. In some areas, such as Los Angeles County, postdivorce counseling services are available for families who remain in litigation over continuing custody and/or visitation conflicts (Elkin, 1977). In many places, self-help support groups such as Parents Without Partners are available to aid in the transition after divorce.

Needless to say, unhappy marriages are unlikely to lead to friendly divorces. Bitterness, chronic frustration, unfinished business, the desire to punish or retaliate—all of these may continue to take a toll on the couple and their children during the divorce period (and perhaps long afterwards), even keeping them from deriving satisfaction from new relationships. According to a survey of 21 highly experienced therapists by Kressel and Deutsch (1977), an especially common predictor of difficult divorce is eagerness to end the marriage on the part of one spouse coupled with reluctance to do so on the part of the other. The guilt feelings experienced by the initiator and the unreasonable, escalating demands made by the unwilling partner (who may feel humiliated about being rejected or anxious about an uncertain future) can further inhibit the couple's ability to reach a workable, equitable settlement. In some cases, opposing lawyers may encourage an adversarial stance in order to get the best settlement for their clients, or may themselves become unwitting pawns in the continuing battle between the hurt, angry, and accusatory divorcing spouses.

A short-term, alternative strategy currently gaining credibility is **divorce mediation,** a nonadversarial approach by which a couple is helped by a trained team of therapists and lawyers to negotiate the emotional mine field of divorce. Developed by Coogler (1978) and elaborated by Haynes (1981) as well as Fisher and Ury (1981) of the Harvard Negotiation Project, divorce mediation is, strictly speaking, neither therapy nor law, but a voluntary process by which couples are helped to arrive at an acceptable and mutually beneficial divorce settlement. Based to some extent on the arbitration model of the American Arbitration Association devised by lawyer Coogler, the process is designed to settle such issues as spousal and child support, custody and visitation, and the division of property while avoiding the emotional intensity and blaming behavior commonly associated with adversarial actions.

Couples must agree upon entering mediation to abide by the settlement or seek arbitration, but not to consult lawyers separately unless both agree to end the mediation. With the guidance of the neutral mediation team (representing expertise in conflict resolution as well as in the relevant legal areas), they define issues, identify their underlying concerns and follow fair procedures to resolve problems, ultimately recognizing the commonality of their interests rather than dwelling on their apparent differences. As a problem-solving, educative rather than therapeutic approach, the focus is on settling practical if mundane questions—Where will the kids live? Who will take them to the dentist? How will finances be arranged to support two separate households? (Vroom, 1983).

Generally speaking, the goal of divorce mediation is an amicable and mutually acceptable end to a marriage, although in some cases reconciliation may even be possible under such nonadversarial negotiating conditions. Other benefits include reduced financial costs as well as reduced emotional stress, more personal and direct control over life decisions, better postdivorce relationships between ex-spouses and children—to say nothing of learning a model for resolving future conflicts. By focusing on the present and future and not reliving the past, the divorcing spouses may be guided to reach reasonable solutions together; their agreements may be presented for review by separate lawyers before they appear in court.

Family mediation organizations came into being in the early 1970s, when Coogler organized the Family Mediation Association to promote the use of his formal process called "structured mediation." Labor mediator Haynes, who helped organize the rival Academy of Family Mediators, offers a less structured approach in which the clients' separate lawyers are involved throughout the mediation process. Training in mediation is provided by both groups, although as yet no licensing or certification is required; the field, still in its infancy, is in the process of developing standards for practice. Nevertheless, interest in divorce mediation is high and for many couples it appears to be, as Vroom (1983) points out, "a more enlightened way of moving through the ordeal of divorce and getting on with their lives" (p. 42).

LARGE-GROUP TREATMENT PROCEDURES

Multiple Family Therapy

Developed from work with hospitalized schizophrenic patients and their families, multiple family therapy (MFT) is an adaptation of group therapy techniques to the treatment of whole families. During the 1950s, Laqueur, then a psychiatrist at Creedmore State Hospital in New York, made the observation that many patients improved steadily while receiving treatment in the hospital, only to return in worse condition after weekend visits with their families. Laqueur originally invited large numbers of patients and their family members to joint informational meetings, but later decided it was more workable to deal with groups of four or five families. Not only did this prove expedient, saving time and personnel, but the interaction between families seemed to bring about desired behavior changes more quickly than working with the individual patient alone or with individual families. The approach also proved useful in helping the patient adjust later from a structured hospital milieu to an unstructured home situation (Laqueur, 1976).

Since its introduction in the early 1950s, MFT has progressed to the point that it is now used with a wide variety of dysfunctional families and in a great number of clinical settings (Strelnick, 1977). Recent efforts to serve heterogeneous outpatient populations (single-parent families, divorced-family groups, groups for families with learning disabled children) generally comprising less seriously disturbed individuals have been described by Gritzer and Okun (1983). Unlike Laqueur's work with groups requiring hospitalization, outpatient treatment usually entails a broader client selection potential, each family voluntarily seeking help for its own particular stresses and crises.

Whether inpatient or outpatient treatment, MFT usually involves four to six families (sometimes randomly selected and sometimes screened in advance) who meet with a therapist and co-therapist weekly for 60–75 minute sessions. The members share problems and help each other in the problem-solving process. In recent years, especially in outpatient facilities, families go through a four- or five-session screening process in order to prepare them for the larger group, reduce their anxieties, and help build a trusting alliance with the therapist (Gritzer & Okun, 1983). The therapist(s) acts as facilitator, guiding the discussion, pointing out transactional patterns, and reviewing at the close of the session what has taken place. Group members do not necessarily sit clustered as individual families; shifts in seating are common as mothers may join together temporarily at one point or perhaps children group together as they learn of their common problems. Groups are open-ended, so that a family leaving the group for whatever reason is replaced by a newly referred family.

Apparently, the benefits of such an approach accrue from the combined benefits of family and group therapy. The group members particularly value group identification and support, the easy recognition of—and quick involvement with—each others' problems, seeing their own family's communication problems portrayed by another family, and learning how other families solve their relationship problems (Goldenberg & Goldenberg, 1975). It is possible to learn new patterns for resolving conflict from observing another family dealing with an analogous conflict situation more successfully. For some children (often, the identified patients), new experiences with parents other than their own may be less threatening and may prove enlightening and therapeutic. A therapist may use the less disturbed families to reach the more disturbed families; the former understand the latter's problems as not totally different from their own, but offer suggestions or serve as models, through their family interaction, of better methods of conflict resolution. This is particularly true in open-ended groups where families new to the group may be helped by other families closer to successful termination.

What are the mechanisms of change in multiple family therapy? Laqueur (1973, 1976), adopting a general systems theory outlook, viewed each individual as a subsystem of a higher system, the family, which in turn represents a subsystem of the MFT group. The MFT group, then, receives input from its various subsystems, processes the information, and through its feedback loops provides output in the form of feedback information to the distressed family and its individual members. Through the circular interaction between the therapist and all groups members, such insights may reverberate throughout the entire MFT system, speeding up progress for all the participating families. The secret codes of a disturbed family's internal verbal and nonverbal communication may be broken by other families. A signal from the therapist may be picked up by a sensitive family member who amplifies it throughout his or her family and onto the entire MFT system. Because so many authority figures—therapist, fathers, mothers—are present, the young identified patient may feel encouraged to work out conflicts over independence through the comparatively nonthreatening mechanisms of analogy and identification. Role-playing a father–son relationship with a father from another family not only helps the son learn new ways of coping with such a situation with his own father, but provides similar insights to all the sons and fathers present.

Over a 25-year period, Laqueur (1976) and his colleagues treated over 1500 families in MFT groups, largely families with hospitalized schizophrenic members. According to Laqueur, only a handful were considered unsuited for this form of family therapy, primarily because exposure of some vital secret might have explosive consequences. Even in these cases, Laqueur acknowledged that such secrets are usually common knowledge within the family despite conspiracies of silence; rather than true secrets, they are more accurately described as barriers to communication and the free sharing of experiences.

An interesting variation of multiple family therapy involves multiple marital-couple therapy, usually consisting of three to five couples. Even when the identified patient is a child, the course of family therapy frequently evolves to the identification and consideration of parental conflict, as we have noted earlier. In such cases, family therapy becomes marital-couple therapy. Bringing together a number of couples to deal with common problems of marriage seems the next logical and efficient step. Framo (1973), Alger (1976b), and Liberman, Wheeler, and Sanders (1976) have all described their work with multiple-couple groups. In some instances, co-therapists who themselves are husband and wife (Low & Low, 1975) add greater personal involvement and authenticity to the group; their ongoing demonstration of problem-solving as a couple serves as a model.

A couples group seems the ideal context for marriage partners to recognize that their problems are not unique, that some conflict is an inevitable part of a marital relationship, that all marital pairs have to work out accommodations in a number of areas (children, sex, money, and so on). Couples may teach each other how to negotiate differences and how to avoid the escalation of conflict. In one sense, a couples group provides a forum where each person can express his or her expectations of marriage and of his or her mate, with feedback from others providing reality testing. Based on his work with over 200 couples, Framo (1973) considers such an approach the most effective therapy for marital couples. A positive support system of peers—other couples contributing as much or more than the therapist—is a significant therapeutic advantage of couples groups (Alger, 1976b). Liberman, Wheeler, and Sanders (1976), adopting a behavioral approach, train couples in communication skills and in learning to recognize, initiate, and acknowledge pleasing interactions. Their goal is to increase the range and frequency of positively experienced interaction between spouses, aided by the support and cohesiveness of the couples group. They contend that as a couple's exchange of positive reinforcements is more equally balanced, marital satisfaction will greatly increase.

Social Network Intervention

Some family therapists choose to work in a troubled person's home, assembling that person's entire social network, including his or her nuclear family as well as friends, neighbors, work associates, significant persons from school, church, various social agencies and institutions—in short, the sum total of human relationships that are meaningful in his or her life. Brought together and led by a team of therapists called "network intervenors," such a group of interrelated people has within itself the resources to develop creative solutions to the distressed individual's current predicaments, according to Speck and Attneave

(1973). Moreover, these therapists contend that much of the behavior traditionally associated with mental illness is instead derived from the individual's feelings of alienation from just such relationships and resources.

Social network intervention (sometimes referred to as network therapy), in which 40 to 50 people who are willing to come together in a crisis are mobilized as a potent therapeutic force, is particularly appealing in an age of increasing depersonalization. Originally developed from work with schizophrenics in their homes, network therapy is based on the assumption that there is significant disturbance in the schizophrenic's communication with all members of his or her social network, not just within the nuclear family. Consequently, this approach works at intensifying the person's network of relationships, intimately involving the entire group as much as possible in each others' lives. Rueveni (1979) sees such networks as analogous to clans or tribal units; they offer support, reassurance, and solidarity to their members. No longer limited to schizophrenics and their families, this technique may be used with any kind of dysfunctional behavior (for example, drug abuse, depression following a suicide attempt) labeled as "sick" by society (Pattison, 1981). In each case, social network intervention attempts to foster an emotional climate of trust and openness as a prelude to constructive encounters between the participants.

In such an assembly, tribal-like bonds can be created or revived not only to cope with the current crisis but also to sustain and continue the process long after formal meetings with a team of therapists are terminated. According to Speck and Attneave (1973), the benefits derive from the "network effect"—a spirited and euphoric group phenomenon seen in peace marches, revival meetings, tribal healing ceremonies, and massive rock concerts, even the seemingly dissimilar group singing at the Lions Club. In such situations, the group takes on an affiliative life of its own and achieves a sense of union and oneness that is somehow larger than what each participant contributes. In the case of social network intervention, the participants, under the influence of the "network effect," focus more energy, more attention, and bring more reality to bear on the tasks to be carried out than could any therapist acting alone during the same brief period of time.

Therapeutic intervention usually gets under way when the network intervention team redefines the troubled person's "symptoms" as a natural reaction to an inadequate social structure, rather than a sign of mental illness. As presented to his or her nuclear family and those people who are daily intimates, the person's present predicaments are further defined in terms of two or three specific issues (for example, the need to find employment, to make more and better friends, to move out of the house) that are potentially resolvable. Next, this close group assembles its social network to meet with the intervention team (usually, two to five professionals possibly joined by nonprofessional "network activists" who can help mobilize and organize group action). Those who are invited are told that they are coming together to help the nuclear family in its crisis and that a team of intervenors will provide leadership, at least at the start. Although the number and length of meetings varies, it is common to hold six evening sessions, each four hours in duration, at one-to-four-week intervals. In rare cases, the network intervenors have only one meeting in which to produce the therapeutic "network effect." More commonly, several sessions take place and the team of intervenors can meet regularly between sessions to plan their strategy.

The goal of network intervention is to capitalize on the power of the assembled network to shake up an overly rigid family unit in order to allow changes in the family system. It is hoped that some new bonds will be strengthened and that others, too constricting, will be weakened. Other goals include changing the members' perceptions of each other, the opening of clearer channels of communication, and the release of latent positive forces within the family and its larger social network.

Each session typically proceeds through several distinct phases. After some informal milling around with the intervenors scattered throughout the group, a number of encounter-group exercises (holding hands, vigorously jumping up and down, screaming out in unison) are employed as warm-up exercises, knitting the group together as a network. Called **retribalization** by Speck and Attneave (1973), this experience enhances the creation or revival of tribal-like bonds so that the network can sustain the process of seeking solutions to the current family crisis. As they reach the point of perceiving themselves as a connected, functioning organic unit, the participants (with the team's help) start to formulate what needs to be done and how to go about doing it. Conflicting viewpoints become apparent as the network becomes polarized (for example, between generations). Subgroups may form inner and outer circles, each in turn listening to the other and presenting its own position (in respect, for instance, to the use of drugs). The point here is to increase tension, generating greater interpersonal involvement and tribal commitment. As the energy developed by polarization starts to become focused, each subgroup trying hard to change the other, the team moves in to mobilize the energy and emotion and channel them constructively. The team conductor, aided by other team members and activists, introduces the task to be dealt with by the network. It is common at this time for the participants to become temporarily depressed, stymied by the difficulties they foresee in solving the problem. Finally the network achieves a breakthrough: the assigned task is accomplished. Exhausted but elated, the team and network terminate the session, experiencing a natural recovery period between meetings. At the conclusion of all meetings, the group participants are likely to have formed a cohesive system as a result of their shared experiences, often (although not necessarily) keeping the network alive long after the formal sessions with the intervention team have ceased. By remaining a supportive, caring, tribal-like group, they may become their own future agents of change, as necessary.

SUMMARY

Four kinds of family therapy techniques that supplement the usual approaches to treatment are considered: nonverbal procedures, crisis-oriented procedures, time-limited interventions and interventions that involve large groups.

In family sculpting, various members are asked to portray how they see the relationships within the family by arranging people in various physical positions in space and time. Family choreography, a related nonverbal technique, physically recreates interactive patterns within the family and thus opens them to examination and possible change. Videoplayback is an adjunctive therapeutic technique for allowing a family to take a look at its own behavioral patterns by filming the family therapy session and immediately showing the participants what signals, messages, and transactions have just transpired. This negative feedback and self-confrontation facilitates change. Other nonverbal techniques include family drawings, the use of puppets, family photos, a family floor plan drawing and a contracting game using a game board.

In multiple impact therapy, a family in crisis (often provoked by the delinquent behavior of an adolescent member) is seen over a two-day period for intensive interaction with a team of mental health professionals. Although essentially a diagnostic procedure, a number of therapeutic guidelines are introduced by the team, who conduct follow-up studies with the family in order to evaluate the extent of any therapeutic gains made. Another crisis-oriented approach, family crisis therapy, is a highly focused technique for mobilizing a family's coping skills to deal with a psychological emergency situation, thereby avoiding psychiatric hospitalization of a family member.

Two noteworthy time-limited treatment procedures are brief family therapy and divorce therapy. As practiced at the MRI, brief family therapy is a pragmatic, strategic, sometimes paradoxical technique for problem resolution in which families learn new, systemic solutions to problems rather than continue the self-defeating "solutions" that become problems in and of themselves. Divorce therapy involves no new techniques but calls for various recommended procedures for different phases of divorce (predivorce, divorce, postdivorce). Divorce mediation is a short-term, nonadversarial intervention by a team trained to deal with the emotional and legal concerns of partners seeking a divorce, to enable the couple to negotiate in an open, fair, direct and equitable manner.

A large-group treatment procedure, multiple family therapy was originally developed for working with hospitalized schizophrenics and their families but in recent years has also been used with an outpatient population. It is a form of group therapy in which several families meet regularly to share problems and help each other in the problem-solving process. A variation is the marital-couples group, which meets to discuss common marital problems and to find solutions together. Another kind of large-group approach, social network intervention (network therapy), brings together family, friends, neighbors, and significant others to aid in the patient's treatment and rehabilitation. The aim is to capitalize on the power of the assembled group to induce change in a dysfunctional family system.

PART FOUR

Training and Evaluation

CHAPTER THIRTEEN

Learning, Practicing, and Evaluating Family Therapy

We have noted a number of times in the previous chapters that preparing to become a family therapist is a new kind of learning experience for a clinician trained in one-to-one psychotherapy. The therapist must learn to view all behavior, including the manifestation of symptoms in an individual, in terms of its social or interpersonal context. The family system, not the symptomatic person, is the therapeutic unit for achieving change. The family therapist is a part of that system, not an outside healer as in many forms of individual treatment. The focus of therapy is on present transactions within the family, rather than retrieval of the past. The goal is to change the family's interactive patterns, not simply to interpret or explain them.

When training a therapist to adopt a family focus, one frequently meets with resistance for several reasons: the therapist sees the identified patient as a victim to be supported; he or she is accustomed to exercising control, being at the center of interactions between family members; and he or she is familiar with the customary role of therapist as outsider and must learn how to be a participant in the family social system, while avoiding entangling alliances. There is great risk that the therapist may be drawn into the family members' ongoing relationships and, if not careful, begin to believe their myths about themselves (for example, jinxed, exploited, or powerless) and adopt their labels for individual family members (such as stupid, selfish, unambitious) (Goldenberg, 1973). In this section, we discuss how best to meet the challenges of training family therapists. We then consider some special professional problems and issues in the family therapy field. Finally, we look at the findings of outcome research on the effectiveness of family therapy and make some comments on the future of family therapy.

BECOMING A FAMILY THERAPIST

A number of mental health and related disciplines—clinical psychology, psychiatry, psychiatric social work, psychiatric nursing, various forms of counseling, the human services—offer direct services to troubled or distressed families. In many cases, practitioners in these disciplines may find themselves, having gathered a family group together, simply treating the individual members separately but in a family setting. As Haley (1970) has observed (see Table 13–1), many therapists continue to perceive individual psychopathology as their central concern while acknowledging the importance of the family con-

TABLE 13–1. A Comparison between Individual-Oriented and Family-Oriented Family Therapy

Individual-oriented	*Family-oriented*
1. Family therapy is one of many methods of treatment.	1. Family therapy is a new orientation to viewing human problems.
2. The individual's psychopathology is the focus of study and treatment; the family is seen as a stress factor.	2. The disordered family system needs some family member to express its psychopathology.
3. The identified patient is the victim of family strife.	3. The identified patient contributes to and is an essential part of family strife.
4. The family is a collection of individuals behaving on the basis of past experiences with each other.	4. The present situation is the major causal factor, since current problems must be currently reinforced if they continue to exist.
5. Diagnosis and evaluation of the family problem should precede intervention.	5. Immediate action-oriented intervention takes place at the first session, which is usually a time of family crisis, when the family is ripe for change.
6. The therapist is an observer evaluating the family's problems.	6. The therapist is a part of the context of treatment; his or her active participation affects the family system.
7. The therapist brings out clients' feelings and attitudes toward each other; he or she uses interpretation to show them what they are expressing.	7. The therapist uses fewer interpretations; he or she is interested in enhancing positive aspects of the relationships.
8. The therapist talks to one person at a time; family members talk largely to him rather than to each other.	8. Family members talk to each other, not the therapist; all members are urged to participate.
9. The therapist takes sides in family conflict, supporting one member (for example, a child, a schizophrenic).	9. The therapist avoids being caught up in factional struggles in the family.
10. Family therapy is a technique for gathering additional information about individuals in the family.	10. Individual psychological problems are social problems involving the total ecological system, including the social institutions in which the family is embedded.

(Adapted from Haley, 1970)

text in which such psychopathology developed. Others find it easier to enlarge their perspective, thus viewing the amelioration of individual intrapsychic conflicts as secondary to improving overall family functioning. In either case, as Skynner (1976) reminds us, the therapist must give up the passive, neutral, nonjudgmental, uninvolved stance developed with so much care in conventional individual psychotherapy. The family therapist must become involved in the family's interpersonal processes (without losing balance or independence); support and nurture at some points, challenge and demand at others; attend to (but not overidentify with) members of different ages; move swiftly in and out of emotional involvements without losing track of family interactions and transaction patterns.

Training Programs

How does one develop family therapy skills: From experience in individual therapy, group therapy, marriage counseling or marital therapy? By having good relationship skills (interpersonal sensitivity, humor, warmth)? By having worked through problems with one's own family of origin? By having raised a family successfully? Through course work in an academic setting, apprenticeship to an established marital/family therapist, or specialized training in a free-standing family therapy institute?

Before 1960, individuals wishing to enter the field typically secured the appropriate education in one of the established professions (psychiatry, clinical psychology, psychiatric social work, psychiatric nursing) and then added further specialized training at the postdegree level (Nichols, 1979). With the advent of the family therapy movement (and the boost it provided for practitioners counseling people in troubled marriages) an alternative developed— direct entry into the field of marital/family therapy at either the master's or doctoral level. Today, both lines of career development are followed, a situation likely to continue in the foreseeable future. An entire issue of the *Journal of Marital and Family Therapy* (Nichols, 1979) is devoted to a description of representative programs, ranging from master's level training in marital/family therapy to the training of psychiatric residents to work directly with problems of marital discord.

A national survey of family therapy training programs by Bloch and Weiss (1981) attests to what the authors term the "exponential" growth of such programs since 1960. Their survey shows that while only 14 training programs in family therapy were established between 1942 and 1960, 37 programs were founded in the years between 1961 and 1970. Moreover, 77 new programs began in the United States between 1971 and 1980, and the number continues to increase.

Bloch and Weiss (1981) confirm the great diversity in training programs that exists today in respect to entrance requirements, degrees or certificates of completion, types and forms of supervision and clinical experiences, clinical affiliations, level of **accreditation,** and so forth. Some training programs aim to produce fully trained practitioners, at least at the journeyman level, while others offer enrichment programs to supplement or improve family therapy skills. Sugarman (1981) describes academic/practicum training programs for psychiatric residents; Cooper, Rampage, and Soucy (1981) describe programs for doctoral students in clinical psychology.

Training in family therapy as a profession in its own right consists of two types of programs: graduate programs offering a terminal degree in marital/family therapy and independent postgraduate family therapy training institutes. Unlike trainees who graduate from the more formal academic programs (with an M.D. Ph.D., Psy.D., M.S.W., Ed.D., or the like) and thus obtain the credentials of their respective professions, graduates of these programs (unaffiliated with universities or teaching hospitals) usually seek to meet the professional standards set up by the American Association for Marriage and Family Therapy (AAMFT). They receive certificates of completion of their training rather than graduate degrees, although in some cases a student may be receiving (or have previously earned) a graduate degree elsewhere and attend these institutes for further specialized training. Table 13-2 provides a sample of some of the better known family therapy training institutes in the United States.

Objectives of Training

While a considerable body of data exists concerning family life, we have seen that there is as yet neither a single theory of family process nor a single set of intervention techniques that is consistently applicable and effective in helping distressed families. Learning family therapy requires theoretical understanding (personality development; family concepts, including cross-cultural studies; research methodology; group dynamics; systems theory; and so on); prob-

TABLE 13-2. A Sample of Freestanding Family Therapy Training Institutes in the United States

Name	Location
Boston Family Institute	Brookline, Massachusetts
Family Institute of Cambridge	Cambridge, Massachusetts
Ackerman Institute for Family Therapy	New York, New York
The Center for Family Learning	New Rochelle, New York
Philadelphia Child Guidance Center	Philadelphia, Pennsylvania
Eastern Pennsylvania Psychiatric Institute	Philadelphia, Pennsylvania
Family Therapy Institute of Washington, D.C.	Rockville, Maryland
Eastern Virginia Family Therapy Institute	Virginia Beach, Virginia
Family Institute of Chicago	Chicago, Illinois
Menninger Foundation	Topeka, Kansas
Houston Family Institute	Houston, Texas
Mental Research Institute	Palo Alto, California
Family Institute of Berkeley	Berkeley, California
Los Angeles Family Institute	Los Angeles, California
Kempler Institute	Costa Mesa, California
California Family Study Center	Burbank, California

ably more important, it requires firsthand contact with families. Since therapy is such a personal encounter, the trainee can learn to do it best by doing it, preferably under supervision. Each trainee must find his or her style of interacting with families and his or her orientation to what makes for successful therapy. Many authorities agree with Mendelsohn and Ferber's (1972) assessment that training is best accomplished in small groups of 5–15 trainees who meet regularly with one or two supervisors over a prolonged period of time, such as a year. The opportunity to work therapeutically with a variety of families (with different structures, from different ethnic backgrounds and socioeconomic situations, with different presenting problems) within a training program offering comprehensive **didactic** course work and clinical supervision seems to represent the ideal learning situation.

What are the learning objectives of a family therapy training program? Goals range from an emphasis on the trainee's personal growth and development to a focus on the acquisition of skills and competencies (Liddle & Halpin, 1978). As an example of the former, Constantine (1976) describes the training offered to members of different mental health professions at Boston State Hospital where supervisors strive to "create an environment conducive to growth and learning" (p. 373). The two-year curriculum in this cognitively and experientially oriented program is designed to gradually prepare the trainee to work with families, particularly nonpathological families.

At the other extreme, Cleghorn and Levin (1973), more behavioral in outlook, set goals of training that are more strictly cognitively based. They teach trainees specific skills and particular ways to intervene in a dysfunctional family system. They distinguish three sets of learning objectives: perceptual, conceptual, and executive. Table 13–3 presents a checklist for the trainee's development of basic observational or *perceptual skills* (recognizing interactions and their meaning and effect on the family members and the family system), *conceptual skills* (formulating the family's problems in systems terms), and therapeutic or *executive skills* (extracting and altering the family's sequences of transactions); these are the skills necessary to be potentially effective with ordinarily func-

TABLE 13–3. Checklist of Basic Objectives in Training Family Therapists

Perceptual and conceptual	*Executive skills*
1. Recognize and describe interactions and transactions.	1. Develop collaborative working relationship with family.
2. Describe a family systematically; include assessment of current problem.	2. Establish therapeutic contract.
3. Recognize effect of family group on oneself.	3. Stimulate transactions.
4. Recognize and describe the experience of being taken into the family system.	4. Clarify communications.
	5. Help family members label effects of interactions.
5. Recognize one's idiosyncratic reactions to family members.	6. Extricate oneself from the family system.
	7. Focus on a problem.

(From Cleghorn and Levin, 1973)

tional families who have been exposed to unusual (and presumably temporary) stress. Having developed these basic competencies, the trainee should be able to deal with families exposed to situational problems (for example, shared grief over a death of a family member), helping to mobilize the family's natural restorative devices in working toward a solution. Essentially, the therapist's role is to facilitate constructive problem-solving communication. Advanced training is required before the therapist can deal successfully with families with chronically fixed, rigid, and unproductive problem-solving transactional patterns. As Table 13-4 suggests, an agent of change must possess different skills than a helper of distressed families. The trainee must learn to catalyze interactions, understand and label relationship messages, and confront family members with what they are doing to each other; he or she must challenge the family to find new solutions, to utilize its strength as a family in order to take the responsibility for change in its members. Finally, the advanced therapist must be able to judge the effectiveness of his or her interventions and to alter the approach whenever necessary to help the family work with greater efficiency and with less distress.

TRAINING AIDS

Family therapy programs utilize three primary methods for training: didactic, supervisory, and experiential (Kniskern & Gurman, 1980). The extent to which each is emphasized, however, varies widely in different programs, depending

TABLE 13-4. Checklist of Advanced Objectives in Training Family Therapists

Perceptual and conceptual	Executive skills
Regarding the family	1. Redefine the therapeutic contract periodically.
1. Conceive of symptomatic behaviors as a function of the family system.	2. Demonstrate relationship between transactions and the symptomatic problem.
2. Assess family's capacity to change.	
3. Recognize that change in a family is more threatening than recognition of a problem.	3. Be a facilitator of change, not a member of the group.
4. Define key concepts operationally.	4. Develop a style of interviewing consistent with one's personality.
Regarding oneself	5. Take control of maladaptive transactions by:
1. Deal with feelings about being a change agent, not just a helper.	a. Stopping a sequence and labeling the process.
2. Become aware of how one's personal characteristics influence one's becoming a family therapist.	b. Making confrontations in the context of support.
3. Assess the effectiveness of one's interventions and explore alternatives.	6. Work out new adaptive behaviors and rewards for them.
4. Articulate rewards to be gained by family members making specific changes.	7. Relinquish control of the family when adaptive patterns occur.

(From Cleghorn and Levin, 1973)

on the skills, experiences, and viewpoints of those offering the training. While the following elements of family therapy training are discussed separately, the reader should be aware that several of the pedagogical techniques are used simultaneously in any training program. Trainees must do more than take a course in family therapy; as in learning any skill—typing, roller skating, driving a car, or lovemaking—practice and firsthand experience are necessary. Reading about families and family therapy, observing teachers demonstrate work with families, seeing films and videotapes of eminent family therapists at work all add to abstract knowledge, but in the last analysis the trainee learns experientially—by treating families, under supervision.

Didactic Course Work

The didactic component of family therapy training includes lectures, group discussion, demonstrations, assigned readings, and role-playing. Typically, the courses examine available theories and the existing scientific evidence for a variety of clinical intervention techniques; the curriculum at the Albert Einstein College of Medicine in New York City is one example (Sander & Beels, 1970). Often courses are team-taught by two supervisors; the teachers not only share the lead in discussion groups but one may comment to the trainees on what is taking place behind a one-way mirror as the other demonstrates intervention with a real or simulated family. In some cases the trainees' formal course work follows the actual experience of conducting family therapy sessions, in order to avoid premature conceptualizing by trainees before they have had firsthand contact with families. This sequence puts trainees in a better position to integrate family therapy concepts into their understanding of family process (Shapiro, 1975). More often, some introductory lectures, assigned readings, and demonstrations precede the trainees' first clinical experiences; the student thus prepared is less likely to be overwhelmed by the abundance of clinical material gathered from the family interview. Following these initial didactic presentations, trainees begin the clinical work of evaluating and treating families while continuing to attend the seminar (Constantine, 1976).

An ongoing controversy surrounds the choice of training method. Is it more effective to present a single, integrated approach to family therapy (for example, Haley's strategic therapy or Minuchin's structural therapy) or to sample a variety of family therapy theories and techniques (as we have done in this book). Kniskern and Gurman (1980) argue that the former method is less confusing or contradictory, and thus conducive to learning, but runs the risk of producing more narrowly focused and less creative practitioners. Whether the latter approach yields more thoughtful, flexible clinicians, or simply more muddle-headed eclectics, is unknown. Family therapist Carlos Sluzki (1974) puts his finger directly on the problem:

> The process of becoming a family therapist includes two tracks: one is identifying with and mimicking as tightly as possible a given teacher, and the other is reading a lot of stuff from different sources with the hope of transforming that melange into one's own private jigsaw puzzle. [Kniskern & Gurman, 1980, p. 226]

We believe the trainee should begin from a broad learning base and then take advanced training in a particular model; those who advocate the reverse sequence argue that it helps a budding clinician develop a consistent sense of self-as-therapist at the beginning, when it is needed most.

Regardless of the sequence in which the trainee attends didactic seminars, or the method of training utilized, readings in the field will constitute a significant part of the training experience. Bodin (1969a) has offered a training guide to the literature in family therapy through the 1960s; for more recent advances in family therapy, see Erickson & Hogan (1981) and Green & Framo (1981). Gurman and Kniskern's (1981b) *Handbook of Family Therapy* and Wolman and Stricker's (1983) *Handbook of Family and Marital Therapy* are single-volume collections of papers, usually by experts in their respective areas. Recent issues of such journals as *Family Process, Journal of Marital and Family Therapy* (the official organ of the AAMFT), *American Journal of Family Therapy, Family Coordinator, Journal of Marriage and the Family, Journal of Sex and Marital Therapy, International Journal of Family Therapy, Marriage and Family Review,* and *Alternative Life Styles* provide up to date references. On a more informal, sometimes chatty level, the popular bimonthly *Family Therapy Networker* keeps students and practitioners alike informed about new books, current workshops, developing controversies in theory and practice and serves as a general clearinghouse for information in the field.

Most of the field's leading theorists have published their papers in book form: Minuchin (1974a), Bowen (1978), Satir (1967, 1972), Framo (1982), Boszormenyi-Nagy (Boszormenyi-Nagy & Spark, 1973), Whitaker (Neill & Kniskern, 1982), Kempler (1981), Haley (1976, 1984), and Ackerman (Bloch & Simon, 1982). Finally, it is a worthwhile and at times exciting experience to read verbatim accounts of family therapy sessions (for example, Haley & Hoffman, 1967; Papp, 1977), following step-by-step what takes place as a master therapist puts theory into practice.

Films and Videotapes

Films showing master therapists at work with real patients came into general use in the 1950s, as the taboos against revealing the privacy of the therapeutic relationship began to diminish. In the years since, a number of films on a variety of techniques have been distributed. Gladfelter (1972) counted 62 films available in the area of group and family therapy alone and since his compilation the list has undoubtedly tripled. Together with videotapes of actual therapy sessions, films now play a significant part in training family therapists because they convey an immediate sense of awareness of the processes by which therapists and patients communicate. Family therapy films in particular rely on cinema verité techniques, allowing the viewer to enter into the multiple verbal and nonverbal transactions going on simultaneously within a family.

In a classic set of eight films, the *Hillcrest Family Series* (available through the Psychological Cinema Register at Pennsylvania State University), Ackerman, Whitaker, Jackson, and Bowen conduct independent assessment interviews with the same family and then discuss (in separate films) the dynamics of the family situation with a therapist who has been working with the family. Although this pioneering film series would probably be considered "quaint" by modern standards, it reveals differences in the therapeutic tactics of four experts dealing with the same family and is worth viewing for that reason alone. In a film entitled *Target Five*, Satir illustrates her therapeutic techniques with a simulated family; four forms of manipulation in a family are considered (see Chapter 6) and the family is then seen engaging in "actualizing" behavior. This film is available from Psychological Films in Santa Ana, California. In a series of films of whole sessions with families, Kempler demonstrates his experiential form of therapy in a variety of family situations (runaway adolescents, working mothers, negotiations in a distrubed family); the series is available from the Kempler Institute in Costa Mesa, California.

In and Out of Psychosis is a two-reel composite of interviews conducted by Ackerman with a family in which the adolescent daughter is labeled psychotic and considered unmanageable. Another Ackerman film, *The Enemy Is Myself*, is a composite of four interviews spanning an 18-month period with a family (including twin 9-year-old sons) who began treatment following the suicide of an older son. Both are available from the Ackerman Institute for Family Therapy.

Videotapes of master therapists demonstrating their techniques in actual sessions with families are readily available from the following organizations: Boston Family Institute; Philadelphia Child Guidance Center; Ackerman Institute for Family Therapy; Georgetown University Family Center; The Center for Family Learning in New Rochelle; The South Beach Psychiatric Center in Staten Island, New York; The Institute of Contextual Growth in Ambler, Pennsylvania; The Eastern Pennsylvania Psychiatric Institute; The Family Therapy Institute of Washington, D.C.; The Kempler Institute; and The Mental Research Institute in Palo Alto.[1]

Clearly one of the greatest boons to the field of family therapy, videotape has opened new avenues of development in therapy (see Chapter 12), training, and research. For example, supervisors can tape initial sessions with a family for later presentation to students; the tapes give students a basis for noting changes in family interactive patterns as they watch "live" demonstrations of subsequent sessions with the same family (Bodin, 1969b). Tape libraries of family therapy sessions from initial interview to termination and follow-up can be compiled for students to view at their leisure or when confronted with a particular kind of technical problem or therapeutic impasse. Of course, the student can monitor his or her own progressive proficiency by comparing tapes made early and late in training.

According to Whiffen (1982), videotaping has three unique properties that

---

[1] All of these centers offer descriptive catalogues of their tapes, which are generally available for a period of 2–3 days and are copyrighted so that they may not legally be reproduced. Most insist that their films and tapes be shown only to audiences made up of students or professionals in the field of family therapy.

make it especially valuable in supervision: 1) it freezes time so that every aspect of a crucial sequence is available for posttherapy review by the therapist, not all of it possible during the session; 2) it enables the therapist to see himself or herself more objectively as part of the whole system; and 3) it allows the effect of a therapeutic intervention to be studied and its success evaluated.

A trainee's verbal report of a family therapy session to a supervisor and/or class has the inherent risks of unreliable recall, defensiveness, distortion, and subjective description. The "instant replay" of the session on tape overcomes these obstacles. Subtle nuances may be more obvious, the interplay of verbal and nonverbal messages and interactions may become clearer. Not only does the trainee confront his or her own behavior with a family but the other viewers provide additional corrective feedback information. Trainees learn from each other's errors as well as successes. The tape can be played and replayed, over and over again, preserved and retrieved for further study and analysis (Berger, 1978).

By observing trainees with families over closed-circuit television, the supervisor and others retain all of the benefits of a one-way mirror along with a permanent videotaped record of precisely what took place. In some cases, the supervisory sessions themselves are videotaped for later playback as the trainee plans further therapeutic strategies with the family.

Clinical research has benefited greatly from videotaping family therapy sessions. By capturing family interaction on film, videotaping allows researchers to examine and code family interactive patterns (see Figure 13–1). Out of the clinical complexity that treatment of a family reveals, researchers can extract meaningful variables and subject them to experimental research (Framo, 1972).

Marathons

A **marathon** is an intensive, uninterrupted group-therapy experience, sometimes extending over several days, that focuses on the ongoing process of encounter among group members. Often used as a device to intensify and accelerate a therapeutic experience by building up group pressure over time, the technique has been adapted for family therapy training purposes.

As an extension of Goldenberg, Stier, and Preston's (1975) group supervision seminar on family therapy at the UCLA Neuropsychiatric Institute, these clinicians reasoned that another dimension might be added to the learning experience if they held an extended group therapy session with their ten trainees and their client families. The trainees were all advanced students who had taken part in the seminar over a year's time. Through viewing videotaped sessions over that extended period, they had become familiar with the various client families. The six-hour, multiple-family marathon was led by the supervisors, who hoped the model of their behavior would provide a useful training experience. No attempt was made during the marathon to identify separate families; the various children and adults (supervisors, trainees, parents) intermingled

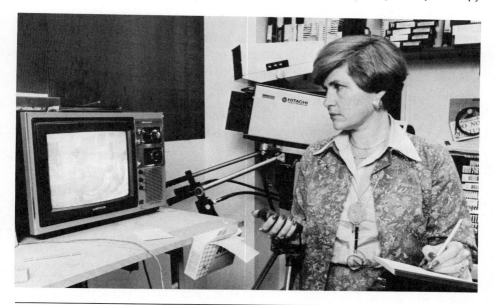

Figure 13–1. Videotaping family therapy sessions preserves these events for research study. This psychologist is rating certain family interactive patterns along previously determined empirical categories in an effort to clarify what distinguishes the functioning levels of different families.

freely. Various role-playing, psychodrama, and encounter group techniques were used throughout the session. A comparison of the student therapists' responses to a premarathon and postmarathon questionnaire revealed that most perceived the experience as a valuable training aid. Most trainees changed their views of the family with whom they had worked previously (for example, "I now recognize that they have the capacity to listen and understand another's viewpoint"). All ten trainees indicated a better and more confident self-image as a family therapist following the marathon session; several acknowledged that through certain self-revelations they had discovered new aspects of themselves personally.

Live Supervision

An effective teaching program in family therapy must meld relevant theory with profitable practical experience. However, clinical contact with families is of limited value without regularly scheduled, careful supervision, especially during the early stages of training. Such supervision, provided by highly competent and experienced family therapists who also have teaching skills, may take a number of forms: review of videotapes of trainee sessions with families, either in a trainee/supervisor conference or in a small group session with several trainees and a supervisor (Stier & Goldenberg, 1975); co-therapy, in which a supervisor and a trainee together work with a family (Skynner, 1976);

observation of a trainee's work through a one-way mirror (Haley, 1976); continuous case conferences during which a trainee presents his or her client family for several class sessions; group marathons, as described in the preceding section; and live, "on the spot" supervision in which the supervisor stays in direct communication with the trainee during a session. Regardless of the form it takes, clinical supervision provides one or more of the following benefits for trainees: (1) ongoing discussion of the behavior of clients; (2) critical feedback on what transpired during the session; (3) the sharing of clinical responsibilities; (4) emotional support, especially when dealing with a difficult family; (5) enhanced opportunity for personal growth (Kadushin, 1973).

Live supervision, in which a supervisor observes an ongoing session through a one-way mirror or watches on a video monitor, introduces a relatively new concept to the supervisory process (Montalvo, 1973); namely, that someone actively guides the therapist's work by providing corrective feedback to what the therapist is doing. The advent of the one-way mirror in the 1950s was a significant breakthrough for clinicians and researchers alike, allowing them to observe live family interviews unobtrusively. By separating the supervisor from the family's ongoing emotional system yet allowing him or her a firsthand look at that system in operation, a new dimension was added to the process of comprehending what is taking place within the family and between the family and therapist. The supervisor is in an ideal position to note developing patterns, and can think about them more objectively than the therapist who is on the "firing line" (and subject to being caught up in, and becoming part of, the family system). Under these conditions, contributions from the supervisor may represent a force for change in the family (Berger & Dammann, 1982).

The supervisor can intervene in several ways: (1) calling the therapist out of the room midway through a session for consultation, the therapist then returning with directives to be given to the family (the technique employed by the Milan associates in their systemic family therapy, described in Chapter 9); (2) calling the therapist by telephone with suggestions during the treatment process (MRI's Brief Therapy Center approach, discussed in Chapter 12); (3) entering the consultation room during a session with comments and suggestions (used at the Brief Therapy Center; also used by Minuchin in structural family therapy as an attempt to reshape or reframe the experience the family is having and thus produce change in their transactional patterns); and (4) using a "bug in the ear" wireless transmitter to communicate directly, and relatively unobtrusively, to the therapist.

When the earphone is used in supervision (Byng-Hall, 1982), the therapist listens through a small "bug" worn in the ear while the supervisor, behind a one-way mirror or at a video monitor, speaks into a microphone. Since the family does not hear the interventions, advocates argue that the technique is superior to the use of the telephone or direct entering of the room by a supervisor. The British psychiatrist Byng-Hall (1982) insists that the earphone is the best tool for supervising the therapy process because the flow of interaction is not interrupted and the family responds as if the interventions came from the trainee, not from others. The technique is controversial, however, and runs the risk of overuse by an exuberant supervisor; the trainee may have the feeling of being simply an "echo" of the supervisor or of having his or her concentration interrupted and autonomy invaded. Whether the intervention is by telephone or "bug," Haley (1976) cautions against indulgence in this procedure, contending that the supervisor should adopt a "call with reluctance" philosophy and offer only one or two very specific suggestions.

According to Byng-Hall (1982), these supervisory interventions are likely to take the form of instructions ("Ask . . ." or "Say to the mother . . ."); suggestions for strategies ("Get father and son to negotiate on that"); efforts to direct the therapist's attention ("Notice how . . ." or "See how they repeat . . ."); moves to increase or decrease intensity ("Encourage mother and father to confront . . ." or "Tell them to stop and listen to one another, instead of . . ."); or perhaps encouragement ("That was well done").

As typically practiced, the person supervising watches the session from behind a one-way mirror (with or without a group of trainees) and intrudes on the session to make suggestions to the therapist at the very moment that the action is taking place; the objective is to help the trainee get disentangled from recurring, nonproductive interactional sequences with the family in order to regain control and direction of the session. Both parties must feel comfortable with the procedure: the trainee must accept the supervisor's right to intervene if the latter believes that a disservice is done to the family by allowing what is occurring to continue; the supervisor must accept the trainee's right to question or challenge the suggestion and ignore it as he or she sees fit.

A basic assumption in live supervision is that any family can direct the therapist away from his or her function as a change agent by maneuvering the therapist into behaving in ways that reinforce the very patterns that brought the members of the family into therapy. The experienced supervisor, not caught up in the action, can help the supervisee correct such missteps at the time they occur. In a sense, the supervisor—as a coach on the sidelines—introduces feedback into the ongoing system, comprising the student therapist and the family.

The advantages of live supervision lie in the timeliness and relevance of supervisor questions or suggestions, and the reduction of possible distortions by the trainee who, in the past, reported to the supervisor what had taken place during the session. Probably the major disadvantage is the added stress felt by the student being observed. According to Loewenstein, Reder and Clark's (1982) description of themselves as trainees receiving live supervision, the experience can arouse intense emotions: the shame of self-exposure in front of others, the potential loss of self-esteem, loss of a sense of autonomy ("feeling under remote control") and of ego boundaries, problems over compliance and the issue of authority. (The authors also report that the anticipatory fantasies of live supervision were far more frightening than the actual experience and that these fears were greatly reduced over time.) In addition, the student therapist may become too dependent on supervisory interventions, the intrusions may be disruptive to the therapeutic process, and they may interfere with the evolution of the therapist's own style (Liddle & Halpin, 1978). Some sense of confidentiality may be jeopardized if the family knows (and it must be told) that it is being observed. Finally, Whitaker (1976c), opposed to live supervision, notes that the procedure tends to make the supervisee less self-confident, more reliant on following a prearranged method rather than relying on the ongoing process for direction.

Despite these objections, authorities such as Haley (1976) consider this method the most effective form of supervision. In the past, all that was revealed about a session was what the therapist chose to reveal, relying on notes taken during or immediately afterward. With the introduction of audiotapes some 35 years ago, the supervisor could learn what was actually said; videotapes reveal both words and actions. But none of these procedures provide guidance at the time the student needs it most—in the act of interviewing. Live supervision not only teaches inexperienced therapists how to do therapy, but protects client families from incompetent practice.

CO-THERAPY: THE USE OF THERAPEUTIC TEAMWORK

Co-therapy—the simultaneous involvement of two therapists in the treatment setting—was originally created as a way to include a trainee in a therapeutic session for teaching purposes; it has been employed successfully in working with individuals, groups, and families (Rubenstein & Weiner, 1967). Whitaker (1967) routinely used a co-therapist in working with individual schizophrenic patients long before doing so with families; today he is perhaps the leading exponent of the co-therapy model for training family therapists as well as for family treatment.

Co-therapy has some obvious training advantages. The trainee has an opportunity to learn a distinctive approach at close range and to see an expert in action without taking the full or even the major responsibility for the family. The trainee has the added benefit of seeing the supervisor as a real person who makes mistakes at times, doesn't always understand all that is happening, and isn't always loving—all very reassuring to a beginning family therapist who has felt exactly the same way at times about himself or herself! The supervisor as co-therapist can provide the supervisee with an opportunity to try creative interventions with the family, assured of skillful support and rescue when trouble arises, as it inevitably does. Family therapy is taught as a personal experience in this way. The process is emphasized, rather than the discussions of abstract theoretical issues that take place in so many supervisory situations (Napier & Whitaker, 1972).

As a training device, co-therapy is not without its disadvantages, real and potential. The trainee may become so identified with the supervisor (especially if the latter's style is colorful and dramatic) that he or she merely mimics the authority figure instead of developing a style more personally authentic. Overdependency may also become a problem. As Haley (1976) points out, the student acting as co-therapist with a more experienced person may simply sit back and not take responsibility for the case, as he or she must ultimately learn to do. Haley prefers live supervision from behind a one-way mirror so that the trainee can receive immediate assistance whenever needed. He argues that co-therapy is set up to support uncertain therapists, not to aid families.

Indeed, the notion of mutual support is often advanced as a rationale for co-therapy by family therapists who prefer working as a team. For example, Whitaker (Napier & Whitaker, 1972) contends that having a co-therapist allows him to become involved with a family in a way and at a level he would not dare if he worked alone. Whitaker—who equates being a therapist with the pursuit of personal growth—can expose many of his own fantasies and free associations to the family knowing that his co-therapist is a backup person, tied to reality and ready to step in with corrective feedback if that should become necessary. That is, as one therapist becomes emotionally involved with the family the other waits silently, remaining less involved and more objective than the more active teammate (Napier & Whitaker, 1978). Co-therapists may also support each other by remaining calm in the midst of intense family anxiety. As Rubenstein and Weiner (1967) note, some families readily arouse anxieties in other people and may experience relief in a new situation in which a team of therapists is not easily provoked.

The nature of the relationship between therapists has a powerful impact on the family they are treating. If therapists like, trust, respect, and remain loyal to each other and if their personalities complement each other, they may serve as models for effective and mutually satisfying relationships (Boszormenyi-Nagy & Spark, 1973). In addition, co-therapists in a male–female partnership can serve as gender role models or sometimes as symbolic parents with a well-defined relationship for all family members to observe. The way the co-therapists *live* their relationship—degrading and undercutting each other or supporting and allowing each other freedom—teaches the family far more about interpersonal relations than what the therapists may *say* about family relationships. As in a good marriage, the co-therapists need to have a caring and accepting involvement with each other in which both struggle actively to grow; such a relationship allows them to take risks such as fighting in front of a family. According to Napier and Whitaker (1972), an intense fight can be enormously beneficial for the family in that it teaches the members how to fight and demonstrates that any two people, no matter how close, are likely to have problems with each other. If the therapists display pseudomutuality as an alternative to fighting, their transparent dishonesty may tempt the family to act out the therapists' unexpressed aggression. A family may also attempt to split the co-therapy team who—like effective parents—must not permit this to happen. On the other hand, if the therapists are competitive and each one wants consistently to be dominant and win favor from the family, such splitting will likely occur and family therapy will be ineffective.

Many therapists working alone may be overwhelmed or "swallowed up" by the family system, seduced or otherwise manipulated by family resistance into maintaining the family status quo. Co-therapists working together can keep a check on each other, meeting after or between sessions to discuss their independent perspectives on what is transpiring. Equally important, either therapist can confront the other's manipulativeness and deception (Holt and Greiner, 1976). In this sense, co-therapy helps to ensure that the therapists actually practice what they intellectually espouse.

There are, of course, practical drawbacks to the use of co-therapy in family treatment; critics cite inefficient use of professional time and the increased expense to the client family.

REGULATING PROFESSIONAL PRACTICE IN MARITAL/FAMILY THERAPY

As we indicated earlier in this chapter, an individual seeking training in marital/family therapy may earn a graduate and/or professional degree from a university or obtain professional preparation at a center offering specialized training in marital/family therapy. A person who follows the academic route and has obtained the requisite training supervision in a program accredited by the appropriate professional association (for example, American Psychological Association)[2] may seek **licensing** or **certification** (according to the law governing practice in a particular state).

A licensing law, the more restrictive of the two, regulates who may practice in the state (for example, licensed psychologist, licensed clinical social worker) by defining education and experience criteria, administering qualifying examinations, and stating the conditions under which a license may be revoked (thereby terminating the right to practice) for ethical or other reasons. A certification law, a weaker and less comprehensive form of regulation, simply certifies who has the right to use a particular professional title. Such a law does not restrict practice or define permissible activities but simply guarantees that the title (for example, "psychologist") will be used only by people who meet the standards established by the law. Like the licensing laws, certification laws set up criteria for issuing and revoking certificates; in that sense they help to monitor practice, at least in regard to the use of the title. Both kinds of laws are designed to ensure that practitioners meet certain minimal standards of education, training and supervised experience. In recent years, regulatory boards in a number of states have mandated that renewal of a license or certificate requires the successful completion of certain continuing education courses (Goldenberg, 1983).

Candidates who elect to receive their training as marital/family therapists have fewer credentialling options at this time, although the situation may be improving in the near future. Since 1978, the U.S. Office of Education of the Department of Health and Human Services has designated the Committee on

---

[2] Accreditation may be granted to an academic institution by an official accrediting agency (such as the regional Association of Schools and Colleges) or to a field-based training facility by the relevant professional organization.

Accreditation of the AAMFT as the official body for accrediting educational and training programs in the field. The committee's sole task is to certify graduate programs and postdegree clinical training centers in marital and family therapy, usually after making site visits and other careful reviews of their programs (Smith & Nichols, 1979). Although there were only sixteen accredited graduate programs and eight accredited postdegree training centers in 1984 (see Table 13-5), the list will undoubtedly grow; however, the committee clearly intends to proceed slowly and with great care in identifying high-quality accredited training programs.

TABLE 13-5. AAMFT Accredited Graduate and Postdegree Programs (1984)

Name	Location
Graduate Programs	
Abilene Christian University	Abilene, Texas
Brigham Young University	Provo, Utah
East Texas State University	Commerce, Texas
Georgia State University	Atlanta, Georgia
Kansas State University	Manhattan, Kansas
Loma Linda University	Loma Linda, California
Northern Illinois University	De Kalb, Illinois
Purdue University	Lafayette, Indiana
Southern Connecticut State	New Haven, Connecticut
Texas Tech University	Lubbock, Texas
University of Bridgeport	Bridgeport, Connecticut
University of Houston at Clear Lake City	Houston, Texas
University of Maryland	College Park, Maryland
University of Southern California	Los Angeles, California
University of Wisconsin–Stout	Menomonee, Wisconsin
Virginia Tech University	Blacksburg, Virginia
Postdegree Programs	
Ackerman Institute for Family Therapy	New York, New York
California Family Study Center	Burbank, California
Family and Children Services	St. Louis, Missouri
Family Institute of Westchester	Mt. Vernon, New York
Family Service of Milwaukee	Milwaukee, Wisconsin
Institutes of Religion and Health	New York, New York
Marriage Council of Philadelphia	Philadelphia, Pennsylvania
Peel Center	Montreal, Canada

(Source: American Association for Marriage and Family Therapy)

Licensing of marital/family therapists is also proceeding slowly, partly because it is easier to establish criteria for licensing the graduates of recognized university programs than those from newly established training programs in freestanding family institutes. In addition, the established mental health professions have presented considerable opposition to an independent profession of marital/family therapists; according to their view, marital/family therapy is but a subspecialty of psychotherapy. However, marital/family therapists argue that traditional professional preparation in the mental health field—especially if it was obtained more than a decade or two ago—generally provides no training in work with families; graduates of such programs should themselves seek additional training and acquire a license in marital/family therapy if they wish to practice in the field. The subject remains controversial and discussion heated, touching on professional issues such as eligibility for third-party payments from health insurance plans to cover the treatment of marital or family dysfunction as well as the updating of professional skills and conceptual knowledge. Clearly, practitioners accustomed to working with individual clients need further training before working with families. Whether most training institutes as they currently operate provide sufficient training in this area is open to debate.

Marital/family therapy is now regulated in eleven states. Licensing laws exist in eight (California, Georgia, New Jersey, Utah, Florida, Connecticut, Arkansas, and Virginia) and three states (Michigan, Nevada, and North Carolina) have passed certification legislation. Sporakowski and Staniszewski (1980) present a detailed survey of the requirements for licensing/certification in each of these states. For example, in California the applicant must possess a two-year Master's degree in marriage, family, and child counseling from an academic institution accredited by the Western College Association or an equivalent accrediting agency, plus at least two years of experience in marriage, family, and child counseling under the supervision of a licensed marriage, family, and child counselor, licensed clinical social worker, licensed psychologist or licensed physician certified in psychiatry. According to this survey, efforts were under way in nearly half the fifty states to produce legislation to regulate the private practice of marriage and family therapy.

THE EFFECTIVENESS OF FAMILY THERAPY

The Question of Psychotherapy Research

Ultimately, all psychotherapeutic ventures must provide some kind of answer to the question "Does it help?" Outcome research in family therapy must address the same problems that hinder such research in individual psychotherapy in addition to the further complications of gauging and measuring the various interactions and changes taking place within a family group. To be meaningful, such research must do more than investigate general therapeutic efficacy; it must determine the conditions under which family therapy is effective: the types of families, the categories of problems or situations, the level of family functioning, the therapeutic techniques, the treatment objectives or goals, and so on. "Does psychotherapy help?" is too vague a question to provide a useful answer; for example, what is the comparison—no formal treatment, individual psychotherapy, another form of family therapy? Moreover, the question presumes that psychotherapy is a unitary phenomenon, which it is not; various forms are practiced and subsumed under the general rubric of psychotherapy.

Another stumbling block to evaluating the outcome of psychotherapy arises from lack of agreement regarding what constitutes success. Strupp (1971) draws a provocative analogy between psychotherapy and education in attempting to answer the question "Does a college education help?" The effectiveness of such an education depends largely on the criterion used to judge success (the graduate is a better person or a happier person than he or she might otherwise be, is able to get a higher paying job or a more fulfilling job, and so forth). Strupp's point is that different educators use different criteria to evaluate success in their work. Since there is a range of good to bad schools, good to bad teachers, students who desire to profit from their experience to those who do not, the question is all but unanswerable unless we evaluate the effectiveness of specific educational programs aimed at specific goals. Similarly, if different schools of individual psychotherapy have different goals (symptom removal for the behaviorist, ego integration for the psychoanalyst), no meaningful comparison can be made of the successes that each claims.

A more precisely stated and thus more useful version of the simple "Does psychotherapy work?" is Paul's (1969) reformulation: "What treatment, by whom, is most effective for this individual with that specific problem, under which set of circumstances, and how does it come about?" (p. 44). Slowly, individual psychotherapy research is becoming more precise in its definitions. In a recent literature survey, Phillips and Bierman (1981) conclude that the trend in research on the outcome of individual treatment is toward greater specificity in respect to client problems, therapeutic operations, treatment goals, and theoretical constructs.

Family Therapy Outcome Studies

Progress in measuring the outcome of treatment has been even slower to develop in the field of family therapy. Several historical factors are involved: (1) family therapy originated in parallel but unrelated ways within different disciplines, each with its own explanatory framework, language, and type of client population (Olson, 1970); (2) most family therapy was practiced in psychiatric (child guidance) or social work (family service agency) settings where the emphasis was more on providing clinical service than conducting research; psychology—the discipline most apt to engage in psychotherapy research— had not yet made a significant impact on the field (Gurman, 1971); (3) during the first half of this century, the general devaluation of direct intervention with a family system and of any kind of clinical practice by nonphysicians had a pronounced negative effect on interprofessional collaboration (Gurman & Kniskern, 1981c).

In addition to these historical factors, outcome research in family therapy faces some critical methodological problems: the unit of study is large and complex; events that occur during sessions usually result from many factors, making it difficult to identify and control the variables; the family unit is in a state of continuous change; the observer (therapist/researcher) is often part of the system and may change with it; the researcher must consider intrapsychic, relationship, communication, and ordinary group variables as well as taking into account such contextual variables as community, culture, and social pressures (Fox, 1976). It is hardly any wonder that, despite the growing number of practitioners, little adequately designed objective research data appeared until the mid-1970s.

Wells, Dilkes, and Trivelli (1972), reviewing outcome studies published between 1950 and 1970, identified only eighteen studies that met their minimal research criteria (three or more families included, outcome measures explicitly stated); of these, only two were found to be adequately designed for research purposes. Most of the other studies lacked a "no treatment" control group against which to compare changes in the experimental group[3] that was undergoing family therapy. Some relied on the therapist's evaluation of his or her own work rather than on an independent judge, or on the family members' subjective self-reports at termination. Most studies neglected to test patients pre- and posttherapy or to carry out adequate follow-up assessments after therapy had terminated. Only the studies of the efficacy of family crisis therapy in preventing hospitalization carried out at the Family Treatment Unit of the Colorado Psychiatric Hospital by Langsley and associates were considered adequate in research design. As reported in Chapter 12, these results showed that patients who were treated at the crisis-oriented Family Treatment Unit instead of being hospitalized functioned as well six months later and had avoided hospitalization during that period (Langsley, Pittman, Machotka, & Flomenhaft, 1968).

Several years later, a more systematic review by Wells and Dezen (1978) of family therapy outcome research between 1971 and 1976 focused specifically on "nonbehavioral" treatment methods. The inquiry included three types of research: (1) uncontrolled, single-group studies; (2) comparisons between treatment and no formal treatment; and (3) comparisons between alternative forms of treatment.

Single-group studies, although flawed because of the absence of a comparable control group, attempt to examine the effects of a particular treatment method on a particular client population ("Does treatment X produce measurable positive changes in population Y?"). Of the sixteen such studies identified by Wells and Dezen (1978), seven were considered to have been designed adequately. The work of Minuchin and colleagues at the Philadelphia Child Guidance Center in treating psychosomatic families (see Chapter 3) was prominent. As Minuchin, Rosman, and Baker (1978) later reported, they based their evaluation on 50 adolescent anorexics seen for therapy together with their

---

[3]It is only fair to point out that most of these studies were meant to exemplify a particular treatment approach rather than being specifically designed as research projects. Under such circumstances, it is not surprising that a control group is missing. However, there is the danger that once a method has begun to be practiced and the results published, readers may assume it to be valid and lose sight of the need for careful and systematic scrutiny of its effectiveness (Wells & Dezen, 1978).

families for an average of six months; they assessed medical outcome (status of anorexic symptoms) and psychosocial functioning (adjustment at home, school, or work, and involvement with peers). They conducted follow-up assessments at intervals from 18 months to seven years after treatment. Of the 50 patients, 43 were judged to have recovered from both the physical symptoms of anorexia and its psychosocial manifestations (see Table 13–6), a figure that compares very favorably indeed with those reported for individually oriented treatment of this seemingly intractable disorder. These highly positive gains persisted at the subsequent follow-up evaluations. Such positive results give considerable credibility to Minuchin's family therapy approach, although the lack of a control group limits further conclusions regarding its advantages over other methods or techniques of treatment.

Is there research-based evidence that a particular form of family therapy produces greater measurable positive change with a particular client population than if that same group received no formal treatment? To acquire such evidence, families must be randomly assigned to receive treatment or not receive treatment; measurements must be made before and after treatment; and a specific method of family therapy must be used with the families in the experimental group. Wells and Dezen (1978) located nine control-group studies in the literature. However, they judged that only five were methodologically adequate according to the above criteria. Of these studies, the work of Bernard

TABLE 13–6. Medical and Psychosocial Assessment of 50 Anorexic Patients following Family Therapy

Rating	Characteristics	Number of cases	Percentage of total
Medical assessment			
Recovered	Eating patterns normal, body weight stabilized within normal limits for height and age	43	86
Fair	Weight gain but continuing effects of illness (borderline weight, obesity, occasional vomiting)	2	4
Unimproved	Little or no change	3	6
Relapsed	Reappearance of anorexia symptoms after apparently successful treatment	2	4
Psychological assessment			
Good	Satisfactory adjustment in family, school or work, and social and peer relationships	43	86
Fair	Adjustment in one or another of these areas unsatisfactory	2	4
Unimproved	Inability to function even at borderline levels; disturbances of behavior, thought, and affect	3	6
Relapsed	Reappearance of anorexia symptoms after apparently successful treatment	2	4

(From Minuchin and Associates, 1978)

Guerney in filial therapy (training parents to function as play therapists with their young children) is especially significant in demonstrating the superiority of a particular technique over no treatment of the parents and children in moderately disturbed families (Guerney, 1976).

Finally, Wells and Dezen (1978) describe studies that compare two forms of treatment in order to determine which produces the greater measurable positive change with a specific population. Once again, random assignment to one group or the other is essential to the design. Of the seventeen studies published, eight were judged adequate. One noteworthy experiment by Wellisch, Vincent, and Ro-Trock (1976) compared the effectiveness of short-term family therapy versus short-term individual therapy with 28 hospitalized adolescents and their parents. This well-designed study utilized objective assessment and observational measures by independent judges before treatment, after treatment, and at a follow-up evaluation of families randomly assigned to the experimental (family therapy) condition or to the control (individual therapy) condition. To eliminate the potential confounding effect of a particular therapist using a particular technique, two therapy teams were used, each one responsible for an equal number of cases in both kinds of therapy. Treatment consisted of eight sessions of either family therapy or individual therapy with the adolescent. Results indicated that family therapy with inpatient adolescents was superior in terms of aiding community adaptation and reducing recidivism (rehospitalization) rates. Compared to those adolescents treated individually, those in family therapy were restored to functioning (in school or at work) more rapidly and remained functional throughout the ordinarily stressful adjustment period immediately following hospital discharge. The authors suggest that in the absence of intervention with the pathological family system, it might be expected that the discharged patient would return to a family situation in which the previous level of dsyfunction could be quickly reinduced, leading to possible rehospitalization; among the 14 adolescents receiving individual treatment but no family therapy, there were six readmitted to the hospital within three months. A three-month follow-up of the 14 family therapy patients found that none had been rehospitalized.

With guarded optimism, Wells and Dezen (1978) noted that research productivity in this key area had increased, as had the quality of research designs in general. However, while acknowledging that some of the uncontrolled studies such as Minuchin's had documented the legitimacy of family therapy as an effective treatment modality, the authors concluded that the overwhelming number of controlled studies (with the exception of Guerney's work) failed to establish that family therapy produces results superior to those achieved by "no-treatment" control groups.

Outcome Studies Revisited

In a continuing series of research reports, Gurman and Kniskern (1978, 1981a, 1981c) reexamined the studies reviewed by Wells and Dezen (1978) as well as others not previously reviewed or of more recent vintage. In a comprehensive survey of behavioral and nonbehavioral studies in both marital and family therapy, Gurman and Kniskern (1978) examined over 200 studies. More favorably impressed than their predecessors, the reviewers found positive evidence for the effectiveness of family therapy as well as the overall status and quality of family therapy research. Regarding the use of family therapy in situations where there are alternatives, they concluded that "every study to date that has compared family therapy with other types of treatment has shown family therapy to be equal or superior" (p. 835).

Specifically, improvement is reported for 65% of the nonbehavioral conjoint marital therapy cases and 73% of the family cases. Behavioral family therapies, compared with no treatment, also produced positive results. As for behavioral marital therapy, Gurman and Kniskern (1981a) reported impressive gains with mildly or moderately distressed couples but somewhat less persuasive evidence of effectiveness with severely distressed couples or with couples in which one or both partners is seriously emotionally disturbed. These data are convincing enough that these researchers question the value of seeing individuals separately for marital problems; couples benefit most when both are involved in therapy, especially when they are seen conjointly.

The most difficult empirical and clinical question remains: what treatment for what problem? Gurman and Kniskern (1981a, 1981c) offer some definite conclusions based on their literature search. To begin with, conjoint treatment for marital discord is clearly the method of choice over the individual, collaborative (each spouse sees separate therapist) or concurrent (one therapist treats marital partners in separate sessions) approaches. Second, the beneficial effects of nonbehavioral marital/family therapy often occur in brief treatment. Third, behavioral marriage therapy is about as effective for minimally distressed couples as nonbehavioral methods, somewhat less so when severe dysfunction is involved. Next, they conclude that increasing a couple's communication skill, however achieved, is the essence of effective marital therapy. Finally, conjoint, behaviorally oriented sex therapy should be considered the treatment of choice for such problems, especially when severe nonsexual problems do not exist.

Gurman and Kniskern (1981a, 1981c) have found family therapy to be more effective than individual therapy, even for problems that seem more intrapsychic in nature than interpersonal. Structural family therapy appears to be particularly helpful for certain childhood and adolescent psychosomatic symptoms. As for the relative efficacy of behavioral and nonbehavioral approaches, no conclusions are justifiable on the basis of published research; however, either strategy is clearly preferable to no treatment at all. No empirical evidence yet exists for the superiority of co-therapy over single-therapist intervention with couples or families.

Finally, clinicians should be aware that a **"deterioration effect"** may be operating in marital/family therapy, producing a harmful effect on the clients, especially when they are being treated by a therapist with poor relationship skills, or a therapist who does little to structure or guide the initial phase of therapy, attacks client defenses too early in treatment, fails to intervene in or interpret family confrontation in ongoing treatment, or fails to support the family members in the therapeutic experience.

THE FUTURE OF FAMILY THERAPY

Whither family therapy? No longer the radical movement it seemed three decades ago, where is it now and where is it headed? Today, many therapists continue to see most of their patients in individual treatment but accept the appropriateness of the family approach for others. An increasing number of therapists now think in terms of nonlinear causality or systems; for these clinicians, the behavior and personality characteristics of an individual and any symptoms he or she may develop are best understood in the context of the person's family life. This group emphasizes that the transactions between family members govern a person's range of experiences and patterns of behavior. As we have attempted to make clear throughout this book, it is the family system—the interdependent parts within the context of "family"—that becomes the focus of intervention. Moreover, to extend the concept of feedback and circular causality, it should be further emphasized that as soon as the therapist begins to "connect" with and treat the family, he or she enters it, coevolves with it, and inevitably becomes a part of the now larger system to be studied and modified.

We think of family therapy as the appropriate method of intervention for our times. Although many of the examples we have offered are of intact families or families striving to remain intact, we recognize that contemporary family life is in a state of transition. High divorce rates, working wives, smaller families, single-parent households, blended families, and other arrangements confront us with new forms of family life, new sets of problems, new kinds of relationships—and the necessity to devise new therapeutic methods for effective intervention. As Bell (1975) forecasts:

> The picture postcard representation of the family as healthy, young parents of three lively children, petting the family dog, joyously indulging in a life that is more leisure than work, setting out on Sunday morning hand in hand for church, conscientiously attending the meetings of the PTA, happily visited by grandmother and grandfather, will be consigned to some kind of antique family album [p. 277].

In fact, such an idealization of a family never really represented how members actually dealt with each other behind the socially acceptable facade. Today, both the realities and varieties of family life are more openly acknowledged.

A number of serious deficiencies still exist in the field of family therapy:

1. *The field requires a broader set of theoretical conceptions.* There is no comprehensive theory of family dysfunction, although pioneers such as Bowen (1978) have made efforts in this direction. As a consequence, no widely prevailing theory of family therapy exists, and this hinders the orderly development of

the field. One promising effort is Auerswald's (1972) ecological approach in which the family system and its interface with other systems becomes the focus of attention. The family as a whole interacts within its subsystems and is itself a part of a larger societal system. The ecological perspective looks at the communication within and between systems, not one or the other. Holistic in outlook, it discourages excessive selectivity in the collection of data and promotes awareness of all the factors relevant to the family in its interplay with the outside environment. Extending the family systems concept, Auerswald proposes that we take into consideration the wide spectrum of systems that impinge on the individual.

2. *Cultural influences on family functioning deserve more attention.* There are significant subcultural, racial, religious, and ethnic variations in families in our own society, to say nothing of transcultural differences. But as Cohen (1974) suggests, many practitioners avoid issues of ethnicity, race, subcultural identity, and bilingualism in their diagnostic or therapeutic efforts. Perhaps they lean over backwards not to show prejudice or discriminate in the clinical setting, but the overall effect is to ignore a potentially rich source of data regarding individual and family functioning. Black ghetto families, rural farm families, families composed of gay couples, Spanish-speaking families, female-led single-parent families, Russian emigré families, refugee Vietnamese families, and intact upper-middle-class suburban families are hardly alike; each group has a different background with its own stresses and pressures, values and attitudes, customs and expectations for family members. To treat all families in the same way is to deny the realities of their lives and to limit therapeutic effectiveness. Lewis and Looney's (1983) study of highly functional working-class Black families is an important corrective step in this direction, supplementing earlier research (reported in Chapter 2) on "healthy" White middle-class families (Lewis, Beavers, Gossett & Phillips, 1976).

3. *Family therapy programs need to be extended to new settings.* During the period of time that the field of family therapy has evolved, there has been a dramatic change in our thinking about the delivery of mental health services (Goldenberg, 1977). As community-based programs (such as aftercare services, emergency services, and day treatment programs) have proliferated, family therapy has remained primarily a method of treatment used in private offices and outpatient clinics (Bell, 1975). Influential clinicians such as Spiegel (1974) urge that family treatment play a more important part in the community health movement and the efforts now under way to develop comprehensive systems of care. By its very nature, the family will have a central role in linking various health and human service delivery systems. The practice of family therapy should be extended to various social agencies, mental hospital inpatient and outpatient units, general hospitals, rehabilitation programs, and other programs that together comprise a community's comprehensive health services.

In this regard, family therapists are beginning to study the relationship between physical illness in the family and the practitioners (physicians, nurses) who provide health care; this area of investigation is labeled "family somatics" by Weakland (1977). In the future, family therapists may make a useful contribution to treatment and rehabilitation by consulting with other health-care providers in hospitals and elsewhere in the community. Donald Bloch, Director of the Ackerman Institute for Family Therapy, has recently founded the journal *Family Systems Medicine* devoted to this important subject.

4. *The assumptions and procedures in family therapy must be evaluated more systematically through research.* As we indicated in Chapter 2, a current controversy among family therapists concerns the "new epistemology"—essentially a reexamination of our world views and paradigms (individual versus system, linear versus circular, and so forth). In a challenge to virtually all of the major assumptions in family therapy developed over the last 35 years, Hoffman (1981), Dell (1982), Keeney (1983) and others have proposed a paradigmatic shift away from the study of *observed systems* (as in physical science) to a study of *observing systems* (the science of living forms) in which the therapist is both observer and participant. One consequence of their thinking is that the therapist does not act unidirectionally to fix the dysfunctional system, but is himself or herself a part of the complex cybernetics. As Keeney and Sprenkle (1982) put it, "a therapist's participation has more to do with being alive than creating specific outcomes" (p. 16).

Would the traditional research strategy regarding the outcome of family therapy—seeking to establish a causal relationship between a method of treatment and its effects on the family—remain relevant if we were to adopt the "new epistemology"? Cybernetically inclined family therapists such as Colapinto (1979) and Keeney and Sprenkle (1982) say "no," arguing that the time-honored ways of doing research on psychotherapy are inappropriate and inadequate to contribute to our knowledge of how complex systems operate and how families actually change. On the other side, Gurman (1983) contends that standard research methods are the only means currently available for assessing the efficacy of family therapy in an ethically responsible manner. He maintains that outcome researchers do attend to context by studying the interactional effects of patient, therapist, treatment and setting variables. Thus Gurman argues that the charge that psychotherapy researchers are overly linear is inaccurate and that there are insufficient grounds for a divorce between standard research (which, in fact, is systems-based) and the "new epistemology."

Most family therapists favor controlled experimental research as a way to tie theoretical understanding to observable behavior. Wynne (1983) has called for a reunion between family therapy and family research, a reference to the situation existing in the early days of the field (see Chapter 4). Wynne lists six areas in which research is needed and is likely to be forthcoming: (1) family therapy outcome studies; (2) the therapeutic process through which outcomes are achieved; (3) development of rating scales and related methods for before-and-after assessments, especially in outpatient settings; (4) renewal of research efforts focused on the ecosystem, the social network, the cultural matrix, and the changing values of the family; (5) longitudinal and developmental studies applicable to programs of prevention and early intervention; and (6) direct clinical observation of therapy sessions by a team of therapists who formulate testable hypotheses and assess their validity in subsequent sessions. This last suggestion (implemented by the Milan group) points to a revival of interest in family theory including the "new epistemology" and, according to Wynne (1983), is closely linked to the clinical research observations of the 1950s.

During the next decade, we predict that a number of current trends will produce the following developments in the field: (1) *greater use of crisis-focused family therapy in a variety of clinical settings.* As an illustration, Cohen, Goldenberg, and Goldenberg (1977) describe a program on the oncology (cancer) ward of a university general hospital in which bone marrow recipients and donors were all helped to develop more adaptive coping strategies while learning to deal realistically, but hopefully, with the life-threatening illness in a family member; (2) *more work with nontraditional families and families with varying membership.* We anticipate that new techniques will be developed for treating alternative families (stepfamilies; dual-career families; gay couples), splintered families (single-parent households; families headed by young, unmarried mothers) or families living separately (dealing with such issues as custody arrangements and visitations); (3) *the growth of brief, even single-session, treatment involving extended families.* We believe that family reunions, the mobilization of natural networks within a family group, the active inclusion of grandparents in the family unit are helpful means to resolving specific problems from the past or present; (4) *the training of parents as therapists or change agents for their children,* as in filial therapy (Guerney, 1976) or the behavioral parent training programs offered by Patterson and associates. The Parent-Adolescent Relationship Development (PARD) program established by Guerney and his associates (Guerney, 1977) is a structured attempt to train families to improve communication and enhance parent–adolescent relationships; (5) *the use of social network intervention on a regular basis.* The retribalization phenomenon described by Speck and Attneave (1973) might be utilized for reviving bonds within extended families, work groups, teacher/student groups, and so on; (6) *the reorganization of child guidance clinic services in order to emphasize family therapy services.* Modeled on the Philadelphia Child Guidance Clinic organized by Minuchin (1974a) and a number of similar institutions in the United States and Canada, an attempt is being made to offer services to families as a whole rather than to children and parents separately; (7) *the implementation of specially targeted early intervention programs.* Such programs will be designed to deal with such alarming problems as family violence, runaway children, battered wives, the physical and sexual abuse of children; (8) *the development of integrative methods of family therapy.* We believe there will be less concern with differences in family therapy approaches and more emphasis on relating specific interventions to phases of treatment, stages in the family's life cycle, type of presenting problem, and so forth; (9) *the integration of family therapy philosophy and values into larger systems.* The interface of family systems with other systems (the schools, industry, social agencies) will encourage the development of more comprehensive theories and new intervention and preventive procedures; (10) *greater use of new observational techniques for research and training.* The use of such devices and methods as one-way mirrors, live supervision, therapy teams working with a single family, rating scales, and videoplayback will increase our knowledge and enhance family therapy training; (11) *the advancement of new ethical standards.* The field has reached the point where a reassessment of its values and ethical commitments is overdue; (12) *the clarification of therapist qualifications for dealing with specific issues or populations.* Considering that a two-track training program now exists, some determinations regarding who is eligible to treat which problems (for example, severe dysfunction versus moderate dysfunction) is necessary; (13) *the reorganization of clinical training programs to include family therapy.* Trainees have traditionally been assigned to adult or children's services, perhaps rotating from one to the other. We anticipate programs where training is offered in working therapeutically with the entire family unit. If no natural family is present (for example, in the case of college students), therapy might be offered to substitute families (friends, roommates). Of all programs to train clinicians, family therapy lends itself best to interdisciplinary training and teamwork.

The next decade promises considerable change in the form and organization of family systems. Bold and resourceful therapeutic programs—based on sound research and a comprehensive theory of family functioning—must be developed to meet the challenge of the future. New methods of training, new populations to serve, new settings for clinical activities, new and improved family therapy techniques—these are our expectations for the future. We can hardly wait!

SUMMARY

Becoming a family therapist is a new kind of learning experience for clinicians trained to understand individual functioning and to offer individual psychotherapy. A theoretical understanding of family relationships, firsthand clinical experience with families, and careful supervision are indispensable elements in a family therapist's education. Training can be obtained from established postgraduate academic programs or from independent family therapy training institutes. Training aids include didactic course work (lectures, demonstrations, assigned readings); the use of master therapist films and trainee videotapes for postsession viewing by the trainee and his or her supervisor and/or classmates; multiple-family marathon sessions including trainees, their client families, and supervisors; and live supervision through active guidance by a supervisor who watches the session behind a one-way mirror and offers corrective feedback by telephone, earphone, or by calling the trainee out of the therapy room.

Co-therapy, simultaneously involving two therapists with a single family, may be used for training purposes as it is when a supervisor and supervisee work together. The technique is sometimes used in practice by family therapists who, like Whitaker, appreciate the mutual support, the teamwork, and the opportunity to freely pursue sensitive areas with a family while knowing the other therapist remains in a backup position, tied to reality. Haley is representative of the family therapists who find co-therapy more useful to the therapist's sense of security than to the family and argue that it is expensive and an inefficient use of professional time.

Family therapists may obtain credentials to practice in one of two ways, depending upon their training: (1) through state licensing or certification in their respecitve mental health professions; or (2) through certification by the AAMFT that they have graduated from an accredited graduate program and received clinical experience in marital/family therapy at an accredited post-degree training center. At present, graduates in marital/family therapy may be licensed or certified to practice that profession in eleven states.

In the past, outcome research in family therapy was deficient and insufficient, due to poor research methodology and an earlier emphasis on exploring new techniques rather than evaluating them scientifically. More recently, better designed research studies have begun to appear. Single-group studies, studies comparing family treatment/no treatment with a particular client population, and studies comparing two forms of treatment with a specific population are the typical types of outcome research in family therapy. Results from these studies indicate that family therapy compares favorably with other types of treatment and is the treatment of choice for certain specific marital/family problems.

The future of family therapy appears bright and the technique appropriate for our times. Family therapy will benefit from broader theories, more attention to cultural factors, application to new settings, and a more systematic research-based evaluation of its existing assumptions, procedures and outcomes. During the forthcoming decade, it is anticipated that the profession will introduce new intervention techniques, serve new populations, offer new observational and training procedures, develop better research methodologies, and clarify the qualifications that are necessary for dealing with specific clinical problems.

APPENDIX

Code of Professional Ethics, American Association for Marriage and Family Therapy

Section I: Code of personal conduct

1. A therapist provides professional service to anyone regardless of race, religion, sex, political affiliation, social or economic status, or choice of lifestyle. When a therapist cannot offer service for any reason, he or she will make proper referral. Therapists are encouraged to devote a portion of their time to work for which there is little or no financial return.
2. A therapist will not use his or her counseling relationship to further personal, religious, political, or business interests.
3. A therapist will neither offer nor accept payment for referrals, and will actively seek all significant information from the source of referral.
4. A therapist will not knowingly offer service to a client who is in treatment with another clinical professional without consultation among the parties involved.
5. A therapist will not disparage the qualifications of any colleague.
6. Every member of the AAMFT has an obligation to continuing education and professional growth in all possible ways, including active participation in the meetings and affairs of the Association.
7. A therapist will not attempt to diagnose, prescribe for, treat, or advise on problems outside the recognized boundaries of the therapist's competence.
8. A therapist will attempt to avoid relationships with clients which might impair professional judgment or increase the risks of exploiting clients. Examples of such relationships include: treatment of family members, close friends, employees, or supervisees. Sexual intimacy with clients is unethical.
9. The AAMFT encourages its members to affiliate with professional groups, clinics, or agencies operating in the field of marriage and family life. Similarly, interdisciplinary contact and cooperation are encouraged.

Section II: Relations with clients

1. A therapist, while offering dignified and reasonable support, is cautious in prognosis and will not exaggerate the efficacy of his or her services.

2. The therapist recognizes the importance of clear understandings on financial matters with clients. Arrangements for payments are settled at the beginning of a therapeutic relationship.
3. A therapist keeps records of each case and stores them in such a way as to insure safety and confidentiality, in accordance with the highest professional and legal standards.
   a. Information shall be revealed only to professional persons concerned with the case. Written and oral reports should present only data germane to the purposes of the inquiry; every effort should be made to avoid undue invasion of privacy.
   b. The therapist is responsible for informing clients of the limits of confidentiality.
   c. Written permission shall be granted by the clients involved before data may be divulged.
   d. Information is not communicated to others without consent of the client unless there is clear and immediate danger to an individual or to society, and then only to the appropriate family members, professional workers, or public authorities.
4. A therapist deals with relationships at varying stages of their history. While respecting at all times the rights of clients to make their own decisions, the therapist has a duty to assess the situation according to the highest professional standards. In all circumstances, the therapist will clearly advise a client that the decision to separate or divorce is the responsibility solely of the client. In such an event, the therapist has the continuing responsibility to offer support and counsel during the period of readjustment.

Section III: Research and publication

1. The therapist is obligated to protect the welfare of his or her research subjects. The conditions of the Human Subjects Experimentation shall prevail, as specified by the Department of Health, Education and Welfare guidelines.
2. Publication credit is assigned to those who have contributed to a publication, in proportion to their contribution, and in accordance with customary publication practices.

Section IV: Implementation

1. In accepting membership in the Association, each member binds himself or herself to accept the judgment of fellow members as to standards of professional ethics, subject to the safeguards provided in this section. Acceptance of membership implies consent to abide by the acts of discipline herein set forth and as enumerated in the Bylaws of the Association. It is the duty of each member to safeguard these standards of ethical practice. Should a fellow member appear to violate this Code, he or she may be cautioned through friendly remonstrance, colleague consultation with the party in question, or formal complaint may be filed in accordance with the following procedure:
   a. Complaint of unethical practice shall be made in writing to the Chairperson of the Standing Committee on Ethics and Professional Practices and to the Executive Director. A copy of the complaint shall be furnished to the person or persons against whom it is directed.
   b. Should the Standing Committee decide the complaint warrants investigation, it shall so notify the charged party(ies) in writing. When investigation is indicated, the Standing Committee shall constitute itself an Investigating Committee and

shall include in its membership at least one member of the Board and at least two members (other than the charging or charged parties or any possible witnesses) from the local area involved. This Investigating Committee or representatives thereof shall make one or more local visits of investigation of the complaint. After full investigation following due process and offering the charged party(ies) opportunity to defend him or herself, the Committee shall report its findings and recommendations to the Board of Directors for action.

c. The charged party(ies) shall have free access to all charges and evidence cited against him or her, and shall have full freedom to defend himself or herself before the Investigating Committee and the Board, including the right to legal counsel.

d. Recommendation made by the Committee shall be:
   1. Advice that the charges be dropped as unfounded.
   2. Specified admonishment.
   3. Reprimand.
   4. Dismissal from membership.

2. Should a member of this Association be expelled, he or she shall at once surrender his or her membership certificate to the Board of Directors. Failure to do so shall result in such action as legal counsel may recommend.

3. Should a member of this Association be expelled from another recognized professional association or his/her state license revoked for unethical conduct, the Standing Committee on Ethics shall investigate the matter and, where appropriate, act in the manner provided above respecting charges of unethical conduct.

4. The Committee will also give due consideration to a formal complaint by a nonmember.

Section V: Public information and advertising

All professional presentations to the public will be governed by the Standards on Public Information and Advertising.

STANDARDS ON PUBLIC INFORMATION AND ADVERTISING

Section I: General principles

The practice of marriage and family therapy as a mental health profession is in the public interest. Therefore, it is appropriate for the well-trained and qualified practitioner to inform the public of the availability of his/her services. However, much needs to be done to educate the public as to the services available from qualified marriage and family therapists. Therefore, the clinical members of AAMFT have a responsibility to the public to engage in appropriate informational activities and to avoid misrepresentation or misleading statements in keeping with the following general principles and specific regulations.

Selection of a marriage and family therapist

A. At a time when the Human Services field is burgeoning and becoming increasingly complex and specialized, few marriage and family therapists are willing and competent to deal with every kind of marital or family problem, and many laypersons have difficulty in determining the competence of psychotherapists in general and marriage and family therapists in particular to render different types of services. The selection of a marriage and family therapist is particularly difficult for transients, persons moving into new areas, persons of limited education or means, and others who have had no previous experience or the degree of sophistication required to evaluate training and competence or because they are in some sort of crisis.

B. Selection of a marriage and family therapist by a layperson should be made on an informed basis. Advice and recommendation of third parties—physicians, other professionals, relatives, friends, acquaintances, business associates—and restrained publicity may be helpful. A marriage and family therapist should not compensate another person for recommending him/her, for influencing a prospective client to employ him/her, or to encourage future recommendations. Advertisements and public communications, whether in directories, announcement cards, newspapers, or on radio or television, should be formulated to convey information that is necessary to make an appropriate selection. Self-praising should be avoided. Information that may be helpful in some situations would include: (1) office information, such as name, including a group name and names of professional associates, address, telephone number, credit card acceptability, languages spoken and written, and office hours; (2) earned degrees, state licensure and/or certification, and AAMFT clinical membership status; (3) description of practice, including a statement that practice is limited to one or more fields of marriage and family therapy; and (4) permitted fee information.

C. The proper motivation for commercial publicity by marriage and family therapists lies in the need to inform the public of the availability of competent, independent marriage and family therapists. The public benefit derived from advertising depends upon the usefulness of the information provided to the community to which it is directed. Advertising marked by excesses of content, volume, scope, or frequency, or which unduly emphasizes unrepresentative biographical information, does not provide that public benefit. The use of media whose scope or nature clearly suggests that the use is intended for self-praising of the therapist without concomitant benefit to the public distorts the legitimate purpose of informing the public and is clearly improper. Indeed, this and other improper advertising may hinder informed selection of a competent, independent professional and advertising that involves excessive cost may unnecessarily increase fees for marriage and family therapy.

D. Advertisements and other communications should make it apparent that the necessity [for] and advisability of marriage and family therapy depend on variant factors that must be evaluated individually. Because fee information frequently may be incomplete and misleading to a layperson, a marriage and family therapist should exercise great care to assure that fee information is complete and accurate. Because of the individuality of each problem, public statements regarding average, minimum, or estimated fees may be deceiving as will commercial publicity conveying information as to results previously achieved, general or average solutions, or expected outcomes. It would be misleading to advertise a set fee for a specific type of case without adhering to the stated fee in charging clients. Advertisements or public claims that use statistical data or other information based on past performance or prediction of future success may be deceptive if they ignore important variables. Only factual assertions, and not opinions, should be made in public communications. Not only must commercial publicity be truthful but its accurate meaning must be apparent to the averge layperson. No guarantees about the outcomes of therapy should be made or implied. Any commercial publicity or advertising for which payment is made should so indicate unless it is apparent from the context that it is paid publicity or an advertisement.

E. The desirability of affording the public access to information relevant to their needs and problems has resulted in some relaxation of the former restrictions against advertising by marriage and family therapists. Historically, those restrictions were imposed to prevent deceptive publicity that would mislead laypersons, cause distrust of the profession, and undermine public confidence in the profession, and all marriage and family therapists should remain vigilant to prevent such results. Ambiguous information relevant to a layperson's decision regarding his/her selection of a marriage and family therapist, provided in ways that do not comport with the dignity of the profession or which demean the amelioration of human problems, is inappropriate in public communications. The regulation of advertising by marriage and family therapists is rooted in the public interest. Advertising through which a marriage and family therapist seeks business by use of extravagant or brash statements or appeals to fears could mislead and harm the layperson. Furthermore, public communications that would produce unrealistic expectations in particular cases and bring about distrust of the profession would be harmful to society. Thus, public confidence in our profession would be impaired by such advertisements of professional services. The therapist-client relationship, being personal and unique, should not be established as the result of pressures, deceptions, or exploitation of the vulnerability of clients frequently experiencing significant stress at the time they seek help.

F. The Regulations recognize the value of giving assistance in the selection process through forms of advertising that furnish identification of a marriage and family therapist while avoiding falsity, deception, and misrepresentation. All publicity should be evaluated with regard to its effects on the layperson. The layperson is best served if advertisements contain no misleading information or emotional appeals, and emphasize the necessity of an individualized evaluation of the situation before conclusions as to need for a particular type of therapy and probable expenses can be made. The therapist-client relationship should result from a free and informed choice by the layperson. Unwarranted promises of benefits, overpersuasion, or vexatious or harassing conduct is improper.

G. The name under which a marriage and family therapist conducts his/her practice may be a factor in the selection process. The use of a name which could mislead laypersons concerning the identity, responsibility, source, and status of those practicing thereunder is not proper. Likewise, one should not hold oneself out as being a partner or associate of a firm if he/she is not one in fact.

H. In order to avoid the possibility of misleading persons with whom he/she deals, a marriage and family therapist should be scrupulous in the representation of his/her professional background, training, and status. In some instances a marriage and family therapist confines his/her practice to a particular area within the field of marriage and family therapy. However, a member should not hold himself/herself out as a specialist without evidence of training, education, and supervised experience in settings which meet recognized professional standards. A marriage and family therapist may, however, indicate, if it is factual, a limitation of his/her practice or that he/she practices within one or more particular areas of marriage and family treatment in public pronouncements which will assist laypersons in selecting a marriage and family therapist and accurately describe the limited area in which the member practices.

I. The marriage and family therapist should support the creation and evolution of ethical, approved plans (such as marriage and family therapist referral systems) which aid in the selection of qualified therapists.

Section II: Regulations

A. The American Association for Marriage and Family Therapy is the sole owner of its name, its logo, and the abbreviated initials AAMFT. Use of the name, logo, and initials is restricted to the following conditions.

1. Only individual clinical members may identify their membership in AAMFT in public information or advertising materials, not associates or students of organizations.

2. The initials AAMFT may not be used following one's name in the manner of an academic degree because this is misleading.

3. Use of the logo is limited to the association, its committees and regional divisions when they are engaged in bona fide activities as units or divisions of AAMFT.

4. A regional division or chapter of AAMFT may use the AAMFT insignia to list its individual members as a group (e.g., in the Yellow Pages). When all Clinical Members practicing within a directory district have been invited to list, any one or more member may do so.

B. A marriage and family therapist shall not knowingly make a representation about his/her ability, background, or experience, or that of a partner or associate, or about the fee or any other aspect of a proposed professional engagement, that is false, fraudulent, misleading, or deceptive, and that might reasonably be expected to induce reliance by a member of the public.

C. Without limitation, a false, fraudulent, misleading, or deceptive statement or claim includes a statement or claim which:

1. Contains a material misrepresentation of fact;

2. Omits to state any material fact necessary to make the statement, in light of all circumstances, not misleading;

3. Is intended or is likely to create an unjustified expectation;

4. Relates to professional fees other than:

   a. a statement of the fee for an initial consultation; a statement of the fee charges for a specific service, the description of which would not be misunderstood or be deceptive;

   b. a statement of the range of fees for specifically described services, provided there is a reasonable disclosure of all relevant variables and considerations so that the statement would not be misunderstood or be deceptive;

   c. a statement of specified hourly rates, provided the statement makes clear that the total charge will vary according to the number of hours devoted to the matter;

   d. the availability of credit arrangements; or

5. Contains a representation or implication that is likely to cause an ordinary prudent person to misunderstand or be deceived or fails to contain reasonable warnings or disclaimers necessary to make a representation or implication not deceptive.

D. A member shall not, on his/her own behalf or on behalf of a partner or associate or any other therapist associated with the firm, use or participate in the use of any form of advertising of services which:

1. Contains statistical data or other information based on past performance or prediction of future success;

2. Contains a testimonial about or endorsement of a therapist;

3. Contains a statement of opinion as to the quality of the services or contains a representation or implication regarding the quality of services, whether thera-

peutic or educational, which is not susceptible of reasonable verification by the public;

4. Is intended or is likely to attract clients by use of showmanship or self-praising.

E. A member shall not compensate or give anything of value to a representative of the press, radio, television, or other communication medium in anticipation of or in return for professional publicity in a news item. A paid advertisement must be identified as such unless it is apparent from the context that it is a paid advertisement. If the paid advertisement is communicated to the public by use of radio or television, it shall be prerecorded, approved for broadcast by the therapist, and a recording of the actual transmission shall be retained by the therapist.

PROFESSIONAL NOTICES, LETTERHEADS, OFFICES, AND DIRECTORY LISTINGS

F. A member or group of members shall not use or participate in the use of a professional card, professional announcement card, office sign, letterhead, telephone directory listing, association directory listing, or a similar professional notice or device if it includes a statement or claim that is false, fraudulent, misleading, or deceptive within the meaning of Section II, C or that violates the regulations contained in Section II, D.

G. A member shall not practice under a name that is misleading as to the identity, responsibility, or status of those practicing thereunder, or is otherwise false, fraudulent, misleading, or deceptive within the meaning of Section II, C or is contrary to law. However, the name of a professional corporation or professional association may contain "P.C." or "P.A." or similar symbols indicating the nature of the organization.

H. A member shall not hold himself/herself out as having a partnership with one or more other qualified therapists unless they are in fact partners.

I. A partnership shall not be formed or continued between or among members in different geographical locations unless all enumerations of the members or associates of the firm on its letterhead and in other permissible listings make clear the limitations due to geographical separation of the members or associates of the firm.

J. Academic degrees earned from institutions accredited by regionally or nationally recognized accrediting agencies or associations may be used or permitted to be used provided that the statement or claim is neither false, fraudulent, misleading, or deceptive within the meaning of Section II, C.

SOLICITATION OF PROFESSIONAL EMPLOYMENT

K. A member shall not seek, by in-person contact, his/her employment as a therapist (or employment of a partner or associate) by a client who has not sought his/her advice regarding employment of a marriage and family therapist if:

1. The solicitation involves use of a statement or claim that is false, fraudulent, misleading, or deceptive within the meaning of Section II, C; or

2. The solicitation involves the use of undue influence; or

3. The potential client is apparently in a physical or mental condition which would make it unlikely that he or she could exercise reasonable, considered judgment as to the selection of a marriage and family therapist.

L. A member shall not compensate or give anything of value to a person or organization to recommend or secure his/her employment by a claim or as a reward for having made a recommendation resulting in his/her employment by a client.
M. A member shall not accept employment when he/she knows or it is obvious that the person who seeks his/her service does so as a result of conduct prohibited by this Section.

SUGGESTION OF NEED OF MARRIAGE OR FAMILY THERAPY

N. A member who has given unsolicited advice to a layperson that he/she/they should obtain marriage or family therapy shall not accept employment results from that advice if:
1. The advice embodies or implies a statement or claim that is false, fraudulent, misleading, or deceptive within the meaning of Section II, C or that violates the regulations contained in Section II, D; or
2. The advice involves the use by the marriage and family therapist of coercion, duress, compulsion, intimidation, unwarranted promises of benefits, overreaching, [or] vexatious or harassing conduct.

GLOSSARY

accreditation The granting of status to an academic institution or training program, indicating that its offerings are in accord with the standards established by the accrediting body.

acting out The overt manifestation of feelings and impulses through behavioral acts rather than through verbalizations.

anorexia nervosa Prolonged, severe diminution of appetite, particularly in adolescent females, to the point of becoming life-threatening.

behavioral The viewpoint that objective and experimentally verified procedures should be the basis for modifying maladaptive, undesired, or problematic behavior.

behavioral analysis An assessment procedure in which a behavioral therapist identifies the behavior to be changed, determines the factors that are currently maintaining the target behavior and formulates a treatment plan that includes specific criteria for measuring the success of the change effort.

behavioral marital therapy The application of behavioral principles and procedures to problems of marital discord.

behavioral parent training Training parents as change agents who apply behavioral principles and techniques to modify undesirable behavior in their own children.

blank screen In psychoanalytic therapy, the passive, neutral, unrevealing behavior of the analyst, onto which the patient may project his or her own fantasies.

blended family A reconstituted family formed by the marriage of divorced persons, establishing stepparent relationships as children from former marriages merge into a new family unit.

boundaries Delineations between parts of a system or between systems.

centrifugal Tending to move outward or away from the center.

centripetal Tending to move toward the center.

certification A state law defining who may call himself or herself by a particular professional title (for example, psychologist) and denying others the right to that title.

circularity The view that causality must be understood as occurring within a relationship context and by means of a network of interacting loops.

circular questioning An information-gathering technique, developed by the Milan associates, aimed at eliciting differences in perception about events or relationships from different family members, particularly regarding points in the family life cycle when significant coalition shifts and adaptations occurred.

classical conditioning A form of learning in which a previously neutral stimulus, through repeated pairing with a stimulus that ordinarily elicits a response, eventually elicits the response by itself.

closed system A system with impermeable boundaries, operating without interactions outside the system, and thus prone to increasing disorder.

cognitive behavior therapy A set of therapeutic procedures that attempts to change feelings and actions by modifying faulty thought patterns or destructive self-verbalizations.

cohabitation A more or less permanent, but not legally binding, living arrangement shared by two unmarried persons of the opposite sex.

common-law family A cohabiting man and woman presenting themselves as married although they have not gone through a formal legal wedding ceremony.

communication deviance According to Wynne, the disordered style of communication primarily characteristic of families with young adult schizophrenics.

complementarity According to Ackerman, the degree of harmony in the meshing of social roles in a family system.

complementary relationship A pattern of communication characterized by inequality and the maximization of differences between people (for example, dominant/submissive).

conductor A type of family therapist who is active, aggressive, colorful, and typically at the center of the family's verbal communication patterns.

conjoint Involving two or more family members concurrently in a therapy session.

conjoint sex therapy Therapeutic intervention with a couple as a unit in an effort to treat sexual dysfunction.

consensus-sensitive families According to Reiss, enmeshed families who view the world as unpredictable and therefore dangerous unless they maintain agreement at all times and on all issues.

contingency contracting An agreement made by two or more family members, specifying the circumstances under which who is to do what for whom, so that they may exchange rewarding behavior with each other.

continuing education Voluntary or mandated postdegree training, typically in the form of professional workshops and in-service training.

contracts As used by behavior therapists, written agreements to make specific behavior changes in the future.

co-therapy The simultaneous involvement of two therapists in working with an individual, group, or family.

counterparadox In systemic family therapy, placing the family in a therapeutic double-bind in order to counteract the members' exchange of paradoxical communications.

countertransference According to psychoanalytic theory, the therapist's unconscious emotional responses to a patient that may interfere with objectivity.

crisis intervention   Brief, direct therapy focused on the here and now in response to an emergency situation.

cybernetics   The study of methods of feedback control within a system.

defense mechanism   According to psychoanalytic theory, the process, usually unconscious, whereby the ego protects the individual from conscious awareness of threatening and therefore anxiety-producing thoughts, feelings, and impulses.

delinquent   A minor who engages in illegal or antisocial behavior.

deterioration effect   The finding, in psychotherapy research, that a certain proportion of clients are worse off after treatment than before.

developmental tasks   Problems to be overcome and conflicts to be mastered at various stages of the life cycle, enabling movement to the next stage of development.

diagnosis   The identification and classification of a specific disorder or abnormality.

didactic   Used for teaching purposes.

differentiation of self   According to Bowen, the separation of intellect and emotion that enables an individual to resist being overwhelmed by the emotional reactivity of his or her family.

disengagement   Family interaction in which members are isolated and unrelated to each other, each functioning separately and autonomously.

divorce mediation   A form of divorce arbitration in which the couple voluntarily learns to negotiate a mutually satisfactory settlement through brief, nonadversarial contact with a team knowledgeable in counseling and the law.

divorce therapy   Intervention by a marital/family therapist with a couple during the predivorce (deliberation) period, divorce (litigation) period or postdivorce (reequilibrium) period.

double-bind message   A set of contradictory messages from the same person to which an individual must respond, although his or her failure to please is inevitable whatever response is made.

dual-career marriage   A marriage in which husband and wife pursue active professional careers as well as active, involved family lives.

dyad   A liaison, temporary or permanent, between two people.

dysfunctional   Abnormal or impaired in functioning.

ego   According to psychoanalytic theory, the mediator between the demands of the instinctual drives (id) and the social prohibitions (superego); thus, it is the rational, problem-solving aspect of the personality.

emotional cutoff   According to Bowen, a flight from unresolved emotional ties to one's family.

emotional divorce   According to Bowen, marked emotional distance between parents, both of whom are equally immature, although one may accentuate the immaturity and the other deny it by acting overly responsible.

enactment   In structural family therapy, a facilitating intervention in which the family is induced to enact its relationship patterns spontaneously during the therapeutic session.

encounter group   A kind of therapy group in which intense interpersonal experiences are promoted to produce insight, personal growth, and sensitivity to the feelings of others.

enmeshment An extreme form of proximity and intensity in family interactions in which members are overconcerned and overinvolved in each others' lives.

entropy The tendency of a system to go into disorder, that is, to reach a disorganized and undifferentiated state.

environment-sensitive families According to Reiss, families in which the members believe they can cope with the world because it is knowable, orderly, and predictable.

epistemology The study of the origin, nature, and methods, as well as the limits, of knowledge.

ethnicity The unique characteristics of a cultural subgroup.

etiology The cause or causes of a disorder.

existential A philosophical view that people define their lives through the choices they make and accept responsibility for their choices and, therefore, for their existence.

experiential The therapeutic approach in which the therapist reveals himself or herself as a real person and uses that self in interacting with a family.

experiential/symbolic family therapy A nontheoretical form of family therapy advocated by Whitaker in which experiences in the therapist-family encounter, especially of a nonverbal kind, are believed to bring about behavior change.

extended family An enlarged and complex family unit in which a married couple and their children plus relatives of other generations (for example, grandparents, uncles, aunts) make up the family structure, all living together or in proximity to one another.

extinction The elimination of behavior as the result of nonreinforcement.

family choreography The charting of shifting transactional patterns within a family through a succession of family sculpting exercises.

family context therapy Bell's therapeutic effort to enhance a family's environment, in order to improve overall family functioning.

family contract game A problem-solving board game, developed by Blechman, for improving a family's negotiating skills.

family crisis therapy A crisis-intervention orientation to family therapy in which the family as a system is helped to restore its previous level of functioning; in some cases, with schizophrenics, hospitalization can be avoided.

family drawings A projective method whereby family members are asked to make pictorial representations of the family as it is organized.

family floor plan A nonverbal assessment device in which a family member draws a floor plan of a current or past dwelling in order to stimulate verbal and emotional responses.

family group therapy The intervention techniques developed by Bell based on social-psychological principles of small-group behavior.

family life chronology Satir's technique in which current family functioning is appraised by first obtaining some understanding of the family's history.

family life cycle Stages of a family's life, beginning with marriage and ending with the death of both marital partners.

family photo reconnaissance An assessment device whereby clients are encouraged to bring significant photos from the past into the therapy session, so that they may be stimulated to retrieve buried emotions connected with the depicted scenes.

family projection process   In Bowen's viewpoint, the mechanism by which parental conflicts are transmitted, through the process of projection, onto children.

family puppet interview   An assessment device directed particularly at young children who lack verbal skills but can act out family scenes through puppets.

family sculpture   An arrangement of the members of a family in space, with the physical placement of each figure determined by an individual family member acting as "director"; the tableau represents his or her view of family relationships.

feedback   Returned information about the consequences of an event.

feedback loop   A circle of responses, in which there is a return flow of information in a system.

first-order changes   Superficial changes within a system that have no effect on changing the structure of the system itself.

functional analysis   A behavioral assessment of a problem in order to determine what elicits and maintains the problem and how to extinguish it.

fusion   In Bowen's theory, a lack of differentiation between the intellect and emotionality, so that the former exists as an adjunct to the latter.

gay couples   Couples of the same gender who develop and maintain a homosexual or lesbian relationship.

general systems theory   The study of the relationship of interactional parts in context, emphasizing their unity and organizational hierarchy.

genogram   A schematic diagram of a family's multigenerational relationship system.

Gestalt family therapy   A form of experiential family therapy loosely based on the principles of Gestalt psychology.

group therapy   A form of psychotherapy in which several persons are treated simultaneously by a therapist and are helped therapeutically through their interaction with each other.

homeostasis   The self-maintenance of a system in balance or equilibrium.

humanistic   The life-affirming viewpoint that emphasizes each person's uniqueness and worth, as well as his or her potential for continued personal growth and fulfillment.

human-potential movement   The movement concerned with expanded sensory awareness, enrichment of life experiences, and fulfillment of the potential for creativity and joy within each person.

hypnotherapy   A psychotherapeutic effort aided by an artificially induced trance-like state that is caused by suggestion.

hypothesizing   As used by Selvini-Palazzoli and the Milan group, therapists' suppositions regarding how and why a family's problems have developed and persisted, formulated in advance of meeting with the family.

identified patient   The family member with the presenting symptoms; thus, the person who initially seeks treatment.

information processing   The gathering, distilling, storing, and retrieving of information; the flow of information through a system, as in a computer program.

insight   Self-awareness, especially regarding one's own motivation and behavior.

intergenerational-contextual therapy   A technique of family therapy, developed by Boszormenyi-Nagy and co-workers, that attempts to build responsible, trustworthy behavior, taking into account the entitlements of all family members.

interlocking pathology   According to Ackerman, multiple forms of disability or dysfunction in a family that are interdependent in the way they are expressed or controlled.

interpersonal   Transactions, verbal and otherwise, between two or more persons.

interpersonal distance-sensitive families   According to Reiss, disengaged families whose members refuse to depend on each other, out of fear that dependence reflects personal weakness and insecurity.

intrapsychic   Within the mind or psyche; this term is used especially in relation to conflicting forces.

introjects   Imprints or memories of the past, usually based on unresolved relationships with one's parents, that continue to impose themselves on current relationships with one's spouse and children.

licensing   A state law defining the practice of a profession (for example, marital/ family therapy) and specifying which services members of that profession are qualified to offer to the public for a fee.

life cycle   See family life cycle.

live supervision   The active guidance of a therapist at work by an observer behind a one-way mirror who offers suggestions by telephone, earphone, or by calling the therapist out of the consultation room.

marathon   An intensive, uninterrupted group experience, generally extending over several days, that is focused on the ongoing process of encounter among group members.

marital schism   According to Lidz, a marital situation characterized by disharmony, self-preoccupation, the undermining of the spouse, and frequent threats of divorce by one or both partners.

marital skew   According to Lidz, a situation in which a marriage is maintained at the expense of the distortion of reality.

medical model   A set of assumptions underlying the view that abnormal behavior patterns are analogous to physical diseases.

metacommunication   A communication that structures and adds meaning to what has already been said (for example, a communication, such as a nonverbal nod, wink, or smile, that qualifies a verbal message).

mimesis   A technique in structural family therapy in which the therapist deliberately mimics the family's style in an effort to join the family and bring about changes from within.

modeling   A form of learning that is based on the imitation of behavior that is observed in others; it is especially common in young children.

multigenerational transmission process   According to Bowen's family theory, the notion that schizophrenia and other severe mental disorders are processes that require several generations to develop.

multiple family therapy   A form of psychotherapy in which the members of several families are seen together as a group.

multiple impact therapy   A form of psychotherapy in which the members of a single family are seen all together or in various combinations for intensive interaction with a team of professionals over a two-day period.

mystification   A masking effect, used by one or more participants in a relationship, in order to obscure the real nature of the conflict and maintain the status quo.

negative reinforcement   The termination of or escape from an aversive event or situation as a result of performing some desired behavior.

negentropy   The tendency of a system to remain flexible and open to change.

network therapy   A form of group therapy carried out in the home of a patient (typically, a schizophrenic) in which family, friends, neighbors, and others participate in treatment and rehabilitation.

neuro-linguistic programming   An approach developed by Bandler and Grinder that draws attention to certain linguistic principles and observable neurological correlates of internal thought processing in an effort to program changes in individuals.

neurotic   A person with a mild or moderate functional disorder marked by subjective feelings of anxiety as well as inadequate coping devices that are used as defenses against anxiety.

neutrality   The effort by systemic family therapists to avoid becoming part of a family alliance or coalition.

nuclear family   A family composed of a husband, wife, and their offspring, living together as a unit.

nuclear family emotional system   In Bowen's view, a family's way of coping with tension and maintaining stability.

object relations theory   The view, first proposed by Fairbairn and adapted to the family by Framo, that the basic human motive is the search for satisfying relationships.

Oedipus complex   According to psychoanalytic theory, the unconscious desire of a boy at the phallic stage to have sexual relations with his mother, with an accompanying fear of castration by his father in retaliation for his rivalry.

open system   A system with more or less permeable boundaries that permit interaction between component parts or subsystems, and is thus likely to function in an orderly manner.

operant conditioning   A form of learning in which correct or desired responses are rewarded or reinforced, thus increasing the probability that these responses will recur.

operant-interpersonal therapy   An approach to marriage counseling, advocated by Stuart, based on operant conditioning theory, particularly the exchange between partners of positive reinforcements.

organization   In systems theory, the notion that the units of a system relate to each other in some consistent fashion, and that the system is structured by those relationships.

paradigm   A set of assumptions, delimiting an area to be investigated scientifically and specifying the methods to be used to collect and interpret the forthcoming data.

paradoxical communication   A family's characteristic way of communicating that is internally inconsistent and contradictory, as in a double-bind message.

paradoxical intervention A clinical intervention technique whereby a therapist gives a patient or family a directive he or she wants resisted; the resulting change takes place as a result of defying the therapist.

parentification The assumption by a child of the nurturing, teaching role of a parent, temporarily or permanently.

pathogenic Pathology-producing.

pathological Concerned with disease or dysfunction.

phenomenological The view in psychology that to understand fully the causes of another person's behavior requires an understanding of how he or she subjectively experiences the world, rather than of comprehending the physical or objective reality of that world.

phobia An intense, irrational fear of a harmless object or situation that the individual seeks to avoid.

positive connotation A reframing technique advanced by Selvini-Palazzoli whereby positive motives are ascribed to family behavior because such behavior helps maintain balance in the system.

positive reinforcement A reward that strengthens a response and increases the probability of its recurrence.

prescribing the symptom A paradoxical intervention, first developed by Jackson, in which the client is put in a position of abandoning a symptom or admitting that it is under voluntary control.

pretend techniques Paradoxical interventions developed by Madanes, based on play and fantasy, in which clients are directed to "pretend" to have a symptom; the paradox is that if they are pretending, the symptom may be exposed as unreal.

prognosis A prediction or forecast about the outcome of a disorder, including an indication of its probable duration and course.

projective systems According to Skynner, the unrealistic expectations, carried over from childhood, of people with relationship difficulties.

projective technique A psychological test that deliberately presents unstructured and ambiguous stimuli to discover the examinee's unconscious processes and the latent aspects of his or her personality.

pseudohostility According to Wynne, a family's inauthentic way of relating in which its chronic conflict and alienation are denied and obscured by superficial bickering.

pseudomutuality A relationship between or among family members that has the appearance of being open and mutually understanding, when in fact it is not.

psychoanalysis A comprehensive theory of personality development and a set of therapeutic techniques that were developed by Sigmund Freud in the early 1900s.

psychodrama An early form of group therapy that was developed by Moreno and is still practiced today; patients role-play themselves or significant others in their lives to achieve catharsis or to resolve conflicts and gain greater spontaneity.

psychodynamics The interplay of opposing forces within a person as the basis for understanding human motivation.

psychonosis Howell's term for a form of psychopathology in which there is a disruption of psychological functioning as well as signs and symptoms indicative of dysfunction.

psychosomatic A physical disorder of the body caused or aggravated by chronic emotional stress, usually involving a single organ system under autonomic nervous system innervation.

punctuation The idea advanced by the communication theorists that, within a family, each participant believes whatever he or she says is caused by what the others say.

reactor A type of therapist whose style is subtle and indirect; the therapist prefers to observe and clarify the family group process rather than serve as an active, aggressive, or colorful group leader.

redundancy principle Repetitive behavior sequences within a family.

reframing Relabeling behavior in a family by putting it in a new, usually more positive perspective ("mother is trying to help" rather than "she's intrusive"), so that new options become available and behavior change can occur.

regression An unconscious defense mechanism in which an individual exhibits behavior that is more appropriate to an earlier developmental level.

reinforcement A reward (positive reinforcement) or punishment (negative reinforcement) that is intended to change the probability of the recurrence of a response.

relabeling Verbal redefinition of an event in order to make dysfunctional behavior seem reasonable and understandable, and thus provoke different kinds of reactions to the behavior on the part of family members.

retribalization In network therapy, the effort to create or strengthen tribal-like bonds between the members of a family in order to facilitate their ability to seek solutions to family crises.

role An expected behavior pattern, socially defined, that accompanies a social position, as in a family.

role overload Stress in a family that occurs when members (for example, husband and wife) attempt to fulfill a greater variety of roles than their energies or available time will permit.

Rorschach test A projective technique that consists of a standard set of ten cards containing patterns that are formed by inkblots; it is used to assess an examinee's basic personality characteristics.

rubber fence According to Wynne, a family boundary that is unstable but so flexible that it stretches to include whatever it considers complementary to its structure or contracts to extrude whatever it considers alien.

sadomasochistic The chronic exchange of pain or humiliation in the relationship between two or more persons.

scapegoat A family member, likely to be the identified patient, cast in a role that exposes him or her to criticism, punishment, or scorn.

schizophrenia A major form of functional psychosis marked by severe disturbances in thinking, restricted affect, delusions, hallucinations, and withdrawal from reality.

schizophrenogenic mother As described by Fromm-Reichmann, a cold, domineering, possessive but rejecting mother whose behavior is thought to be a determinant of schizophrenia in her offspring.

second-order changes Fundamental changes in a system's structure and functioning.

sets   The assumptions, manner, and expectations with which a family approaches and intends to deal with problem situations.

shaping   A form of behavior therapy, based on operant conditioning principles, in which successive approximations of desired behavior are reinforced until the desired behavior is achieved.

sibling position   In Bowen's view, the notion that interactions between spouses may be influenced by their family of origin birth order (for example, oldest child married to youngest child).

single-parent family   Household led by one parent (mother or father) due to divorce, desertion or death of a spouse, or because of never having married.

social-learning theory   The view that a person's behavior is best understood when the social conditions under which he or she learned that behavior are taken into consideration.

social network intervention   See network therapy.

societal regression   An extension of Bowen's thinking about the emotional forces operating in society during the last several decades: as the level of anxiety has increased in society, the forces leading to togetherness in the family have become more intense and the forces leading to individuation have been eroded.

strategic family therapy   A therapeutic approach advanced by Haley and Madanes in which the therapist develops a plan or strategy for solving the presenting problem.

structural family therapy   A family therapy approach, identified with Minuchin, directed at changing the family organization or structure in order to alter behavior patterns in its members; the therapist changes the system by actively participating in its interpersonal transactions.

subsystem   An organized unit within an overall system; every system contains within it a number of such coexisting component parts.

symmetrical escalation   A spiraling effect in the communication between two people whose relationship is based on equality, so that vindictiveness leads to greater vindictiveness in return, viciousness to greater viciousness, and so on.

symmetrical relationship   A pattern of communication characterized by an emphasis on equality and the minimization of difference between people.

symptom   A medical term for an observed physical, emotional, or behavioral sign of a disorder or disease.

system   A set of units and the interrelationships between those units.

systemic family therapy   The therapeutic approach of Selvini-Palazzoli and the Milan associates based on a systematic inquiry into how different family members process information and construe events in order to keep the family system stabilized.

Thematic Apperception Test (TAT)   A projective technique in which the examinee, by making up stories in response to a series of semi-ambiguous pictures depicting various scenes, reveals his or her inner fantasies and conflicts.

therapeutic double-bind   A general term for a variety of paradoxical techniques, used primarily by Jackson and other communication therapists, in which clients are directed to continue to manifest their symptoms; caught in a bind, they must give up the symptom or acknowledge control over it.

time-out   A behavior therapy procedure, based on operant-conditioning principles, in which undesirable behavior is reduced by temporarily removing the person (most often a child) from a setting that supplies the reinforcers for the behavior.

token economy A behavior therapy system, based on the principles of operant conditioning, in which institutionalized patients are given rewards (such as poker chips) for socially constructive behavior; the rewards are later exchangeable for special privileges not available to other patients.

tracking In structural family therapy, a technique by which the therapist deliberately remains aware of the symbols, style, language, and values of the family, and uses them in order to communicate with the family more effectively.

transference In psychoanalytic treatment, the unconscious shifting to the analyst of a patient's feelings, drives, attitudes and fantasies (both positive and negative) that are displacements from reactions to significant people in the patient's past.

triad A three-person relationship.

triadic-based therapy A family therapy approach advocated by Zuk in which the therapist, as a third person, acts as go-between in working with a couple in order to disrupt the partners' chronic patterns of relating to one another.

triangle According to Bowen, the tendency of a two-person emotional system under stress to recruit a third person into the system in order to lower the intensity and anxiety and to gain stability.

typecasting Ascribing or assigning a stereotypical role to someone.

undifferentiated family ego mass Bowen's early term for intense interdependency (symbiosis) in a family; an individual sense of self fails to develop in members because of the existing fusion or emotional oneness.

videoplayback The videotape recording and replaying of a family therapy session for therapeutic or training purposes.

wholeness The systems theory view that combining units or elements produces an entity greater than the sum of its parts.

Zeitgeist The spirit of the time; the prevailing cultural climate at a particular period in history.

REFERENCES

Ackerman, N. W. The family as a social and emotional unit. *Bulletin of the Kansas Mental Hygiene Society*, 1937, 12, No. 2.

Ackerman, N. W. Interlocking pathology in family relationships. In S. Rado & G. Daniels (Eds.), *Changing concepts of psychoanalytic medicine*. New York: Grune & Stratton, 1956.

Ackerman, N. W. *The psychodynamics of family life*. New York: Basic Books, 1958.

Ackerman, N. W. *Treating the troubled family*. New York: Basic Books, 1966.

Ackerman, N. W. Family psychotherapy and psychoanalysis: The implications of difference. In N. W. Ackerman (Ed.), *Family process*. New York: Basic Books, 1970. (a)

Ackerman, N. W. (Ed.). *Family therapy in transition*. New York: Little, Brown, 1970. (b)

Ackerman, N. W. The growing edge of family therapy. In C. Sager & H. Kaplan (Eds.), *Progress in group and family therapy*. New York: Brunner/Mazel, 1972.

Ackerman, N. W., & Behrens, M. L. Family diagnosis and clinical process. In S. Arieti & G. Caplan (Eds.), *American handbook of psychiatry II: Child and adolescent psychiatry, sociocultural and community psychiatry* (2nd ed.). New York: Basic Books, 1974.

Alexander, J., & Parsons, B. V. *Functional family therapy*. Monterey, Calif.: Brooks/Cole, 1982.

Alger, I. Audio-visual techniques in family therapy. In D. A. Bloch (Ed.), *Techniques of family psychotherapy: A primer*. New York: Grune & Stratton, 1973.

Alger, I. Integrating immediate video playback in family therapy. In P. J. Guerin, Jr. (Ed.), *Family therapy: Theory and practice*. New York: Gardner Press, 1976. (a)

Alger, I. Multiple couple therapy. In P. J. Guerin, Jr. (Ed.), *Family therapy: Theory and practice*. New York: Gardner Press, 1976. (b)

Anderson, C. M., & Stewart, S. *Mastering resistance: A practical guide to family therapy*. New York: Guilford Press, 1983.

Andolfi, M. *Family therapy: An interactional approach*. New York: Plenum, 1979.

Anthony, E. J., & Rizzo, A. Adolescent girls who kill or try to kill their fathers. In E. J. Anthony & C. Koupernik (Eds.), *The child in his family II: The impact of disease and death*. New York: Wiley, 1973.

Aponte, H. J. Underorganization in the poor family. In P. J. Guerin, Jr. (Ed.), *Family therapy: Theory and practice*. New York: Gardner Press, 1976.

Aponte, H. J., & Van Deusen, J. M. Structural family therapy. In A. S. Gurman & D. P. Kniskern (Eds.), *Handbook of family therapy*. New York: Brunner/Mazel, 1981.

Auerswald, E. H. Interdisciplinary versus ecological approach. In C. J. Sager & H. S. Kaplan (Eds.), *Progress in group and family therapy*. New York: Brunner/Mazel, 1972.

Back, K. W. Intervention techniques: Small groups. In M. R. Rosenzweig & L. W. Porter (Eds.), *Annual review of psychology* (Vol. 25). Palo Alto, Calif.: Annual Reviews, 1974.

Bandler, R., & Grinder, J. *The structure of magic* (Vol. 1). Palo Alto, Calif.: Science and Behavior Books, 1975.

Bandler, R., Grinder, J., & Satir, V. M. *Changing with families*. Palo Alto, Calif.: Science and Behavior Books, 1976.

Bandura, A. *Social learning theory*. Englewood Cliffs, N.J.: Prentice-Hall, 1977.

Baruth, L. G., & Huber, C. H. *An introduction to marital theory and therapy*. Monterey, Calif.: Brooks/Cole, 1984.

Bateson, G. *Naven* (2nd ed.). Stanford, Calif.: Stanford University Press, 1958.

Bateson, G. *Steps to an ecology of mind*. New York: Ballantine, 1972.

Bateson, G. *Mind and nature*. New York: Dutton, 1979.

Bateson, G., Jackson, D. D., Haley, J., & Weakland, J. Towards a theory of schizophrenia. *Behavioral Science*, 1956, *1*, 251–264.

Beavers, W. R. *Psychotherapy and growth: Family systems perspective*. New York: Brunner/Mazel, 1977.

Beavers, W. R. Healthy, midrange, and severely dysfunctional families. In F. Walsh (Ed.), *Normal family processes*. New York: Guilford Press, 1982.

Beck, D. F., & Jones, M. A. *Progress on family problems*. New York: Family Service Association of America, 1973.

Beels, C., & Ferber, A. Family therapy: A view. *Family Process*, 1969, *8*, 280–332.

Bell, J. E. *Family group therapy* (Public Health Monograph No. 64). Washington, D.C.: U.S. Government Printing Office, 1961.

Bell, J. E. *Family therapy*. New York: Aronson, 1975.

Bell, J. E. A theoretical framework for family group therapy. In P. J. Guerin, Jr. (Ed.), *Family therapy: Theory and practice*. New York: Gardner Press, 1976.

Bell, J. E. Family group therapy. In B. B. Wolman & G. Stricker (Eds.), *Handbook of family and marital therapy*. New York: Plenum, 1983.

Berger, M., & Dammann, C. Live supervision as context, treatment, and training. *Family Process*, 1982, *21*, 337–344.

Berger, M. M. (Ed.). *Videotape techniques in psychiatric training and treatment* (Rev. ed.). New York: Brunner/Mazel, 1978.

Berkowitz, B. P., & Graziano, A. M. Training parents as behavior therapists: A review. *Behavior Research and Therapy*, 1972, *10*, 297–317.

Bertalanffy, L. von. *General systems theory: Foundation, development, applications*. New York: Braziller, 1968.

Bing, E. The conjoint family drawing. *Family Process*, 1970, *9*, 173–194.

Bion, W. R. *Experiences in groups*. New York: Basic Books, 1961.

Blechman, E. A. The family contract game: A tool to teach interpersonal problem solving. *Family Coordinator*, 1974, *23*, 269–281.

Bloch, D. A. The family of the psychiatric patient. In S. Arieti (Ed.), *American handbook of psychiatry I: The foundations of psychiatry*. New York: Basic Books, 1974.

Bloch, D. A., & La Perriere, K. Techniques of family therapy: A conceptual frame. In D. A. Bloch (Ed.), *Techniques of family psychotherapy: A primer*. New York: Grune & Stratton, 1973.

Bloch, D. A., & Simon, R. (Eds.). *The strength of family therapy: Selected papers of Nathan W. Ackerman.* New York: Brunner/Mazel, 1982.

Bloch, D. A., & Weiss, H. M. Training facilities in marital and family therapy. *Family Process*, 1981, *20*, 133–146.

Bodin, A. M. Family therapy training literature: A brief guide. *Family Process*, 1969, *8*, 729–779. (a)

Bodin, A. M. Videotape in training family therapists. *The Journal of Nervous and Mental Disease*, 1969, *148*, 251–261. (b)

Bodin, A. M. The interactional view: Family therapy approaches of the Mental Research Institute. In A. S. Gurman & D. P. Kniskern (Eds.), *Handbook of family therapy.* New York: Brunner/Mazel, 1981.

Bodin, A. M. Family therapy. Unpublished manuscript. 1983.

Boszormenyi-Nagy, I., & Framo, J. L. *Intensive family therapy: Theoretical and practical aspects.* New York: Harper & Row, 1965.

Boszormenyi-Nagy, I., & Krasner, B. R. The contextual approach to psychotherapy: Premises and implications. In G. Berenson & H. White (Eds.), *Annual review of family therapy* (Vol. 1). New York: Human Sciences Press, 1981.

Boszormenyi-Nagy, I., & Spark, G. M. *Invisible loyalties: Reciprocity in intergenerational family therapy.* New York: Harper & Row, 1973.

Boszormenyi-Nagy, I., & Ulrich, D. Contextual family therapy. In A. S. Gurman & D. P. Kniskern (Eds.), *Handbook of family therapy.* New York: Brunner/Mazel, 1981.

Bowen, M. A family concept of schizophrenia. In D. D. Jackson (Ed.), *The etiology of schizophrenia.* New York: Basic Books, 1960.

Bowen, M. The use of family theory in clinical practice. *Comprehensive Psychiatry*, 1966, *7*, 345–374.

Bowen, M. Family therapy after twenty years. In S. Arieti, D. X. Freeman, & J. E. Dyrud (Eds.), *American handbook of psychiatry V: Treatment* (2nd ed.). New York: Basic Books, 1975.

Bowen, M. Theory in the practice of psychotherapy. In P. J. Guerin, Jr. (Ed.), *Family therapy: Theory and practice.* New York: Gardner Press, 1976.

Bowen, M. Family systems theory and society. In J. P. Lorio & L. McClenathan (Eds.), *Georgetown family symposia: Volume II* (1973–1974). Washington, D.C.: Georgetown Family Center, 1977.

Bowen, M. *Family therapy in clinical practice.* New York: Aronson, 1978.

Broderick, C., & Smith, J. The general systems approach to the family. In W. R. Burr, R. Hill, F. I. Nye, & I. L. Reiss (Eds.), *Contemporary theories about the family* (Vol. 2). New York: Free Press, 1979.

Broderick, C. B., & Schrader, S. S. The history of professional marriage and family therapy. In A. S. Gurman & D. P. Kniskern (Eds.), *Handbook of family therapy.* New York: Brunner/Mazel, 1981.

Brody, E. M. Aging and family personality: A developmental view. *Family Process*, 1974, *13*, 23–38.

Byng-Hall, J. The use of the earphone in supervision. In R. Whiffen & J. Byng-Hall (Eds.), *Family therapy supervision: Recent developments in practice.* London: Academic Press, 1982.

Carter, E. A., & McGoldrick, M. The family life cycle and family therapy: An overview. In E. A. Carter & M. McGoldrick (Eds.), *The family life cycle: A framework for family therapy.* New York: Gardner Press, 1980.

Cleghorn, J. M., & Levin, S. Training family therapists by setting learning objectives. *American Journal of Orthopsychiatry*, 1973, *43*, 439–446.

Cohen, M., Goldenberg, I. T., & Goldenberg, H. Treating families of bone marrow recipients and donors. *Journal of Marriage and Family Counseling*, 1977, *3*, 45–51.

Cohen, R. E. Borderline conditions: A transcultural perspective. *Psychiatric Annals*,

1974, 4, 7–20.

Colapinto, J. The relative value of empirical evidence. *Family Process*, 1979, *18*, 427–441.

Colapinto, J. Structural family therapy. In A. M. Horne & M. M. Ohlsen (Eds.), *Family counseling and therapy*. Itasca, Ill.: F. E. Peacock, 1982.

Colon, F. The family life cycle of the multiproblem poor family. In E. A. Carter & M. McGoldrick (Eds.), *The family life cycle: A framework for family therapy*. New York: Gardner Press, 1980.

Constantine, L. L. Designed experience: A multiple, goal-directed training program in family therapy. *Family Process*, 1976, *15*, 373–387.

Constantine, L. L. Family sculpture and relationship mapping techniques. *Journal of Marriage and Family Counseling*, 1978, *4*(2), 13–24.

Coogler, O. J. *Structural mediation in divorce settlement*. Lexington, Mass.: Lexington Books, 1978.

Cooper, A., Rampage, C., & Soucy, G. Family therapy training in clinical psychology programs. *Family Process*, 1981, *20*, 155–166.

Cooper, D. *The death of the family*. New York: Vintage, 1970.

Cooper, S. Treatment of parents. In S. Arieti & G. Caplan (Eds.), *American handbook of psychiatry II: Child and adolescent psychiatry, sociocultural and community psychiatry* (2nd ed.). New York: Basic Books, 1974.

Coppersmith, E. The family floor plan: A tool of training, assessment, and intervention in family therapy. *Journal of Marital and Family Therapy*, 1980, *6*, 141–145.

Corey, G. *Theory and practice of counseling and psychotherapy* (2nd ed.). Monterey, Calif.: Brooks/Cole, 1982.

Cromwell, R. E., Olson, D. H. L., & Fournier, D. G. Diagnosis and evaluation in marital and family counseling. In D. H. L. Olson (Ed.), *Treating relationships*. Lake Mills, Iowa: Graphic, 1976.

D'Andrade, R. G. Sex differences and cultural institutions. In R. A. Le Vine (Ed.), *Culture and personality: Contemporary readings*. Chicago: Aldine-Atherton, 1974.

Dell, P. F. Beyond homeostasis: Toward a concept of coherence. *Family Process*, 1982, *21*, 21–42.

Dicks, H. V. *Marital tensions*. New York: Basic Books, 1967.

Dilts, R., Grinder, J., Bandler, R., Cameron-Bandler, L., & De Lozier, J. *Neuro-linguistic programming* (Vol. 1). Cupertino, Calif.: Meta Publications, 1980.

Dinkmeyer, D., & McKay, G. D. *Systematic training for effective parenting*. Circle Pines, Minn.: American Guidance Service, 1976.

Doyle, A. M., & Dorlac, C. Treating chronic crisis bearers and their families. *Journal of Marriage and Family Counseling*, 1978, *4*(3), 37–42.

Duhl, F. J., Kantor, D., & Duhl, B. S. Learning, space, and action in family therapy: A primer of sculpture. In D. A. Bloch (Ed.), *Techniques of family psychotherapy: A primer*. New York: Grune & Stratton, 1973.

Duvall, E. M. *Marriage and family development* (5th ed.). New York: Lippincott, 1977.

Elkin, M. Postdivorce counseling in a conciliation court. *Journal of Divorce*, 1977, *1*, 55–65.

Epstein, N., Bishop, D. S., & Baldwin, L. M. McMaster model of family functioning: A view of the normal family. In F. Walsh (Ed.), *Normal family processes*. New York: Guilford Press, 1982.

Erickson, G. D., & Hogan, T. P. *Family therapy: An introduction to theory and technique* (2nd ed.). Monterey, Calif.: Brooks/Cole, 1981.

Fairbairn, W. R. *An object-relations theory of personality*. New York: Basic Books, 1954.

Falloon, I. R. H., & Liberman, R. P. Behavioral therapy for families with child management problems. In M. Textor (Ed.), *Family pathology and its treatment*. New York: Aronson, 1982.

Feldman, L. B. Sex roles and family dynamics. In F. Walsh (Ed.), *Normal family processes*. New York: Guilford Press, 1982.

Ferber, A., & Ranz, J. How to succeed in family therapy: Set reachable goals—give workable tasks. In C. Sager & H. S. Kaplan (Eds.), *Progress in group and family therapy*. New York: Brunner/Mazel, 1972.

Ferreira, A. J. Family myths. *Psychiatric Research Reports* (No. 20), 1966, 86–87.

Fisch, R., Weakland, J. H., & Segal, L. *The tactics of change: Doing therapy briefly*. San Francisco: Jossey-Bass, 1982.

Fisher, L. Dimensions of family assessment: A critical review. *Journal of Marriage and Family Counseling*, 1976, *2*, 367–382.

Fisher, R., & Ury, W. *Getting to yes: Negotiating agreement without giving in*. Boston: Houghton Mifflin, 1981.

Fleck, S. A. A general systems approach to severe family pathology. *American Journal of Psychiatry*, 1976, *133*, 669–673.

Fox, R. E. Family therapy. In I. B. Weiner (Ed.), *Clinical methods in psychology*. New York: Wiley, 1976.

Framo, J. L. Rationale and technique of intensive family therapy. In I. Boszormenyi-Nagy & J. L. Framo (Eds.), *Intensive family therapy: Theoretical and practical aspects*. New York: Harper & Row, 1965.

Framo, J. L. (Ed.). *Family interaction: A dialogue between family researchers and family therapists*. New York: Springer, 1972.

Framo, J. L. Marriage therapy in a couples group. In D. A. Bloch (Ed.), *Techniques of family psychotherapy: A primer*. New York: Grune & Stratton, 1973.

Framo, J. L. Personal reflections of a family therapist. *Journal of Marriage and Family Counseling*, 1975, *1*, 1–22.

Framo, J. L. Family of origin as a therapeutic resource for adults in marital and family therapy: You can and should go home again. *Family Process*, 1976, *15*, 193–210.

Framo, J. L. In-laws and out-laws: A marital case of kinship confusion. In P. Papp (Ed.), *Family therapy: Full length case studies*. New York: Gardner Press, 1978.

Framo, J. L. The integration of marital therapy with sessions with family of origin. In A. S. Gurman & D. P. Kniskern (Eds.), *Handbook of family therapy*. New York: Brunner/Mazel, 1981.

Framo, J. L. *Explorations in marital and family therapy: Selected papers of James L. Framo*. New York: Springer, 1982.

Franklin, P., & Prosky, P. A standard initial interview. In D. A. Bloch (Ed.), *Techniques of family psychotherapy: A primer*. New York: Grune & Stratton, 1973.

Franks, C. M., & Wilson, G. T. (Eds.). *Annual review of behavior therapy: Theory and practice* (Vol. 3). New York: Brunner/Mazel, 1975.

Freeman, D. S. *Techniques of family therapy*. New York: Aronson, 1981.

Freud, S. Analysis of a phobia in a five-year-old boy (1909). *The standard edition of the complete psychological works of Sigmund Freud* (Vol. 10). London: Hogarth, 1955.

Freud, S. Fragments of an analysis of a case of hysteria (1905). *Collected papers* (Vol. 3). New York: Basic Books, 1959.

Fromm-Reichmann, F. Notes on the development of treatment of schizophrenics by psychoanalytic psychotherapy. *Psychiatry*, 1948, *11*, 263–273.

Gazda, G. M. Group psychotherapy and group counseling: Definitions and heritage. In G. M. Gazda (Ed.), *Basic approaches to group psychotherapy and group counseling* (2nd ed.). Springfield, Ill.: Charles C Thomas, 1975.

Gelles, R. J. *The violent home: A study of physical aggression between husbands and wives*. London: Sage, 1972.

Gladfelter, J. Films on group and family psychotherapy. In C. J. Sager & H. S. Kaplan (Eds.), *Progress in group and family therapy*. New York: Brunner/Mazel, 1972.

Glick, I. D., & Kessler, D. R. *Marital and family therapy* (2nd ed.). New York: Grune & Stratton, 1980.

References

Goldenberg, H. *Is training family therapists different from clinical training in general?* Paper presented at the American Psychological Association annual meeting, Montreal, Canada, 1973.

Goldenberg, H. *Abnormal psychology: A social/community approach.* Monterey, Calif.: Brooks/Cole, 1977.

Goldenberg, H. *Contemporary clinical psychology* (2nd ed.). Monterey, Calif.: Brooks/Cole, 1983.

Goldenberg, H., & Goldenberg, I. Homicide and the family. In B. L. Danto, J. Bruhns, & A. H. Kutscher (Eds.), *The human side of homicide.* New York: Columbia University Press, 1982.

Goldenberg, I., & Goldenberg, H. A family approach to psychological services. *American Journal of Psychoanalysis,* 1975, *35,* 317–328.

Goldenberg, I., & Goldenberg, H. *Treating a family following an adolescent member's suicide.* Paper and videotape presented at the International Congress on Suicide Prevention and Crisis Intervention, Helsinki, Finland, 1977.

Goldenberg, I., & Goldenberg, H. Historical roots of contemporary family therapy. In B. B. Wolman & G. Stricker (Eds.), *Handbook of family and marital therapy.* New York: Plenum, 1983.

Goldenberg, I., & Goldenberg, H. Treating the dual-career couple. *American Journal of Family Therapy,* 1984, *12*(2), 29–37.

Goldenberg, I., Stier, S., & Preston, T. The use of multiple family marathon as a teaching device. *Journal of Marriage and Family Counseling,* 1975, *1,* 343–349.

Goldstein, M. J., Rodnick, E. H., Jones, J. E., McPherson, S. R., & West, K. L. Familial precursors of schizophrenia spectrum disorders. In L. C. Wynne, R. L. Cromwell, & S. Matthysse (Eds.), *The nature of schizophrenia: New approaches to research and treatment.* New York: Wiley, 1978.

Gordon, S. B., & Davidson, N. Behavioral parent training. In A. S. Gurman & D. P. Kniskern (Eds.), *Handbook of family therapy.* New York: Brunner/Mazel, 1981.

Gorod, S., McCourt, W., & Cobb, J. The communications approach in alcoholism. *Quarterly Journal of Studies on Alcohol,* 1971, *32,* 651–668.

Gray, W., Duhl, F. J., & Rizzo, N. D. *General systems theory and psychiatry.* Boston: Little, Brown, 1969.

Green, R. J., & Framo, J. L. (Eds.). *Family therapy: Major contributions.* New York: International Universities Press, 1981.

Greenberg, G. S. The family interactional perspective: A study and examination of the work of Don D. Jackson. *Family Process,* 1977, *16,* 385–412.

Gritzer, P. H., & Okun, H. S. Multiple family group therapy: A model for all families. In B. B. Wolman & G. Stricker (Eds.), *Handbook of family and marital therapy.* New York: Plenum, 1983.

Group for the Advancement of Psychiatry. *The field of family therapy* (Report No. 78). New York: Group for the Advancement of Psychiatry, 1970.

Guerin, P. J., Jr. Family therapy: The first twenty-five years. In P. J. Guerin, Jr. (Ed.), *Family therapy: Theory and practice.* New York: Gardner Press, 1976.

Guerin, P. J., Jr., & Fogarty, T. Study your own family. In A. Ferber, M. Mendelsohn, & A. Napier (Eds.), *The book of family therapy.* New York: Science House, 1972.

Guerin, P. J., Jr., & Pendagast, E. G. Evaluation of family system and genogram. In P. J. Guerin, Jr. (Ed.), *Family therapy: Theory and practice.* New York: Gardner Press, 1976.

Guerney, B. J., Jr. *Relationship enhancement: Skills-training programs for therapy, problem prevention, and enrichment.* San Francisco: Jossey-Bass, 1977.

Guerney, L. F. Filial therapy program. In D. H. L. Olson (Ed.), *Treating relationships.* Lake Mills, Iowa: Graphic, 1976.

Gurin, G., Veroff, J., & Feld, S. *Americans view their mental health.* New York: Basic Books, 1960.

Gurman, A. S. Group marital therapy: Clinical and empirical implications for outcome research. *International Journal of Group Psychotherapy*, 1971, *21*, 174–189.

Gurman, A. S. Dimensions of marital therapy: A comparative analysis. *Journal of Marital and Family Therapy*, 1979, *5*, 5–18.

Gurman, A. S. Behavioral marriage therapy in the 1980's: The challenge of integration. *American Journal of Family Therapy*, 1980, *8*(2), 86–95.

Gurman, A. S. Family therapy research and the "new epistemology." *Journal of Marital and Family Therapy*, 1983, *9*, 227–234.

Gurman, A. S., & Kniskern, D. P. Research on marital and family therapy: Progress, perspective, and prospect. In S. L. Garfield & A. E. Bergin (Eds.), *Handbook of psychotherapy and behavior change: An empirical analysis* (2nd ed.). New York: Wiley, 1978.

Gurman, A. S., & Kniskern, D. P. Family therapy outcome research: Knowns and unknowns. In A. S. Gurman & D. P. Kniskern (Eds.), *Handbook of family therapy*. New York: Brunner/Mazel, 1981. (a)

Gurman, A. S., & Kniskern, D. P. (Eds.). *Handbook of family therapy*. New York: Brunner/Mazel, 1981. (b)

Gurman, A. S., & Kniskern, D. P. The outcome of family therapy: Implications for practice and training. In G. Berenson & H. White (Eds.), *Annual review of family therapy* (Vol. 1). New York: Human Sciences Press, 1981. (c)

Gurman, A. S., & Knudson, R. M. Behavior marriage therapy: I. A psychodynamic-systems analysis and critique. *Family Process*, 1978, *17*, 121–138.

Haley, J. *Strategies of psychotherapy*. New York: Grune & Stratton, 1963.

Haley, J. Family Therapy. *International Journal of Psychiatry*, 1970, *9*, 233–242.

Haley, J. Approaches to family therapy. In J. Haley (Ed.), *Changing families: A Family therapy reader*. New York: Grune & Stratton, 1971. (a)

Haley, J. Family therapy: A radical change. In J. Haley (Ed.), *Changing families: A family therapy reader*. New York: Grune & Stratton, 1971. (b)

Haley, J. *Uncommon therapy: The psychiatric techniques of Milton H. Erickson, M.D.* New York: Norton, 1973.

Haley, J. *Problem-solving therapy*. San Francisco: Jossey-Bass, 1976.

Haley, J. *Ordeal therapy: Unusual ways to change behavior*. San Francisco: Jossey-Bass, 1984.

Haley, J., & Hoffman, L. *Techniques of family therapy*. New York: Basic Books, 1967.

Hare-Mustin, R. T. Paradoxical tasks in family therapy: Who can resist? *Psychotherapy: Theory, Research and Practice*, 1976, *13*, 128–130.

Hare-Mustin, R. T. A feminist approach to family therapy. *Family Process*, 1978, *17*, 181–194.

Hare-Mustin, R. T. Family therapy may be dangerous to your health. *Professional Psychology*, 1980, *11*, 935–938.

Hareven, T. K. American families in transition: Historical perspectives on change. In F. Walsh (Ed.), *Normal family processes*. New York: Guilford Press, 1982.

Hatcher, C. Intrapersonal and interpersonal models: Blending Gestalt and family therapies. *Journal of Marriage and Family Counseling*, 1978, *4*, 63–68.

Haynes, J. M. *Divorce mediation: A practical guide for therapists and counselors*. New York: Springer, 1981.

Heiman, J. R., Lo Piccolo, L., & Lo Piccolo, J. The treatment of sexual dysfunction. In A. S. Gurman & D. P. Kniskern (Eds.), *Handbook of family therapy*. New York: Brunner/Mazel, 1981.

Hetherington, E. M., Cox, M., & Cox, R. Effects of divorce on parents and children. In M. E. Lamb (Ed.), *Nontraditional families: Parenting and child development*. Hillsdale, N.J.: Erlbaum, 1982.

Hines, P., & Hare-Mustin, R. T. Ethical concerns in family therapy. *Professional Psychology*, 1978, *9*, 165–171.

Hirsch, S., & Leff, J. *Abnormalities in parents of schizophrenics.* Oxford: Oxford University Press, 1975.

Hoffman, L. Deviation-amplifying processes in natural groups. In J. Haley (Ed.), *Changing families: A family therapy reader.* New York: Grune & Stratton, 1971.

Hoffman, L. The family life cycle and discontinuous change. In E. A. Carter & M. McGoldrick (Eds.), *The family life cycle: A framework for family therapy.* New York: Gardner Press, 1980.

Hoffman, L. *Foundations of family therapy.* New York: Basic Books, 1981.

Hoffman, L. W. Changes in family roles, socialization, and sex differences. *American Psychologist,* 1977, *32,* 644–657.

Holt, M., & Greiner, D. Co-therapy in the treatment of families. In P. J. Guerin, Jr. (Ed.), *Family therapy: Theory and practice.* New York: Gardner Press, 1976.

Howells, J. G. *Principles of family psychiatry.* New York: Brunner/Mazel, 1975.

Irwin, E., & Malloy, E. Family puppet interview. *Family Process,* 1975, *14,* 179–191.

Jackson, D. D. Family interaction, family homeostasis, and some implications for conjoint family therapy. In J. Masserman (Ed.), *Individual and family dynamics.* New York: Grune & Stratton, 1959.

Jackson, D. D. *The etiology of schizophrenia.* New York: Basic Books, 1960.

Jackson, D. D. Family rules: Marital quid pro quo. *Archives of General Psychiatry,* 1965, *12,* 589–594. (a)

Jackson, D. D. The study of the family. *Family Process,* 1965, *4,* 1–20. (b)

Jacobson, N. S. Behavioral marital therapy. In A. S. Gurman & D. P. Kniskern (Eds.), *Handbook of family therapy.* New York: Brunner/Mazel, 1981.

Jacobson, N. S., & Margolin, G. *Marital therapy: Strategies based on social learning and behavior exchange principles.* New York: Brunner/Mazel, 1979.

Jacobson, N. S., & Martin, B. Behavioral marriage therapy. *Psychological Bulletin,* 1976, *83,* 540–556.

Justice, B., & Justice, R. *The abusing family.* New York: Human Services Press, 1976.

Kadushin, A. *Supervision in social work.* New York: Columbia University Press, 1973.

Kanner, L. Emotionally disturbed children: A historical review. *Child Development,* 1962, *33,* 97–102.

Kantor, D., & Lehr, W. *Inside the family: Toward a theory of family process.* San Francisco: Jossey-Bass, 1975.

Kaplan, H. S. *The new sex therapy: Active treatment of sexual dysfunctions.* New York: Brunner/Mazel, 1974.

Kaplan, M. L., & Kaplan, N. R. Individual and family growth: A Gestalt approach. *Family Process,* 1978, *17,* 195–206.

Kaslow, F. W. History of family therapy in the United States: A kaleidoscopic overview. *Marriage and Family Review,* 1980, *3,* 77–111.

Kaslow, F. W. Divorce and divorce therapy. In A. S. Gurman & D. P. Kniskern (Eds.), *Handbook of family therapy.* New York: Brunner/Mazel, 1981.

Kaslow, F. W., & Friedman, J. Utilization of family photos and movies in family therapy. *Journal of Marriage and Family Counseling,* 1977, *3*(1), 19–25.

Kaufman, E., & Kaufman, P. From a psychodynamic orientation to a structural family therapy approach in the treatment of drug dependency. In E. Kaufman & P. Kaufman (Eds.), *Family therapy of drug and alcohol abuse.* New York: Gardner Press, 1979.

Kazdin, A. E. *Behavior modification in applied settings* (3rd ed.). Homewood, Ill.: Dorsey Press, 1984.

Keeney, B. P. *The aesthetics of change.* New York: Guilford Press, 1983.

Keeney, B. P., & Sprenkle, D. Ecosystemic epistemology: Critical implications for the aesthetics and pragmatics of family therapy. *Family Process,* 1982, *21,* 1–19.

Keith, D. V., & Whitaker, C. A. Experiential/symbolic family therapy. In A. M. Horne &

M. M. Ohlsen (Eds.), *Family counseling and therapy.* Itasca, Ill.: F. E. Peacock, 1982.

Kempler, W. *Principles of gestalt family therapy.* Costa Mesa, Calif.: The Kempler Institute, 1974.

Kempler, W. *Experiential psychotherapy within families.* New York: Brunner/Mazel, 1981.

Kempler, W. Gestalt family therapy. In A. M. Horne & M. M. Ohlsen (Eds.), *Family counseling and therapy.* Itasca, Ill.: F. E. Peacock, 1982.

Kerr, M. E. Family systems theory and therapy. In A. S. Gurman & D. P. Kniskern (Eds.), *Handbook of family therapy.* New York: Brunner/Mazel, 1981.

Kinder, B. N., & Blakeney, P. Treatment of sexual dysfunction: A review of outcome studies. *Journal of Clinical Psychology,* 1977, *33,* 523–530.

Kniskern, D. P., & Gurman, A. S. Research on training in marriage and family therapy: Status, issues and directions. In M. Andolfi & I. Zwerling (Eds.), *Dimensions of family therapy.* New York: Guilford Press, 1980.

Kressel, K., & Deutsch, M. Divorce therapy: An in-depth survey of therapists' views. *Family Process,* 1977, *16,* 413–443.

L'Abate, L., & Frey, J., III. The E-R-A model: The role of feelings in family therapy reconsidered: Implications for a classification of theories of family therapy. *Journal of Marital and Family Therapy,* 1981, *7,* 143–150.

Laing, R. D. Mystification, confusion, and conflict. In I. Boszormenyi-Nagy & J. L. Framo (Eds.), *Intensive family therapy: Theoretical and practical aspects.* New York: Harper & Row, 1965.

Laing, R. D., & Esterson, A. *Sanity, madness and the family.* Middlesex, England: Penguin, 1970.

Lamb, M. E. Parental behavior and child development in nontraditional families: An introduction. In M. E. Lamb (Ed.), *Nontraditional families: Parenting and child development.* Hillsdale, N.J.: Erlbaum, 1982.

Langsley, D. G., & Kaplan, D. M. *The treatment of families in crisis.* New York: Grune & Stratton, 1968.

Langsley, D. G., Machotka, P., & Flomenhaft, K. Avoiding mental hospital admission: A follow-up study. *American Journal of Psychiatry,* 1971, *127,* 1391–1394.

Langsley, D. G., Pittman, F. S., Machotka, P., & Flomenhaft, K. Family crisis therapy: Results and implications. *Family Process,* 1968, *7,* 145–158.

Laqueur, H. P. Multiple family therapy: Questions and answers. In D. A. Bloch (Ed.), *Techniques of family psychotherapy: A primer.* New York: Grune & Stratton, 1973.

Laqueur, H. P. Multiple family therapy. In P. J. Guerin, Jr. (Ed.), *Family therapy: Theory and practice.* New York: Gardner Press, 1976.

Lazarus, A. A. Has behavior therapy outlived its usefulness? *American Psychologist,* 1977, *32,* 550–554.

Lewis, J. M., Beavers, W. R., Gossett, J. T., & Phillips, V. A. *No single thread: Psychological health in family systems.* New York: Brunner/Mazel, 1976.

Lewis, J. M., & Looney, J. G. *The long struggle: Well-functioning working-class black families.* New York: Brunner/Mazel, 1983.

Liberman, R. P. Behavioral approaches to family and couple therapy. *American Journal of Orthopsychiatry,* 1970, *40,* 106–118.

Liberman, R. P., Wheeler, E. G., de Visser, L. A. J. M., Kuehnel, J., & Kuehnel, T. *Handbook of marital therapy: A positive approach to helping troubled relationships.* New York: Plenum, 1980.

Liberman, R. P., Wheeler, E., & Sanders, N. Behavioral therapy for marital disharmony: An educational approach. *Journal of Marriage and Family Counseling,* 1976, *2,* 383–395.

Liddle, H. A., & Halpin, R. J. Family therapy training and supervision: A comparative review. *Journal of Marriage and Family Counseling*, 1978, *4*, 77–98.

Lidz, R., & Lidz, T. The family environment of schizophrenic patients. *American Journal of Psychiatry*, 1949, *106*, 332–345.

Lidz, T., Cornelison, A., Fleck, S., & Terry, D. The intrafamilial environment of schizophrenic patients. II. Marital schism and marital skew. *American Journal of Psychiatry*, 1957, *114*, 241–248.

Loewenstein, S. F., Reder, P., & Clark, A. The consumers' response: Trainees' discussion of the experience of live supervision. In R. Whiffen & J. Byng-Hall (Eds.), *Family therapy supervision: Recent developments in practice*. London: Academic Press, 1982.

Lo Piccolo, J., & Lo Piccolo, L. (Eds.). *Handbook of sex therapy*. New York: Plenum, 1978.

Low, P., & Low, M. Treatment of married couples in a group run by a husband and wife. *International Journal of Group Psychotherapy*, 1975, *25*, 54–66.

Lowe, R. N. Adlerian/Dreikursian family counseling. In A. M. Horne & M. M. Ohlsen (Eds.), *Family counseling and therapy*. Itasca, Ill.: F. E. Peacock, 1982.

MacGregor, R. Multiple impact psychotherapy with families. In J. G. Howells (Ed.), *Theory and practice of family psychiatry*. New York: Brunner/Mazel, 1971.

MacGregor, R., Ritchie, A. N., Serrano, A. C., & Schuster, F. P. *Multiple impact therapy with families*. New York: McGraw-Hill, 1964.

MacKinnon, L. Contrasting strategic and Milan therapies. *Family Process*, 1983, *22*, 425–440.

McGoldrick, M. Ethnicity and family therapy: An overview. In M. McGoldrick, J. K. Pearce, & J. Giordano (Eds.), *Ethnicity and family therapy*. New York: Guilford Press, 1982.

McGoldrick, M., & Carter, E. A. The family life cycle. In F. Walsh (Ed.), *Normal family processes*. New York: Guilford Press, 1982.

McGoldrick, M., Pearce, J. K., & Giordano, J. *Ethnicity and family therapy*. New York: Guilford Press, 1982.

McPherson, S. R., Brackelmanns, W. E., & Newman, L. E. Stages in the family therapy of adolescents. *Family Process*, 1974, *13*, 77–94.

Madanes, C. *Strategic family therapy*. San Francisco: Jossey-Bass, 1981.

Madanes, C. *Behind the one-way mirror: Advances in the practice of strategic therapy*. San Francisco: Jossey-Bass, 1984.

Madanes, C., & Haley, J. Dimensions of family therapy. *The Journal of Nervous and Mental Disease*, 1977, *165*, 88–98.

Malcolm, J. A reporter at large: The one-way mirror. *New Yorker*, May 15, 1978, 39–114.

Manus, G. Marriage counseling: A technique in search of a theory. *Journal of Marriage and the Family*, 1966, *28*, 449–453.

Margolin, G. Ethnical and legal considerations in marital and family therapy. *American Psychologist*, 1982, *37*, 788–801.

Margolin, G. Behavioral marital therapy. In B. B. Wolman & G. Stricker (Eds.), *Handbook of family and marital therapy*. New York: Plenum, 1983.

Martin, J. P. *Violence and the family*. New York: Wiley, 1978.

Martin, P. A., & Bird, W. H. An approach to the psychotherapy of marriage partners: The stereoscopic technique. *Psychiatry*, 1963, *16*, 123–127.

Masnick, G., & Bane, M. J. *The nation's families: 1960–1990*. Cambridge, Mass.: Joint Center for Urban Studies, 1980.

Masters, W. H., & Johnson, V. E. *Human sexual inadequacy*. Boston: Little, Brown, 1970.

Meissner, W. W. The conceptualization of marriage and family dynamics from a psychoanalytic perspective. In T. J. Paolino & B. S. McCrady (Eds.), *Marriage and marital therapy: Psychoanalytic, behavioral and systems theory perspectives.* New York: Brunner/Mazel, 1978.

Mendelsohn, M., & Ferber, A. A training program. In A. Ferber, M. Mendelsohn, & A. Napier (Eds.), *The book of family therapy.* New York: Science House, 1972.

Menninger, K. *The vital balance.* New York: Viking Press, 1963.

Midelfort, C. F. *The family in psychotherapy.* New York: McGraw-Hill, 1957.

Miller, J. G. *Living systems.* New York: McGraw-Hill, 1971.

Minuchin, S. *Families and family therapy.* Cambridge, Mass.: Harvard University Press, 1974. (a)

Minuchin, S. Structural family therapy. In S. Arieti & G. Caplan (Eds.), *American handbook of psychiatry II: Child and adolescent psychiatry, sociocultural and community psychiatry* (2nd ed.). New York: Basic Books, 1974. (b)

Minuchin, S. Constructing a therapeutic reality. In G. Berenson & H. White (Eds.), *Annual review of family therapy* (Vol. 1). New York: Human Sciences Press, 1981.

Minuchin, S. Foreword. In J. R. Neill & D. P. Kniskern (Eds.), *From psyche to system: The evolving therapy of Carl Whitaker.* New York: Guilford Press, 1982.

Minuchin, S., & Barcai, A. Therapeutically induced family crisis. In C. J. Sager & H. S. Kaplan (Eds.), *Progress in group and family therapy.* New York: Brunner/Mazel, 1972.

Minuchin, S., & Fishman, H. C. *Family therapy techniques.* Cambridge, Mass.: Harvard University Press, 1981.

Minuchin, S., Montalvo, B., Guerney, B. G., Jr., Rosman, B. L., & Schumer, F. *Families of the slums: An exploration of their structure and treatment.* New York: Basic Books, 1967.

Minuchin, S., Rosman, B. L., & Baker, L. *Psychosomatic families: Anorexia nervosa in context.* Cambridge, Mass.: Harvard University Press, 1978.

Mittelman, B. The concurrent analysis of married couples. *Psychoanalytic Quarterly,* 1948, *17,* 182–197.

Montalvo, B. Aspects of live supervision. *Family Process,* 1973, *12,* 343–359.

Moos, R. H. *Combined preliminary manual: Family, work and group environment scales.* Palo Alto, Calif.: Consulting Psychologists Press, 1974.

Morrison, J. K., Layton, D., & Newman, J. Ethical conflict in decision making. In J. C. Hansen & L. L'Abate (Eds.), *Values, ethics, legalities and the family therapist.* Rockville, Md.: Aspen Systems Corporation, 1982.

Mudd, E. H. *The practice of marriage counseling.* New York: Association Press, 1951.

Napier, A. Y., & Whitaker, C. A. A conversation about co-therapy. In A. Ferber, M. Mendelsohn, & A. Y. Napier (Eds.), *The book of family therapy.* New York: Science House, 1972.

Napier, A. Y., & Whitaker, C. A. *The family crucible.* New York: Harper & Row, 1978.

Nass, G. D. *Marriage and the family.* Reading, Mass.: Addison-Wesley, 1978.

Neill, J. R., & Kniskern, D. P. (Eds.). *From psyche to system: The evolving therapy of Carl Whitaker.* New York: Guilford Press, 1982.

Neugarten, B. Adaptation and the life cycle. *The Counseling Psychologist,* 1976, *6,* 16–20.

Nichols, W. C. Introduction to Part I. Education and training in marital and family therapy. *Journal of Marital and Family Therapy,* 1979, *5*(3), 3–5.

O'Leary, K. D., & Turkewitz, H. Marital therapy from a behavioral perspective. In T. J. Paolino & B. S. McCrady (Eds.), *Marriage and marital therapy: Psychoanalytic, behavioral and systems theory perspectives.* New York: Brunner/Mazel, 1978.

Oliveri, M. E., & Reiss, D. Family styles of construing the social environment: A perspective on variation among nonclinical families. In F. Walsh (Ed.), *Normal family processes.* New York: Guilford Press, 1982.

Olson, D. H. Marital and family therapy: Integrative review and critique. *Journal of*

Marriage and the Family, 1970, *32,* 501–538.

Olson, D. H., Russell, C. S., & Sprenkle, D. H. Marital and family therapy: A decade review. *Journal of Marriage and the Family,* 1980, *42,* 973–993.

Olson, D. H., Sprenkle, D. H., & Russell, C. S. Circumplex model of marital and family systems: I. Cohesion and adaptability dimensions, family types, and clinical applications. *Family Process,* 1979, *18,* 3–28.

Papero, D. V. Family systems theory and therapy. In B. B. Wolman & G. Stricker (Eds.), *Handbook of family and marital therapy.* New York: Plenum, 1983.

Papp, P. Family choreography. In P. J. Guerin, Jr. (Ed.), *Family therapy: Theory and practice.* New York: Gardner Press, 1976.

Papp, P. (Ed.). *Family therapy: Full length case studies.* New York: Gardner Press, 1977.

Papp, P. Setting the terms for therapy. *The Family Therapy Networker,* 1984, *8*(1), 42–47.

Patterson, G. R. *Families: Application of social learning to family life.* Champaign, Ill.: Research Press, 1971.

Patterson, G. R. Parents and teachers as change agents: A social learning approach system. In D. H. L. Olson (Ed.), *Treating relationships.* Lake Mills, Iowa: Graphic Publishing, 1976.

Patterson, G. R., & Reid, J. Reciprocity and coercion: Two facets of social systems. In C. Neuringer & J. Michael (Eds.), *Behavior modification in clinical psychology.* New York: Appleton-Century-Crofts, 1970.

Patterson, G. R., Weiss, R. L., & Hops, H. Training of marital skills. In H. Leitenberg (Ed.), *Handbook of behavior modification and behavior therapy.* New York: Prentice-Hall, 1976.

Pattison, E. M. Clinical applications of social network therapy. *International Journal of Family Therapy,* 1981, *3,* 241–320.

Paul, G. L. Behavior modification research: Design and tactics. In C. M. Franks (Ed.), *Behavior therapy: Appraisal and status.* New York: McGraw-Hill, 1969.

Pepitone-Rockwell, F. (Ed.). *Dual-career couples.* Beverly Hills, Calif.: Sage Publications, 1980.

Perls, F. S. *Gestalt therapy verbatim.* Lafayette, Calif.: Real People Press, 1969.

Perry, H. S. *Psychiatrist of America: The life of Harry Stack Sullivan.* Cambridge, Mass.: Harvard University Press, 1982.

Phillips, J. S., & Bierman, K. L. Clinical psychology: Individual methods. In M. R. Rosenzweig & L. W. Porter (Eds.), *Annual review of psychology* (Vol. 32). Palo Alto, Calif.: Annual Reviews, 1981.

Private violence. *Time,* September 5, 1983, pp. 18–29.

Prochaska, J., & Prochaska, J. Twentieth century trends in marriage and marital therapy. In T. J. Paolino, Jr., & B. S. McCrady (Eds.), *Marriage and marital therapy: Psychoanalytic, behavioral and systems theory perspectives.* New York: Brunner/Mazel, 1978.

Rapoport, R., & Rapoport, R. The dual-career family. *Human Relations,* 1969, *22,* 3–30.

Reiss, D. *The family's construction of reality.* Cambridge, Mass.: Harvard University Press, 1981.

Ritchie, A. Multiple impact therapy: An experiment. In J. Haley (Ed.), *Changing families: A family therapy reader.* New York: Grune & Stratton, 1971.

Robinson, L. R. Basic concepts in family therapy: A differential comparison with individual treatment. *American Journal of Psychiatry,* 1975, *132,* 1045–1054.

Rosenberg, J. B. Structural family therapy. In B. B. Wolman & G. Stricker (Eds.), *Handbook of family and marital therapy.* New York: Plenum, 1983.

Rosenblatt, B. Historical perspective of treatment modes. In H. E. Rie (Ed.), *Perspectives in child psychopathology.* Chicago: Aldine-Atherton, 1971.

Rubenstein, D., & Weiner, O. R. Co-therapy teamwork relationships in family psychotherapy. In G. H. Zuk & I. Boszormenyi-Nagy (Eds.), *Family therapy and disturbed
families.* Palo Alto, Calif.: Science and Behavior Books, 1967.

Rubenstein, E. Childhood mental disease in America: A review of the literature before
1900. *American Journal of Orthopsychiatry,* 1948, *18,* 314–321.

Rueveni, U. *Networking families in crisis.* New York: Human Sciences Press, 1979.

Sager, C. J. The treatment of married couples. In S. Arieti (Ed.), *American handbook of
psychiatry* (Vol. III). New York: Basic Books, 1966.

Sager, C. J., Brown, H. S., Crohn, H., Engel, T., Rodstein, E., & Walker, L. *Treating the
remarried family.* New York: Brunner/Mazel, 1983.

Sander, F. M., & Beels, C. C. A didactic course for family therapy trainees. *Family
Process,* 1970, *9,* 411–423.

Satir, V. M. *Conjoint family therapy.* Palo Alto, Calif.: Science and Behavior Books,
1964.

Satir, V. M. *Conjoint family therapy* (Rev. ed.). Palo Alto, Calif.: Science and Behavior
Books, 1967.

Satir, V. M. *Peoplemaking.* Palo Alto, Calif.: Science and Behavior Books, 1972.

Satir, V. M. The therapist and family therapy: Process model. In A. M. Horne & M. M.
Ohlsen (Eds.), *Family counseling and therapy.* Itasca, Ill.: F. E. Peacock, 1982.

Satir, V. M., Stachowiak, J., & Taschman, H. A. *Helping families to change.* New York:
Aronson, 1975.

Schultz, S. J. *Family systems therapy: An integration.* New York: Aronson, 1984.

Segal, L. Brief family therapy. In A. M. Horne & M. M. Ohlsen (Eds.), *Family counseling and therapy.* Itasca, Ill.: F. E. Peacock, 1982.

Segal, L., & Bavelas, J. B. Human systems and communication theory. In B. B. Wolman
& G. Stricker (Eds.), *Handbook of family and marital therapy.* New York: Plenum,
1983.

Selvini-Palazzoli, M. *Self-starvation.* New York: Aronson, 1978.

Selvini-Palazzoli, M. Why a long interval between sessions? The therapeutic control of
the family–therapist suprasystem. In M. Andolfi & I. Zwerling (Eds.), *Dimensions
of family therapy.* New York: Guilford Press, 1980.

Selvini-Palazzoli, M., Boscolo, L., Cecchin, G., & Prata, G. *Paradox and counterparadox: A new model in the therapy of the family in schizophrenic transaction.* New
York: Aronson, 1978.

Selvini-Palazzoli, M., Boscolo, L., Cecchin, G., & Prata, G. Hypothesizing–circularity–
neutrality: Three guidelines for the conductor of the session. *Family Process,* 1980,
19, 3–12.

Shapiro, R. J. Problems in teaching family therapy. *Professional Psychology,* 1975, *6,*
41–44.

Shapiro, R. L. The origin of adolescent disturbance in the family: Some considerations
in theory and implications for therapy. In G. H. Zuk and I. Boszormenyi-Nagy
(Eds.), *Family therapy and disturbed families.* Palo Alto, Calif.: Science and Behavior Books, 1967.

Shean, G. *Schizophrenia: An introduction to research and theory.* Cambridge, Mass.:
Winthrop, 1978.

Silverman, H. L. Psychological implications of marital therapy. In H. L. Silverman
(Ed.), *Marital therapy: Moral, sociological, and psychological factors.* Springfield,
Ill.: Charles C Thomas, 1972.

Simon, R. M. Sculpting the family. *Family Process,* 1972, *11,* 49–57.

Singer, M. T., & Wynne, L. C. Principles of scoring communication defects and devi-
ances in parents of schizophrenics: Rorschach and TAT scoring manuals. *Psychiatry,* 1966, *29,* 260–288.

Skinner, B. F. *Science and human behavior.* New York: Macmillan, 1953.

Skolnick, A. S., & Skolnick, J. H. Introduction: Family in transition. In A. S. Skolnick & J. H. Skolnick (Eds.), *Family in transition: Rethinking marriage, sexuality, child rearing, and family organization* (2nd ed.). Boston: Little, Brown, 1977.

Skynner, A. C. R. *Systems of family and marital psychotherapy.* New York: Brunner/Mazel, 1976.

Skynner, A. C. R. An open-systems, group-analytic approach to family therapy. In A. S. Gurman & D. P. Kniskern (Eds.), *Handbook of family therapy.* New York: Brunner/Mazel, 1981.

Slavson, S. R. *A textbook in analytic group psychotherapy.* New York: International Universities Press, 1964.

Sluzki, C. E. *Treatment, training and research in family therapy.* Paper presented at the Nathan W. Ackerman Memorial Conference, Cumana, Venezuela, February, 1974.

Sluzki, C. E. Marital therapy from a systems theory perspective. In T. J. Paolino & B. S. McCrady (Eds.), *Marriage and marital therapy: Psychoanalytic, behavioral and systems theory perspectives.* New York: Brunner/Mazel, 1978.

Sluzki, C. E., & Ransom, D. C. (Eds.). *Double-bind: The foundation of the communicational approach to the family.* New York: Grune & Stratton, 1976.

Smith, V. G., & Nichols, W. C. Accreditation in marital and family therapy. *Journal of Marital and Family Therapy,* 1979, *5,* 95–100.

Speck, R. V., & Attneave, C. L. *Family networks.* New York: Pantheon, 1973.

Spiegel, J. P. *Transactions: The interplay between individual, family and society.* New York: Science House, 1971.

Spiegel, J. P. The family: The channel of primary care. *Hospital and Community Psychiatry,* 1974, *25,* 785–788.

Sporakowski, M. J., & Staniszewski, W. P. The regulation of marriage and family therapy: An update. *Journal of Marital and Family Therapy,* 1980, *6,* 335–348.

Stanton, M. D. Strategic approaches to family therapy. In A. S. Gurman & D. P. Kniskern (Eds.), *Handbook of family therapy.* New York: Brunner/Mazel, 1981.

Stanton, M. D., Todd, T. C., & Associates. *The family therapy of drug abuse and addiction.* New York: Guilford Press, 1982.

Steinglass, P. The conceptualization of marriage from a systems theory perspective. In T. J. Paolino, Jr., & B. S. McCrady (Eds.), *Marriage and marital therapy: Psychoanalytic, behavioral and systems theory perspectives.* New York: Brunner/Mazel, 1978.

Steinglass, P. Family therapy with alcoholics: A review. In E. Kaufman & P. Kaufman (Eds.), *Family therapy of drug and alcohol abuse.* New York: Gardner Press, 1979.

Stewart, A. J., & Platt, M. B. Studying women in a changing world: An introduction. *Journal of Social Issues,* 1982, *38,* 1–16.

Stier, S., & Goldenberg, I. Training issues in family therapy. *Journal of Marriage and Family Counseling,* 1975, *1,* 63–68.

Stierlin, H. *Separating parents and adolescents.* New York: Quadrangle, 1972.

Stierlin, H. *Psychoanalysis and family therapy.* New York: Aronson, 1977.

Strelnick, A. H. Multiple family group therapy: A review of the literature. *Family Process,* 1977, *16,* 307–325.

Strupp, H. H. *Psychotherapy and the modification of abnormal behavior.* New York: McGraw-Hill, 1971.

Stuart, R. B. Operant-interpersonal treatment for marital discord. *Journal of Consulting and Clinical Psychology,* 1969, *33,* 675–682.

Stuart, R. B. An operant-interpersonal program for couples. In D. H. L. Olson (Ed.), *Treating relationships.* Lake Mills, Iowa: Graphic, 1976.

Stuart, R. B. *Helping couples change: A social learning approach to marital therapy.* Champaign, Ill.: Research Press, 1980.

Sugarman, S. Family therapy training in selecting psychiatry residency programs. *Family Process*, 1981, *20*, 147–154.

Sullivan, H. S. *The interpersonal theory of psychiatry.* New York: Norton, 1953.

Terkelsen, K. G. Toward a theory of the family life cycle. In E. A. Carter & M. McGoldrick (Eds.), *The family life cycle: A framework for family therapy.* New York: Gardner Press, 1980.

Textor, M. R. An assessment of prominence in the family therapy field. *Journal of Marital and Family Therapy*, 1983, *9*, 317–320.

Thaxton, L., & L'Abate, L. The "second wave" and the second generation: Characteristics of new leaders in family therapy. *Family Process*, 1982, *21*, 359–362.

Thibaut, J. W., & Kelley, H. H. *The social psychology of groups.* New York: Wiley, 1959.

Toman, W. *Family constellation: Its effects on personality and social behavior.* New York: Springer, 1961.

Towards a differentiation of self in one's family. In J. L. Framo (Ed.), *Family interaction: A dialogue between family researchers and family therapists.* New York: Springer, 1972.

Ulrich, D. N. Contextual family and marital therapy. In B. B. Wolman & G. Stricker (Eds.), *Handbook of family and marital therapy.* New York: Plenum, 1983.

U.S. Bureau of the Census. *Household and family characteristics: March 1981* (Current population reports, Series P-20, No. 371). Washington, D.C.: U.S. Government Printing Office, 1982.

Visher, J. S., & Visher, E. B. Stepfamilies and stepparenting. In F. Walsh (Ed.), *Normal family processes.* New York: Guilford Press, 1982.

Vroom, P. The anomalous profession: Some bumpy going for the divorce mediation movement. *The Family Therapy Networker*, 1983, *7*(3), 38–42.

Walrond-Skinner, S. *Family therapy: The treatment of natural systems.* London: Routledge & Kegan Paul, 1976.

Walsh, F. Conceptualizations of normal family functioning. In F. Walsh (Ed.), *Normal family processes.* New York: Guilford Press, 1982.

Warkentin, J., and Whitaker, C. A. The secret agenda of the therapist doing couples therapy. In G. H. Zuk and I. Boszormenyi-Nagy (Eds.), *Family therapy and disturbed families.* Palo Alto, Calif.: Science and Behavior Books, 1967.

Watson, J. B., & Rayner, R. Conditioned emotional reactions. *Journal of Experimental Psychology*, 1920, *3*, 1–14.

Watzlawick, P. A structural family interview. *Family Process*, 1966, *5*, 256–271.

Watzlawick, P., Beavin, J. H., & Jackson, D. D. *Pragmatics of human communication.* New York: Norton, 1967.

Watzlawick, P., & Weakland, J. H. (Eds.). *The interactional view: Studies at the Mental Research Institute, 1965–1974.* New York: Norton, 1977.

Watzlawick, P., Weakland, J., & Fisch, R. *Change: Principles of problem formation and problem resolution.* New York: Norton, 1974.

Waxler, N. The normality of deviance: An alternate explanation of schizophrenia in the family. *Schizophrenia Bulletin*, 1975, *14*, 38–47.

Weakland, J. H. Communication theory and clinical change. In P. J. Guerin, Jr. (Ed.), *Family therapy: Theory and practice.* New York: Gardner Press, 1976.

Weakland, J. H. "Family somatics": A neglected edge. *Family Process*, 1977, *16*, 263–272.

Weathers, L., & Liberman, R. P. The family contracting exercise. *Journal of Behavior Therapy and Experimental Psychiatry*, 1975, *6*, 208–214.

Weeks, G. R., & L'Abate, L. *Paradoxical psychotherapy: Theory and technique.* New York: Brunner/Mazel, 1982.

Wellisch, D. K., Vincent, J., & Ro-Trock, G. K. Family therapy versus individual therapy: A study of adolescents and their parents. In D. H. L. Olson (Ed.), *Treating relationships.* Lake Mills, Iowa: Graphic, 1976.

Wells, R. A., & Dezen, A. E. The results of family therapy revisited: The nonbehavioral methods. *Family Process,* 1978, *17,* 251–274.

Wells, R. A., Dilkes, T. C., & Trivelli, N. The results of family therapy: A critical review of the literature. *Family Process,* 1972, *11,* 189–207.

Whiffen, R. The use of videotape in supervision. In R. Whiffen & J. Byng-Hall (Eds.), *Family therapy supervision: Recent developments in practice.* London: Academic Press, 1982.

Whitaker, C. A. The growing edge in techniques of family therapy. In J. Haley & L. Hoffman (Eds.), *Techniques of family therapy.* New York: Basic Books, 1967.

Whitaker, C. A. Psychotherapy of the absurd: With a special emphasis on the psychotherapy of aggression. *Family Process,* 1975, *14,* 1–16.

Whitaker, C. A. A family is a four dimensional relationship. In P. J. Guerin, Jr. (Ed.), *Family therapy: Theory and practice.* New York: Gardner Press, 1976. (a)

Whitaker, C. A. The hindrance of theory in clinical work. In P. J. Guerin, Jr. (Ed.), *Family therapy: Theory and practice.* New York: Gardner Press, 1976. (b)

Whitaker, C. A. Comment: Live supervision in psychotherapy. *Voices,* 1976, *12,* 24–25. (c)

Whitaker, C. A. Process techniques of family therapy. *Interaction,* 1977, *1,* 4–19.

Whitaker, C. A., & Malone, T. P. *The roots of psychotherapy.* New York: Blakiston, 1953.

Whitaker, C. A., & Miller, M. H. A re-evaluation of "psychiatric help" when divorce impends. *American Journal of Psychiatry,* 1969, *126,* 57–64.

White, S. L. Family theory according to the Cambridge Model. *Journal of Marriage and Family Counseling,* 1978, *4,* 91–100.

Wolman, B. B., & Stricker, G. (Eds.). *Handbook of family and marital therapy.* New York: Plenum, 1983.

Wolpe, J. *Psychotherapy by reciprocal inhibition.* Stanford, Calif.: Stanford University Press, 1958.

Wynne, L. C. The study of intrafamilial splits and alignments in exploratory family therapy. In N. W. Ackerman (Ed.), *Exploring the base for family therapy.* New York: Family Service Association of America, 1961.

Wynne, L. C. Some indications and contraindications for exploratory family therapy. In I. Boszormenyi-Nagy & J. L. Framo (Eds.), *Intensive family therapy: Theoretical and practical aspects.* New York: Harper & Row, 1965.

Wynne, L. C. Some guidelines for exploratory conjoint family therapy. In J. Haley (Ed.), *Changing families: A family therapy reader.* New York: Grune & Stratton, 1971.

Wynne, L. C. Family research and family therapy: A reunion? *Journal of Marital and Family Therapy,* 1983, *9,* 113–117.

Wynne, L. C., Jones, J. E., & Al-Khayyal, M. Healthy family communication patterns: Observations in families "at risk" for psychopathology. In F. Walsh (Ed.), *Normal family processes.* New York: Guilford Press, 1982.

Wynne, L. C., Ryckoff, I. M., Day, J., & Hirsch, S. I. Pseudomutuality in the family relationships of schizophrenics. *Psychiatry,* 1958, *21,* 205–220.

Wynne, L. C., & Singer, M. Thought disorder and family relations of schizophrenics, I and II. *Archives of General Psychiatry,* 1963, *9,* 191–206.

Yalom, I. D. *The theory and practice of group psychotherapy* (2nd ed.). New York: Basic Books, 1975.

Zeig, J. K. (Ed.). *A teaching seminar with Milton H. Erickson.* New York: Brunner/Mazel, 1980.

Ziegler-Driscoll, G. The similarities in families of drug dependents and alcoholics. In E. Kaufman & P. Kaufman (Eds.), *Family therapy of drug and alcohol abuse.* New York: Gardner Press, 1979.

Zimmerman, J., & Sims, D. Family therapy. In C. E. Walker & M. C. Roberts (Eds.), *Handbook of clinical child psychology.* New York: Wiley, 1983.

Zuk, G. H. Family therapy. In J. Haley (Ed.), *Changing families: A family therapy reader.* New York: Grune & Stratton, 1971.

Zuk, G. H. Family therapy: Clinical hodgepodge or clinical science? *Journal of Marriage and Family Counseling,* 1976, 2, 299–303.

Zuk, G. H. *Family therapy: A triadic based approach* (Rev. ed.). New York: Human Sciences Press, 1981.

Zuk, G. H., & Boszormenyi-Nagy, I. (Eds.). *Family therapy and disturbed families.* Palo Alto, Calif.: Science and Behavior Books, 1967.

Zuk, G. H., & Rubenstein, D. A review of concepts in the study and treatment of families with schizophrenics. In I. Boszormenyi-Nagy & J. L. Framo (Eds.), *Intensive family therapy: Theoretical and practical aspects.* New York: Harper & Row, 1965.

NAME INDEX

SUBJECT INDEX

CREDITS

CHAPTER ONE

18, Figure 1-1 from Figure 7-2, p. 148, from *Marriage and Family Development*, 5th Ed., by Evelyn Millis Duvall. Copyright © 1957, 1962, 1967, 1971, 1977 by J. B. Lippincott Company. By permission of Harper & Row, Publishers, Inc. Based on data from the U.S. Bureau of Census and from the National Center for Health Statistics, Washington, D.C. **19–21,** Figure 1-2 and Table 1-2 from "The Family Life Cycle and Family Therapy: An Overview," by E. A. Carter and M. McGoldrick. In *The Family Life Cycle: A Framework for Family Therapy* by E. A. Carter and M. McGoldrick (Eds.). Copyright © 1980 by Gardner Press. Reprinted by permission.

CHAPTER TWO

34, Figure 2-1 from "The Study of the Family," by D. D. Jackson, *Family Process*, 1965, 4, 1–20. Reprinted by permission. **35,** Figure 2-2 from *Living Systems*, by J. G. Miller. Copyright 1978 by McGraw-Hill, Inc. Reprinted by permission. **39,** Figure 2-3 reprinted by permission of the publishers from *Families and Family Therapy*, by Salvador Minuchin. Cambridge, Mass.: Harvard University Press. Copyright © 1974 by the President and Fellows of Harvard College. **40,** Table 2-1 from "Sex Roles and Family Dynamics," by L. B. Feldman. In *Normal Family Processes*, by F. Walsh (Ed.). Copyright 1982 by The Guilford Press. Reprinted by permission. **45,** Figure 2-4 from "Circumplex Model of Marital and Family Systems: I. Cohesion and Adaptability Dimensions, Family Types, and Clinical Applications," by D. H. Olson, D. H. Sprenkle, and C. S. Russell. In *Family Process*, 1979, *18*, 3–28. Copyright 1979 by *Family Process*. Reprinted by permission. **46,** Table 2-2 from "Family Styles of Construing the Social Environment: A Perspective on Variation among Nonclinical Families," by M. E. Oliveri and D. Reiss. In *Normal Family Processes* by F. Walsh (Ed.). Copyright © 1982 by The Guilford Press. Reprinted by permission. **49,** Figure 2-5 from *No Single Thread: Psychological Health in Family Systems*, by J. M. Lewis, W. R. Beavers, J. T. Gossett, and V. A. Phillips. Copyright 1976 by Brunner/Mazel, Inc. Reprinted by permission. **52,**

Figure 2-6 from "Healthy, Midrange, and Severely Dysfunctional Families," by W. R. Beavers. In *Normal Family Processes* by F. Walsh (Ed.). Copyright 1982 by The Guilford Press. Reprinted by permission.

CHAPTER THREE

60, Figure 3-1 reprinted from *Progress on Family Problems*, by Dorothy Fahs Beck and Mary Ann Jones, by permission of the publisher. Copyright 1973 by Family Service Association of America, New York. **71,** Figure 3-2 from Figure 1 of *Families of the Slums: An Exploration of Their Structure and Treatment* by Salvador Minuchin et al. © 1967 by Basic Books, Inc., Publishers, New York. Reprinted by permission. **62–65,** Quotes are reprinted from *Pragmatics of Human Communication*, by Paul Watzlawick, Ph.D., Janet Helmick Beavin, A.B., and Don D. Jackson, M.D., with the permission of W. W. Norton & Company, Inc. Copyright © 1967 by W. W. Norton & Company, Inc. **82–83,** Table 3-1 from *Marital and Family Therapy*, 2nd Edition, by I. D. Glick and D. R. Kessler. Copyright 1980 by Grune and Stratton. Reprinted by permission.

CHAPTER FOUR

91–93, Table 4-1 (pp. 127–129) from *Marriage and Family Development*, 5th Edition, by Evelyn Millis Duvall. Copyright © 1957, 1962, 1971, 1977 by J. B. Lippincott Company. By permission of Harper & Row, Publishers, Inc. **98,** Figure 4-1 from Sundberg/Tyler/Taplin, *Clinical Psychology: Expanding Horizons*, 2nd Ed., © 1973, p. 101. Reprinted by permission of Prentice-Hall, Inc., Englewood Cliffs, New Jersey. Based on the theory presented by Miller, 1971. **104,** Table 4-2 from Table 10.1 in *Americans View Their Mental Health* by Gerald Gurin, Joseph Veroff, and Sheila Feld, © 1960 by Basic Books, Inc., Publishers, New York. Reprinted by permission. **116,** Tables 4-4 and 4-5 from *The Field of Family Therapy*, GAP Report No. 78. Copyright 1970 by the Group for the Advancement of Psychiatry, Inc. Reprinted by permission of the Committee on the Family, Group for the Advancement of Psychiatry.

CHAPTER SIX

154–158, Quotes from *Experiential Psychotherapy within Families* by W. Kempler. Copyright © 1981 by Brunner/Mazel, Inc. Reprinted by permission.

CHAPTER TEN

210–211, Quotes from "Behavioral Approaches to Family and Couple Therapy," by R. P. Liberman. Reprinted, with permission, from *American Journal of Orthopsychiatry*, 1970, 40, 106–118. Copyright 1970 by American Orthopsychiatric Association. **214,** Figure 10-1 from "An Operant Interpersonal Program for Couples," by R. B. Stuart. In D. H. L. Olsen (Ed.), *Treating Relationships*. Copyright 1976 by Graphic Publishing Company. Reprinted by permission. **216,** Figure 10-2 from "An Operant Interpersonal Program for Couples," by R. B. Stuart. In D. H. L. Olsen (Ed.), *Treating Relationships*. Copyright 1976 by Graphic Publishing Company. Reprinted by permission. **217,** Figure 10-3 from *Helping Couples Change: A Social Learning Approach to Marital Therapy*, by R. B. Stuart. Copyright 1980 by The Research Press, Champaign, Ill. **219,** Figure 10-4 from "Behavioral Therapy for Families with Child Management Problems," by I. R. H. Falloon and R. P. Liberman. In M. Textor (Ed.), *Helping Families with Special Problems*. Copyright 1983 by Jason Aronson, Inc. Reprinted by permission. **221,** Figure 10-5 from

CHAPTER ELEVEN

CHAPTER TWELVE

CHAPTER THIRTEEN

APPENDIX